P9-EGM-727

EMOTIONAL FREEDOM

"*Emotional Freedom* is a valuable guidebook for anyone who believes that greater possibilities await them but has not yet realized them. Dr. Judith Orloff is a gentle, compassionate expert whose wisdom can lead you to a deeper, more fulfilled life."

—LARRY DOSSEY, M.D., author of *Healing Words*

"If you, like myself, wish for a deeper and truer life, a wiser understanding of yourself and your emotions, this book will provide you with answers, with companionship, and, most powerful of all, the clarity and faith of an extraordinary teacher."

—MARY OLIVER, Pulitzer Prize–winning poet

"This breakthrough book is a lifesaver for people who are frustrated, stressed, and anxious, or who have minds that won't shut off. If you long for more joy, give yourself a gift and read this book!"

—MARCI SHIMOFF, bestselling author of *Chicken Soup for the Woman's Soul* and *Happy for No Reason*

"I carry around Dr. Orloff's book *Emotional Freedom* like a bible! I keep re-reading it to remind myself to stay positive and that it is a *choice* not to go to a negative place. It taught me to feel good about my own sensitivities and deal with difficult personalities without going mad! We have the power to change any negative emotion into a positive one."

—ROSANNA ARQUETTE

ALSO BY JUDITH ORLOFF, M.D.

Positive Energy:
10 Extraordinary Prescriptions for Transforming Fatigue,
Stress, and Fear into Vibrance, Strength, and Love

Dr. Judith Orloff's Guide to Intuitive Healing

Second Sight

EMOTIONAL FREEDOM

LIBERATE YOURSELF FROM NEGATIVE
EMOTIONS AND TRANSFORM YOUR LIFE

JUDITH
ORLOFF, M.D.

HARMONY BOOKS / NEW YORK

The information presented in this book is the result of years of clinical experience by the author. The stories in this book are true. The names and identifying characteristics of the patients have been changed to protect their privacy.

Copyright © 2009 by Judith Orloff, M.D.

All rights reserved.
Published in the United States by Harmony Books, an imprint of the Crown Publishing Group, a division of Random House, Inc., New York.
www.crownpublishing.com

Harmony Books is a registered trademark and the Harmony Books colophon is a trademark of Random House, Inc.

Grateful acknowledgment is made to HarperCollins Publishers for permission to reprint three lines from #27 from TAO TE CHING BY LAO TZU, A NEW ENGLISH VERSION, WITH FOREWORD AND NOTES by Stephen Mitchell, translation copyright © 1988 by Stephen Mitchell. Reprinted by permission of HarperCollins Publishers.

Library of Congress Cataloging-in-Publication Data
Orloff, Judith.
    Emotional freedom : liberate yourself from negative emotions and transform your life / Judith Orloff.—1st ed.
        p. cm.
    1. Emotions. 2. Negativism. 3. Self-actualization (Psychology) I. Title.
BF531.O74   2009
152.4—dc22   2008021482

ISBN 978-0-307-33818-1

Printed in the United States of America

Illustrations by Nicole Kaufman

10 9 8 7 6 5 4

First Edition

FOR LEONG TAN

ACKNOWLEDGMENTS

I'm grateful to the many people who've generously supported my writing:

Richard Pine, literary agent of my dreams
Betsy Rapoport, hardworking and dedicated editor, whose caring was invaluable
Shaye Areheart, publisher, goddess, champion of my work
Thomas Farber and Susan Golant, who helped me define and map out this book
Berenice Glass, my best friend, who laughs irresistibly and with whom I can always speak my truth
Stephan Schwartz, friend, mentor, and Renaissance man

A special thanks for the extraordinary team at Harmony Books: Annsley Rosner, Philip Patrick, Jenny Frost, Kate Kennedy, Katie Wainwright, Kira Walton, Linda Kaplan, Sarah Breivogel, Laura Duffy, Cindy Berman, Jie Yang, Shawn Nicholls, and Karin Schulze.

In addition, I offer my deep appreciation to friends and family for their inspiration, encouragement, life stories, and countless hours spent helping me distill the essence of my message: Ron Alexander, Barbara Baird, Patricia Bisch, Barbara Biziou, Charles Blum, Rabbi Mark Borovitz, Reverend Laurie Sue Brockway, Cary Brokaw, Ann Buck, Janus Cercone, Ilene Connoly, Jennifer Cook, Lisa Davis, John Densmore, Vic Fuhrman, James Grotstein, Barry Haldeman, Ping Ho, Melinda Jason, Cathy Lewis, Frank Lowree, Michael Manheim, Mignon

McCarthy, Meg McLaughlin-Wong, Richard Metzner, Caroline Myss, Daoshing Ni, Mary Oliver, Dean Orloff, Maxine Orloff, Phyllis Ostrum-Paul, Dean Radin, Charlotte Reznick, Jillian Robinson, Harriet Rosetto, Mark Seltzer, Rabbi Don Singer, David Smith, Christina Snyder, James Spar, Ira Streitfeld, Leong Tan, Russell Targ, Roy Tuckman, Niki Vettel, Mary Williams, and Beth Zacher. Finally, my parents Maxine Ostrum-Orloff and Theodore Orloff, still with me, though now on the Other Side.

Finally, I am indebted to my patients and workshop participants from whom I continue to learn so much. I have disguised their names and identifying characteristics to protect their privacy.

CONTENTS

Earth is the right place for love.

—ROBERT FROST

EMOTIONAL FREEDOM

INTRODUCTION

EMOTIONAL FREEDOM:

THE SECRET TO SERENITY

I INVITE YOU on a remarkable journey where you can embrace more happiness, peace, and mastery over negativity than you may have ever known. You possess the ability to achieve such emotional freedom; it's closer than you might think. No matter how stressed your life is currently, the time for positive change is now.

Our society is in the midst of an emotional meltdown. People are restless, volatile, our tempers about to blow. In the past year, Prozac was prescribed for over thirty million people. Domestic violence occurs in one out of six households. Fifty percent of drivers who're cut off respond with horn honking, yelling, obscene gestures, or even road rage. Half of our marriages end in divorce.

None of this is how we want life to be. Our pressure cooker society pushes us to our emotional limits. We deserve relief from getting crucified by daily stresses. We deserve to be happier, to be more comfortable in our own skins, to have nurturing relationships. This book empowers you to attain this high quality of life and to handle stress artfully. I'm excited to present practical new tools for mastering your emotions because conventional coping mechanisms just aren't sufficient in our hypertense world. It's lunacy to put up with being

1

chronically anxious, fatigued, or depressed, as so many of us have. I rebel against that cheerless status quo, and hope you will too.

Emotional Freedom offers the answer to reclaiming your happiness and heart. What is emotional freedom? It means increasing your ability to love by cultivating positive emotions and being able to compassionately witness and transform negative ones, whether they're yours or another's. This fundamental living skill liberates you from fear and lets you navigate adversity without going on the attack, losing your cool, or being derailed by it. The result? With true emotional freedom, you can *choose* to react constructively rather than relinquishing your command of the situation whenever your buttons get pushed, as most people do. This lets you communicate more successfully and gain more confidence in yourself and empathy for others. Then you own the moment no matter whom or what you're facing.

Though we commonly think of freedom as uncensored speech, emancipation from slavery, and the right to vote and worship as we choose, you can't achieve total freedom until you learn to take charge of emotions, instead of them running you. This is a radical paradigm shift we all can make, regardless of our present anxieties or past hardships. If you are painfully driven by emotions, this book will show you how not to be.

Your well-being matters to me. My mission is to increase your emotional freedom. It has always been within you, but you must know how to connect with it. I consider it my great privilege to help you say farewell to anything that imprisons—that keeps you afraid, small, or disconnected. Then you won't inexorably be locked in combat with yourself or anyone else. I want you to be more fiercely alive. I'm presenting *Emotional Freedom* as a lifelong guide to release you from the compulsive tyranny of negative emotions such as worry and anger so you can choose more joy.

I'm compelled to write this book because, as a board-certified psychiatrist in private practice and an assistant clinical professor at the University of California, Los Angeles (UCLA), I work in a mainstream medical system where emotions are only partially understood. Even today, they don't receive the total respect that they warrant. All too often, doctors ignore scientific data clearly linking emotions and health. During my psychiatric training at UCLA, I was chief resident of the Affective Disorders Clinic. We treated emotional "disorders," including depression and anxiety, as biochemical imbalances requiring medication. I'd meet with patients for fifteen minutes every few weeks, write a prescription, then send them home. Though I never saw medications as the whole solution to their problems (despite the zeal of some of my colleagues), I did watch many patients experience at least partial symptom relief, an undeniable blessing and alleviation of suffering. However, in my subsequent two decades of medical practice, I've learned that emotional freedom is rarely just about removing a symptom. It involves much, much more.

Over years of working with patients and seminar participants, I've seen that emotional freedom comes from many sources, mainstream and beyond. This book gives me the opportunity to help expand psychiatry to include a larger vision of emotional freedom and to wed my fondest loves: traditional medicine, intuition, energy, and dreams—a mystical yet practical marriage. I've coined the term Energy Psychiatry to describe a new kind of psychotherapy I'm pioneering that synthesizes these multiple forms of knowledge. I'll explain how I use each of them to help my patients find emotional freedom so you can find it too.

The intellect, stunningly incisive as it may be, has restricted vision when it comes to emotions. This is why bringing intuitive awareness to the feeling realm is so liberating: it pushes beyond the limits of linear understanding. Intuition is a potent wisdom not mediated by the linear mind—a practical, smart decision-making aid. Intuition can be a hunch, a dream, a "knowing," specific guidance, or a warning of danger. During troubled times, intuition is a voice in the wilderness to get you through, and when things are good, it'll help them stay that way. Contrary to what you might suppose, intuition is the antithesis of "woo-woo." It can actually be perceived physically as a "gut feeling." Cutting-edge science associates this with a separate "brain" in the gut called the enteric nervous system, a network of neurons that learn and store information. Interestingly, Harvard researchers have linked the overall capacity for intuition to the basal ganglia, a part of the brain that informs us something's not right and we'd better act on it.

Emotions also have an intuitive language that silently begs to be decoded in our bodies—"subtle energies" that move through us that can be sensed. These are what Chinese medicine calls *chi,* our vital life force, a growing area of scientific study. We feel emotions internally, while their energy expands beyond our bodies, affecting the world we touch, determining our affinities. Similarly, other people's emotional energy impacts us.

Today, I am a woman who travels many worlds. My approach to emotional freedom utilizes the best of traditional and nontraditional realms to map the territory of the heart. In this book, I'll discuss the four major components of emotions that shape your health and mood: biology, subtle energy, psychology, and spirituality. Why do I emphasize spirituality? I want to acknowledge that there's a heightened sense of mystery to emotions. Albert Einstein said, "The most beautiful experience we can have is the mysterious. It is the fundamental emotion which stands at the cradle of true art and true science." To tap this, we must appreciate that we are spiritual beings having a human experience. It's impossible to grasp how we tick emotionally without a cosmic perspective; everything about us, including our biology, is an expression of the divine. Seeing emotions as a training ground for the soul frames every victory over fear, anxiety, and resentment as a way to develop your spiritual muscles and be better able to love and cultivate goodness. Anything that keeps you from your light distances your spiritual connection too.

I'm unrelentingly dedicated to helping my patients and you combat the emotional forces of darkness that cause suffering. This has to be done. We all have suffering. When unaddressed, it ends up hurting others and ourselves. I've seen too frequently how the ravages of suffering can deform people. I'll teach you how to dissipate negativity so suffering can be lifted and you can be more loving. Goodness doesn't shy away from the dark. But achieving emotional freedom doesn't mean becoming bland, numbing our feelings, or spewing them indiscriminately toward others. It entails striving to develop everything that is positive within us as well as being accountable for our full spectrum of feelings, mastering them, and realizing we're so much larger than they are.

I'm also compelled to write this book as a testament to my own progress on the path toward emotional freedom. I come from a lineage of powerful, caring women who, despite their accomplishments, often grappled with fears of inadequacy that kept them from reveling in their own magnificence. My mother and my aunt, for instance, as very young physicians in Philadelphia during World War II, staffed an inner-city emergency room. And my grandmother was a flamboyant seer who'd heal her neighbors with her hands during the lean years of the Great Depression. These wonderfully talented and complex women were my role models; for better and for worse, I've shared both their strengths and apprehensions on my own path to self-realization.

I learned much about the consequences of emotions from my mother. At seventy, with a thriving Beverly Hills practice in family medicine, her credentials in order, she nonetheless chose to take the national board exams to prove she was as "competent" as doctors fresh out of medical school. Everybody, including my father (also a physician), her other doctor friends, and me, said to her, "Why put yourself through it?" But, as usual, Mother was stubborn. Maddeningly, she still had something to prove. We were just spectators, loving her the best we could, hurting as she hurt. Preparation for the test was Herculean, requiring months of intense study. Even though she'd been an impeccably skilled, compassionate doctor, beloved by her patients for four decades, she was possessed by a sense of inadequacy. A thousand people could tell her how incredible she was, but if one person said something derogatory, she'd believe him. It was so much easier for her to be kind to others than to herself—a paradox shared by many of us. Twenty years earlier, Mother had been diagnosed with a slow-growing type of lymphoma. It hadn't spread, but it hadn't gone away. Soon after the national board exam, however, the tumor changed to an aggressive form of leukemia. Though she heroically did pass her boards, she died within six months of doing so. Near the end, she told me she believed that the stress and fears that ate at her had accelerated her death.

Witnessing my mother's struggle with self-doubt gave me vital insights into emotional freedom. As a daughter, I saw the horrible toll negative emotions took on the person dearest to me. I ached with pow-

erlessness as I watched her weaken. Even before she died, I experienced the cellular chill of having lost my mother. I stayed very close to
her until the moment she turned bright gold and was no longer of this
earth. During those heartrending days, the mind-body connection
was never more apparent. Ironically, not one iota of my mother's
being consciously wanted to die, but stress and fear don't care about
that. They beat relentlessly at her seventy-year-old immune system,
already taxed by cancer, and her body broke down.

My mother, myself: even now, at times I can't stop my fears or inner
slave driver, and it's hell. However, one make-or-break difference is
that I'm explicitly committed to not being ruled by negative emotions.
I'll fight to the finish to overcome them. This is my eternal vow, and
I'm making sweet and steady progress. But Mother came from the old
school where you tough things out, believe in achievement as scrip-
ture, and shy away from psychotherapy. It's not that she didn't want
her fears to go away; during many conversations at our Saturday
afternoon teas I'd listen to her yearning for inner peace. But she just
wouldn't commit the time and energy to get there, whether through
contemplative introspection or with the assistance of a guide. And
though she devoutly believed in Judaism, the traditional services she
attended didn't focus on the everyday spiritual meaning of emotions
or help her get down to the nitty-gritty of how to relieve fear. Even at
the end, she lacked the tools for change. It breaks my heart that
Mother, so gutsy and skilled, never fully realized her own worth. If
she had, then maybe she would have lived longer and discovered
another chapter of satisfaction in her life—a chapter that had nothing
to do with achievement. But this is a passage that must be negotiated
as you age, a grace one must seek.

My mother gave me many gifts, including the tenacity to follow my
dreams and a love of learning. But from her life, I also learned the dire
necessity to heal negative emotions in order to achieve my own inner
peace and to help my patients do the same. The power of love is the
champion of emotional freedom. We must respect the voice within
that says, "Honey, be kind to yourself. You are enough. You are beautiful." Compassion is in each of us: it is the ultimate answer, the one
I aspire to, to teach my patients, and shout from the rooftops.

In the spirit of compassion, you can use *Emotional Freedom* to grow joyful and strong. My book is divided into two parts. Part One, "Tapping the Power of Emotional Freedom," introduces you to the four components of emotions. It offers a self-assessment test to help you evaluate your current level of emotional freedom so you can record its growth as you practice the principles contained in this book. I'll also invite you into my romance with sleep and dreams, revolutionary states of consciousness that offer liberating wisdom. Everyone can access this realm, even if you've never been able to remember your dreams. You'll gain relief from insomnia and learn to see nightmares and all dreams as allies and healing forces. Finally, I'll show you how to stay open without getting overwhelmed by an often insensitive world. I take particular pleasure in sharing these solutions—including discovering your emotional type and how to optimize it—since I well know what it's like to be a sponge absorbing the angst of people around me. I'll also offer an "emotional vampire survival guide," crucial tips to protect yourself from friends, family, or coworkers who emotionally suck you dry.

In Part Two, "Your Tools for Liberation," I offer a hands-on approach for facing the seven most prevalent difficult emotions and building positive ones. Each chapter is called a "transformation" and tackles different emotions; some may be hotter issues for you than others. I present negativity as a means to an end, a form of suffering to confront and transform. It'll periodically arise, but you'll learn to quickly shrink it again. I've paired negative and positive emotions in each chapter because freedom comes from practicing these transformations rather than getting stuck in pessimism. For instance, I'll offer techniques to overcome fear with courage or jealousy with self-esteem. Similarly, I'll show you ways to address loneliness, anxiety, frustration, depression, and anger to create a compassionate, vibrantly connected life. With each transformation, I'll illustrate how the four components of emotions—their biology, spirituality, energetic power, and psychology—can help you achieve a more serene wholeness. Though misery loves company, so does inner peace. I'll share my personal journey with each emotion, my challenges and my victories. You'll also discover ways my patients, workshop participants, and

friends have found emotional freedom so you can learn how to wel-
come it too.

I dedicate this book to people under emotional stress who're overwhelmed but lack tools to implement change—those with demanding
jobs, overextended superparents, or chronic worriers who long to
master the exhale of life—and to everyone who feels lonely but
yearns for a greater sense of connection. It's aimed at those who suffer from problems labeled "psychosomatic," such as chronic fatigue
syndrome and fibromyalgia, which are fueled by negative thoughts
and feelings. You'll also benefit from this book if you're in a good emotional place but want to feel better.

Let *Emotional Freedom* guide you through your emotional terrain.
Go at your own pace. I swear by baby steps: they foster a sense of
safety and comfort and they prevent you from getting overloaded. I've
had it with epiphanies! As revelatory as these life-changing aha!
moments can feel, they're often hard to sustain. A burning bush is
miraculous, but I wouldn't wait around for one or have your growth
depend on it. I encourage you instead to make small changes with
great love—then they'll accumulate and last. Stitch by golden stitch,
you'll be sewn together, more whole. Keep it slow and simple. Use the
strategies offered in each chapter. In my medical practice, I've seen
everyone from stressed-out moms to hard-charging business execu-
tives benefit. During this process, you may move forward, then back-
slide a bit. Don't worry: that's just how it goes. A mistake is only a
mistake when you don't learn from it. Be aware that even with the
best intentions, emotions can sometimes discombobulate us. They
know just how to catch us off guard if we're not centered.

Take frustration, the great tester of equanimity when obstacles, be
they mundane or extreme, arise. Recently, I was running late for a
dental appointment. As I pulled out of my condo, a monster U-Haul
blocked the exit; I wasted precious minutes tracking down the owner
to have it moved. While en route, I got a disappointing call on my cell
phone informing me that a project for which I had high hopes had
fallen though. Then, muddled by that frustration, I realized that my
dentist had just moved his office, and I had parked in the wrong lot.

So, in haste, I took a shortcut through a nearby bank, and got lost. Now I was really late. Then I lucked out. There was a security guard, decked out in a neatly pressed uniform and shiny gun, who could give me directions. I started feverishly asking him to point the way, but got no response. Suddenly, I realized he seemed awfully quiet. And then it dawned on me—I was talking to a dummy! I touched him . . . yep, he was stuffed. I heard someone chuckling behind me. I turned and spotted the real security guard on duty a few feet away.

"The dummy looks so real," I said sheepishly.

"It's okay," he replied. "People do what you did all the time. They don't realize he's a work of art."

Although I'm shamelessly amused by my own foibles, my mounting frustrations had gotten the best of me. There I was, asking directions from a dummy! A delectable, cogent reminder of how important it is to be mindful of our emotions. We don't want to be blind to whom we're talking, let alone follow some dummy's advice. But if you do, be sure to get a good laugh out of it. Then immediately correct your course. Through all the emotional twists and turns of life, a sense of humor has been my salvation.

As I'm writing to you, a winter storm passes over the Pacific. An expanse of white crests dapple my beloved ocean outside my living room. The tide is receding at twilight, my favorite time. Wind is whipping, whistling hard as golden rays penetrate the steely grayness that threatens to engulf the world. I love sitting here watching. I feel like the luckiest person as I gaze upon this glorious scene. Dark, light, or the infinity of shades in between—I've come to cherish it all. Be apprised: my native tongue is intuition, that invisible, unspoken language that peers into the poetry of things, a mode of sensing and knowing that moves me more than any linear analysis or most words. Throughout the book, I'll bring this aesthetic to our exploration of emotions and impart it to you. Be gentle with yourself on this remarkable journey. Enjoy the ride. Though we humans have a way to go, we are luminous still.

Judith Orloff, M.D.
Marina del Rey, California

Part One

TAPPING THE POWER OF EMOTIONAL FREEDOM

I live my life in widening rings.
—RAINER MARIA RILKE

1

THE PATH TO EMOTIONAL FREEDOM: BEGINNING TO LEARN TO LOVE

YOUR LIFE IS about to get better.

I see great things in your future, a time when wishes come true.

All the notes you put in a bottle were found.

Right here, right now, consider: what do you wish for most? Is it happiness? Love? Less struggle? An unbumpable ticket to stress relief? As you'll soon learn, the power is within you to achieve these. Or maybe you've completely sworn off wishing in response to a pile-up of disappointments. Of course, I've known that sentiment: "What's the use?" Right? Wrong! Such woe-is-me resignation corners you in some godforsaken dead-end unfit for serenity. My determined hope is that you'll give wishing for what's wonderful another chance. There are moments when opportunities arise. This is one, the staking out of your emotional freedom. Freshly fallen snow, not a single footprint— the path of new beginnings. Your first steps are truly memorable. Don't ever forget them. Let me tell you about mine.

The door to emotional freedom cracked open for me as a teenager in southern California. It was 1968. I was sixteen, a flower child in paisley crop tops, holey jeans, and leather combat boots or barefoot, heavily into the drug scene. My parents were frantic. They kept trying to get through to me, but I made that impossible. My rebellion wasn't just against them but to save myself. Though Mother and Dad couldn't have loved me more, I felt suffocated by their mainstream vision of who they thought I should be, what would make me happy. Jewish country clubs, "presentable" clothes, conservative friends . . . I didn't think so. Some nights, I even slept in my beloved jeans (my mother despised them) to feel more free. At the same time, I didn't want to be who I was—so sensitive, not quite of this world. Since childhood I'd experienced many intuitions and dreams that came true, like the times I predicted my grandfather's death and my parents' friends' divorce, when no one else saw either coming. These and other similar incidents unsettled and confused me. To make matters worse, my parents became so unnerved that I was forbidden to talk to them about my intuitions. Then I was sure there was something really wrong with me, a dread I was totally alone with. I didn't choose to predict these things. They just kept happening. I had huge forces churning inside and no way of reconciling them.

Finally, one night, my parents became hell-bent on ending my flirtation with disaster. In a show of gutsy unity, they packed my things, marched me into the car, and checked their only child into a private locked adolescent substance abuse unit of Westwood Psychiatric Hospital. I felt set up, betrayed, and howled my indignation. I did everything in my power to hide my fear. This was where my path to emotional freedom began.

Every moment in that hospital seems so alive to me now. How I fought the kindness I was offered. Initially I felt like a prisoner. Cooperate? Not a chance. I tried everyone's patience. In daily group therapy sessions I refused to talk. The leader, a tough-love former biker babe in denim, would confront me: "Judi [my nickname then], why are you so angry?" "Huh? I'm fine," I'd snap, tight-lipped and seething. The more she'd probe, the more I'd clam up, pretending to everyone, including myself, just how fine I was. I'd be equally forthcoming with my psychiatrist. At meals twenty of us teenagers would sit in a beige cafeteria with plastic utensils (silverware can become weapons) eating some rubberized version of food. I fully intended to isolate myself, until Windy, a fellow hippie patient who lived in her long-fringed brown suede jacket, befriended me. My prickly exterior didn't seem to faze her. Windy's innocent nature quickly won me over; we became inseparable.

Comrades in captivity, during downtime we'd huddle in my room with its barred windows, plotting our escape. How we'd slip past the night cleaning crew after they wheeled their mops and brooms through the entrance of our locked unit. Then we'd hitch a ride to the coast highway, a few miles away, and head to parts unknown. No parents. No authorities. Just free. Though our great escape never came to fruition, all our scheming, giggling, and singing to the Stones ("You can't always get what you want . . . but you just might find you get what you need") made confinement more palatable.

Still, I loathed being locked up, and saw no reason to examine my life or change. But other mysterious influences beyond my control seemed to be operating too. I remember there was a door at the end of our green linoleum hall. It stood between us and a fenced yard where we played volleyball. The most brilliant light would shine through its wired panes. I couldn't take my eyes off the light. Something loving within that brilliance quieted my snarl, soothed me when words couldn't. Ever since I was a child, I'd felt a loving presence keeping track of me, an invisible friend offering comfort. Usually it stayed in the background, but now it was stepping forward. There was a change wanting to happen within me, and despite my protests, it began with a velocity all its own. Slowly, miraculously, I softened during my fourteen days in this unit.

With the guidance of a wise psychiatrist who understood me and knew how to intervene, I started to realize that I hadn't been free in my life before being confined here. I was rebelling against my parents, but without clarity or focus. I was reactive, not proactive. Rebellion and living on the margins were how I'd survived, yet they weren't the endpoint. Over the next few years, this angel of a man showed me how to better deal with my emotions so I could come from a place that was truer for me. He also helped me begin to embrace my intuitive side, so vital to knowing my soul. Our work together set into motion my calling to become a physician and bring intuition into medicine—

a genuinely unexpected destiny. Though both my parents were physicians and there were twenty-five physicians in my extended family,
given my artistic nature, they'd never urged this career on me. Getting
an M.D. was the last thing I thought I wanted.

Life went on. Two decades later I was a psychiatrist seeing patients
in that same hospital. In my case, the (former) inmate truly was running the institution! I felt deliciously subversive. How enlightening
to have been a patient on the inside with a bird's-eye view of being
incarcerated and at the mercy of strangers. What better way to develop compassion for people in the same position . . . and to learn
how to risk receiving the compassion the staff had once shown me?
These are some of the jewels I've taken with me in my search for
emotional freedom.

The hospital was flattened by the Northridge earthquake in 1994,
and I must admit, I miss not seeing it when I drive by the site. Mother
and Dad shared none of my nostalgia. My teenage self was a nightmare
from which they never quite recovered. Incredibly, even in their elder
years, they occasionally felt obliged to set the record straight. Summoning up looks of horror I knew so well, they'd half jokingly say to me—
a grown woman, for decades a doctor of whom they were extremely
proud—"Judith, we've never gotten over your adolescence."

THE BASICS OF EMOTIONAL FREEDOM:
THE START OF YOUR LIBERATION

Your life is brimming with opportunities to learn about emotional
freedom. Every success. Every heartbreak. Every loss. Every gain.
How you transport yourself through these portals determines how
free you can be. I want you to start viewing your emotions in a nonor-
dinary way: as vehicles for transformation (the word *emotion* comes
from the Latin meaning "to move") rather than simply as feelings that
make you happy or miserable. Expect them to test your heart; that's
the point. What you go through—what we all go through—has a
greater purpose. Always, the imperative of emotional freedom is for
the love in us to evolve. Albert Camus says, "Freedom is nothing else

but a chance to be better." To make this a reality, you must begin to see each event of your life, uplifting or hurtful, earthshaking or mundane, as a chance to grow stronger, smarter, more light-bearing.

But here's where many of us hit a wall. We're ashamed of feeling afraid, inadequate, lonely, as if we've failed or done something wrong. None of these conclusions are true. It's a misguided expectation that we're supposed to be serene all the time. A depressed patient once apologized, "I wish I could be coming to you for something more spiritual." I felt for him, but like so many people in pain with that commonly held perception, he was mistaken. Facing emotions—all of them—is a courageous, spiritually transformative act.

As you look into yourself, this is a failproof formula for liberation: dare to keep expanding your heart even if you've been justifiably wounded by pain or disappointment. The effort is never wasted. As you do, ferociously resist selling out by becoming cynical or shutting down (claustrophobic states worse than death to me). No matter what you've experienced, there is always hope for change and healing. It's a miracle within reach. Don't be afraid to want it.

The way to start is to understand the basics of emotional freedom. Here's a mission statement that summarizes the process. To stay clear about your purpose and goals, you can refer to it while exploring the principles of this book.

WHAT DOES EMOTIONAL FREEDOM MEAN?

It's the capacity to give and receive more love. Getting there entails building positive emotions as well as facing and releasing negative ones. Instead of spinning out with, say, anger after you've been hurt, you'll respond from a centered, more empathic place. Emotional freedom includes both personal and spiritual evolution. Learning to work with negative emotions, rather than collapsing into them, helps you grow spiritually and rise above what is small within you. Becoming free means removing counterproductive emotional patterns and viewing yourself and others through the lens of the heart.

WHY DO I NEED IT?

To liberate yourself from the quicksand of negative emotions. When these accumulate, they disrupt your calmness and compassion, destroy relationships, and ultimately distance you from the joy and wonder of the world.

HOW DO I ACHIEVE IT?

Emotions become a springboard for higher consciousness once you see that each one has a lesson to impart. I'll show you, for instance, how to build patience to counter frustration. Sometimes, though, as with acute grief, you'll learn that you need to just be with the feelings, whereas you can aim to heal and transform envy. There are two stages of processing emotions. First is healthily acknowledging the raw feeling rather than stuffing or airbrushing it. The second is transforming negativity. I'll explain many methods to do this with a variety of emotions.

THE OUTCOME?

You'll feel happier, more flexible and alive; you'll also be kinder to yourself, your friends, and family. You'll have increased patience with coworkers and be able to effectively resolve conflicts. You'll connect with your deepest instincts and the power of the heart to surmount even the most disappointing situations. You'll feel nurtured and protected by a spiritual force that will let you know you're never alone.

I SAVOR THIS Native American story because it speaks to the essence of emotional freedom:

A chief is talking to his tribe about two dogs inside his mind: one a white dog that is good and courageous, the other a black dog that is vengeful and angry. Both dogs are fighting to the death. A young brave, unable to wait for the end of the story, asks, "Which one will win?" The chief responds, "The one I feed."

Remembering this dynamic, set your intention to feed what's best and most beautiful within you, a stance that will impel your liberation.

The goal of emotional freedom is balance. Although in Western culture, being in touch with emotions has become a pop religion—making the expression of feelings an end in itself—the point here isn't to self-indulgently emote or to wall off your feelings. Rather it's to become a more caring, aware person. Another goal is to reconnect with your vital essence, which thrives if it's not pulverized by stress and pessimism. What a gorgeous feeling when you're tapped into it!

You can't just think your way to emotional freedom. Throughout this book I'll keep underscoring that it grows from a linear understanding of biology and behavior, as well as an intuitively sparked transformation in your soul. To create the positive change you desire, get ready to fire up all of your perceptual capacities, even those you never realized you had. You want to see more than a sliver of what's possible for yourself.

EVOLVING BEYOND CONVENTIONAL MEDICINE: INTEGRATING INTUITION TO BETTER GRASP EMOTIONS

A gift of being a psychiatrist is that others entrust me with their deepest feelings and confidences. Over the years, I've had the opportunity to help countless patients and workshop participants mired in fear, worry, or depression fight to be free. I'm no stranger to such predicaments, having endured my own share of emotional trials by fire. We've all done our time in anguished places. But, as I'll describe, there's a way out, sooner rather than later. My role with patients and with you is to be a midwife to the emergence of your finest, freest selves.

Along with my conventional medical training, today I utilize intuition to help my patients achieve emotional freedom. In psychotherapy sessions, I combine nonlinear messages from images, knowings, energy, and dreams with insights provided by my analytic mind. This organic blending of sensibilities lets me make the most of my traditional education and also listen to what emerges from my intuition—the knower behind the thinker. Intuition provides access to the psyche's deep recesses, which don't speak in sentences or paragraphs and are where unexpected connections are made. Further, I teach patients to access their own intuitive abilities to gain greater emotional knowledge of themselves and others and so their lives aren't marred by false notes. But this integration hasn't always felt so natural, nor have I always practiced psychotherapy in this way.

I received my basic training in emotions as a fledgling psychiatric resident in the early 1980s. I was working in the emergency room every third night at UCLA and the Veterans Administration hospitals. I learned volumes about emotions in these cauldrons of intensity. I was riveted and heartbroken by the in-your-face hard truths of this deeply human experience. The work asked everything of me. But it was good work and it was real. During those endless nights, I saw it all. A stick-thin anorexic girl (who thought she was fat) with a ruptured esophagus from vomiting repeatedly to lose weight. Suicidal patients who could've been our mothers, sisters, sons, with slashed wrists, hemorrhaging. People so crippled by panic they could hardly breathe. Being so close to such suffering was different than I'd imagined. In part, the numbing adrenaline rush made this surreal experience tolerable. At the same time, I was completely taken over by an instinct to relieve my patients' pain and offer hope. In the heat of the crises, I didn't think, see, or smell anything but them. It was a spontaneous, exhilarating selflessness I'd never known. Though my medical school classes had spoken about compassion, no one had ever mentioned such an utterly altered state of being—or of how it was protective, keeping me clear, quick, less prone to drain. But in fact compassion was the very essence of healing.

Those formative days of medical training were full of awe. I was privileged to bear witness to the unvarnished details of my patients' lives. No sugarcoating. No censoring. The noble honesty of what is, whether joyous or terrifying, is why being a physician moved my soul then, and powerfully continues to do so now. I'm endlessly curious about why you feel what you feel or why you don't feel something. This has great meaning for me.

In retrospect, I realize that during my psychiatric residency, I just skimmed the surface of emotional freedom. This was true whether I was treating patients with life-threatening problems or others who sought psychotherapy for insight into quandaries ranging from poor self-image to difficult relationships. As invaluable as psychotherapy and/or medications can be in appropriate situations, I've found that they often can't catalyze the level of emotional freedom my patients craved. Relieving symptoms and pinpointing their causes is essential. But we can't stop there. I've had to offer my patients other skills that went far, far beyond my traditional medical roots.

I've long been fascinated by ways science interfaces with intuitive knowledge in the area of health—the elegant dance between our physicality and the nonmaterial. I refuse to turn my back on either realm in favor of the other. I want to make absolutely real how both disciplines can be woven together to create a fuller and more interesting sense of who you are emotionally. (I describe my process of incorporating intuition with science in my books *Second Sight, Dr. Judith Orloff's Guide to Intuitive Healing,* and *Positive Energy*).

This pairing would've been a no-brainer for medieval alchemists, who aspired to join science and instinct in hope of unmasking secrets of the universe. These sixteenth-century philosophers wouldn't have considered music, astronomy, or mathematics without noting their emotional and divine capacities. As when they tried to turn lead to gold, they sought the transformation of a base substance into something higher. From an alchemist's perspective, geometry is more than sterile calculations of lifeless points, lines, and angles. Rather, it's a consciousness-enhancing art in which the design of, say, a cathedral or school could awaken many levels of awareness, including emotions. I thank God for all alchemists, past and present, those in every profession who address our complete essence, no part omitted. This holistic view must not be kept underground, as it too often has been throughout the ages.

Carl Jung says, "Alchemy sets itself the task of acquiring this 'treasure hard to attain' and of producing it in visible form." I held this vision as I began to develop the field I would call Energy Psychiatry. My aim was to contemporize alchemy in medicine and to help reinvent psychiatry so that my field retains magic and breadth and isn't reduced to a prescription mill. I've come to realize that emotional freedom in the largest sense is contingent on amending our accepted agreements of what constitutes reality. It's not that there are two worlds—ordinary reality and the other. It's all one, when we sense with our complete attributes.

Today, I realize the naturalness of this union and can't wait to keep learning more. Not so back in 1983 when I first opened my Los Angeles private practice. The turning point for me happened while working with one patient in particular. I was nearly struck by lightning with an intuition about her but didn't know what to do with it. Christine, a bank teller at fifty, had come to me with severe depression, a melancholy stranger in her own skin. Over six months, her symptoms had dramatically improved on the antidepressants I'd prescribed. It was gratifying to see her looking and feeling so animated and hopeful. But then one day I was conducting a psychotherapy session with Christine when my mind wandered to a large white cloud drifting past my eighteenth-story window. For a few moments, though my mind was lucid, Christine's voice seemed eons away. In this state of complete stillness, and despite her progress, I had a crystal-clear, terrible sense that she would attempt suicide.

My insight shocked and confused me as a physician. I'd been so engrossed in the rigors of science, I hadn't had such a distinct intuition for years. I wanted to dismiss it, explain it away. After all, medical school had trained me to revere concrete evidence, and I had none to indicate that Christine wanted to harm herself. Thus, with real ambivalence, I decided not to mention my intuition to her. Also, I could make no urgent argument to intervene. I resolved that in future sessions, I'd try to see if Christine had undisclosed feelings of hopelessness or despair I'd somehow overlooked.

But Christine didn't make it to the following week's appointment. The next time I saw her was in a grim, windowless ICU; she'd overdosed on antidepressants. There her ghostly gray comatose body lay, bound by tubes to life support, jerkily breathing only when the respi-

rator chugged. In this sickeningly medicinal microuniverse I felt as if
a locomotive had slammed me. By discounting my intuition, I'd failed
both Christine and myself. I felt I'd harmed her by not utilizing a vital
piece of intuitive information. From then on, I knew that, as a responsible physician, I had to bring intuition into my practice.

After three weeks in a coma, blessedly, Christine began to recover.
Had she not survived I would've been devastated. When she and I
started psychotherapy sessions again, I had a more explicit understanding that "feeling better" is only one aspect of achieving emotional freedom. It turned out that despite her strides, Christine had plummeted
into a vortex of worthlessness after feeling belittled by a close relative,
which prompted the suicide attempt. In that near-lethal instant of
panic, Christine was unable to counter a cascade of destructive emotions. Previously, we'd focused on uncovering the roots of her depression and treating its biochemical imbalance. Now, in addition, calling
on everything I knew, I engaged Christine more interactively. I taught
her the behavioral methods I'd learned at that point to weather negativity: calling a friend or me when stressed, relaxation techniques,
journaling, rehearsing how to deal with stressful people. (Alas, I hadn't
yet developed spiritual or intuitive tools that would've been crucial
here.) Further, I helped her build self-esteem so she wasn't so fragile
when criticized. As a result, Christine became stronger. But I knew I
needed more than these available mainstream strategies and solutions.

To assist my patients—and for the sake of my own emotional freedom—I had to enter uncharted territory in search of knowledge I
hadn't yet tapped. This meant reopening an intuitive part of myself
that had been long shut down, and with which I wasn't clear or at
peace. Also, I understood that bringing intuition into my medical
practice carried the risk of being condemned by my peers. Still, fears
and all, I tentatively ventured down this new path. I didn't know
where I was going or how to get there, but I said a prayer and started
exploring possibilities.

As grace would have it, I began meeting pivotal guides, including
the spiritual teacher with whom I've now studied for twenty years.
After I'd experienced a parade of wannabe gurus—from an ex-
housewife who channeled an age-old entity to a celebrity pet psychic

who specialized in poodles—a friend told me about a teacher whose meditation techniques had helped her. A week later I walked up a flight of creaky stairs in an older office building in Santa Monica. A middle-aged Asian man wearing a nondescript cotton shirt and pants just sat there quietly waiting for me, utterly unassuming. The room felt extraordinarily still, as if time had stopped. Suddenly, I was completely absorbed with his eyes, two deep pools I'd known somewhere before. These eyes knew me—my virtues, my flaws—before I even said a word. I wanted to study with him. But when I asked about his weekly meditation classes, he said, smiling mischievously, "Oh, you don't really need these!" "Yes I do," I protested, as he well knew I would. I began to attend every Sunday. From the start, he had my contrary side pegged: he knew to tell me not to do something, so I'd do it. So I commenced learning from him, and I've been lucky to do so since that auspicious first day.

I'm convinced that every doctor (and teacher) could benefit from a spiritual guide, though such a notion would surely make some colleagues roll their eyes. Unfortunately, spiritual guides don't grow on trees. This relationship is one of those fated bondings similar to finding a soul mate. You can search for years and come up with nothing. Then one day you're just walking down the street minding your own business, and he or she appears. Meeting my teacher was a blessing. Our paths crossed when the time was right.

My teacher has shown me more about emotional freedom than any medical text could. Our practice comes from Daoism, which venerates the power of the heart, intuition, and spirituality (a connection with a loving higher power). It emphasizes compassion, helping others, and that the miraculous isn't abstract—it's intermixed in every moment. Keeping these priorities in mind brings perspective to all situations. My teacher also introduced me to meditating regularly, my direct line to spirit and the heart. Because of this practice, my life force has become utterly alive in me. Over the years, he's also taught me how to be vulnerable but strong, no matter what happens. I've learned how to keep loving despite feeling unsure and afraid, especially during those wrenching days when both my parents were dying. I'm profoundly grateful for these benefits of emotional freedom. It wasn't that I became immune to pain; rather, I was better equipped to handle it. Always, my teacher advocates cultivating an unswayable inner center so that negativity, in all its cunning incarnations, can't own me. He doesn't baby or indulge my fears, which can feel infuriating when I'm overwhelmed. In the long run, however, the compassion of this tack has proven itself, spurring me to summon my own strengths to become self-reliant.

Of all his lessons about freedom, one of the trickiest (and most necessary) to live has been embracing my own power as a woman and as a teacher—not in an egotistical way, but by speaking up, shining my light without apology. You'd think this would've been a cinch compared to the trials of confronting inner demons, but for me it wasn't always so. For a long time I mightily resisted my power, as many of us tend to do. Something about it petrified me. Let me explain.

Adjusting to change can sometimes be hard for me, though I'm getting much better. Never mind that change is inevitable. The Capricorn in me is stubborn like a billy goat, often preferring things just as they are. In my mid-twenties, I had a prescient moment when I was curled up in bed under the covers, realizing there would be a point in my distant future when things wouldn't be the same anymore. This went beyond finishing medical school, but I couldn't foresee the particulars. Though the difference in me was going to be positive, still I was threatened: I didn't recognize who I'd become, and that change felt scary.

Flash-forward to 1996. *Second Sight,* my first book, was being released. It had been thirteen years since I'd opened my private practice, where I'd see patients five days a week. I'd rarely done any public speaking. I'm quiet, shy, basically an introvert; I require much solitude and do lots of staring at the ocean. So at my first book signing, when I was handed the microphone, I couldn't have been more flabbergasted at how fluently my story about embracing intuition emerged from between my lips. Me, the one who could barely eke out a word when my mother held court at Hillcrest Country Club during those interminable dinners. Her regal presence, Chanel suits, and take-no-prisoners cleavage (she had a terrifyingly ample bosom) left me tongue-tied, obscured in her shadow. But there I was at the bookstore, astonishing myself by being so articulate with no preparation at all. I'd simply been determined to speak from my heart. I felt like Judith, but it was a new Judith too. An inner switch had flipped on. My power was flowing. It was just happening.

Incredibly, that night wasn't a fluke. For over a decade, I've been addressing enthusiastic audiences, large and small, about intuition and emotional freedom. It's been a joy and feels completely natural. I'm thrilled that so many people, including many medical colleagues, are open to listening to their inner voice. I only wish my mother could've seen this part of me, as my father did. But she died right before that Judith appeared. I'd give anything to have Mother sitting there dressed to the nines in the front row, just once, even though I know she's cheering from the Other Side. Claiming my power through writing and teaching has continued to entail opening my heart. In your life may you open yours too.

HOW EMOTIONALLY FREE ARE YOU?

Emotional freedom is a homecoming to your own heart and fullest power. It salutes authenticity, not conforming to someone else's notion of what to feel or how to be. I vow to leave no stone unturned to get you to freedom. Over the years, I've been delighted to watch patients and workshop participants experience emotional break- throughs using my techniques when conventional therapy wasn't enough. No hocus-pocus. The proof is in the results. I think of Leon, an accountant on hyperrev. He'd whip himself into a frenzy of worry about everything from bills to a Howard Hughes–like dread of germs until he learned to achieve a yearned-for inner calm with meditation. Or Sheri, an attorney and self-confessed "control freak" who suffered bouts of panic. Her micromanaging began to relent only when I showed her how to feel safer by intuitively connecting with a support- ive, loving spiritual force. Similarly, you'll discover new methods to get past your dilemmas.

My approach to emotions is avidly solution-oriented and practical, and involves radical self-appraisal. I'll prepare you to be more street-smart than ivory tower. I want you to get down and dirty with feelings such as fear or frustration so you'll know what you're dealing with and take charge. Then you won't be a sucker for negative forces. However, to achieve freedom, you must go further and also activate your strengths. Why? If you keep focusing on tragedy, you'll become that tragedy; if you focus on hope, you'll become that too. Negativity has no chance of overpowering you once you know how to confront and transform it. You can be this brave if you try. Such remaking of emotional protoplasm is the alchemy that creates freedom.

An initial step toward achieving emotional freedom is to know where you currently stand. Take the following Emotional Freedom Test. It's a self-assessment tool that consists of twenty questions for reflection covering a range of positive and negative emotions. Answer "not true," "sometimes true," or "mostly true" to each question. This will help you identify ways you typically respond to a variety of emotionally charged situations in your life today, including the most mundane. How you deal with, say, traffic or an obnoxious neighbor is not trivial. The microcosm of daily aggravations is in fact a practice lab for larger, more serious issues. Behavior in both dimensions can impact your quality of emotional freedom. Take the test to find out about yourself. The purpose is to get a baseline score; mark it down for future reference, then watch it improve as you practice the techniques I'll be recommending. It'll highlight your strong points and those in need of loving attention.

Emotional Action Step

TAKE THE EMOTIONAL FREEDOM TEST

20 QUESTIONS FOR REFLECTION

This test will help you assess your level of emotional freedom at this time. Place a check mark in the blank that most corresponds to how seldom or often you experience these reactions.

	Not True **0**	Sometimes True **1**	Mostly True **2**
1. If I'm angry with someone, I'll breathe and center myself before I react.	___	___	___
2. When I'm filled with self-doubt or fear, I treat myself lovingly.	___	___	___
3. When stuck in traffic or if something doesn't happen on my timetable, I have patience.	___	___	___
4. After a hard day, I focus on what I'm grateful for rather than beating myself up for what has gone wrong.	___	___	___
5. I rarely get snippy or cop an attitude if people frustrate me.	___	___	___
6. I feel connected to a sense of spirituality, however I define it.	___	___	___
7. I check in with my intuition—my gut feelings—when making choices.	___	___	___
8. If I'm blamed for something, I rarely lash out and say things I regret.	___	___	___
9. I fall asleep quickly and don't worry about tomorrow's to-do list.	___	___	___
10. If my heart gets broken, I don't give up on love.	___	___	___
11. I'm a positive person and don't make small problems into big ones.	___	___	___
12. I don't seek revenge if someone treats me poorly.	___	___	___
13. I'm not jealous of other people's success if it surpasses mine.	___	___	___
14. I quickly let go of negative emotions and don't brood on them	___	___	___
15. I'm not easily crushed by disappointments.	___	___	___

16. I don't compare myself to others.   ____   ____   ____

17. I have empathy for others but I don't
    become their therapist or get drained
    by their emotional pain.   ____   ____   ____

18. I live in the Now, rather than dwelling
    on the past or future.   ____   ____   ____

19. I feel happy with my life, not that it's
    just passing me by.   ____   ____   ____

20. I am good at setting limits with people
    who drain my energy.   ____   ____   ____

HOW TO INTERPRET THIS TEST

To calculate your emotional freedom score, total the numbers corresponding to your responses.

- A score of 30–40 suggests that you're experiencing a considerable level of emotional freedom in your life.

- A score of 15–29 suggests a moderate level.

- A score of 14 or below suggests a beginning level.

- A zero score (and it takes courage to admit that) indicates you haven't found emotional freedom yet, but the good news is that you can start discovering it now.

Whatever your score, be compassionate when you identify areas you'd like to improve. Realize that we all have a ways to go. Emotional freedom isn't some place you arrive at and just stay there. It's an ongoing blossoming.

KEEP IN MIND: EMOTIONAL DIFFERENCES BETWEEN MEN AND WOMEN

I've observed that there's often a yin and yang (male/female) factor to emotional freedom. When my patients first take the test, both sexes tend to answer certain questions differently, particularly regarding affinities for logic versus intuition and styles of countering life's energy drains. These answers represent their emotional modus operandi at the onset of our work, prior to achieving positive changes. Remember this with your initial test scores too. Intriguing, though, is that as my patients' emotional fluency and freedom expands, there's an increasing similarity of responses. Both men and women become more able to assimilate the best in each other to complement their own strengths. This is the divine miracle of growth: hallelujah! Though I'm loath to lump people into polarizing categories or make sweeping generalizations, clarifying certain gender tendencies—assets *and* shortcomings—can offer sharper understanding of yourself and the opposite sex. These tendencies aren't set in stone and aren't applicable to everyone, and of course each of us embodies them to different degrees at different points of our lives. But I do present the following variables to consider in your quest to expand beyond unconscious emotional habits.

Many (but not all) men:

- Are more comfortable with the language of logic than of emotion
- Are externally less reactive under stress
- Aren't as apt to be drained by other people's negativity
- Have an easier time setting limits with others
- Are bottom-line and results-oriented when solving problems, less interested in processing emotions to get there
- Gravitate toward doing before being

Many (but not all) women:

- Have a greater ease with intuition
- May trust the heart more instinctively
- Experience increased empathy and patience
- More readily express emotions
- Want to process emotions as a way of solving problems
- Gravitate toward being before doing

Also evident from my patients' initial scores is that neither sex appears to have an innate talent for transforming negative emotions, though women tend to relieve stress by sharing their feelings more, while men often suffer silently.

What accounts for these variations? In part, our culture supports them. Additionally, our brains are hardwired based on what's necessary for our species' survival. A picture tells a thousand words: in brain imaging studies, women show stronger connections between parts of the brain that process emotions and language. In the most primal sense, showing feelings is vital for empathic mothering and to preserve community. Brain scans indicate that men aren't as anatomically programmed to talk about feelings; they may need to work harder at it. In days of yore this wasn't mandatory in order to hunt or protect their families from hordes of barbarians. Women also have denser links between the brain's left side (analytic) and the right side (intuitive/emotional), which allow them to merge both capacities, whereas men excel at being more logically focused, left-brain problem solvers.

How can this information, as reflected in your test scores, enhance your understanding of emotional freedom? You'll have sharper insight into ways you or others are conditioned to respond. This makes you more self-aware and a smarter communicator. It behooves us to learn synergy and balance from each other, remembering that both male and female DNA are necessary for creation. We can all profit from drawing on the voltage of both yin and yang. Women can often show men how to be freer by teaching them to be more intuitive and emotionally articulate. Men can often show women how to be freer by teaching them to maintain a strong center of gravity under stress and not be a perpetual shock absorber for people's pain. But most revelatory, emotional freedom helps you evolve beyond cultural stereotypes or your brain's wiring to more enlightened ways of treating yourself and the world.

THE BUDDHA SAYS, "There is no external refuge." To be free you must go inside. A defining moment of emotional freedom is when you begin to become more conscious of who you are and what your motivations are. It's so spectacular because light penetrates inner crevices and growth commences. At this stage of emotional evaluation, you may like or dislike what you see about yourself, but the most important thing is seeing it. Where you are now and where you want to be will come together. You're awakening—that's what counts. It sends a message to all things negative within that their days of usurping your serenity are numbered, that change is imminent.

Still, as you get closer to freedom, note this paradox. Even if every atom in you wants to be free and you're bone-tired of stale habits of relating, change often engenders resistance. Change can feel intimidating. You're on the verge of making headway with a major block, yet, weirdly, a stubbornness resists the breakthrough. How does this manifest? You may temporarily revert to emotional ruts, feel fatigued, feel restless, or be overtaken by inertia. No need to panic. Internally, you're stirring things up, invoking emotional growth, which may take some adjustment. Try to ease into this shift, breathing your way through it. Be sweet to yourself; this phase will pass. Keep moving forward as you develop more trust in your new direction. Becoming free involves learning to be carried by a force greater than fear of change, greater than anything.

To facilitate the process, this book will teach you to map the world of emotions. Its geography can be known. Emotions are an intimate part of who we are. Our right and duty as seekers of consciousness is to know how they function. Keeping this a mystery keeps you in the dark, and that won't serve you. In the next chapter I'll share four practical secrets that will empower your emotional life and enlarge your repertoire of coping skills.

The best way to keep a prisoner from escaping is to make sure he never knows he's in prison.

—FYODOR DOSTOEVSKY

2

FOUR PRACTICAL SECRETS
TO EMPOWERING YOUR
EMOTIONAL LIFE

EMOTIONS CAN COME at you hard and fast. You must be prepared.

In a flash, negativity can spin you into a tizzy, your center blown to smithereens. Not to worry. You're about to replace that "been there, done that" scenario with more successful ways to cope. I'm going to provide you with strategies for dealing with every angle of emotions—cerebral and intuitive, from earth to heaven. These have repeatedly rescued me, friends, and patients from losing our emotional balance. The four secrets I'll discuss will expose the workings of negativity so that it can't steal your peace of mind or mute your awe for the mind-blowing universe we inhabit.

This chapter offers an overview of the four major components of emotions: their biology, spirituality, energetic power, and psychology. This is the unifying theme I'll develop throughout this book. Together, these components create an elegant portrait of your emotional self, revealing breakthroughs about how you operate that will lead to freedom. To omit even one impairs your inner vision; it's as partial a sight as color blindness. Without a healthy respect for them all, your effort to master emotions will be thwarted—an unacceptable limitation if you want to be free. By paying attention to each component, you'll become adept at transforming negative to positive, achieving a true integration of your powers. You'll taste the freedom of conquering the bad boys of fear and their relations, a natural high to look forward to. I'll describe how to parlay basic information about each component into simple daily actions that will propel you forward.

SECRET 1: REPROGRAM THE BIOLOGY OF YOUR EMOTIONS

To know thyself, you must know some basics of your biology. Outrageously, most people remain uninformed. Biology lends piercing insights into our emotions. It is the awesome science of life (from the Greek *bios,* meaning "life," and *logos,* meaning "reason") that defines the laws of how living things relate, both physically and emotionally. True, high school or college rarely imparts the subject's magic. And the harrowing sight of that poor limp frog pinned belly up for us to dissect in the ninth grade remains branded in my brain. However, the essence of biology I want to transmit involves dazzling life force; I'll show you how to ignite the biochemicals of happiness, turning your mind and body into a finely tuned, mean machine. Taking responsibility for your biology and developing emotional habits to support its highest functioning is a fundamental step toward freedom.

A revelation of twenty-first-century science is that anxiety and loneliness aren't just feelings. Nor are love and hope. All emotions trigger biological reactions that shape your health just as distinctly as what you choose to eat or how you choose to exercise. When you learn to change your emotional reaction to a situation, you change your biological reaction as well. I want to emphasize: *how you react emotionally is a choice in any situation—and those cumulative choices can make or break your chances for well-being.* Appreciating the physical repercussions of emotions makes you more perceptive about how to react, a life-altering realization.

There are two biological scenarios I want you to memorize: (1) how emotional stress depletes your body and (2) how calm revives your body. To clarify both, I'll present explanations and diagrams to etch in your awareness the architecture of these mind-body connections. Why is this important? Stress is the enemy of emotional freedom. We can't afford to indulge it or remain oblivious to the biological deple- tion it causes. Alternatively, calm is an ongoing state we can seek to counteract stress's wear and tear.

How Emotional Stress Depletes Your Body

Short-Term Effects

Your brain processes emotions. When it senses a potential threat—say, a car screeching to a halt right in front of you or your beet-faced boss flipping out—it poises the body for protection, a primitive, lifesaving instinct. The amygdala, your brain's emotional center, goes on high alert. It sets off a fight-or-flight response. This stimulates your adrenal glands (capping the kidneys) to produce the stress hormones cortisol and adrenaline. In the blink of an eye, you're transformed into your hyperattentive superself: your eyes dilate, and your blood pressure, heart rate, blood sugar, and muscle tension increase. (Think Popeye after he eats his spinach.) All systems reactive to the max, you're thrust into survival mode with extra energy and focus to conquer danger.

Long-Term Effects

Your body is brilliantly adaptive to sudden threats, but chronic emo- tional stress can make it degenerate. Your superself inevitably poops out. While those stress hormones have primed you to respond effec- tively to a physical threat—running away from a mugger, dashing into the street to rescue a toddler from an oncoming car—in most cases, the stress chemicals coursing through your system are an excessive reaction to contemporary aggravations that aren't about physical sur- vival. Yet your body doesn't know this; it behaves as if you're in a per- petual crisis. It clenches and defends to get through the day. If someone cuts you off in traffic or is rude, you're apt to react as if a tiger in the woods attacked. Emotional stress comes from outer sources—a bullying coworker, a snooty relative—but it's also what you do to yourself in your own head. The stress hormones that you need for emergencies now become silent assassins as worry, anger, or fear beat at your immune system. You're a sitting duck for hypertension, heart disease, some cancers, and depression (serotonin, a neurochemical that helps regulate mood, gets sapped, which can lead to anxiety and depression). Moreover, those inflammatory chemicals can incite nasty conditions such as rashes, ulcers, and irritable bowel syndrome. Stress's slow burn has been shown to make you age faster, die sooner, and lead an unhealthy, unhappy life.

You Under Stress: The Fight-or-Flight Response

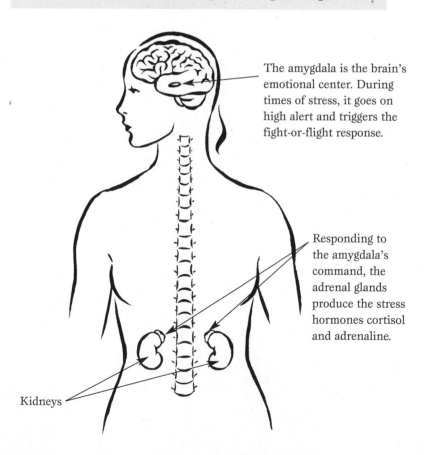

The amygdala is the brain's emotional center. During times of stress, it goes on high alert and triggers the fight-or-flight response.

Responding to the amygdala's command, the adrenal glands produce the stress hormones cortisol and adrenaline.

Kidneys

How Calm Revives Your Body

Finding calm is an emotionally stressed-out person's salvation, a humane time-out from turmoil when you're centered and at ease. A state of calm floods the body with the bliss of endorphins, your brain's opiate-like natural painkillers. Serotonin becomes replenished, putting you in a good mood and making daily irritations tolerable. Stress hormones wane as spasms in your shoulders and gut loosen, heart rate and blood pressure lower, mental frenzy relents. The pretzel in you untwists on all levels. Your body can breathe freely again and gratefully releases its guard to become more open, soft, expansive. Harvard University's Dr. Herbert Benson calls this the "relaxation response," an antidote for the fear-based fight-or-flight style of emotional coping.

The Calm You: The Relaxation Response

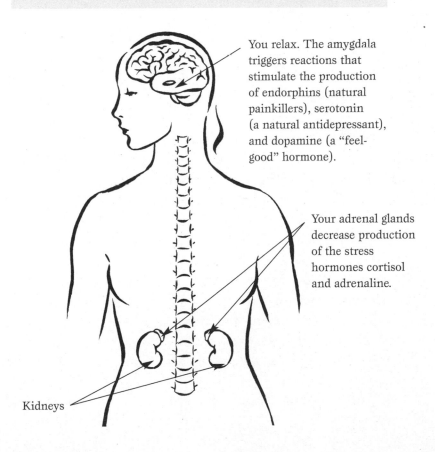

You relax. The amygdala triggers reactions that stimulate the production of endorphins (natural painkillers), serotonin (a natural antidepressant), and dopamine (a "feel-good" hormone).

Your adrenal glands decrease production of the stress hormones cortisol and adrenaline.

Kidneys

To find calm, you must be an activist. Realize this distinction: calm is something you must go after, whereas stress comes after you. True, you may drift into calm while gazing at a turquoise sea or listening to the song of doves, but in our manic world, you must learn to deliberately cultivate such peacefulness. It's a mistake to think it'll just descend on you.

The biology of emotional freedom depends on getting your endorphins flowing and turning off your stress hormones. How do you achieve this? Laughter, exercise, meditation, and doing anything that makes you feel loved, including making love. Set out to experience a little bit more calm each day. Here's how to get started.

Meditate to Experience Emotional Freedom

Feelings of freedom begin to percolate in us when we calm down. Meditation is the gold standard of calming techniques. For millennia, it's been used by traditions from Zen to Judaism to attain inner stillness. I was overjoyed to see a *Time* magazine cover story, "The Science of Meditation," a tribute to how Eastern mysticism and Western medicine are finally merging their truths. It's useable in the here and now, not on some rarefied plane. I swear by meditation, practice it daily, and teach it to my patients. It has saved me many times from losing my marbles when life amps up and emotions are swirling. If I stop meditating, even for short spurts, I'll start feeling squirrelly, irritable, and more overwhelmed by the jitter of the world.

Meditation quiets your mind and reprograms your biology (aside from its spiritual and energetic advantages, which you'll discover). The miracle of brain imaging has done wonders to demystify meditation, pinpointing cerebral changes responsible for the calm you feel. Most striking, regular meditation has been shown to literally change the brain by promoting growth in a region responsible for integrating thoughts and emotions; this wires us to deal with stress better. I'm happy to report that it also works fast. In just minutes, meditators have shown increased alpha activity, the brain waves indicating relaxation.

My patient "Mister C" was a poster boy for someone who needed meditation. At thirty, a gifted, adrenaline-addicted, African American rap musician, his songs had topped the charts. Mister C's badge of honor was to be in perpetual motion. I recognized that he was a rare bird in the rap business, committed to getting positive messages out. The death of his only brother from a heroin overdose made Mister C about as clean and sober as you can get. I respected his integrity, his refusal "to sell out for the big bucks by hyping gangstas, guns, and crack dealers." At our first session, he was the epitome of cool in baggy pants, backward baseball cap, and mirrored shades. But I soon saw that he was a nail-biting, jaw-clenching, acid-reflux-singed bundle of nerves. Mister C arrived with a very long list of symptoms, all deemed stress-induced by his referring internist: he was a casualty of his own stress hormones.

Using Energy Psychiatry, we focused on Mister C going slower and calming down. I suggested that he meditate. At first, he bristled. "Oh, c'mon. I'll lose my edge. It's boring. A waste of time. Mumbo-jumbo." He was giving me a dose of attitude, showing off his inner tough guy. (Too late: I'd already gotten glimpses that he was a softy, a dutiful son, and a Robin Hood to kids in South Central L.A.)

Perhaps you're like Mister C: too driven and restless to believe that you can be both a high achiever and a calm person. You may be unable to release the outdated image of the patchouli-scented, laid-back navelgazer, so far from the efficient person you want to be. This is why appreciating the biological breakthroughs of meditation is so crucial. Many people have such misconceptions before they see how much sharper they get navigating busy lives from a calm emotional place. I explained to Mister C how neuroscientists have documented that daily meditation improves the ability to focus. Though Mister C had "no comment" about anything "New Age," he did go for the biological reasons to meditate. Despite all the glitz of his life as a performer, he was a pragmatist. As is true for many of my patients, once a technique's science is substantiated, they're comfortable with it. Previously, all Mister C knew was how to drive himself; my job was to show him ways to calmly just Be. Discomfort can motivate; it got him to try what had only recently seemed "ridiculous."

To begin, I started Mister C with the short meditation I'll describe below, and taught him others I'll cover later. Because calm can feel like an alien state, it's best to acclimate slowly. Merely sitting still for a few seconds can be nerve-wracking when you're addicted to the adrenaline surge of constant activity. Over the next few weeks, as I taught Mister C the basics of meditation, I watched more squirming, fidgeting, scratching, throat clearing, and twitching eyelids than I've ever dreamed I'd see. Mister C was like a dog that couldn't find the right position. Though I concluded he set the world record for being antsy, such reactions were, to me, a familiar part of the learning process. To varying degrees, everyone gets antsy, especially at the beginning of meditation. But soon, Mister C was actually sitting still for sixty seconds, then for three minutes. He practiced these short meditations many times throughout the day. He was starting to get a better grip on de-escalating stress by becoming calmer. To the surprise of this take-charge, macho guy, so successful at making things happen in the real world, meditation was giving him a feeling of mastery, but this time of himself. And this mastery in turn translated into even greater success in the world.

In the footsteps of Mister C, get ready to prime your biology for emotional freedom with the following meditation. It's only three minutes, a quick way to access your inner calm. (However, if, like Mister C, you find it hard to sit for three minutes, it's fine to start with even a few seconds, then build up.) Set a timer if necessary so you stick to three minutes. In future exercises, as you become more proficient, you can meditate as long as you like, but more isn't better now. Here, the goal is to hone your focus, then notice results. The turnaround of tension will be fast. When stress strikes or simply to become more mellow, practice this meditation. Try it once daily, then gradually increase the frequency to two or three times a day.

Emotional Action Step

APPLYING THE FIRST SECRET: REPROGRAM THE BIOLOGY OF YOUR EMOTIONS

Reduce Stress with This Three-Minute Meditation

1. *Find a comfortable, quiet place.* Wearing loose clothing, settle into a relaxed position in a spot where you won't be interrupted by phones, beepers, or people. It's best to sit upright on a couch, chair, or cushion, so you don't fall asleep. You can be cross-legged or with legs extended, whatever makes you most at ease.

2. *Focus on your breath to quiet your thoughts.* Eyes closed, gently place your awareness on your breath. Be conscious only of breathing in and breathing out. When thoughts come, and they will, visualize them as clouds passing in the sky. Notice your thoughts, but don't attach any judgment to them. Just let them float away and gently return to focusing on your breath. Maintain a centered state of calm by continuing to follow the movement of your breath.

3. *Breathe in calm, breathe out stress.* Let yourself feel the sensuality of inhaling and exhaling as air passes through your nostrils and chest like a cool breeze. Take pleasure in the breath's hypnotic rhythm, what the Buddha described as "breathing in and out sensitive to rapture." With each slow, deep breath, feel yourself inhaling calm, sweet as the scent of summer jasmine, then exhaling stress. Inhale calm, then exhale fear. Inhale calm, then exhale frustration. All negativity is released. Your body unwinds, lulling your biology. You're cocooned by the safety of stillness. Keep refocusing on your breath and the calm. Only the calm.

This simple, stress-busting meditation is an initial action step you can take to forge a winning partnership with your biology. Practicing it, you'll become increasingly adept at upping endorphins and short-circuiting your flight-or-flight response, biological gifts of meditation. Once you get the hang of neutralizing stress, it's a merciful reprieve for the body. You'll feel a load lift when uptightness dissipates.

SECRET 2: UNCOVER THE SPIRITUAL MEANING OF YOUR EMOTIONS

As a psychiatrist, I'm in the sacred position of getting to hear what goes on in people's heads, from soccer moms to movie stars. I wish you could be a fly on the wall in my office. Then you'd see why I'm so struck by our basic emotional commonalities, despite how externally different we may seem. To cope with the ongoing saga of life's conundrums, we all have the same set of emotions to choose from (there are only so many) and often keep getting similarly sabotaged. Here's the double bind: everyone wants love, but negativity, our own or another's, often subverts us. So we stay stuck in an unfree limbo of lovelessness for extended periods. Simply put, what is our suffering for? The puzzle can be solved, but it requires a spiritual perspective.

Spirituality, as I'm defining it, is a quest for meaning that goes beyond the linear mind to access a vaster force of compassion to frame everything. Our emotional landscapes are practically unintelligible without this. Why? Because if you don't have an expanded context within which to decipher emotions, the bare bones of many experiences can seem bleak or punishing—a dead-end conclusion that imprisons. Spirituality is freeing because it means opening the heart and doing your darnedest to see every nanosecond of existence through this aperture. Always, you must ask, "How can a situation— any situation—help me grow and develop loving-kindness toward myself or others?" Both with patients and personally, I've seen the authority this question has to recast despair. Adversity of any kind can yield hidden gifts. During boyhood, one of my patients had to walk miles each day to school and thus became great at whistling, a talent that continues to enchant him and his young daughter. Similarly, we can mine goodness in all experiences when we learn to find the spiritual message within emotional turmoil.

I became very aware of the existence of spirit when I was a child up on the roof of our garage. I'd lie there in my white flannel nightgown, mesmerized by the night sky, quietly certain that the moon and the stars were my friends. But in addition, I felt that a large force was loving me, something I couldn't name but knew was real. Though my parents, not unreasonably, hoped that I'd find God in Judaism, the religion in which I was raised, I mostly found spirituality gazing at the heavens. In my life, the thread runs from there to the last two decades with my Daoist teacher, whose tenets are grounded in revering nature.

Spirituality isn't static. It's an evolving optimism that won't let hardship get the best of you. It apprises you that something good can show up at any time. From my own instincts and from my spiritual teacher, I've also come to define spirituality not just as recognizing that there's more than the material realm, but that we're all points of light bonded together in a vaster continuum. In the context of emotional freedom, a spiritual vantage point is liberating for numerous reasons:

1. By opening yourself to something larger, a compassionate higher power of your own (God, Goddess, nature, love, or something nameless), you'll gain strength beyond your own to conquer adversity. You're not alone. Never have been. You'll feel the safety in that.
2. You'll learn how to be released from what Buddhists call "monkey mind," the circular insecurities that incarcerate you in your smallest self. In Energy Psychiatry I've seen how a problem often can't be solved on a problem's level. To put distance between yourself and negativity, you must view it from higher ground.
3. You'll realize that there's something greater than the emotion of the moment. If you don't know this—and most people don't—you'll think your anger is all there is. You'll get into how justified you are to hold on to it, a lethal stance that fuels war in your kitchen or globally. When you think and act from the framework of spirituality I'm presenting, you'll see anger as an impetus to grow, to resolve differences, to rise above them. You won't stay

angry because you believe it's deserved or lose your temper as a pressure-release valve. You won't want to hurt others, rather, you'll seek to become more expanded in yourself.

Here's my gospel about how to conceptualize emotions in spiritual terms: view each one as a trusted guide whose purpose is to enlarge your heart. I'm presenting emotions as a path to spiritual awakening, a way to break through to the light inside you. Specific emotions play specific roles. For instance, consider how the misery of depression can teach you to develop hope or how bitter jealousy can prompt the cultivation of self-esteem. These key transformations are more than psychological. *They refine your soul, which is your reason to be. There is nothing as important.* Remember this when life gets hard or lonely. I want you to understand that there is meaning and beauty in these difficult experiences too.

My spiritual teacher has helped give me an appreciation of the big-picture reasons for why we're here, a reference point sorely lacking in our spiritually phobic medical system. (Happily, though, I do see a growing recognition that spirituality is integral to good medicine. In fact, over half our medical schools, from Stanford to Harvard, now offer courses in spirituality and healing or incorporate the theme into their curriculum.) It's beyond me how to make complete sense of your purpose without it. Understanding the big picture gives you a shot at freedom because it defines the role emotions play in your awakening. My teacher says to look at life as your main career and as a divine classroom. Your spirit is in human form to learn what the body and emotions can teach about love, including how to overcome a slew of obstacles. The way you approach everything—your job, family, friends, health—must be in service to that aim.

If the following scheme resonates with your views, let it help you make sense of the role your emotions play. However, if you don't believe in anything other than this world but value being a compassionate person, let that stellar goal guide you in your explorations; don't fret about the rest. Or if what I'm proposing is something you'd never considered, see how it intuitively sits as you gauge fresh possibilities.

A Simple Breakdown of Life: Your Purpose in a Nutshell

What is this talked-of mystery of birth
But being mounted bareback on the earth?
—ROBERT FROST

Your soul is on a journey. You're born here as part of that journey. You live a certain number of years with the unique chance of developing your soul as a human being (emotions are catalysts for this). Your body dies. Your soul's growth continues to the next phase.

The great news about this trek is that you have a lot more longevity than you probably thought. In the grander plan, we all belong to no-time and all time. During your short stay here (I know it can feel like forever sometimes), don't lose sight of how fortunate you are to have a body, with all its tribulations and reasons to cheer, because it helps the spirit grow in many ways. Perhaps emotions are tailored for mammalian physiology, are exclusive to this realm. I'd like you to appreciate the specialness of their role as springboards to freedom.

Spirituality is a strength that can work for you. Some path-forging scientists are downright passionate about how our brains are programmed for it. Dr. Andrew Newberg, a radiologist at the University of Pennsylvania, and his colleague Eugene D'Aquili scanned the brains of meditating Buddhist monks and Franciscan nuns in prayer. They found that in these states of spiritual communion, distinct changes were set off in the brain. Most significant, the part that orients you to time and space, that defines your usual identity, was inhibited. This is a gigantic deal! It unlocks the doors of perception ordinarily guarded by the linear mind. With this tireless watchdog gone, the Buddhist meditators were free to experience a blissful "oneness with the universe," and the Franciscans sensed "the presence of God." Even the medical lab's wires, meters, and electrodes didn't inhibit these meditators' transcendent connection. (The authors documented how we're "hardwired for spirituality" in their book *Why God Won't Go Away*.) Impressively, this study was the forerunner of others that have mapped the brain's programming for spirituality, charting how such experiences are biologically observable, scientifically real.

How does this inform your emotional freedom? We now have

scientific evidence that spirituality can transport your brain to some pretty elevating places where it wouldn't ordinarily go. At the very least, you'll see emotions—and everything else—from a juicier panorama. But further, embracing your spiritual side will secure your relationship with a loving force that's realer than real. There's no downside to such an alliance. It'll give you the edge you need to combat negativity and touch the ecstasy of the heart.

The upcoming Heart-Centering Meditation forms the bedrock of my own spiritual practice, and it's one I teach to my patients. It's crucial to emotional freedom because it shifts you from vicious rants about yourself into compassion. I know how easily these hate-fests can gather steam; this meditation averts them quickly. But as my spiritual teacher, who's a realist, says, "Progress occurs when we beat ourselves up a little less every day." So, with that modest but quite respectable goal, we'll look at how the meditation applies to self-nurturing. The key to opening the heart—what Daoists call the "little sun"—is to use your intuition. Analyzing won't work: the linear mind can't viscerally grasp what the knower behind the thinker can. In this centering meditation I'll describe ways your body can intuitively sense the heart's nuances, a sanity saver to utilize whenever you're upset or tired or when you start mentally flogging yourself. Activating your heart turns the tables on negative feelings.

Emotional Action Step

APPLYING THE SECOND SECRET: UNCOVER THE SPIRITUAL MEANING OF YOUR EMOTIONS

A Heart-Centering Meditation to Counter Negative Self-Talk

1. *Settle down.* In a tranquil setting, sit comfortably and close your eyes. Take a few long, deep breaths to relieve tension. Even if your negative thoughts are going a mile a minute (you know that broken record: "I'm not good enough, smart enough, spiritual enough," yada yada), keep concentrating on your breath as best you can.

2. *Tune in to your heart.* Lightly rest your palm over your heart in the midchest. This energy center is the entryway to compassion and spirit. In a relaxed state, inwardly request to connect with a higher power, a force greater than yourself that links you to love. It can be God, the starlit sky, or a beneficent intelligence, whatever stirs you. Then, in your heart area, notice what you intuitively *feel,* not what you *think.* You may experience a soothing warmth, comfort, clarity, even bliss. I often get shivers, feel a wave of goose bumps, or am moved to tears. It's easiest to first feel spirit inside you. From that home base, you can better sense it everywhere. Stay aware of your heart as it opens more and more, infusing you with compassion. If negative self-talk still arises, keep your compassion flowing. The spiritual meaning of doing this is learning to have mercy on yourself for any perceived lacking, to know that you're enough just as you are. With that meaning in mind, let the freedom of compassion flood your body, a balm for all that ails.

This meditation is a surefire antidote to negative self-talk. I've never seen anyone able to sustain a denigrating diatribe when they're centered in the heart. I'm indefatigable when it comes to equating compassion with freedom. I hope the potency of this pairing really clicks for you. Compassion is the great transformer, of the self and the world. No matter how things seem, your compassion doesn't fall on deaf ears. Remember: Jesus talked about love and the people listened. Whenever you feel lost, return to your heart. It's the doorway to heaven.

SECRET 3: LEARN THE ENERGETIC POWER OF YOUR EMOTIONS

In Energy Psychiatry I've learned to see emotions as a stunning expression of energy. Positive ones nurture you. Negative ones deplete you. In terms of wattage, hope, self-acceptance, and compassion make you brighter, freer; shame, envy, and desire for revenge dim your brightness. You feel emotions internally, while their energy extends beyond your body, affecting everyone you contact. Similarly, the emotions of others register in you.

Since childhood, I've been able to sense energy around people. I didn't know what to call it then, but it felt as real as the nose on my face. I knew when people were scared, peaceful, or distraught, though these intuitions, particularly negative ones, often didn't jibe with the persona they showed the world. A happy face without a happy heart was a cinch to sense. Take Eric, a dashing British businessman who had it all. The night my parents introduced us, Eric looked like James Bond in his tux as he whisked them off to a party in his chauffeured Rolls. Eric was friendly to everyone, yet in his presence an intense whiff of desperate sadness hit me like pungent perfume—such a strange but distinct sensation. I was spooked, and recoiled. The next day I told Mother about my feelings. She looked part blank, part exasperated, assuring me that Eric was fine. The subject was dropped. I felt like a troublemaker, doubted my perceptions, until a few months later. My parents received an overseas call: Eric had killed himself. Mother and Dad were dumbfounded because Eric's bravado had so successfully masked his depression. For me, this news was a creepily unnerving validation I'd rather not have had. I had no way of framing it as an affirmation of my maturing sensitivity. Ultimately, my parents wrote off my forecast as a peculiar coincidence. Much as they adored me, they didn't know what emotional energy was, why I sensed it, or how to support my intuitive abilities.

Now, as an Energy Psychiatrist, I want to convey to you that emotions are intuitively palpable; you can learn to access their force field to enhance your freedom. I'd like you to begin to think of emotions in terms of subtle energy, a "vibe" emanating from yourself and others, an intimate sensing. Subtle energy is right in front of you but isn't visible. It can be felt inches or feet from the body. I'll describe how to sense it with intuition. Indigenous healing traditions revere subtle energy as our life force. In Chinese medicine it's called *chi*. It's *mana* to Hawaiian kahunas, *prana* to Indian yogic practitioners. Though the molecular structure of subtle energy isn't yet fully defined, scientists have measured increased photon emissions and electromagnetic readings around healing practitioners.

For an unforgettable visual of how the energy of emotions can impact the body, take a look at Dr. Masuro Emoto's book *The Hidden Messages of Water.* His high-speed photographs of frozen water crystals send a valuable message. Listen to what he observed. When sentiments such as "I love you" or "You're wonderful" were directed to water, symmetrical, rainbow-hued snowflake patterns took form, unfolding universes of delight. However, the negative emotions of "I hate you" or "You make me sick" created fractured, ugly shapes with muddled colors—not what you want in your body. (Though some consider this work controversial, Dr. Dean Radin at the Institute of Noetic Sciences has successfully replicated it, and other similar experiments are under way). Take time to assimilate these findings. They have momentous implications for your emotional freedom: since you're composed mostly of water, you must generate maximal positivity to stay healthy and whole. Also, you can't afford to nurse resentments or self-loathing without suffering toxicity.

I realize that it's one thing to know this, yet another to live it. The problem is that negative emotional energy is basically louder and wilder than the positive, and more seductively grabs your attention. Picture a bucking bronco versus a contented cat warming its belly in the sun. If both were in front of you, where would your attention go? Positive emotions, delicious as they are, don't have as dramatic an energetic pull. That's why as a child and intuitive novice, I'd have dead-on intuitions about unspoken pain such as Eric's as well as illnesses and disasters, but was less apt to pick up happier events. Needless to say, this can be a disconcerting phenomenon until it's understood. On an intuitive level, emotions such as grief and terror are easier to sense than the lower-keyed vibes of calmness or confidence. It's important that you channel this knowledge into new behaviors so you're not the doomed moth eternally drawn to the flame.

Take Action: Harness the Energy of Words and Tone

The Zen of emotional freedom entails learning to resist negativity's flash and turn up the volume on the positive. Let's make this maneuver practical by examining your words and tone, areas where you can have total control if you exert it. As Dr. Emoto's work indicated, words impart energy that can be enlivening or malignant. This is true whether you direct words to yourself or others. You think them. You want to express them. Ready. Aim. Fire. Whether words set off a love bomb or a noxious explosion, they transfer energy to the target, eliciting a response. You can wield this force for construction or destruction. The aim is always to treat yourself and others well.

Words ride on the energy of tone, its warmth or coldness; think of tone as the music of how words are expressed. You want this music to be soulful, whether you're giving sweet talk or tough love. With patients I'm keenly aware of the positive impact of a compassionate, heartfelt tone. That energy quickens healing, lets me be heard better, makes it safer for patients to be vulnerable. A little snip or judgment in my tone, and therapy can be sunk. But with a little compassion, we're cookin'!

My patient Phoebe, at nineteen a painfully shy, trembly-voiced college student, has torturous anxiety attacks she's valiantly trying to get a grip on. I respect Phoebe's tenaciousness—she shows up every week on the dot. She's brave and getting braver. Still, she berates herself for not improving "fast enough." My compassion for Phoebe overflows, but recovery can take time. So, in a caring tone, which comes so easily with her, I reassure her, "You're doing the best you can." Phoebe feels the support. Coincidentally, her sister, a "pull-yourself-up-by-your-bootstraps" vigilante and professional motivational speaker, says the very same words to her. But as Phoebe puts it, her sister speaks "with a snicker that makes me feel like a pathetic weakling, a lost cause." Same syllables, two tones. See the difference. Freedom begets freedom. When you're coming from a conscious, empathic place, that energy fills you and extends to others. This won't make you into a Pollyanna or a pushover. Rather, you can get across almost anything if you say it the right way.

Boy, did I learn that a few years ago. At the time, my father's Parkinson's disease had become so debilitating that he couldn't live on his own anymore. Excruciating as it was, I explored assisted-living facilities. My father the physician, so surefooted on the tennis court (his heaven), now couldn't walk on his own. He needed complete care: diapers, someone to feed him and even brush his teeth. God, it had come to this: the Ocean Villa in Santa Monica, the fifth of ten such facilities on my list. Why do they always name these last resorts as if they were cheery holiday getaways? Most are overcrowded and dark and smell awful. The manager led me through a small city of wheelchairs: elderly residents with Alzheimer's or Parkinson's, heads drooped, drool on bibs, though there were still a few bright eyes. This man in a spotless suit led me to the second floor where my father's single room would be. At least it had a view of the Pacific, I thought. He'd like that.

However, while looking out the window onto Ocean Avenue I did a double take. Across the street I saw my white Volkswagen convertible where I'd parked it. But there were these teenagers dressed like gang members, jiggling the lock of the driver's side, attempting to break in. I couldn't believe it. Everything in me rallied. This wasn't going to happen. I charged down the stairs of Ocean Villa. I could hear the manager's voice fading: "Do you think you should go out there?" I didn't think. I just went. In the two minutes it took me to reach my car, they'd stolen my radio. A muscle-bound, tattooed kid smoking a cigarette was holding it on his lap in the backseat of his car, gloating. He was flanked by two husky girls with some serious mascara and sizeable hair, who looked even more intimidating.

You'd think I would've been a basket case but, amazingly, I was the picture of composure. Not angry. Not frightened. Just calm. I intuitively knew what to do, and did it—a feat I credit to years of meditation practice spontaneously kicking in. I looked straight at this guy who would've scared the bejesus out of a sane person and said, "If you give me the radio back, I won't call the police." Where that sentence came from I do not know. It sounded laughably naive when I was saying it. Even so, my tone was gentle, firm, even loving, and remarkably without blame. I surprised myself as I listened. Miracles do happen. The next thing I knew he was handing over the radio, flailing wires and all. I'll never forget how shockingly obedient he seemed, like a puppy just wanting to please. I smiled. I thanked him. Then, muffler roaring, that low-rider Chevy drove away.

In hindsight, I realize how foolish and dangerous my actions were. I was risking my life for a blasted radio. Get real: these "kids" could've harmed me. But, in the crazed altered state of slowly losing my father,

I instinctively needed to take back control. I couldn't allow anything more to be stolen from us. I'm well aware that there might've been a very different outcome had my tone been demanding, angry, or fearful. This drama, compliments of Life 101, hammered home the influential energy of words and tone—how they can turn negativity around, are peacemakers with adversaries, and can create outcomes that seem inconceivable.

Remember this when you're up against some nemesis, whether another person or within yourself. The art of communicating is to speak with a nonjudging sensitivity and mean it rather than impulsively verbalizing whatever feelings arise; there's no better way to make a point. It doesn't mean you don't have negative feelings; you just don't come from that place. As you become more practiced at sensing the energy of emotions, you'll get better at identifying and responding to them. The next exercise will take you beyond theory to give you that direct experience.

Emotional Action Step

APPLYING THE THIRD SECRET: LEARN THE ENERGETIC POWER OF YOUR EMOTIONS

Try an Intuitive Experiment: Sense the Difference Between Positive and Negative Emotions

In this experiment, you're going to compare two scenarios. With both observe how your words and tone affect your body and emotional state. Spend at least a few minutes trying these words on.

Scenario 1. Stand in front of a mirror and sincerely say to yourself in a loving, appreciative tone, "I look terrific and I'm a fantastic person." Stay focused on your positives. Then feel, don't think. Notice how your body reacts. Are you breathing easier? Do your shoulders relax? Does your gut untighten?

Does your energy rise? Do you feel happier? Lighter? Freer?
Also, note any other changes.

Scenario 2. Stand in front of the mirror and say in your nastiest,
most hateful tone, "I look horrible and I despise myself." Really
mean it. Flare those negatives up. How does your body react
now? Notice your shoulders, your gut, your chest. Is your
energy higher or lower? Are you clenching? Breathing
shallowly? Do you feel depressed? Are your aches and pains
aggravated? Whatever you sense, note it. Stew in this negativity
awhile so you won't forget the feel of toxic energy.

I'm so taken by this exercise because it spells out that positive and
negative energy are about as opposite as you can get. No confusing
them. Ask yourself which you prefer. It's time to make a choice and go
after it. The launching pad for emotional freedom is always yourself.
Words, tone, and the positive or negative energy of emotions all figure
in. You must become accountable for the vibes you expose yourself and
others to. The next time someone speaks to you, note the physical reaction within your body, not how your brain processes the actual words.
Feel the energy beneath those words; notice how your body responds
to that. If the content of someone's words is positive, yet the energy
beneath it causes you to contract, respect that physical reaction.
Energy doesn't lie. Keep sensing it, trusting it, letting it liberate you.

SECRET 4: MAP THE PSYCHOLOGY
OF YOUR EMOTIONS

Why do you feel what you feel? Where do fear of commitment, alpha
achieving, or looking on the bright side begin? Which emotional coping styles hinder or serve you? These urgent questions are the
lifeblood of psychology's study of emotions and behavior. You need to
know your psychological self so unhealthy patterning doesn't stifle

you. I get a special charge out of picturing all the psychotherapists and their patients around the world valiantly tackling hard issues. Two people sitting across from each other in reverence to growth, a noble undertaking. I've seen it from both sides. Part of my role as psychiatrist is helping patients attain psychological insights, sparkling as always when they pop from the void; my therapist continues to work the same magic for me. Whether I'm the healer or healing recipient, I'm wowed. I lust for those light-bursts of clarity that edge me closer to love and freedom or lift confusion, secrets you'll tap in to yourself.

Here's a first look at how psychology can liberate your heart and head. I'll focus on one principle—"You are not your parents"—which is so central to your emotional freedom that it can dictate how you treat yourself and everyone you love.

You Are Not Your Parents: Learn from Their Assets and Shortcomings

To know your psychology, there's no detour around your parents. Beloved or dreaded, these two people emotionally molded you. Spiritual teacher Ram Dass nails it when he says, "If you think you're enlightened, go spend a week with your parents." There you have it: the good, bad, and the ugly. I say, stir up that pot; examine the relationship with your parents. Why? To achieve emotional freedom, you want to disentangle yourself from their worst traits and embody the best.

Who you are emotionally often reflects who your parents are. While growing up, it's frequently monkey see, monkey do. For better or worse, you emulate your parents' virtues and faults. If your mother was anxious or a worrywart, chances are she transmitted some of that to you. If your father was a bastion of hope, that came through too. In addition, you may contain interesting dualities of both parents. For example, my mother was a people person, my father more a loner. I have both in me, and I've learned to embrace each. You can do likewise with the dualities you've inherited.

Sometimes, in an attempt to be different from your parents, you may develop completely opposite emotional coping styles. For example, if your mother was an inveterate nagger, you may shun all confrontation. If your father was intensely critical, you may be reluctant to be honest with others when you disagree. These styles also deserve examination so that instead of simply doing the opposite of what your parents did, you can find a truly authentic, balanced way to be.

With patients and workshop participants, I've repeatedly seen how one member of a family seems chosen to change generational patterns. He or she didn't ask for this job, yet it's given to that person. Take my patient Connie, at twenty-three a single working mother. For generations the women in her family—including herself—had been physically abused by one or both parents. Then they became abusers of their own children, a tragically predictable programming. Connie was forced to face her own capacity for violence after punching her four-year-old daughter, who was having a tantrum, in a fit of rage. This was hardly the first time, though in remorse she'd promised herself to stop, but over and again she'd failed. Connie cherished her child and felt tremendous shame. She said, "Hurting my baby feels barbaric. Sickening." But now, having finally sought help and working with me, she vowed, "I won't be a monster. The violence is over." Connie had long known she was out of control, but finally, finally screamed "no" to her programming. That "no" changed everything. The robotic cycle of generational abuse stopped with her. In our sessions, Connie was committed to being vigilant, to deal with simmering stress before she snapped into violence. Also, she was ready to face the rage and misery of having herself been abused. Then she could avoid becoming what was done to her by purging the poisoned childhood within. These efforts—to me, deeply moving—along with anger management classes and a single mothers' support group released Connie from the bondage of her negative inheritance. Courageous self-scrutiny and a dedication to healing furthered her emotional freedom, the freedom of her daughter, and of future generations.

Similarly, in situations large and small, you have the choice to evolve past your parents' limitations. This choice and the changes that ensue exorcise the unhealthy habits you're unconsciously reenacting. When you refuse to be afraid because your father is fear-ridden, or reject being the victim your mother has become, that's real emancipation. The flip side of freedom is also accepting your parents' positive emotional legacy, the smarts and goodness they've handed down.

With parents it's nearly always a mixed bag. Freedom comes from going with the good and striving to shed the rest.

Emotional Action Step

APPLYING THE FOURTH SECRET: MAP THE PSYCHOLOGY OF YOUR EMOTIONS

TAKE AN EMOTIONAL INVENTORY OF YOUR PARENTS

To get a well-rounded picture of your parents, I'd like you to take an inventory of their top five positive and negative traits. Were they caring, good listeners, always there for you? And/or depressed, disappointed in life, blaming? Try using the format below. Identifying these traits, do your best to see your parents as human rather than idealizing or demonizing them. Get their pluses and minuses down on paper so they can stare right back at you. When reviewing the inventory, consider ways your parents' assets or liabilities impacted you. Which traits on your list instilled confidence? Humor? A sense of safety? Which ones impaired your well-being? Also, be truthful about the traits you too possess. If they are positive, embrace them. If they are negative, begin to work with one at a time to free yourself. You don't have to worry about turning into your parents if you take action not to parrot their dysfunction. Then decide what you want to retain. Let this inventory begin to help you rewire your psychological programming so it suits the freest you.

Trait	Mother	Father
Positive	1._____	1._____
	2._____	2._____
	3._____	3._____

4._____   4._____

5._____   5._____

Negative 1._____   1._____

2._____   2._____

3._____   3._____

4._____   4._____

5._____   5._____

Let me describe how I applied this inventory to my mother. She was my hero in so many ways. Mother fearlessly spoke her mind, seized every moment, and dedicated her life to helping people. Plus, she taught me the satisfaction of good conversations, something I treasure in my relationships now, a way to make close friendships that last. At dinner, in the car, or walking on the beach, we talked: about me, her, our patients, the state of the universe. I relished our repartee, our woman-to-woman sharing. These and other qualities she conveyed helped me blossom.

In contrast, one of my mother's most disturbing traits was her persistent criticism of my father, though she clearly loved him. In relationships peevishness often directs itself to what's closest at hand. Her digs included, "Teddy, you're so antisocial. Why do I always have to drag you places?" "You're a fixture in front of that damn television set." Or sometimes she'd call him "Little Lord Fauntleroy" after that well-mannered prissy boy in his tidy suit from the English novel. My father would pretend to ignore her or would growl with irritation, "Oh, Maxine, for God's sake, cut it out." Accepting my father as is wasn't in her repertoire. I asked Mother why. She said, "What's the point if I can't change him?" Never mind that he hadn't changed much over forty years of marriage (or that trying to coerce change typically ensures resistance).

That didn't stop her from trying. I'd wince at my mother's jabs, badly wished my father would stand up for himself more.

Conditioned patterns die hard. As the sixties song by P. F. Sloan goes, "The sins of the family fall on the daughter." It didn't take a rocket scientist to understand why I too sometimes made similar cutting remarks to my romantic partners, but it took me forever to see it. One past relationship woke me up to this. My boyfriend was an attractive, caring chiropractor whose humor kept me in stitches. But when my implacable inner criticizer sized him up on her clipboard, she noted that he was awfully skinny (bird bones, I thought). He also drank this gross, thick green algae concoction with each meal (mainly salads—also green). And he didn't go out much. The list went on. I heard myself ragging on him: "You know, I think you really should put on some weight." "Why can't we ever just eat at a regular restaurant?" "How come we don't go out more?" I shudder to remember these lines, but back then I couldn't stop myself. Criticisms just spurted out. I couldn't put two and two together that I was mimicking Mother. To his credit, this man had excellent self-esteem and wasn't about to apologize for what warranted no apology. He refused to let me speak this way to him. Further, he knew my parents and said to me, "The sad truth is, Judith, you sound just like your mother." Okay, this I didn't want to hear, but when I wrote down my inventory, I was forced to examine my behavior and to start to make changes.

Subsequently, my challenge has been quieting my mother's hypercritical voice as it wants to speak through my lips—a kind of possession—and striving to lovingly accept my partner basically as he is (though of course we have disagreements and seek compromise to improve communication). This means staying alert to the part of me that would be determined to improve even a saint if I were romantically involved with him. I strive not to obsess about the gratuitous barbs that go through my head and to refrain from expressing them to my partner. Rather I refocus on appreciating him and letting him simply be. My saving grace is that, unlike my mother, I don't want to criticize. Reviewing my inventory, I recognized that I didn't like that part of her and don't choose to perpetuate it. Though I have to stay on top of my conditioning, I've come a long way.

Freedom is about taking charge of who you want to be. Keep referring to this inventory on your journey with emotions. Whenever a feeling comes up, especially a negative one, ask yourself, "Who is reacting—me or my parents?" This is a telling question that reveals if you're a parent clone but don't know it. Like many of us, you may be stuck in the unconscious rut of responding like them, say, being a complainer or a drama queen. However, once you determine who's really running the show, you can decide to behave differently. At this point, before we zero in on transforming specific emotions in Part Two, it's enough to recognize arthritic coping habits as you consider alternatives. Doing so lets you locate your true voice and identity.

AS EVERYONE WITH even a little awareness understands, any gutless wonder can walk around oblivious to the effect of his or her emotions. What's it to them to keep acting out and hurting other people with disastrous results? Freedom asks more of you than that. Now that you've been initiated into the four secrets to emotional freedom, you've sampled the collective wisdom of your biology, spirituality, energetic power, and psychology. The more you know about these ingredients of emotions, the more they'll increase consciousness and a connection to your heart. Self-knowledge is a most impressive oracle, crystallizing who you are and can be. As it mounts, expect to feel a coming together inside of you, a beautiful feeling of awakening. I praise consciousness so unflinchingly because it's the path to freedom. The fog will never offer asylum. In all circumstances, make this your mantra: "I will keeping moving toward the light, toward compassion." I promise: it's the right direction. You won't be let down. The bigger your heart grows, the better things will get. Now and always, celebrate the freedom of your life. There's more to come in this adventure.

All human beings are dream beings. Dreaming ties mankind together.

—JACK KEROUAC

3

DREAMS AND SLEEP: ACCESSING REVOLUTIONARY STATES OF CONSCIOUSNESS

RECENTLY, I WENT THROUGH a phase of complaining a lot. Everything seemed to be falling through—projects, relationships. Even the plumber couldn't get it together to fix my toilet. I started getting grouchy, becoming generally ungrateful, none of which is going to make me free. Then I had this dream:

> *I'm with my father, who passed away a few years ago. He is moving from one location to another. I want to help him. I ask, "Daddy, is there anything I can get you?" Smiling, he says, "No, darling, I don't need anything except a pen and piece of paper in case I want to write a thank-you note."*

I can't imagine a more tender wake-up call. This dream's message highlights the importance of gratefulness, here and in the hereafter. It was all I needed to adjust my attitude. The genius of the dream was that it didn't pound me emotionally about what I was doing wrong. Rather, it spoke so poignantly that change was irresistible.

Dreams are revolutionary states of consciousness that impart intuitive wisdom about how to be free. They'll save you eternities trying to figure the meaning of your emotions by highlighting which ones liberate or not. Sleep is an avant-garde level of awareness that makes dreams possible. You're going to learn about both because their power is linked. I crave the sweet surrender of sleep and my dreams' uncensored communication: no tiresome small talk, sucking up to impress, or tiptoeing around charged topics. Dreams are naked truth; get ready for it. Dreams are the fast track to freedom. Your cage is bound to be rattled. I say, bring that excitement on.

Revolutions aren't about ambivalence; they require stepping forward, fears and all, toward a healthy reinvention of your emotional persona. Sleep stills your mind so dreams can offer tools to teach you how to walk your talk. They're quick, keen problem solvers at your disposal every night. In dreams, the star is always you; they put your emotions on center stage so you can more clearly see your strengths and areas that need healing. Whether dreams are nightmares or feel heavenly, each plotline and character are devoted to your emotional freedom.

The concept of "seizing every moment" takes on new meaning when you consider that over a seventy-year period, you'll spend at least a quarter of your life asleep and devote fifty thousand hours or more to dreaming, the equivalent of 5.7 years. So much lost time and information—who'd want to waste that? I'll help you prevent this amnesia. After all, each night you dream during the REM (rapid eye movement) cycle, whether you remember or not. It's a phase of heightened brain activity. Your eyes wildly dart back and forth. Heart rate and breathing speed up. Blood rushes to your genitals. Your limb muscles are temporarily paralyzed (so you don't act out your dreams), but you're highly aroused. Then, bingo: a dream hatches. This is your big chance. To gain self-knowledge, you can work with it. Here are answers you've been waiting for, not-to-be-missed revelations.

In this chapter I'll discuss sleep and dreams as evocative facilitators of emotional freedom. I want to help you rest better, dream well, and become increasingly enlightened emotionally. Because dreams are intuitive communications, they can't be understood in an ordinary way. I'll make them immediately relevant to your life by explaining in simple terms how to remember and analyze them, skills you'll fine-tune throughout the book. Even if dreams seem nonsensical or weird now, they won't be for long. You'll see how their advice can unshackle you from fear, jealousy, and anger, and develop your best self. Applying dream wisdom to the everyday is my favorite kind of translation. It gives voice to the ethereal while you sleep, making tangible what had no words. Your intellect can't do this, but intuition can. Dreams are poetry in motion; intuition is their language.

SLEEP AS THE GREAT AWAKENER OF FREEDOM: A BODY-AND-SOUL APPROACH

To understand dreams, it's important to understand sleep. Sleep is the conduit for dreams. I experience it as utter freedom. Each day I'm prepared to be awake only sixteen hours max. For me, that's it for linear time and the jitter of the mundane world. I can't wait to wriggle out of this skintight form before it cramps my style. Sometimes I wish I could melt into sleep for a thousand years. My safest place is in my dreams. There I become more me. I effortlessly replenish myself with images, energy, and insights about my emotions that otherwise require far more effort to assimilate.

Sleep is a liberating state in many ways. First, it supports emotional freedom by refreshing your body. Shakespeare's Macbeth calls it "the chief nourisher of life's feast." Think of sleep as a mini-vacation you take every night, a balm for your being. It's necessary for sanity and survival. Without adequate sleep, you'll snap at a flea, have mind fog, and be prone to high drama and pained nosedives into the negative. (Sleep deprivation has been used as a method of torture, causing paranoid hallucinations and psychosis; without any sleep humans last only about eleven days.) Talk about priorities: sleep is as precious as oxygen, food, water. Life tires you out even if you treasure it, and we need regular repairs from the wear and tear of living. Thus, to rejuvenate your body and emotions, you get a nightly break from being awake. Sleep blesses you with this. The hubbub recedes as your metabolism slows, your senses switch off, and your body clicks into healing mode.

Sleep revives you because it:

- *Recharges the part of your brain that controls emotions.* Neurons that regulate emotions become dormant and rest so you can have emotional stamina while awake.
- *Sharpens your memory and ability to learn.* Your brain encodes new information and its learning centers are activated while you're asleep. With sleep deprivation, your nervous system is on overdrive and can't perform as efficiently.
- *Strengthens your immune system and elevates your mood.* Sleep enables the immune system to protect your body from infections and other illnesses by increasing immune cell production. When you're healthy, your mood improves.
- *Keeps you beautiful.* Every night you get a "beauty sleep"—skin cells regenerate and damage is repaired from stress, aging, and ultraviolet radiation. With too little sleep, the skin doesn't renew itself and looks dull—plus you get dark circles around your eyes (the badges of fatigue) caused by tiny blood vessels seeping from lack of rest. When you look better, you feel better.

Along with these wonders, sleep is also freeing because it resuscitates your spirit by giving it room to roam. Sleep transports you past the physical—all those chores and deadlines—to intuitively experience a larger reality that holds insights about your emotional freedom. It lets you see what your intellect can't. Sleep is a socially sanctioned altered state, the sacred medium for dreams. I call sleep the "little death." (In Greek mythology, sleep is the brother of death.) Ponder it: while you are asleep, the awareness of your body and the everyday world are suspended. You close your eyes and shift from being body-centric to the nonmaterial, a supercreative metamorphosis. The big difference between sleep and death, however, is that with one you wake up in bed, while with the other your spirit just keeps going. No one instructs us in how to fall asleep or what to do after we've left our bodies. We must be trained to travel to our dreams and back without fear, a freedom to traverse boundaries.

Sleep plays by different rules. While awake, you may sell girdles for a living, chase after your kids, or win a Miss or Mrs. America pageant, but in dreams you can go beyond such partial identities. You can fly over canyons and oceans, be in the presence of the greats, or even visit with the dearly departed, all of which feels second nature. Your dreaming self isn't fazed that the laws of physics are kaput. You widen what's possible, experience states that boggle the linear mind. From this perspective, you see your emotional self more clearly.

My patient Denise, thirty, was a telephone operator. Five days a week, she dealt with the public, an often thankless job that made her feel invisible. Denise deserves a medal for ten years of "trying to be kind, even to rude people." This conscientious woman with stoic tolerance felt "cramped" in her job, yet "frozen, numb, and afraid to change." Initially, our sessions slogged along as Denise's inertia kept us in slow motion. She suffered from the kind of low self-esteem that coagulates when no one ever really sees you, which is how Denise felt not only at work but in her meager personal life: there were slim pickings among her family and friends, mostly good ol' boys with pickups and their compliant wives. Denise had one and only one refuge: she loved the blues—Bessie Smith, Lightnin' Hopkins, Mississippi John Hurt. One night, Denise's number one hero—someone who truly moved her soul—appeared to her in a dream. It was the man himself, the king of the Delta blues, Robert Johnson. As Denise recounted:

> *I'm in a nightclub, a juke joint where Robert Johnson is performing. I know he died in 1938 at twenty-seven, but there he is. Unbelievable. I start dancing to "Crossroad Blues," real sensual. It goes: "I went to the crossroad, fell down on my knees / Ask the Lord above, 'Have mercy, now save poor Bob if you please.'"*
>
> *Then he smiles at me and winks. I'm amazed he notices me. Our eyes lock. He sings as if I'm the only one there. My temperature is off the charts. God, my blouse has actually started smoking! I'm afraid I'll get burned. But I'm okay. Really, really okay. The harmonica wails, the guitar moans. I'm still dancing. Robert's eye is on me the whole time.*

The next day Denise awoke feeling more emotionally alive. The blues can do that to you. But sometimes you got to dream it to feel it. At Denise's crossroad, she did. Who knows the spell Robert Johnson cast that night? When someone like him sings the blues just to you, a flame is bound to be lit. Denise's was. For her, this dream of being seen was real. She felt acknowledged by a legend, no longer invisible. Freudians might dismiss it as a wish fulfillment fantasy, but I disagree. In sessions, I intuited an ongoing shift in her energy from sluggish to smokin', compliments of her dream. We both embraced this break-through. I watched it begin to free her frozen self, in part because there was more of Denise present in our work. Also, as her self-esteem grew, she was able to move forward.

A few months later, Denise gave the phone company notice. Then she returned to school to get her teaching credential. Wish fulfillment fantasies? Years of medical practice have convinced me that they just don't have the power to elicit such transformation. The visceral con-tact Denise made in the dream, this visitation, though allegedly "unreal," nonetheless stimulated constructive change. Today Denise teaches first grade, a nurturing of children she was born for. Some-times she plays the blues for her kids, Robert Johnson and others. They take to it. All those little bodies boogeying in that Long Beach classroom must be quite a sight.

Emotional freedom has many champions. Some reside in your wak-ing life, while others appear during sleep. What's to gain from reject-ing help in any form? My mother's favorite saying was "Never say never" (at her request, it's carved on her tombstone to inspire others). This applies day and night. Be playful. See what happens. Let sleep be a catalyst for the incredible.

THE MAGICAL BIOLOGY OF YOUR SLEEP CYCLE

To consciously partake of sleep, it's important to be cognizant of what's going on in you then. Many people perceive it as just one big blank, a zoning out into nothingness. But actually the reverse happens: new worlds open. The body brilliantly helps you ease the transition from waking to dreaming to deep sleep in five stages. Each cycle lasts approximately ninety minutes, then typically repeats four to five times in an average night's sleep. Once you attune yourself to this rhythm, you can maximize the freedom it offers.

Emotional Action Step

LEARN THE STAGES OF YOUR SLEEP CYCLE

Stage 1: You drift into drowsiness for a few minutes as your mind quiets and muscles relax.

Stage 2: For about half the night, overall, you're in light sleep when your brain waves and metabolism slow.

Stages 3 and 4: For about a quarter of the night, you're in deep "delta wave" sleep. Your eyes and muscles don't move; you're hard to rouse and you'll feel disoriented if awakened. Night terrors and sleepwalking can occur here.

Stage 5: Your brain shifts gears into the super-alert wildness of REM, the dream state. REM, occurring in roughly fifteen-minute spurts, constitutes a quarter of the sleep cycle. Heart rate and blood pressure increase; you may become sexually aroused. Dreams originate in the limbic system, a part of the brain that controls emotions. It explodes into activity during REM, a blazing orange firework visible on PET scans. That's why so many dreams are emotional events. REM helps you process emotions by enacting them. If REM is disrupted, the next night you'll go straight there (bypassing other sleep stages) until you catch up, as if the body craves it.

I marvel at the cleverness of our brain's programming, how it recalibrates us so we may dream. The stages of sleep aren't merely electrical blips on an EEG. They generate biological rhythms that enable us to jump realities, natural as can be. The stages of sleep are stages of surrender in which you go deeper and deeper, past your mind's addiction to the limiting A + B = C formula for problem solving.

Sleep is anything but passive. It produces just the right conditions in your brain for dreams to hatch. Familiarize yourself with the stages of sleep so you get the gist of what's transpiring in the wee hours. You and your brain are one, and being informed about its activities puts you in closer touch with how you function. If you go to sleep with an adventurous attitude, "I'm going to learn about becoming freer tonight," then you prompt your brain to have liberating discoveries. The mindfulness you bring to sleep increases the insights you'll find there.

WHAT PREVENTS SLEEP: OVERCOMING INSOMNIA

Of course, falling asleep or staying asleep isn't always easy. You try to let go but just can't. Insomnia is a cruel condition that plagues the nicest people—seventy million Americans suffer from it. One night of tossing and turning, staring at the clock, can push the most sensible person over the edge. How emotionally free can you be in this wretched condition?

What causes insomnia? An obsession with daily concerns won't let your mind shut off. Negative emotions keep you up. This makes you anxious. Then you worry about being unable to fall asleep. A vicious cycle starts. Chemical substances also contribute to not getting enough rest. A Jack Daniel's nightcap might let you doze off (or pass out), but you don't stay deep enough to dream well or get restorative sleep. Heavy smokers also tend to sleep lightly, barely dream, and jerk awake during the night in nicotine withdrawal. Caffeine, diet drinks, sugar, and other stimulants exacerbate insomnia, especially if you have a sensitive system like mine. I'm loath to admit it, but I fall asleep quicker when I don't drink my one relished mug of strong morning coffee. But insomnia can also echo a deeper, unconscious fear of loss of control, even death. If letting go is subliminally associated with death, who wouldn't resist sleep? Like many of my patients struggling with insomnia, you may be defending against fears you're unaware of. I'll help you through them (Chapter 10 specifically addresses new ways of understanding death that reduce fear). Your ease in falling asleep depends on a comfort level with what you'll find there.

Don't fret if sleep is a problem. The following strategies quiet inflamed emotions and relax the body so you can rejuvenate even if you're a light sleeper like me. Experiment with each. See which are most effective.

Emotional Action Step

TRY THESE CURES FOR INSOMNIA

1. *Avoid sleep robbers.* Stay away from stimulants, excess alcohol, sugar, a large meal, or too many drinks, which can prompt a full bladder. Likewise, avoid emotional stimulation, including arguments, discussing charged emotional issues, violent newscasts, or stressful chores such as paying bills. Before sleep, consider a soothing cup of decaffeinated herbal tea. Some people find the preparation ritual as calming as the tea itself.

2. *Practice deep breathing to be free of negative emotions.* When you're tense, you tend to hold your breath and grind your teeth. So practice breathing yourself into relaxation. Deeply breathe in. Breathe out. If you have rushes of worry, panic, or fear, keep exhaling that toxicity. Breathing ushers them out of your body, as if carried by the wind. Keep focusing on your breath's hypnotic rhythm, not the disturbing emotion. Let it lull you to sleep.

3. *Visualize delta brain waves.* Holding a mental picture of the delta waves of deep sleep can relax you. The diagram below is what they look like on an EEG readout. To disarm negative thoughts and emotions burn this visual in your mind. Doing so for a few minutes will retrain your brain to sleep.

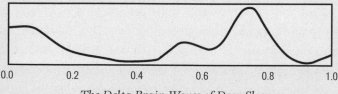

0.0   0.2   0.4   0.6   0.8   1.0

The Delta Brain Waves of Deep Sleep

4. *Repeat the serenity prayer.* If you're kept up by a pressing problem (which you may not even remember a year from now) or escalating anxiety, say this prayer as frequently as needed to relieve pressure before it gains momentum. This prayer is a trusty mantra that saves you from insomnia: *God, grant me the serenity to accept the things I cannot change, the courage to change the things I can, and the wisdom to know the difference.*

5. *Calm your mind.* To banish negative emotions, meditate on an uplifting image. My father used to see himself making the perfect tennis shot. One of my patients pictures George Hamilton doing the cha-cha, a scene that cracked him up on television. Yours can be a tranquil mountain lake, a seagull hovering, anything calming. Have the image ready so you don't have to scramble for it if you can't sleep.

Another way to help calm a jittery mind is to create a relaxing, cozy sleep environment. You want everything about sleep to feel comfortable and safe. How you sleep, where you sleep, and with whom you share a bed affect the quality of your restfulness and dreams. Your sleep environment is more than a place to plop yourself down after a long day. It's your launching pad to mind expansion. Whether you're in bed alone or with another, try these practical solutions.

Happiness Is the Right Mattress

I consider mattresses to be holy ground. You sleep there, dream there, make love there, heal there, or escape from the world. The right mattress can alleviate back pain, align your spine, and prime your energy system while you dream. The wrong one can aggravate sleep, induce horrible nightmares, and distract you from remembering dreams. A mattress is to be revered. Go all out to find one that suits you.

My worship of mattresses began when my lower back started aching from the unholy relic I was sleeping on. I went shopping for a new one at a chi-chi store on Melrose that a friend had recommended. The showroom had about twenty different mattresses. Girard, a peppy salesman who was a ringer for Ricky Ricardo, told me, "Try them all out. Choose the one that feels best." So I did. The next week they delivered it. The mattress was fine—at first. But the ultra-enthusiastic Girard hadn't conveyed that the top-of-the-line memory foam would form a head-to-toe body dent after ten minutes. Thus, I had to hoist myself out of this trench when I changed positions, which scrunched my poor back. No wonder I had recurring dreams I was in quicksand. Following Girard's ever hopeful advice, I tried to get used to the mattress, but just couldn't. I returned it. (A friend, however, swears by the memory foam; the mattress mutes all her husband's tossing and turning, and she credits it for curing her bad back.) Then, still under Girard's tutelage, I ordered a firmer model. But, to my mortification, it soon revealed itself to be unforgivingly rock-like. I kept dreaming I was behind bars on a ratty bunk, and woke up haggard with Johnny Cash's "Folsom Prison" on my mind. I now understand why a patient said her mattress was torturing her! That version went back too.

Bleary-eyed, I trekked to numerous stores in L.A. I'd lie down on bed after bed, pumping the salesmen for information, describing my plight. They were a pretty understanding bunch. Sometimes it felt like they were my therapists. "It'll be all right," they assured. "You'll find what you're looking for." Thankfully, after several months, I found "the one"— the perfect combination of soft and firm. Now, sleeping is nirvana.

It's worth every hour of searching to be sure your mattress supports your body and your ability to sleep and dream. There are many options. Some eliminate motion transmission and also allow couples to separately adjust firmness. Don't settle or be deterred by people who imply you're "neurotic" or "overly picky." The princess had it right about the pea. Your sensitivity is non-negotiable; it isn't anybody's business to judge. Even if you have to audition a few mattresses, try not to see this as drudgery, but rather as a testament to self-care. Your dream life and well-being will benefit.

Get Under Luxurious Sheets, Blankets, and Comforters

The feel of what you sleep on and between can texture your dreams. Soft 100 percent cotton linens with a high thread count (300 or greater) allow your body to relax more than scratchy, synthetic, or starched material. (At sixteen, I was initiated into the wonders of bedding during my first job at the May Company. My fellow saleswomen, who'd worked in the department over twenty years, transmitted a love of linens to me.) Today's options are ingenious. For instance, if you and your partner have different temperature preferences, get sheets that are split—thick fleece on one side, light cotton on the other. Also, some comforters are half thick and half thin, and there are mattress pads with dual heating controls. Since I'm the freezing type and have a gift for finding partners who are part polar bear, easily overheated in southern California, these alternatives are a relief. The days of having to silently suffer while you sweat or shiver are gone. Splurge on the most sensually satisfying, functional sleep accoutrements possible.

Make Your Bedroom Peaceful and Quiet

A tranquil atmosphere promotes the freedom of dreaming. To block out distracting sounds such as snoring or traffic, use earplugs. A white noise machine is invaluable for lulling you to sleep. Some simulate waves breaking on the shore, while others generate a gentle whirring sound. In hotels, I always request a floor fan so I can sleep without hearing slamming doors or my neighbors' romantic epiphanies. Invest in light-blocking shades.

If you're a late-night television devotee, don't allow the television set into your bedroom. Turn your alarm clock away from you so you won't be distracted by its light—or, if you're tossing and turning, its relentless countdown (only three more hours before the alarm, two more hours, one more hour . . .).

Dismayingly, a National Sleep Foundation survey of American couples found that a quarter complained their partner interfered with a good night's rest. Talk about too close for comfort! The most common gripe was snoring. Next was tossing and turning, blanket stealing, teeth gnashing, and monopolizing the mattress. Get this: when one person moves in bed, there's a *75 percent* chance that the partner will be disturbed. This isn't just a pesky inconvenience—it can derail good sleep. There's an old joke: Why do female black widow spiders kill their males after mating? To stop the snoring before it starts. If snoring is a problem, instead of contemplating either murder or suicide, consult your physician to find available cures (as with treatable polyps or allergies). The moral: for snorers of both sexes, get help! Also, if you or your partner has to arise early, there's a wrist alarm clock you can wear to spare the sleeper a rude awakening. There are also miniature book lights that allow one partner to enjoy a novel without disturbing the other.

Have a Free Flow of Fresh Air

Stuffiness or lingering smells such as food or perfume can unsettle you and prevent your mind from switching off. They're reminders of the day and all its challenges, making it harder to forget the world. Fresh air purifies, clears out your space, and is conducive to dreaming. Ventilation is especially important since your body cools down during sleep. An open window or a fan can help drop the room temperature and let you sleep more soundly.

Putting these elements into place sets the stage for restful sleep and vibrant dreaming. When you feel cocooned, you're more able to trust what comes next. What your skin touches, the freshness around you, and your body's sense of support all feed into your ability to surrender to sleep. Such loveliness and comfort can enable you to dream with more ease.

INSOMNIA AND THE HYPNAGOGIC STATE: ENTER THE DOORWAY BETWEEN SLEEP AND WAKEFULNESS

The hypnagogic state is the mysterious doorway between sleep and waking. Most people pass through this usually relaxing period with no problem. Others make a beeline into psychedelic central, where far-out waking dreams occur that aren't associated with REM. Eyes open or shut, images, sounds, and sensations are startlingly vivid. These may be consoling or frightening and may hijack sleep: visions of your dead aunt Mabel, a sudden falling sensation, crashing or knocking noises, your name being called, angels singing, loving or ominous presences by your bed. One of my patients, as sane as you get, had the creepy feeling that she was being "nibbled at" in this state. What's going on? Traditional psychiatry calls these waking dreams hypnagogic "hallucinations" linked to unbalanced brain chemistry and emotional stress. Yes, valid explanations—sometimes. But as an Energy Psychiatrist, here's what I also know: the moment you fall asleep is supervulnerable, neurologically and intuitively. It's an in-between juncture when your brain hasn't quite reoriented itself to sleep and your waking psychological defenses are down. There's a crack between worlds, and you're in it. From my own experiences and accounts of patients, I know that this zone can have a whole lot of intuitive shaking going on.

If your hypnagogic state keeps you awake, identify the disturbance's root to relieve insomnia. I learned firsthand the havoc a haywire brain signal can wreak. Intermittently for months, I kept getting jarred awake by a loud, repetitive, high-pitched squeaking noise beside my bed. It sounded like one of those yellow duckies that children squeeze in the bathtub. The noise was weird, even to me. It wasn't my neighbors. They were quiet as mice. I kept thinking it'd go away. But that confounded squeaking continued. I wondered if some impish energies might be getting a charge out of bugging me. You know the kind: you misplace your keys and empty your purse or pockets searching for them, but nada, yet later the keys are right where you looked. My spiritual teacher has always taught us to order away negative energies (we have more power than them and must assert it). So I did this a few nights; the noise still returned. I was exasperated, getting more anxious and tired. When I asked my therapist, a neuroscientist who respects intuition, he said matter-of-factly, "Your brain is simply replicating a daytime noise you hear. Falling asleep is a time when synaptic signals get crossed, especially if you're stressed." (I was then.) So I scanned my environment and found the culprit: a curly-topped toddler with a mean hold on his squeaky toy; I jogged by him daily on the Venice boardwalk. Why my brain chose to replay this sound eludes me, but locating its source relieved my anxiety. I didn't get so worked up by the squeak, so I could sleep. Also I resolved a clash with a friend, and it wasn't weighing on me. Soon the sound disappeared. As open as I am to extrasensory explanations, this incident seemed to be physiological and stress related.

Alternatively, there are true hypnagogic intuitions that can enhance emotional freedom. Because of our extreme receptivity when falling asleep, it's easier for intuitions to surface. My father saw his closest friend in a black mourning dress sitting beside him the night she died; this brought him comfort in his grief after he got past being startled by it. One patient heard a friend's voice saying, "I'm so happy." The next morning he got her e-mail: "I'm pregnant." For both, it was a special communication that brought them closer. An incident I'll never forget is feeling my aunt, who lives in Philadelphia, tenderly stroking my cheek when I was feverish with a virus, which soothed me.

Hypnagogic experiences push the envelope of emotional freedom by heightening your intuitive receptivity. But they're a liability if they incite insomnia. Be sure to eliminate stressors that could cause jumbled brain signals. Also, realize you have the right to tell negative or spooky waking dreams to stop. It's fine to ignore them or insist they desist, either inwardly or aloud. As the Buddhists say, detach. Negativity is fed by fear. When you don't give it juice it will probably fade. However, also realize that potent intuitions may occur when falling asleep, which may take some getting used to, but these are natural, especially when they concern those you love. My approach to waking dreams is to embrace only what's healthy and whole. Setting that parameter makes you the gatekeeper of your experiences. This will help you get a better night's rest.

SLEEP IS THE GREAT AWAKENER. Your mind, body, and spirit are the recipients of its grace. During sleep you'll gather input about keeping your total self in mint condition. From here on out, we'll get down to logistics. Talking about sleep has been preparing you to dream. Now you're ready. As you practice my techniques, freedom builds in this way: you'll become emotionally self-aware through dreams so you can see farther than your own nose, toward infinity. Go with it as your vision expands. You've got everything to gain from seeing more. I'm right there with poet Jack Kerouac who says, "I like to sleep so I can tune into . . . the big show." I don't want to miss a moment of it. Whenever I go to sleep I'm excited. Let yourself be too. Every night is opening night. You're all invited.

DREAMS AS OPPORTUNITIES FOR FREEDOM

In dreams you'll make a new kind of sense of your emotions.

Science magazine recently reported that sleeping on something, or "unconscious thought," often results in smarter decisions than over-thinking—especially with important choices. Here's how this applies to your emotional freedom. Let's say you're going crazy analyzing the pros and cons of a romantic relationship on the skids. The *Science* study says that won't get you very far. Rather, it proposes a plan B: think less and sleep on the dilemma, a valuable opportunity to let what's "unsolvable" marinate in your subconscious.

I subscribe to the "sleep on it" school of decision making. Dreams are the engine driving this successful intuitive process. From an emotional standpoint, why do we dream? To find answers, resolve conflicts, and discharge negativity. Also to stabilize our biochemistry and mood. But to me, an equally interesting question is, why do we wake up? Native American and Aboriginal cultures revere dreamtime over waking life, even basing tribal law on information obtained there. The Maoris believe that when we die, we return to the dream world. Kalahari Bushmen say, "There is a dream and it is dreaming us." So as you pursue emotional freedom, remember that your dreams summon advice that goes beyond the *Annals of Internal Medicine.*

Dreaming isn't just a sideline for me. It's been a link to my freedom since childhood. When I was growing up, my bedroom faced our backyard, which had one of those turquoise, kidney-shaped swimming pools popular in suburbia in the sixties. At night, hugging my floppy-eared stuffed bunny under the covers (who's still in my closet today), I'd crack open the blinds and watch the moon's reflection in the pool. It seemed enchanted, that white light on water. Gazing into it, I forgot about how "different" I felt—and how my classmate "Monkey" Myerhoff, the big cheese at the jungle gym, made shameless fun of my shyness. As moonlight became sleep, none of that mattered anymore. It was just me and my dreams. How freeing it was not to have to talk to be heard, to fly, to hear angels sing, to be home again.

In this section, I'll tell you how to find freedom in dreams too. I'll outline an approach to dreamwork: how to ask questions of your dreams and act on the answers. I'll describe the different types of dreams and how to use intuition to interpret them. Later in the book you'll utilize this foundation to conquer every emotion that scares happiness away.

THE ESSENTIALS OF DREAMWORK: STRATEGIES TO LET DREAMS LIBERATE YOU

Now, let's get down to the business of dreamwork, a system of decoding messages to find answers. Emotional freedom doesn't just strike willy-nilly. To let dreams liberate you requires a plan. I'll describe two simple strategies that I use in my Energy Psychiatry practice and which I've personally cherished for years. They'll give you entry to a wisdom without borders, a spiritual dimension, and timelessness too. But the trick is getting in. I'll show you how. With practice everyone can do it, even if this endeavor is new.

Strategy 1: Remember Your Dreams

Remembering dreams sharpens emotional intelligence by mining the memory banks of your experiences. *Webster's Dictionary* defines memory as "the power of recalling what has already been learned." Recovering what happens during REM lets you use what you've learned there to improve your emotional life. The memories that surface are stunning. You'll remember things about your childhood and your past, about your present, perhaps even your future. You may even remember God. What this all adds up to is remembering your whole self, your essence.

Here's the mind tickler: Have you ever awakened at night with the most extraordinary dream you were sure you'd recall, but next morning it was gone? The "unforgettable" evaporates. Why? You're trying to capture dreams with linear thought. No can do. You need your intuitive memory. The irony is that being awake conspires against contacting intuition. Why? The instant you start talking to others or begin your day, you click into a "get things done" mode, putting the kibosh on dream recovery. To counteract interferences that obscure intuition, you must mindfully slow down your pace of awakening.

I've seen that patients don't remember dreams for two principal reasons. First, they get up too fast, don't know to linger in the hypnagogic state, the creatively versatile transition between sleep and waking. The edge you get from being a regular there is being able to straddle both worlds. You're asleep enough to tap into dreams and alert enough to retrieve them.

The second reason my patients don't remember their dreams is that they fail to record them to preserve their content. Instead of bounding into e-mails, phone calls, or caffeine, you must program yourself to recall dreams, whether they're spontaneous or in response to a question you pose before sleep. Seeking to remember is a kind of prayer. Keep trying every night. Don't force the process or get scared that you can't do it. Simply stay receptive and loosen up. Your dreams will come. (To encourage them, I've been known to throw kisses to the moon—its energy is conducive to dreaming. You can try it too.) The more relaxed you are, the more successful you'll be. I recommend the following technique:

Emotional Action Step

HOW TO REMEMBER YOUR DREAMS

1. *Keep a dream journal permanently installed by your bed.* Pick one you like the looks of and that magnetizes you to write in it. The journal can be a simple spiral notebook, or you can splurge on one created especially for dreamwork. I've seen some graced with Mahatma Gandhi, star maps, even adorable hippopotami. My

current one has bluebirds on it, an intuitively astute birthday gift
from a friend who didn't know I'd dreamed of the most beguiling
bluebirds of happiness the week before. Make your journal
exclusively about dreams, a notebook devoted to your emotional
liberation. Place it by your bed with a pen so you can reach it
without a hassle. The less you bumble around, the easier it will
be to drift off again. You might also get a "dream pen," which
shines light while you transcribe, or a voice-activated tape player
to record a dream during the night. Keep your journal private,
off-limits to everyone unless you decide to share it. You must feel
safe to be honest, especially about painful, embarrassing, or scary
themes. Such courageous dream-keeping augments freedom.

2. *Write a question about an emotional dilemma on a piece of paper
before you go to sleep.* For example, "How can I be happier?" Or
"What can cure my loneliness?" Formalize your request. Ask
only one question each night to get the clearest answer. (There's
plenty of time for others later.) Place it on a table beside your bed
or under your pillow.

3. *Set your intention to remember a dream.*

4. *In the morning, try to wake up slowly.* Keeping your eyes shut,
focus on the feeling behind your eyes, a way to activate intuition.
Avoid talking right away so that your intellect isn't engaged.
Also, try to keep the same posture as when you were asleep—
this can prologue the memory of a dream. For at least a few
minutes, luxuriate under the covers in the hypnagogic state, a
peaceful feeling between sleep and waking. Then open your eyes.

5. *Record your dream immediately.* You may recall a face, object,
color, or scenario, or feel an emotion. It doesn't matter if it makes
perfect sense or if you retrieve a single image or many. Get
everything down without censoring, especially what may seem
weird or unsettling. Also, don't interpret the dream yet; this will
stop you from remembering.

Committing your dreams to a journal lets you uncover emotional blocks and obtain subconscious information on how to relieve them. Once recorded, these details can't slip away. You want raw. You want primal. You want uncut. Then growth can happen. Dreams aren't about looking good; they're about seeing. Prettying them up dumbs them down, which neuters their message. So be courageous in your journal; let it rip. I still have piles of old ones dating back to my teenage escapades, some with frayed bindings that my beloved dog Pipe teethed on. They let me recall the pangs and exhilarations at the time of the dream. Keeping a regular diary has never appealed to me because what happens in dreams more forcefully chronicles the emotional pulse of my life force.

Allen Ginsberg called Jack Kerouac "the great rememberer," a supreme compliment from where I stand. In his *Book of Dreams* Kerouac wrote: "I got my weary bones out of bed and though swollen from sleep I scribbled in pencil in my dream notebook till I had exhausted every remarkable item—I wrote nonstop so the subconscious world could speak for itself in its own form . . . uninterruptedly flowing and rippling. Everyone interested in their dreams should use the method of fishing their dreams out *in time* before they disappear forever."

Strategy 2: Recognize Three Types of Liberating Dreams

During my heavily neurobiological training in psychiatry at UCLA, medications were the operant treatment modality, and dreams were given short shrift. I was fortunate to have a supervisor who valued them at all. Believe me, I was grateful to discuss my patients' dreams with that dignified Freudian professor in his preternaturally unrumpled suits—but it was always from a psychological angle. Pertinent as this was, I often left our weekly meetings itching for more, sure I wasn't doing some dreams justice. Dreams are big, very big. They warrant a multilayered dissection. My approach in Energy Psychiatry goes beyond the conventional to show how spirituality and intuition pervade our dream's messages about emotional freedom. There's a spirituality to all dreams when they're viewed as ways to develop your soul, to take your life to a more compassionate place.

To me, there is no such thing as a bad dream. Even the most

bloodcurdling nightmare that leaves you slithering in sweat, heart exploding, is intended to set you free from suffering. Sure, these dreams are frightening, but why get intimidated? Being fear-driven condemns your sorry emotional self back to prison yet again. Aren't you sick of it there? Nightmares have been given a bum rap by our discomfort-phobic culture. You have a choice. You can keep running scared or rethink your attitude about nightmares. This is the turnabout: view them as opportunities to face insecurities so they don't keep yanking your chain. Nightmares recur only if you ignore them. Sometimes you have to fight for your spirituality, that connection to the light—and this means taking your dark side on. It's an inestimable relief to identify what persecutes you, to overcome it with awareness and love. Our emotions must be sensitively reckoned with, but freedom can't always be spoon-fed; it may require a wake-up call from nightmares.

I'll introduce you to three basic types of liberating dreams: psychological, predictive, and guidance. Though they may overlap, each has an expertise and spiritual mission related to awakening you. Most dreams are psychological, depicting your emotional quandaries and strides. Don't get fooled into believing that these are less "spiritual" than the others—they're uniquely qualified to disable the time bombs of trauma and negativity so their fallout doesn't pulverize you. In contrast, predictive dreams extend forward in time to present information about enlightening your emotional future. Guidance dreams specialize in giving you direction about confusing situations. Get into the routine of generating an ongoing dialogue with your dreams. There's no reason to stew in frustration or self-pity. Keep asking your dreams questions about how to resolve waking dilemmas. If something's unclear, ask again. Consider dreams as friends, really smart ones. Their advice is coming from your intuitive self, and spirit too, a special delivery from the Mystery.

Psychological Dreams

Let me tell you about a dream I once had about an ex-boyfriend.

I'm at dinner with my best friend, Berenice. I announce that I want to get back together with a man I'd been with for years, a relationship she knew was hugely complicated. Berenice just smiles Buddha-like, as if seeing all, and says, "Not in your dreams!" Her certainty irritates me. I snap, "What do you know?" In a snit, I stomp off to the phone to call my ex. I leave a message on his voice mail: "I miss you. Let's be together." Instantly, I know this is the wrong move. Every good reason why we'd split up flashes before my eyes. I panic that I've opened a can of worms that spells trouble.

I woke up squirming with regret, then thanked my lucky stars I hadn't made that call. This psychological dream was a commentary on my ambivalent emotions. I'd adored this man, yet he hadn't wanted to live together or take the relationship deeper; he liked us as we were, but I couldn't stop there. The thing about me is that I must keep growing, and I need a partner who wants that too. I'm not capable of limiting where love can go without feeling that my life force is rotting. Despite this possibly once-in-lifetime connection, we'd reached an impasse. Impossible as it seemed, following months of painful indecision, we'd said good-bye. I intuitively knew then and know now that this was the right choice, despite my heartbreak, despite feeling I'd lost part of my soul. After many moons, I still have tremors of missing him, his big bear self, all that poetry. I cop to the fact that at a few lonely moments, I've called his answering machine just for the familiar comfort of his voice, but left no message. At those moments I wonder, "Maybe he's changed. What if . . . ?"

My dream warned against such unrealistic thinking. In it, Berenice, at seventy-seven a truth-teller with razor wit, didn't indulge me. Reconciliation wasn't going to happen. She couldn't have said "not in your dreams" any plainer! Even during sleep, Berenice busted me. But, as in the dream, I'm sometimes willful, impulsive. I was being cautioned this could instigate emotionally destructive consequences, a certainty that made it easier to let go and stopped me from regressing. In my bones, I knew I couldn't resurrect us. I knew I had to lovingly and patiently keep healing my feelings of loss—an emotional and spiritual cleansing that would keep my light bright and prevent me from shutting down. By providing these realizations, my dream led me toward emotional freedom; I was able to face my heart's delusion and move on.

Psychological dreams have two main intentions. They are cries for help from something in you that can't bear to carry some emotional cross anymore. Also, they are advocates for your finest qualities, rather than letting you huddle in some shrunken version of yourself. Their emotional intensity, positive or negative, gives them away. What can you expect from working with these dreams? You'll send your demons packing so you can make decisions that support emotional freedom, removing barriers that keep you from feeling your magnificence.

What intrigues me about psychological dreams is that we have so many similar ones. They're an intuitive voice for our species's communal zeitgeist, what psychiatrist Carl Jung calls the collective unconscious. No matter how different we are on the surface, our inner struggles and needs are often similar. So are the symbols our unconscious uses to articulate itself. At times, our emotional narratives in dreams are universal. Imagine it: a Burmese pygmy, a Siberian huntress, and you may all be worried about a masked villain lurking nearby. Collective dreams unveil our human family's interconnections, our nocturnal apprehensions and bliss. The vocabulary of collective dreams is so universal, in fact, that entire books have been written to help decipher its codes.

A GUIDE TO COMMON PSYCHOLOGICAL DREAMS

DREAMS ABOUT YOUR FEARS, ANXIETIES, AND INSECURITIES

- You're standing buck naked in front of a group of people who are pointing at you.
  Meaning: You feel exposed, vulnerable, and unsafe about a situation.

- You're taking a test and panic that you don't know the answers.
  Meaning: You feel unprepared to meet a challenge or solve an emotional dilemma.

- You're being chased by a horrifying pursuer.
  Meaning: You're trying to escape a scary person or emotion (past or present) instead of facing it.

- You lose your wallet and are stranded without credit cards or cash.
  Meaning: You're afraid you're without the emotional resources to cope with one or more aspects of your life.

- Your teeth fall out, crack, or decay.
  Meaning: You feel that a source of power has been taken away in your life; you can't bite back or assert your needs in a situation. Also, you may experience a lack of energy or nurturing from others. (Without strong teeth, it's hard to chew food and assimilate its nutrients, necessary for vitality.)

- You're wandering around lost, unable to find your way home.
  Meaning: You lack a sense of inner or outer direction. You don't know how to get back on track with a situation or relationship and don't feel emotionally supported.

DREAMS AFFIRMING YOUR STRENGTHS, EMOTIONAL
ACHIEVEMENTS, AND LARGENESS OF SPIRIT

- You're able to fly, a natural, joyous feeling.
  Meaning: You're empowered, creative, unfettered by the drag of negativity.

- You triumph over impossible odds—there is a flood, landslide, or a war and you survive.
  Meaning: You have the courage, strength, and heart to overcome difficult emotional obstacles.

- You give birth or watch someone give birth.
  Meaning: You're coming into your own, thriving. It's a time of new beginnings for relationships, career, or revitalizing health and emotions.

- You feel vibrant, eating (not overeating) a delicious meal in good company.
  Meaning: You're nourishing yourself emotionally and others are nourishing you.

- You're getting married or celebrating someone else's wedding.
  Meaning: You're becoming whole. Your physical, emotional, and spiritual sides are becoming integrated. You're ready for more of an emotional commitment to yourself, your work, or another person.

As you begin dreamwork, it's edifying to identify your collective dreams or other defining psychological patterns. Pinpointing the emotional conflict, you can solve it. For instance, if that was you standing naked before a group of jeering coworkers, ask yourself, "Might I have feelings of being exposed or berated at work?" Then take steps to feel more protected in that environment. Or if, in a dream, you're wandering aimlessly, consider, "Where am I lost in my life, and how can I find my way?" Also, it's crucial to celebrate messages of encouragement dreams send. Sometimes, reflexively, my patients breeze over these affirmations and fixate on what's negative. (Bad news not only travels fast, it lingers.) I refuse to let them get away with this. Emotional freedom is cause to celebrate again and again. It's about believing in yourself, maturing into that personal and spiritual authority.

When my patient Fred, a nice man with an inferiority complex, started psychotherapy, he couldn't find anything redeeming about himself. At forty, he owned a small computer business that paid his bills, and he volunteered in homeless shelters, but he was his own worst critic. A self-described "inept putz," he had a doofus-in-over-his-head look plastered on his face. True, he'd done some really dumb things. At seventeen, on Quaaludes (one of the few times he ever used drugs) he'd held up a convenience store with a water pistol on the dare of a high school buddy—a bungled heist that got him a grand total of $56 and a juvenile prison stint. Most of his life, Fred hadn't quite been on the wavelength of the functioning world. He said, "I'm the type who tries to change a lightbulb and ends up blowing out the house's entire electrical system." Of course, I got the picture, but I knew I couldn't help Fred by feeding into his intractably denigrating self-image. He was stuck and needed a better biographer.

One way I work intuitively is to "see" other people's dreams, a gorgeous feeling. I may get a Polaroid-like flash in my head of what a patient dreamed the previous night, or thirty years ago; time frame is harder to read than content. Or as someone recounts a dream I'll receive intuitive flashes elucidating it. During our first session, Fred bemoaned the missteps of his history while slumped so low in the chair he was becoming one with the fabric. Even so, I kept seeing an image of him flying over vast land masses in his dreams, elated and elegantly airborne. Between Fred saying "I mess up this" and "I mess up that," I sensed the masterful navigator he could become. Same man, two aspects. I've gotten used to the seeming discrepancies between how patients paint themselves and what's hankering to emerge. I shared my intuition with Fred, who'd sought me out just for this ability. I asked him directly, in an apparent non sequitur, "Have you ever dreamed you can fly?" Fred looked startled, as if my question came out of left field. Intuition may initially seem so because it isn't a linear association. He thought it over, then became lost in gloom. Finally, sighing, he said, "Oh, that was ages ago. As a boy, I'd have incredible flying dreams. My dreams were the one place I could escape my dad, who constantly criticized me." Fred was like many children from emotionally difficult or abusive homes who instinctively turn to dreams as a safe haven. Flying is a respite from trauma, also a return to the comfort of our spirits' original form. But, as an adult, Fred had forgotten that experience. My function was to jog his memory, make such freedom palpable in his current life.

Our sessions became Fred's flight school. Through talking and meditations, we resurrected Fred's bodily experience of flying—sun baking his shoulders, hair tousled in the wind, feeling joyful, confident, strong. I also asked him to request a flying dream before he went to sleep. He said, "I'm game, but you know how I am—I'll probably come up empty-handed." Reliable Fred: his negativity was second nature. Nonetheless, he asked and he received. The next morning the dream came, as if it'd never left his orbit. Fred looked unusually upbeat when he brought his dream journal in to read aloud. "It worked!" he exclaimed, as though I'd be surprised. But I'd never doubted he'd succeed. Our natural state is flying. Nobody loses that ability. We just get a little earthbound. Fred simply had to reacquaint himself with flying. His dream was that vehicle. It allowed him to feel the boundlessness of his spirit, to connect with his true capabilities, a long overdue boost to his mental health. Now, after a year of psychotherapy, whenever he feels inferior or self-critical, he conjures the freedom of flying, that remarkable competence—a healthy coping mechanism that short-circuits the negativity transmitted by his father. It's an ongoing behavioral and spiritual modification. Fred's opinion of himself is slowly becoming more positive, which is no minor feat, I can tell you. It's a heartening shift for him to experience, and for me to witness.

You can use your psychological dreams to understand emotions that boggle or brighten. Both will surface, but don't get overwhelmed if the information comes through too fast and furious. Even though dreams are messengers, it's fine to ask them to turn down the volume or come at a slower rate. Maintain an active dialogue with your dreams. Some of my patients wrongly assume they are passive recipients of whatever dreams come down the pike, that they don't have a say in the pacing. Then they get barraged by nightmares and burn out. As much as I support emotional self-evaluation in service of becoming free, you must assimilate information at your own pace. You always have input in the matter of timing.

Now, I'd like you to request a psychological dream before you go to sleep, and follow its wisdom. Whether you get a snippet or saga, save it in your journal. If nothing comes the first night, ask again every night for a week. I'll give you tips for interpreting these dreams. Use them along with the techniques for remembering I've discussed in this chapter.

To uncover the message you need to hear, keep this in mind: *the key to grasping psychological dreams is to concentrate on the most emotionally charged segment.* Get down to what infuriates, astounds, or depresses you, as these feelings are the mother lode of transformation. Your intuition is a heat-seeking missile for the emotional energy in dreams. Feel it in your gut. Your churning stomach can lead to freedom. Keep tuning in, but don't try too hard. After a dream, follow these directions.

Emotional Action Step

EXPLORE A PSYCHOLOGICAL DREAM

FIVE TIPS FOR INTERPRETING YOUR DREAM

1. Give the dream a fitting title (for instance, "Escaping the Enemy" or "Passing a Test").

2. Identify the part that's most upsetting, embarrassing, or inspiring.

3. Select one emotion that stands out, such as anxiety, hope, or fear.

4. Identify the main area of your life, past or present, to which the dream's emotional theme relates.

5. Consider, "How can facing this enhance my life? How can it help me become more loving to myself or others?"

This exercise gives you options to psychologically evolve rather than being ruled by neuroses. Your responses to the above questions will locate a pertinent emotional hot spot. With this knowledge, you can gain control. How? As with all dreams, if something isn't working in your life, make it right. If something is beautiful, embrace it. Use cues from the dream's content to liberate yourself. Be practical. If you're being chased by a terrorist who turns out to be your mother-in-law, honestly examine how your mother-in-law terrorizes you. Or if a lover transports you with a luscious kiss, your sexuality either wants to be ignited or is reveling in how ignited it is. I'm presenting dreamwork as a way to teach your subconscious to produce solutions. I could care less about mulling over emotions unless the result is freedom. So take action, then observe if circumstances improve—concrete feedback on the validity of your dream's intuitions. At this stage, get the wheels of dreamwork turning. You'll get better at it. Dreamwork is a craft to refine through the labor of love.

Predictive Dreams

Predictive dreams were part of the sophisticated Hellenic culture's repertoire. The ancient Greeks revered dreams, believed in their capacity to foresee the future. Healing shrines were devoted to this purpose. One of the most famous was Delphi. Pilgrims journeyed from far and wide to consult the Oracle for her dreams' predictions. The Oracle influenced the elite from many professions—what she saw shaped politics and religion. Emperors sought her counsel before declaring war; others came for cures to emotional and physical maladies.

A few years ago, I had the privilege of visiting Delphi, which had lived in my imagination since childhood. Delphi is known as the omphalos, the navel or center of the world. (Legend says that Zeus released two eagles from opposite ends of the earth, and they met in Delphi.) It's situated atop a remote plateau beside Mount Parnassus, cradled by sensuous breast-shaped hills. I went with a friend on a chilly December day, when tourists were scarce, so I could intuitively absorb every detail of this terrain without distractions.

Possessed by wonder, bundled in my hooded parka, I walked the same dirt path the Oracle took. I began by the sacred spring in the woods where she would bathe before readings. Then I wound upward through the cedars to the cool, dark underground tunnel-entrance of the public amphitheater. Following it to the stage, I paused in silence and tuned in. Sensing the Oracle at work was breathtaking: how she sat in trance, poised on a tripod (Apollo's symbol of prophecy), so vulnerable, yet undaunted by the risk of ridicule or persecution. My every fiber vibrated in recognition. Such intuitive naturalness was something my DNA knew. No shame, no muzzles, just the sheer abandon of letting your hair down as visions come. And in Delphi dreams flowed through me. In one, I gave all of Delphi's citizens a book of my poems, and everyone saw the soul in them. I ache for such understanding in my world, to have my subtleties truly seen in a time and place where quietness is often undervalued. I ache to live in a society that's secure and smart enough to trust its own instincts, one that makes reliable predictions aligned with its promises. Delphi exemplifies an intuitive flowering we can emulate personally and culturally. After a week there, I left phenomenally energized by all its possibilities. Through your dreamwork, I want to transmit this to you too.

Know it or not, you have at least a little bit of oracle in you. I'd like you to get comfortable with the idea of having predictive dreams, an opening that coincides with mounting emotional freedom. These dreams impart specific intuitions, compared to gut feelings or hunches, which are more general. What are the mechanisms by which predictions operate? In intuitive states, time is relative. It's not arranged in orderly sequences as it appears to your waking mind. Albert Einstein got it right: "For us physicists the distinction between past, present, and future is only an illusion, even if a stubborn one." We all know Einstein was a genius, so consider the hypothesis that receiving information about your future is doable. Don't overintellectualize yourself out of letting these dreams help you.

In medicine, we've lost the healing art of prophecy. I'm not talking about the thundering commands Moses heard from God about parting the Red Sea, a prediction compelled into consciousness by an instinct to free his people so they could survive. I'm referring to everyday prophecies that can make your emotional life easier if you pay attention. Predictive dreams can lighten your load if you let them.

Let me tell you about my patient Sue. She was a twenty-four-year-old law student with anxiety that was off the charts about her upcoming bar exam. Three weeks prior to it, she dreamed:

> *I see myself in the room taking the test. I'm on the essay portion, and answer the first question easily. I go to the second question, which is on freedom of religion. I freak out because our bar review teacher assured us, "You can skip this subject. They never ask about it." I'm heartsick because I'm totally unprepared.*

Sue awoke hyperventilating at 5:00 A.M. She later told me, "The weird part of the dream was that I was calmly watching my reactions while experiencing them. I flipped on the light and furiously wrote the dream down. I immediately got out my constitutional law books and spent hours thoroughly briefing the answer." Then she continued with more weeks of determined study. Still, on exam day, Sue felt nervous. She said, "You can't imagine the pressure. They have trash cans in the middle of the room for people to throw up. It's embarrassing, but I did. Then I somehow pulled myself together and began the essay portion. The first question wasn't a problem. Then I looked at the next one. I couldn't believe my eyes. It was on freedom of religion, exactly as I'd dreamed! I started to tear up, I felt so relieved. This time I was prepared for that question!" A month later, an ecstatic Sue learned she'd passed the bar on the first try, though there's a failure rate of over 50 percent. Just when Sue's anxiety could've sabotaged her, a predictive dream provided a brilliant study tip. To Sue's credit, she took seriously what we'd worked on, following the dream's lead, though she could've allowed her legal mind's ironclad logic to argue her out of it. With a little help from her dream, Sue made it through the rite of passage to become an attorney and was spared stressful months of having to cram for the bar exam again.

Though predictive dreams aren't as common as psychological or guidance dreams, they can convey hope, spare you heartache, or prepare you for challenges. Whether the subject is romance or overcoming depression, you'll be given information to make a better choice. Predictive dreams can take many forms. You observe an event. A person or a voice counsels you. You have conversations with people you've never met before. Sometimes it seems that you're taking dictation from an outside force. Train yourself to listen. You have a strong hand in shaping your future (though some events in life are unavoidable), but these dreams don't do the work for you. You can't sit back and think, "Oh well, it's going to happen anyway. I don't have to lift a finger." After a dream announced in my twenties that I'd become a doctor, I had to go to medical school to make it a reality. Predictions may come unbidden or upon request. Use their data to determine your best direction.

Predictive dreams feel different from psychological ones in distinctive ways. To learn the difference, routinely scan your dreams for the following giveaways. Then see what their message is. To get the clear-est results, before you go to sleep, simply ask to be shown what you most need to know about the future, rather than asking a specific question. In the beginning this minimizes expectations and enhances intuitive accuracy.

Emotional Action Step

EXPLORE A PREDICTIVE DREAM

WATCH FOR THESE SIGNS

- Exceptionally vibrant imagery, colors, sounds
- An oddly impersonal tone, neutrally conveying information
- A sense of indisputable "knowing" in your body
- A crispness and clarity to segments
- Feeling like a witness, as if you're in a theater watching a movie
- You may feel calm, perhaps even detached during the dream itself. (Emotional reactions to the dream often occur later, when you wake up.)

LISTEN TO THE MESSAGE

- Record your dream and ask yourself, "What is it trying to tell me?"
- Use common sense when applying this input. For instance, if you're warned that a potential love interest is bad news, keep your antennae up and don't elope. Or if you're shown that a new job will be hectic but rewarding, consider accepting it despite the demands. Still, go in with your eyes open.
- Observe how heeding this message makes your emotional life freer. Doing so will offer positive reinforcement to listen again.

The key to interpreting predictive dreams is to zoom in on a seg-ment with a quality of neutral detachment, as though you're merely a witness, elements conspicuously absent in psychological dreams. Identifying them helps you distinguish true intuition from fear, anxiety, or wishful fantasies. When my patient kept having recurring nightmares about her husband of five years divorcing her, the dream's pervasive agitation (and his devotion to their marriage) tipped me off that this wasn't a prediction. Rather, it was a childhood flashback of being abandoned by her alcoholic father, a fear she was projecting onto her husband. That's where our therapy needed to focus, not on some needlessly upsetting wild-goose chase about a divorce. Compared to the high drama of psychological dreams, predictions can take you by surprise by their blandness. You could be watching World War III erupt, yet you're an impartial observer.

I'll never forget the afternoon I took a nap on Edgar Cayce's couch during a lunch break from an intuition workshop I was giving at his institute in Virginia Beach. I was so eager to doze on the same brocade cushions where he gave his medical "readings." (Cayce, perhaps America's most famous seer of the twentieth century, was called the "sleeping prophet"; his intuitions didn't manifest while awake.) I curled up under a cover and peacefully drifted off. Then time warped. Suddenly, I was realms away, dreaming of apocalyptic hurricanes ripping through the South—walls of water shattering glass, demolishing homes, people marooned, so much suffering. During the dream, I nonchalantly noted this, no reaction in particular. In contrast to that cool sense of detachment, I woke up flailing on the edge of these famous cushions, pumped with adrenaline, astounded by what I'd so quickly seen. I didn't know its relevance until a month later, when Hurricane Katrina devastated New Orleans and other southern cities. I watched the agony unfold on television, intimately attuned to these events by virtue of having intuited them. I was aghast at the victims' monumental loss and pain. Even so, as strange as it may seem, I greatly valued my predictive dream, wouldn't have chosen not to have it. The act of seeing, of bearing witness—independent of outcomes—possesses an uncompromising integrity that feels pure and real to me, the direness of Katrina included. Cayce's intuitively high-voltage couch catapulted me into that future. My dream's lack of emotionality was the signature for its accurate foreshadowing.

What's marvelous about predictive dreams is that you're privy to emotional history in the making, personal or collective. What's disturbing about them is that they can rock your world by revealing more than you may want to know. My philosophy about these dreams is this: take constructive action on predictions that can improve your life or someone else's, but try not to feel guilty or responsible if you can't prevent what's going to transpire. As was true of my hurricane dream, you may not have the ability to alter events, though you're given a window to acclimate to them. I consider all predictive dreams as evidence of the depth of the intuitive connection we can have with ourselves and humankind. They link us to all shades of life, a knowledge I cherish. Happy or unhappy, truth is freedom if you view it from that perspective.

Guidance Dreams

You can be your own best intuitive and *still* not be able to read certain situations.

Guidance dreams are expert at dispelling confusion. Whenever I'm in an emotional funk or too involved to see a person or predicament accurately, I turn to them. No matter how flummoxed I get—feeling hurt or rejected can still sometimes put me into a tailspin—I know the escape hatch from that dismal prison. Guidance dreams offer the distance and smarts to grasp how I may be tripping myself up or perpetuating a going-nowhere situation. Nightly I track my dreams for spontaneous guidance, and I'm not shy about collaborating with them when I'm stumped or want a second opinion. I'll ask about a patient, family member, friend, lover, work, health—any issue that's still muddled after my intellect and daytime intuition have had a stab at it. Just because I've hit a wall while awake, I don't assume the answer isn't there. Dreams tap a creative universe that dwarfs logic, materializing options from the void.

Dreams are the mothers of invention when it comes to right-on guidance. Note these hefty testimonials:

> Elias Howe cracked the puzzle of the lock-stitch sewing
>   machine in a dream that showed him where to place the
>   eye of the needle.

Paul McCartney dreamed the melody of "Yesterday," deemed
   the number one pop hit since 1963 by *Rolling Stone*
   magazine.
Robert Louis Stevenson was inspired in a dream to write
   Dr. Jekyll and Mr. Hyde.
Jonas Salk used dreams to shape his thinking when inventing
   the polio vaccine.
Conrad Hilton, who was famous for "Connie's hunches,"
   purchased the first Hilton Hotel after he dreamed the
   amount necessary to outbid a competitor.

Here and in future chapters, you'll learn to solicit guidance in
dreams. How can this help? Perhaps you're addicted to frustration
and don't know how not to be. Or you're tired of being commitment-
phobic and want to unearth what's condemning you to loneliness.
Maybe you keep getting your hopes smashed but are enslaved to that
battering rerun. The problem with overanalyzing emotional stale-
mates is that you may be too stuck in denial or circular reasoning to
make a breakthrough. Dreams circumvent stagnancy by presenting a
novel take on the situation.

My friend Paul, a bookstore owner and idealist, needed a reality
check on a family member. Paul sees the best in others and forgives
easily, sometimes overlooking more hard-nosed input from logic or
intuition. When it came to his ne'er-do-well sister Edie, he had a blind
spot the size of Texas. One night at dinner, Paul shared a decision he
was struggling with: "Should I get involved in a real estate project
with Edie?" Perfectly straight-faced, he added, "I know she's been a
hotheaded, impulsive daredevil. I know she's been irresponsible with
money, and she's burned me before. But recently Edie seems so much
better. I really want to do it. What does your intuition say?" Honestly,
my only reaction was, "You must be kidding! Who in their right mind
would hook up with such a maniac? It's a setup for emotional and
financial disaster." But I didn't blurt that out, as tempting as it was,
because my instinct was that it wouldn't do any good. Paul's family
had already read him the riot act about the arrangement. I knew my
friend well enough to realize he'd never hear me if he perceived I was

in cahoots with them. Instead, I was a sly fox and appealed to his interest in dreams. I suggested, "Why don't you ask one for guidance?" No threat in this. He liked my idea. That night Paul dreamed:

I'm in a souped-up car with Edie. She revs it, then speeds off. I'm apprehensive. She's driving too fast, swerving around a series of large boulders. We barely avoid them. The brakes squeal. The car jerks. I hold on to my seat. The ride is hair-raising but we make it to our destination.

Paul called in the morning to tell me his dream. He said, "It was so real, like I was there. My whole body was shuddering. The ride was rough but we made it! Does this mean to go ahead?" I smiled to myself, reminded that denial isn't just a river in Egypt; it can distort an ordinarily wise man's good sense. Then, I supplemented his interpretation: "Yes, you made it, but the dream also warns that your project will be perilous. It might financially succeed, but at what cost? Do you want all that stress? But if you decide to move forward, at least closely oversee Edie to rein her in." The strength of my position was that the final authority was his dream, not my personal opinion. I was simply deciphering the content. Since I wasn't judging him or Edie, Paul was able to consider my interpretation without getting defensive, and soon felt the rightness of it. As much as he wanted to help his sister or believe that she'd changed, the dream's straightforward intuitive guidance dissolved his denial. In the end, he opted to say no to Edie, averting the pitfalls of working with someone so irresponsible.

The saving grace of querying your dreams for guidance is that you don't have to be on an even keel to get results. Your clarity while awake and your clarity while asleep may be radically different. To pick out the pearls of this aspect of dreamwork, listen carefully to your body, the central nervous system of intuition. Its reactions will flag what you need to know. For an experience of how this works, try asking a dream for guidance. Write a specific question down in a journal. To receive the most direct answer, make it succinct and heartfelt. For instance, "How can I stop giving away my power to men I'm attracted to?" If you dream of sticking up for your needs with a dominating ex-spouse, consider this new behavior as a place to start, and reevaluate the temperament of your romantic choices. When interpreting a dream, notice what viscerally resonates and what doesn't. You've got to feel that rightness in your body to get the message. Note how different this feels from the typically detached reaction that indicates a predictive dream.

Emotional Action Step

EXPLORE A GUIDANCE DREAM

WATCH FOR THESE SIGNS

- A word, image, or scenario zings with energy and grabs your attention.
- Your body is sensually responsive—you feel a sudden wave of goose bumps, a chill, the hair on the back of your neck standing on end, your face flushing. These are indications you're on track.
- You experience an aha! recognition, as if a gong is sounding in your body, affirming the answer.
- The advice sits well in your gut.
- Your energy brightens, tension lifts; you may feel teary, relieved, or uplifted, experiencing an emotional release.

IDENTIFY THE GUIDANCE

- Record the dream and pinpoint your answer.
- You'll know it's accurate if at least one of the above signs is present. You can't force these intuitions; they're either there or not. If you're unsure, keep asking; don't act until the answer comes.
- Never do anything that feels harmful to yourself or others. Authentic guidance is always compassionate and will make you emotionally freer, even if it involves tough love.
- Follow your dream's suggestions and note positive changes.

The guidance you receive doesn't have to be a matter of life or death to be meaningful. Good advice about everyday emotions goes a long way. Say your husband is snapping at you. You mention this, nicely; he shrugs it off; the snapping continues. Don't resort to nagging. Try a different tactic that will be more freeing for both of you. Ask a dream, "What's going on?" If, for example, you dream you see his supervisor yelling at him, it's a clue. Feel your husband out about the climate at work or mention the dream if he's receptive. Give him room to respond. A nudge based on a dream's cue may be all that's needed to uncover the root of his irritability.

What continually touches me about guidance dreams is that they may also respond to your heart's desires, even though you didn't think to ask. As a writer, I spend countless hours, even days, in solitude, immersed in birthing a book. I've given so much of my life to writing, and writing has given so much life to me. This pursuit is utterly fantastic, though sometimes lonely. It's often just me and the ocean. Some nights I go to dinner or movies with friends. On others it's only the gym and a hot bath. Then I head for bed, dream madly, and it's morning again. In this time tunnel, I occasionally wonder if God has lost track of me. It's not something I concentrate on a lot, more of an undercurrent. Still, my lament was heard. One night I dreamed:

> *A man in a crowd who I've never met before asks God: "Do you know Judith Orloff?" God answers endearingly, "Yes. She's the one who always has her hand raised with another question!"*

A much-appreciated reminder: God hadn't forgotten me. I felt that love. In my aloneness I wasn't alone. My guidance dream offered the solace I needed. Dreams want us to know that we are seen and supported.

A divine impulse is behind the guidance we're given. Don't think that what you're going through is too mundane to qualify. Your effort to master your daily emotional conflicts is far more impressive to me than any burning bush. Staying calm when picking up your kids, feeling okay with yourself even after a crushing blow: these are sacred paths and notable accomplishments. Help in dreams is available for all of this and more. Whenever you're confused about something, remember to ask. Then use the guidance well. As my spiritual teacher says: "Make life light, not heavy." Try to stay positive and learn from everything.

SLEEP AND DREAMS are integral to emotional freedom. Use this chapter as a primer to be referred to again and again. Add the strategies I've presented to your compendium of coping skills. They'll strengthen your stance with any emotion that diminishes you and will make you more confident and serene. Keep focused: what you're after is an ongoing transformation of negative feelings and attitudes to positive ones. This can't be accomplished only by sitting in a therapist's office talking, as beneficial as this may be. You must become an emotional street scientist, dealing with what arises moment to moment, a kinetic improvisation.

Watch and listen. Life will unfold. You've got to be on your toes to transform fear into courage or anxiety into calm. Sometimes it can be done then and there. An arrogant associate grunts a rude remark, but you don't retaliate or get down on yourself. Now, that's a win. A tit-for-tat mentality only condemns you to a loser pattern that signals war. However, in instances when you're not so centered—intense feelings notoriously impair intuition and balance—be savvy enough to admit, "I'm too close to this situation to make a clear call." Then get out of your own way by consulting your dreams.

Emotional freedom is a twenty-four-hour-a-day happening. I want you to value all phases of awareness: wakefulness, dreaming, and the mystical place in between. You'll become agile at going back and forth. Dreams retrieve wisdom that's always been there; they make your inner universe visible. Let their encyclopedic vision help you conquer all emotions that impede your freedom, and move you toward everything that's good and beautiful.

Know thyself.

—SOCRATES

4

FROM INTELLECTUALS TO EMPATHS: WHAT IS YOUR EMOTIONAL TYPE?

EMOTIONAL FREEDOM MEANS being able to remain sensitive but centered in an often overwhelming world. It means taking charge of how you respond to people, especially emotional vampires who can savage your equanimity and suck you dry. While interacting with others, remember that you emit emotional energy and they're sending it right back to you. Emotions are catchy. Envy. Greed. Confidence. Caring. They're all part of the matrix of human relationships and can bring you up or down. I'll give you efficient strategies to attract what's positive and not get blindsided by negative people or situations. Many of my patients have been unwitting targets who go down for the count, clueless about how they got there. Freedom increases when you master these emotional interchanges.

It's time to discard our culture's testosterone-fueled equation of sensitivity with weakness. I've had it with being told to "get a thicker skin" or that I'm "overly sensitive," uninformed remarks that my well-meaning parents, and perhaps yours, used to spout and that should have been laid to rest long ago. These days, I prize my receptiveness, its gentle sensuality, and will describe ways you can feel resilient enough to do the same. As a healer and a woman, I want to be penetrable to emotions. I have no desire to become calloused, numb, or hermetically sealed to give the frightened part of me the illusion I'm safer. That would be an outright deception, crippling my intuition, eclipsing my romance with life. Of course, you don't want to get overloaded. But feeling less isn't the answer; building a solid core and learning to protect your emotional accessibility are.

With these skills in place, you'll be more liberated in innumerable ways. You'll be able to respond with an open heart, to stand in other people's shoes rather than just seeing your side of any story. Yet you'll also become a ninja at combating emotional vampires and setting clear limits. The integrative emotional style I'm suggesting for both men and women is to be vulnerable but strong, the union of apparent opposites that my spiritual teacher continues to help mature in me.

My diagnosis of the human condition is that it's mortifyingly hard for us all to just get along, though not impossible. The media is maxed out with grisly war stories and tales of horrific murders and betrayals. How many more salacious televised court cases does the public need? It's always this side against that, us versus them, ad nauseam. I'm offering viable alternatives to such defeatist, self-perpetuating posturing. There's a better way. The quantum leap of emotional freedom is the capacity to identify our addiction to negativity and move beyond it. The place to begin is with you. Getting along with yourself will lead to getting along with others and ultimately, mercifully, more camaraderie and contentment for us all.

WHAT IS YOUR EMOTIONAL TYPE?

To pin down your style of relating, it's edifying to know your emotional type. This is the filter through which you see the world, the default setting of your personality to which you revert, especially under duress. Each type is determined by inborn temperament and who you imprinted on while growing up. Becoming more sensitive to your nature will help you increase self-mastery and freedom. I've seen many patients without these insights dysfunctionally hunker down for decades in their emotional type, not examining which aspects serve them. It's time to come to terms with the pluses and minuses of your type, and to see what qualities from the others you'd like to adopt: the more emotionally well endowed you are, the freer you'll be. Don't sell yourself short by thinking you're just one thing. No one is. Be big. Grow wings. The most scintillating intellect will soar even higher with fire in your belly. A heart as big as the world will only grow wiser with a discerning mind. I'll describe how to accrue the benefits of each type and counteract the disadvantages.

To determine your emotional type, begin by reviewing the descriptions below and comparing them to your history from childhood on. Ask yourself, "What's my primary template for dealing with life? Through my intellect? Empathy?" (Empathy is central to my work; I've discussed it in all my books. Here, I present it as a distinct emotional type that momentously affects emotional freedom.) "Am I the rock who supports others but only emotes reluctantly? Or do I typically gush the blow-by-blows of my feelings?" Of course, you may contain aspects of each type. Even so, to begin, I'd like you to select a type that feels most like you as a reference point. From there, refine your emotional persona by blending attributes from all categories. If you don't fit one, try to embody the best qualities in those you relate to. No type is better than another when it's balanced. During this evaluation, be kind; don't make it an excuse to beat up on yourself. Your emotional type is a baseline to build on, not a life sentence. It also isn't etched in stone, but simply represents general tendencies. My intention isn't to stereotype. Nor am I suggesting you change your basic personality. But I do want to help you enhance what you've got and be able to branch out to become freer.

Emotional Type 1: The Intellectual

Intellectuals are bright, articulate, incisive analysts who are most comfortable in the mind, tending toward a cerebral approach to emotions. When stress hits, they often take refuge in their head as the first line of coping. Their world is powerfully filtered through rational thought. Picture the highbrow *New Yorker* literary scene in the sixties: Gore Vidal and John Updike, thinkers who heatedly wrestled with opinions and ideas. Intellectuals can also be scientists, teachers, housewives, anyone who's predominantly focused on mental pursuits, Ivy League pedigree or not. Some of these brainiacs may consider intuition or spirituality drivel because they don't sufficiently inhabit their gut to experience them viscerally or confirm their benefits. Whether flamboyant or reserved, their kingdom is more mind than body—no earth mothers here. For intellectuals locked into their head (not all are), it can be like pulling teeth to get them to talk about feelings, let alone act from a noncerebral place. Some just don't know how *not* to think; they're enslaved by reason.

It can feel hellish to be stuck in one's mind. Intellectuals are at risk for becoming cut off from their emotions, dismissing them as too "soft" or illogical. When feelings do register, they may attempt to digest them entirely through the mind, disconnected from the body, which means they glean only a fraction of their import. In other instances, intellectuals may passively experience emotions in a hit-or-run way. Think of author Truman Capote, a biting intellect whose paroxysms of anger and joy were famous amongst New York literati. But his emotions controlled him, not the other way around; he suffered a lot and descended into alcoholism. Problematically, some intellectuals misconstrue suffering for aliveness, indulging it rather than working through painful feelings. The result isn't freedom. Despite their smarts, they may not know a dang about how to banish negativity or fight for a more positive take on life.

I've always been a groupie for those with brilliant minds. In medical school, I was rapt hearing an attending physician make a well-argued point about how to treat disease or save a life. I trailed those academic beacons, soaked up their knowledge. I eagerly used the scientific method to deduce solutions to ease my patient's pain. Then and now, I respect my analytic mind and get a kick out of applying it. But I also don't want to be trapped there. A few years ago I had this nightmare:

I'm presenting a patient to a group of doctors on hospital rounds. The chief of psychiatry, a professorial man in a suit, tells me, "Dr. Orloff, give us your diagnosis, but you can't use your intuition to make it." Huh? I think, stunned. Why do I have to edit this information?

I woke up in a spasm about his repressive proposal. It would be unfair to my patients. In good conscience, I wouldn't and couldn't censor what I had to give. It'd feel like dismembering a part of me. I'm thankful I don't have to. Balancing intellect with instinct is the answer. Being both is being free.

Intellectuals often pay a high price by letting their braininess co-opt an organic sense of spirituality that transcends linear understanding or rules. I once had a boyfriend, a devout Orthodox Jew and religious scholar, who used to pray daily using rituals his faith prescribed. Still, he'd tell me, "I do everything right, but I can't feel God"—a "failure" that he was tormented by. I sympathized, but frustratingly, I couldn't help much. If one believes there isn't anything more authoritative than the linear mind, there won't be. This stubborn but lovely man wouldn't deviate from his prescribed intellectual format for contacting God, though his religious faith and devotion were strong. He shot down any option I presented, such as other prayer techniques, because it didn't fit into his scheme. Eventually our relationship ended when his synagogue's rabbi, his spiritual leader, heard about my dream in which my dying grandfather came to say good-bye. "Judith's a witch," the rabbi said, the equivalent in Orthodox circles of branding the sign of the beast on my forehead. This declaration made my scholar run for the hills, leaving me stung by the loss, feeling like a pariah. Nevertheless, this situation taught me how the intellect can turn against you if it's too rigid, how it can stop you from knowing the spirit's passion.

To determine whether you qualify as an intellectual, take the following quiz.

QUIZ: AM I AN INTELLECTUAL?

Ask yourself:

- Do I believe that I can think my way to any solution?
- When presented with a problem, do I immediately start analyzing the pros and cons rather than noticing how it makes me feel?
- Am I uncomfortable when people get highly emotional?

- Do I tend to get overly serious?
- Do I distrust decisions made by the gut?
- Do I prefer planning to being spontaneous?

Answering yes to between one and three of these questions suggests that you tend to process emotions intellectually. Responding yes to more than three questions indicates that you've found your emotional type.

Recognizing that you're "the intellectual" will alert you to the importance of balancing mind and intuition so that you can become more whole. Among the Hopi prophecies is a rock carving that predicts the dangers of our overintellectualized culture: figures of humans with their heads detached from their bodies, an eerie vision of the schism between intellect and feeling. The Hopis say this can lead to civilization's demise. As a psychiatrist, I know it can cause emotional and spiritual annihilation. To avoid this, realize you can be the most strident intellectual without becoming a disembodied talking head with shriveled intuition. I was tickled to see a *Forbes* magazine cover that read, "Chrysler: Company of the Year: Smart, Disciplined, Intuitive," referring to their chairman, who prided himself on using both intellect and intuition. Keeping this model in focus, I'll summarize the attributes and disabilities of this emotional type to consider.

THE INTELLECTUAL'S UPSIDE

- You're an impeccable analyzer with a killer sense of logic.
- You're comfortable in the world of ideas and abstract thought.
- You're able to debate a point.
- You respect and utilize what's scientifically proven.
- You can keep calm in emotionally heated situations.

THE INTELLECTUAL'S DOWNSIDE

- You may live from the neck up, have difficulty connecting with your own feelings or another's.

- You may seem emotionally cold, withholding, or snobbish about anything that doesn't fit your system.

- You can't turn your brain off at night, obsess about problems.

- You may believe in spirituality but are hard-pressed to feel it in your soul.

- You often forget to be playful.

If you belong to this emotional type, it won't be a stretch to relate to these traits. The freeing part is, you can choose who you want to be. It's up to you to bring out the intellectual's richest side and strut its stuff. Still, the intellect can never keep you warm at night or sustain the human spirit. Plus, scientific data proves you can think yourself into exhaustion, particularly as you age, by depleting glucose, a brain nutrient. So, identify what's working or not about this type, and prepare to grow. The following exercise sparks that metamorphosis.

Emotional Action Step

HOW TO FIND BALANCE

To be conversant with feeling as well as thinking, spend more time in your physical/sensual self. I suggest these three beginning techniques.

1. *Remember to breathe.* To intellectualize less, focus on your breath, a quick fix for a hyperactive mind. Day or night, if you're mentally gridlocked, take a time-out to breathe. It distracts the mind and creates more psychic space to decompress. For a few minutes, simply inhale and exhale deeply and slowly. Breathe in through your nose, out through your mouth. Appreciate breathing as a sensual pleasure. Let yourself feel the cool air gently passing through your nostrils, the slow expansion and decompression of your chest. Breathing relaxes your mind and body and enhances your ability to solve problems.

2. *Exercise.* Whether you're Rollerblading, walking, or poised in
a yogic sun salutation, exercise imparts an in-the-now body
awareness that gives the intellect a rest. I especially recommend
yoga, qigong (which combines movement with meditation), or
t'ai chi ch'uan (graceful motions to find inner stillness). These
techniques make you fit and also catalyze a direct experience of
spirituality, an intelligence larger than your mind that naturally
flows from the movements.

3. *Empathize.* To get more in sync with your emotions or another's,
always ask yourself, "How can I respond from my heart, not just
my head?"—the essence of empathy. An intellectual typically tries
to solve a dilemma before empathizing with the feelings it evokes,
a backward approach that can come off as robotic, dismissive, or
cold. Instead, if your spouse is having a meltdown about work or
the kids, first empathize. This emotionally aligns you with him
or her, an effort your spouse will appreciate. "I know how you're
feeling" can go a long way. When your spouse feels heard,
tension melts. Then you can gently suggest tactical fixes.
Similarly, when you're upset, empathize with what prompted
this feeling before forcing an answer or self-flagellating. Such
kindness paves the way for speedier resolutions.

Emotional Type 2: The Empath

*You never really understand a person until you see it from his point of
view . . . until you climb into his skin and walk around in it.*
—ATTICUS FINCH IN *TO KILL A MOCKINGBIRD*

Empaths are highly sensitive, finely tuned instruments when it comes
to emotions. They feel everything, sometimes to an extreme, and are
less apt to intellectualize feelings. Intuition is the filter through which
they experience the world. Empaths are naturally giving, spiritually
attuned, and good listeners. If you want heart, empaths have got it.
Through thick and thin, they're there for you, world-class nurturers.

The trademark of empaths is that they know where you're coming from. Some can do this without taking on people's feelings. However, for better or worse, others, like myself and many of my patients, can become angst-sucking sponges. This often overrides the sublime capacity to absorb positive emotions and all that is beautiful. If empaths are around peace and love, their bodies assimilate these and flourish. Negativity, though, often feels assaultive, exhausting. (It took one empath patient, a journalist, weeks to recover after reporting on a tsunami's devastation in Thailand.) Thus, they're particularly easy marks for emotional vampires, whose fear or rage can ravage empaths. As a subconscious defense, they may gain weight as a buffer. When thin, they're more vulnerable to negativity, a missing cause of overeating explored in my book *Positive Energy*. Plus, an empath's sensitivity can be overwhelming in romantic relationships; many stay single since they haven't learned to negotiate their special cohabitation needs with a partner, a topic I'll discuss in Chapter 8.

When empaths absorb the impact of stressful emotions, it can trigger panic attacks, depression, food, sex and drug binges, and a plethora of physical symptoms that defy traditional medical diagnosis. The Centers for Disease Control and Prevention report that more than two million Americans suffer from chronic fatigue. It's likely that many of them are misdiagnosed empaths. Also, others of this emotional type become agoraphobic, recluses too spooked to venture outdoors.

Typically an empath, beset by these terrible symptoms, runs to the doctor for a million-dollar workup—blood tests, MRIs, scans up the wazoo—but not much is found. Next stop: the psychiatrist's office. Over the years, many well-intended mainstream doctors have asked me to prescribe Prozac for these patients, usually not the right call. A strength of Energy Psychiatry is that it recognizes empathy as a rewarding form of intuition to be developed with the proper skills. Once empaths get the hang of sensing in this way, their lives deepen. But for empaths to achieve freedom and enjoy their assets, they must learn to protect their sensitivity and find balance.

Since I'm an empath, I want to help all my empath patients cultivate this capacity and be comfortable with it. If you primarily process emotional energy this way, you probably have had certain signs and

symptoms since childhood. See if my experiences resonate. I've always been hyperattuned to other people's moods, good and bad. Before I learned to protect my energy, I felt them lodge in my body.
Crowded places amplified my empathy. Girlfriends couldn't wait to go
to shopping malls, but I perceived them as war zones. I could sense
people's emotions ricocheting in the atmosphere like artillery fire. I
wished I could've ducked them, but they darted right into me. I'd start
out feeling fine but leave anxious, depressed, or tired. When I got
home, I'd just crawl into bed, yearning for peace and quiet. Chagrined,
I'd tell my physician-mother, a fashion hound who shopped with fer-
vor. She'd respond, "Darling, you're just not tough enough," a comment that had nowhere to take me but down. My caring mother didn't
realize that crowds can emotionally overload an empath. I can easily
identify with one patient's description of her early empathy: "As a
little girl, I thought God had left a window open in me, that he forgot
to seal me up completely."

Empathy doesn't have to make you feel too much all the time. Now
that I can center myself and refrain from shouldering civilization's
discontents, empathy continues to make me freer, igniting my compassion, vitality, and sense of the miraculous.

To determine whether you're an emotional empath, take the following quiz.

QUIZ: AM I AN EMPATH?

Ask yourself:

• Have I been labeled as "too emotional" or overly sensitive?

• If a friend is distraught, do I start feeling it too?

• Are my feelings easily hurt?

• Am I emotionally drained by crowds and require time alone to revive?

• Do my nerves get frayed by noise, smells, or excessive talk?

• Do I prefer taking my own car places so that I can leave when I
  please?

- Do I overeat to cope with emotional stress?
- Am I afraid of becoming engulfed by intimate relationships?

If you answer yes to between one and three of these questions, you're at least part empath. Responding yes to more than three indicates that you've found your emotional type.

Recognizing that you're an empath is the first step in taking charge of your emotions instead of constantly drowning in them. As one empath to another, I want to legitimize your sensitivity so you don't think you're losing your gourd. I'd had numerous patients who've said, "Judith, I thought there was something wrong with me. I feel like such a sissy." We're not sissies. Our systems are just more permeable. Also realize that the fact that you're the only person feeling something doesn't invalidate your perceptions. For instance, when an empath patient, timid to begin with, asked his wannabe rock star neighbor to turn down "Adam Bomb," an earsplitting heavy metal band, the neighbor's response was, "Why? You're the only one who ever complains." This scenario is crazy-making for an empath, since it wrongly implies that a majority vote is necessary to justify one's stance. To maintain resolve in an emotionally coarse world, empaths must have enough self-knowledge to clearly articulate their needs. Otherwise, like my patient, you may slink away from such encounters feeling beaten and defenseless, licking your wounds. Staying on top of empathy will improve your self-care and relationships. Here's a summary of this emotional type.

THE EMPATH'S UPSIDE

- You've got a big heart, are gifted in helping others.
- Your sensitivity makes you passionate and exquisitely sensual.
- You're intuitive about people's thoughts and feelings.
- You're emotionally responsive, can relate to another's feelings.
- You're in touch with your body and emotions.
- You have a palpable sense of spirituality.

THE EMPATH'S DOWNSIDE

- You're an emotional sponge, absorbing people's negativity.

- You're so sensitive to emotions, you feel like a wire without insulation.

- You're prone to anxiety, depression, and fatigue.

- You may feel hemmed in living in the same space with other people.

- You may have chronic, debilitating physical symptoms.

- You have difficulty setting boundaries with draining people and get run over by them.

Candidly tallying which traits are productive or not makes you freer. Of course, you want to be emotionally charitable, intuitive, and open, the empath's well-deserved badges of honor. These qualities prevent the retardation of your life force that happens when you're imprisoned in your head. However, empathy won't make you free if you walk around perpetually raw, are easily fractured, or have your wildness go out in a whimper because you're constantly having to emotionally defend yourself. To be comfortable in your own skin, this emotional type must find the right mix of intellect, feeling, and groundedness. The next exercise, along with upcoming ones to combat emotional vampires, will help you achieve this.

Emotional Action Step

HOW TO FIND BALANCE

Practice these strategies to center yourself.

- *Enlist your intellect.* When you're emotionally wrung out or suspect you've taken on someone's distress, think things through to counter anxiety. Use both positive self-talk and logic to get grounded. Here's how: First, tell yourself that you can handle this circumstance while taking a few deep breaths to unwind. Second, repeat this mantra: "It is not my job to take on the emotions of

others. I can be loving without doing so." This belief must make
sense for you to stay sane and happy. It forms the intellectual
foundation for how you healthily cope with empathy.

- *Allow quiet time to emotionally decompress.* Get in the habit of
taking calming mini-breaks throughout the day. Breathe in some
fresh air. Stretch. Take a short walk around the office. These
interludes will reduce the excessive stimulation of going nonstop.

- *Practice guerilla meditation.* To counter emotional overload, act
fast and meditate for a few minutes. Find a private place to close
your eyes. Lower your expectations—it doesn't have to be
Shangri-La. My salvation has often been the bathroom (particularly in airports, the bane of my existence—human hordes
crawling through security, loudspeakers screeching). Bathrooms
are the one socially sanctioned location to be alone. Anytime,
anywhere, be game to recenter yourself and release unwanted
emotions. Do two things while meditating. First, keep exhaling
pent-up negative emotions—loneliness, worry, and more. Feel
them dissipate with each breath. Second, put your hand over
your heart and visualize loving-kindness permeating you from
head to toe. (See Chapter 2's Heart-Centering Meditation.) These
actions will quickly relax you.

- *Define and honor your empathic needs.* Safeguard your sensitivities.
In a calm, collected moment, make a list of your top five most
emotionally rattling situations. Then formulate a plan for handling
them so you don't fumble in the moment. Here are some practical
examples of what to do in situations that predictably stymie
empaths.

  ○ If someone asks too much of you, politely tell them no. It's
  not necessary to explain why. As the saying goes, "*No* is a
  complete sentence."

  ○ If your comfort level is three hours max for socializing—
  even if you adore the people—take your own car or have an
  alternative transportation plan so you're not stranded.

○ If crowds are overwhelming, eat a high-protein meal beforehand (this grounds you) and sit in the far corner of, say, a theater or a party, not dead center.

○ If you feel nuked by perfume, nicely request that your friends refrain from wearing it around you. If you can't avoid it, stand near a window or take frequent breaks to catch a breath of fresh air outdoors.

○ If you overeat to numb negative emotions, practice the guerilla meditation mentioned above before you're lured to the refrigerator, a potential vortex of temptation. As an emergency measure, keep a cushion by the fridge so you can be poised to meditate instead of binge.

○ Carve out private space at home. Then you won't be stricken by the feeling of too much togetherness. (Chapter 8 discusses nontraditional living settings compatible with an empath's comfort zone.)

Over time, I suggest adding to this list to keep yourself covered. You don't have to reinvent the wheel each time you're on emotional overload. With pragmatic strategies to cope, empaths can have quicker retorts, feel safer, and their talents can blossom.

Emotional Type 3: The Rock

Rocks are emotionally strong for themselves and others, as well as being practical. When you're reeling from emotions, rocks won't lose their cool. You can sob, complain, rant. They don't pull away or judge. But rocks are no empaths; there's a solid border between themselves and the world. They genuinely care about your delight and pain (you can curl up in a rock's arms anytime) but don't bear the brunt of these feelings. Though they prefer life to be on an even keel, they won't shirk difficulties. You can put a rock's name on your doctor's emergency contact form; during a health crisis, they'll bust their butt to be there for you. They'll gladly show up on your birthday and special occasions—they're not the type who's constantly too busy but makes sure to RSVP "I'll be there in spirit." However, supportive as rocks can be, they tend to internalize their own stressful emotions; these gnaw at them and box them into an unfree place. But they don't realize that examining their feelings will help. Unless rocks are spurred to do so by a mate or friend, they generally won't. They're wired more to keep on keeping on. Overall, rocks aren't the most passionate persons on the planet. In fact, they can seem like slow-moving herbivores when it comes to showing emotion. Because unspoken feelings jam their circuits, they may appear bland, without an edge.

To determine whether you're a rock, take the following quiz.

QUIZ: AM I A ROCK?

Ask yourself:

- Is it easier to listen than to share my feelings?
- Do I often feel like the most dependable person in the room?
- Do people tend to come to me with their troubles?
- Am I able to stay calm when others are upset?
- Would I rather avoid introspection?
- Am I generally satisfied with the status quo in relationships but others are often trying to draw me out emotionally?

If you answer yes to between one and three questions, you have some rock-like qualities. Responding yes to more than three questions suggests that this is your emotional type.

Recognizing you're a rock allows you to increasingly be more open to the richness of feelings and life. Rocks often risk becoming couch potatoes, watching a lot of television or frequently taking naps. As Simon and Garfunkel's song suggests—"I am a rock / I am an island"—this type can be emotionally insular, detached. One patient described her rock husband as "loving but dense," a man who "always listens to me but doesn't reciprocate with what's going on in him." Emotionally, it may be a one-way street with a rock. Not that they don't have feelings. Rocks just need some nudging to bring them out. Consider the following summary of this emotional type's pros and cons.

THE ROCK'S UPSIDE

- You're a pillar of strength for others.
- You're consistent and loyal.
- You enjoy giving.
- You respect people, wish the best for them.
- You get along with nearly everyone.

THE ROCK'S DOWNSIDE

- You can be detached from your feelings.
- You harbor anger and frustration.
- Your relationships may lack excitement and depth.
- You don't make waves or challenge yourself to grow emotionally.
- You'd rather avoid conflict than confront difficult issues in relationships.

Emotional Action Step

HOW TO FIND BALANCE

- *Light your fire with an attitude update.* For freer, more spontaneous interactions, you've got to stir things up. This means deciding to initiate emotional exchanges rather than only responding when needed. Otherwise your relationships are out of whack. Life is in session. Engage it. Remember that showing emotion is a form of generosity, just as being dependable is. With loved ones, expressing your feelings generates sparks, which generates passion, yours and theirs.

- *Express a feeling a day.* In a daily journal, record one (and only one) emotion you're experiencing. Don't mince words: You're

pissed off. You're content. You're in love. Whatever it is, bravo!
Then share the emotion with someone. Take the risk. This means
opening your mouth and heart, remaining present enough to be
authentic. If you don't suppress your emotions, stress lessens, and
there's more of you to connect with. Also, when a friend offers
support, take it in, whether it's simply "I know what you mean,
brother" or a pat on the back. Resisting being on the receiving end
is a way of chickening out of growth. Embracing the give-and-take
of communicating makes you more attractive and available.

Emotional Type 4: The Gusher

Gushers are virtuosos at knowing their emotions and were born to
share them. They're the opposite of rocks—no one has to wonder
where they're at. Elated, bored, or miserable, they tell you. What you
see is what you get. They tend to be spontaneous, direct, authentic,
and trusted confidants. The gusher unloads stress by verbalizing it.
I, for one, know how freeing this can be. I bow to my treasured circle
of friends, who deserve trophies for listening to my fears, hopes, and
quandaries over the years. However, some gushers get antsy when
there's no one to tell. Also, they may resist making independent decisions, trusting their intuition, or staying emotionally grounded without external input. I have a patient who's an aide in a convalescent
home, a true friend to the elderly. Though he finds helping others
gratifying, the setting can be arduous: understaffing and budget cuts
compromise the care he gives to the demented or physically disabled,
a brutal neglect he had difficulty stomaching. Each night, he depended
on being able to vent his stress to his wife and could work himself into
a delirium of anxiety if she wasn't around. My patient didn't know
how else to calm down and release stress until I taught him the techniques in this topic's action step. In addition to healthily venting, he
learned to tap the power within to find inner peace.

To determine whether you're a gusher, take the following quiz.

QUIZ: AM I A GUSHER?

Ask yourself:

- Is it easy for me to express my emotions?
- Do I get anxious if I keep my feelings in?
- When a problem arises, is my first impulse to pick up the phone?
- Do I need to take a poll before finalizing a decision?
- Are my friends often telling me, "Too much information"?
- Do I have difficulty sensing other people's emotional boundaries?

If you answer yes to between one and three of these questions, you possess some gusher tendencies. Responding yes to more than three suggests that this is your emotional type.

Recognizing you're a gusher enables you to become a better communicator by learning to balance self-sufficiency with emotional expression. Sometimes gushers are so hungry to share that they turn people off. At a party, in the market, they're all over you, compulsive emotional purgers. (The joke goes that such motormouths qualify for the twelve-step program On-and-on-and-on-and-on.) Although it's liberating to voice feelings, a gusher must strike a balance between healthily emoting and drawing on the wisdom within. Consider the following profile summarizing a gusher's traits.

THE GUSHER'S UPSIDE

- You're emotionally articulate.
- Negativity doesn't fester in you if you express it to others.
- You have a supportive network of friends.
- You value intimate relationships, are a sensitive listener.
- You deal with hard issues and process them quickly.

THE GUSHER'S DOWNSIDE

- You're a candidate for becoming a drama king or queen.

- You may turn friends into therapists.

- You seek external feedback before you consult your intuition for answers.

- Your need to share excessively may burn other people out.

- You haven't fully embraced your own inner power or spiritual strengths.

Emotional Action Step

HOW TO FIND BALANCE

EMPOWER YOURSELF WITH SELF-SUFFICIENCY

Experiment with centering your feelings before soliciting support. Here's how: First, define the upset. Let's say your Cruella De Vil boss has made mincemeat out of your self-worth yet again. Second, ask yourself, "How does this make me feel? Seething? Demoralized? Plotting murder?" Let yourself experience those emotions uncut, not acting them out, an essential stage before transformation can happen. Third, work with your feelings using these techniques:

- Set your intention to clear the emotion.

- Keep exhaling negativity.

- Use positive self-talk to love yourself back to center again. Inwardly say, "I did my best. I even deserve kudos for graciousness." Affirm everything you did right; try to forgive where you might've fallen short, a loving inner dialogue that reinstates your power.

- Tune in to intuition to find a solution. Spend a few quiet moments meditating to see what images, impressions, or ah-ha!s come to you about improving the situation.

As a gusher, if you skip these steps and go straight to the phone, you'll cheat yourself out of the opportunity to build the emotional muscles necessary for more freedom and autonomy.

THE MOST IMPORTANT relationship you'll ever have is with yourself. If this is good, you'll be capable of fruitful relationships with others. Knowing your emotional type provides a platform to evolve emotionally. Remember, though, it's a start to self-knowledge, not an endpoint. There are many layers to that mysterious onion. Still, at this point, go with what you've got. You'll be tackling emotions in diverse shapes and forms in Part Two of this book. For now, let's focus on the next chapter, which addresses defanging the emotional vampires that drain your energy.

Remember, no one can make you feel inferior without your consent.

—ELEANOR ROOSEVELT

5

COMBATING EMOTIONAL VAMPIRES: HOW TO UNDERSTAND AND PROTECT YOUR SENSITIVITY

TO BE FREE, you can't remain naive about relationships. Some people are positive, mood-elevating, sustaining. Others can suck optimism and serenity right out of you. To protect your sensitivity, it's imperative to name and combat these emotional vampires. They're everywhere: coworkers, neighbors, family, friends. In Energy Psychiatry I've treated a revolving door of patients who've been hard hit by drainers—truly a mental health epidemic that conventional medicine doesn't see. I'm horrified by how many of these "emotionally walking wounded" (ordinarily perceptive, intelligent individuals) have become resigned to chronic anxiety or depression. Why the blind spot? Most of us haven't been educated about draining people or how to emancipate ourselves from their clutches, requisite social skills for everyone desiring freedom. Emotional drain is a touchy subject. We don't know how to tactfully address our needs without alienating others. The result: We get tongue-tied, destructively passive. We ignore the SOS from our gut that screams, "Beware!" Or, quaking in our boots, we're so afraid of the faux pas of appearing "impolite" that we become martyrs in lieu of being respectfully assertive. We don't speak out because we don't want to be seen as "difficult" or uncaring. (Emily Post's *Etiquette,* published in 1922, lumps difficult people under the category of "rudeness" along with belching and spitting on the sidewalk.)

Here, I'm presenting a sequel to my section on energy vampires in *Positive Energy.* The concept struck such a collective chord that I'm compelled to extend it to illustrate how it applies to emotional freedom. Why? Vampires do more than drain our physical energy. The supermalignant ones can make you believe you're an unworthy, unlovable wretch who doesn't deserve better. The subtler species inflict damage that's more of a slow burn. Smaller digs here and there can make you feel bad about yourself: "Dear, I see you've put on a few pounds" or "It's not ladylike to interrupt." In a flash, they've zapped you by prodding areas of shaky self-worth.

This is my credo for vampires: their antics are unacceptable, so you must develop a successful plan for coping with them. I deeply believe in the merciful message of the Lord's Prayer to "forgive people their trespasses," but I'm also a proponent of preventing the unconscious or mean-spirited from trespassing against us. Taking a stand against draining people is a form of self-care and canny communication that you must practice to give your freedom legs.

What turns someone into an emotional vampire? First, a psychological reason: children often reflexively mimic their parents' most unflattering traits. A self-absorbed father can turn you into a self-absorbed son. Early modeling has impact. Studies of Holocaust survivors reveal that many become abusive to loved ones themselves. The second explanation involves subtle energy. I've observed that childhood trauma—mistreatment, loss, parental alcoholism, illness—can weaken a person's energy field. This energy leakage may condition those with such early wounds to draw on the vitality of others to compensate; it's not something most are aware of. Nevertheless, the effects can be extreme. Visualize an octopus-like tendril extending from their energy field and glomming onto yours. Your intuition may register this as sadness, anger, fatigue, or a cloying, squirrelly feeling. The degree of mood change or physical reaction may vary. A vampire's effects can stun like a sonic blast or make you slowly wilt. But it's the rare drainer who sets out to purposely enervate you. The majority act unconsciously, oblivious to being an emotional drain.

Let me tell you the secret of how a vampire operates so you can outsmart one. *A vampire goes in for the kill by stirring up your emotions. Pushing your buttons throws you off center, which renders you easier to drain.* Of all the emotional types, empaths are often the most devastated. However, certain emotional states increase everyone's vulnerability. They are:

- Low self-esteem
- Depression
- A victim mentality
- Fear of asserting yourself
- Addiction to people-pleasing

I myself am most susceptible to emotional vampires when I feel desperate, tired, or disempowered. For a few years, I'd been trying to get a project dear to me off the ground. It was close to happening. I was getting my hopes up. But just at that juncture, I discovered that the person pivotal to the project's success, whom I'd just then met, was an emotional vampire. He had a pleasant veneer and an ear-to-ear smile, but when he extended his hand, I got the message that he expected me to kiss it, not shake it. He kept insinuating that the project wouldn't move forward unless he saved the day. This man insisted on calling me "Judy" even after I nicely told him several times that I preferred to be called "Judith"—a kind of verbal power play. I'd been so ready to like him, but my intuition insisted over and again, "Scram. This is toxic." The empath in me felt smothered. Following the meeting, I started feeling desperate, afraid that without him, the project would fall apart. Then I paused to take a deep breath and emotionally regroup. My fear-based reaction was not the direction I wanted to go. In my gut, it felt better to wait for a more positive partnership rather than to work with an emotional vampire. So I went on trust that if the project was meant to be, the right people would present themselves. Now, a year later, I'm happy to report that they have. This incident reinforced how desperation can work to override intuition, that it's freeing to say no to drainers and hold out for relationships that feel right.

When encountering emotional vampires, see what you can learn. It's your choice. You can simply feel tortured, resentful, impotent. Or, as I try to do, ask yourself, "How can this interaction help me grow?" As I've mentioned, every nanosecond of life, good, bad, or indifferent, is a chance to become emotionally freer, to enlarge the heart. If we're to have any hope of breaking war-mongering patterns, we must each play a part. As freedom fighters, strive to view vampires as opportunities to enlist your highest self and not be a sucker for negativity. Then you'll leave smelling like a rose, even with major-league Draculas.

EMOTIONAL VAMPIRE SURVIVAL GUIDE: WHO THEY ARE AND HOW TO PROTECT YOURSELF

To come out ahead with drainers, you must be methodical. Emotional vampires can't savage your peace of mind or prick you to death with corrosive remarks if you're on to them. This survival guide covers everything from recognizing an initial exposure to deploying techniques to deflect negativity. It will enable you to stay centered in difficult relationships.

The First Guideline: Determine If You're Being Sapped by an Emotional Vampire

Anyone who has ever shared an office, been in a car pool, or attended a family dinner with a vampire can attest to experiencing some common emotional side effects. Even after a brief contact, you feel worse; they feel better. To find out if you've been bled, watch for these signs. Experiencing even one indicates you've met a drainer on the prowl.

- Your eyelids get heavy—you're ready for a nap.
- You feel put down or like the rug was pulled out from under you.
- Your mood takes a nosedive.

- You have a yen to binge on carbs or comfort food.
- You feel sniped at, slimed, or agitated.

In addition, sometimes intuitive flashes and dreams can raise a red flag. Pay attention. For instance, following a dinner I attended where the guests had something negative to say about everything, I dreamed I was bombarded by a storm of leeches. Similarly, after a critical friend skewered one of my patients, she felt as if she'd fallen to the bottom of a well. Another patient dreamed that a pigeon pooped on her head— *splat,* there it was: her reaction to a nasty altercation with her apartment's superintendent. Whether you're awake or asleep, notice telling imagery that conveys emotion. This will help you identify a vampire.

The Second Guideline: Practice These General Dos and Don'ts with Emotional Vampires

Whenever possible, eliminate drainers from your life. However, with those you can't or don't want to remove—for example, friends going through a rough patch or relatives who are fixtures—follow these tips:

DO

- Take a breath to center yourself
- Listen for intuitions signaling danger (i.e., you get the creeps, a bad taste in your mouth, a tired or tense feeling)
- Stay calm and matter-of-fact instead of going for their bait
- Pause and develop a plan to handle the situation before you react (refer to the fourth guideline, below)
- Communicate clearly, firmly, and with a neutral tone when setting limits

DON'T

- Panic
- Talk yourself out your intuitions or call yourself neurotic

- Blurt out something you'll regret later or use an accusatory tone

- Fight with the person

- Overeat to medicate stress

Also consider what kind of emotional vampires you're facing; we often attract what we haven't emotionally resolved in ourselves. If you're fearful, you may find yourself surrounded by legions of fearful people. However, once you've begun to heal an emotion, you're less likely to magnetize it toward you, nor does it possess the same ability to wear you out.

If you decide that the pros outweigh the cons of remaining with an emotional vampire, such as a bullying colleague or mate, you must take responsibility for that decision and the way you respond. Ask yourself, "How can I stay in the relationship and not feel oppressed?" Along with practicing the strategies I'll suggest, this means concentrating on the good and accepting someone's limitations.

The Third Guideline: Could You Be an Emotional Vampire? How Do You Know?

We've all got a smidgeon of vampire in us, especially when we're stressed. So cut yourself a break. It's admirable to admit, "I think I'm emotionally draining people. What can I do?" You can't be free without such honesty. Then you can change. These are some common indications that you're becoming a drainer.

- People avoid you or glaze over during a conversation.

- You're self-obsessed.

- You're often negative.

- You gossip or bad-mouth people.

- You're critical, controlling.

- You're in an emotional black hole but won't get help—this strains relationships and won't free you.

The solution is always to own up to where you're emotionally stuck and change the related behavior. For instance, one patient in computer graphics kept hammering his wife with a poor-me attitude about how he always got stuck with boring projects at work. Instead of trying to improve the situation, he just kvetched. She started dreading those conversations, and diplomatically mentioned it to him. This motivated my patient to address the issue with his supervisor, which got him more stimulating assignments. Similarly, whenever I slip into vampire mode, I try to examine and alter my behavior or else discuss the particulars with a friend or a therapist so I can change. Don't hesitate to seek assistance when you're stumped. Also, review the types of emotional vampires in the next section to make sure you're not one of them.

The Fourth Guideline: Identify and Combat Emotional Vampires

To be free of vampires, you must know the nature of the beast. Each one has a special talent for emotionally disabling you. The good news is that vampires are predictable. Once you get their number, you won't be caught off guard. I'll present emotional vampires as variants of textbook personality disorders (ongoing maladaptive behaviors that impair social functioning), but with Energy Psychiatry's spiritual and intuitive twist. Understanding vampires from multiple angles gives you the upper hand. So does having empathy for their emotional wounds—intuitively, these feel as real to me as physical injury. Think about it: no one becomes a vampire because he or she is happy. Whether or not they know it, vampires are driven by insecurity and weakness, infirmities that impede goodwill. This doesn't excuse their predatory acts. Rather, it allows you to show compassion for people you may not like while setting limits, a paradigm for emotional diplomacy that frees you and reduces drain. I'll discuss narcissistic, dependent, obsessive, critical, and borderline personalities, nightmares for friends and family to deal with. This framework will help clarify your relationships, but realize there's much more to a human being than any single definition. To protect yourself from each vampire, try my straightforward methods, which you can mix and match. Stay focused: your aim isn't to rehabilitate vampires, merely to counter them with uncommon grace. Here are the types.

Emotional Vampire 1: The Narcissist (Narcissistic Personality)

Their motto is "Me first." Everything's all about them. They have a grandiose sense of self-importance and entitlement, hog attention, and crave admiration. They're a legend in their own minds, and the world is reflected in their image. They'll corner you at a party and interminably recount their life saga. Some narcissists are unlikeable, flagrant egotists. Others can be charming, intelligent, caring—that is, until their guru status is threatened. When you stop stroking their ego or beg to disagree, these vampires turn on you and become punishing. Once you catch on to this pattern, a narcissist seems about as charming as a banana peel. *These vampires are so dangerous because they lack empathy and have a limited capacity for unconditional love.* Sadly, their hearts either haven't developed or have been shut down due to early psychic trauma, such as being raised by narcissistic parents, a crippling handicap both emotionally and spiritually. (The damage of narcissistic parenting is outstandingly detailed in Alice Miller's *Drama of the Gifted Child.*) Hard as it may be to comprehend, these vampires have little insight into their actions, nor do they regret them. Though often highly intuitive, they mainly use intuition for self-interest and manipulation. Spiritually speaking, the narcissist is cruisin' for a bruisin'. As the Hasidic proverb cautions, "There is no room for God in him that is full of himself." Egotism inevitably curdles the soul, liberating nothing.

It's important to know if you're dealing with a narcissist—then you can decide what tack to take with them to make your life easier. To find out, ask yourself the following questions.

QUIZ: AM I IN A RELATIONSHIP WITH A NARCISSIST?

- Does the person act as if life revolves around him?
- Do I have to compliment him to get his attention or approval?
- Does he constantly steer the conversation back to himself?
- Does he downplay my feelings or interests?
- If I disagree, does he become cold or withholding?

If you answer yes to one or two questions, it's likely you're dealing with a narcissist. Responding yes to three or more questions suggests that a narcissist is violating your emotional freedom.

Narcissists are hard nuts to crack. With these patients, the best I can do is align with their positive aspects and focus on behaviors that *they agree* aren't working. Still, even if one wants to change, progress is limited, with meager gains. My professional advice: don't fall in love with a narcissist or entertain illusions they're capable of the give-and-take necessary for intimacy. In such relationships you'll always be emotionally alone to some degree. If you have a withholding narcissist spouse, beware of trying to win the nurturing you never got from your parents; it's not going to happen. Also, forget about having your sensitivity honored. Such vampires eat empaths for dinner; they sour love with all the hoops you must jump through to please them. Ultimately, they'll break your heart and steal your freedom.

I'm touched by Bernard Cooper's portrayal of a narcissistic parent in his memoir *The Bill from My Father.* When Bernard was twenty-eight, his father, Ed, a divorce attorney, sent him an invoice for his paternal services typed on his law firm's onionskin stationery. No joke. It itemized the money his father had spent raising him: $2 million. That tops every war story I've ever heard about entitlement. Poor Bernard didn't pay the bill. But amazingly, for ensuing decades of grudges and disappointments, he kept trying to compassionately understand this man and not follow in those footsteps. When his father was in his eighties, it was up to Bernard (and a live-in nurse who quickly became Ed's lover) to care for him. I'm most impressed by how Bernard emerges with a luminous heart, a rare survivor of a narcissistic parent.

If a narcissist is draining you emotionally, the next exercise will help you get your power back and mindfully deal with his or her self-centeredness.

Emotional Action Step

LOWER YOUR EXPECTATIONS AND STRATEGIZE YOUR NEEDS

Use these methods to deter narcissists.

- *Keep your expectations realistic.* Don't be gurued into anything. Enjoy their good qualities, but understand they're emotionally limited, even if they're sophisticated in other ways. Accepting this, you won't continue asking something of friends, family, or coworkers they can't give. Consider this definition of insanity: when you repeat the same actions but expect a different response.

- *Never make your self-worth dependent on them.* Don't get caught in the trap of always trying to please a narcissist. Also protect your sensitivity. Refrain from confiding your deepest feelings to someone who won't cherish them.

- *Show how something will be to their benefit.* To successfully communicate with narcissists, the hard truth is that you must frame things this way. Stating your needs clearly rarely works, nor does getting whiny, angry, or demanding. Alternatively, speak to what floats their boat. Instead of saying to your spouse, "I'd really enjoy going to a family dinner," reframe it as "Everyone really likes you. They'd be delighted to have you there." Or instead of saying to your employer, "I'd prefer to work fewer nights," say, "I can bring in more revenue for your company during these hours." Naturally, it's better not to have to contend with the tedious ego stroking of a narcissist. But if the relationship is unavoidable, use this technique to achieve your desired outcome.

Emotional Vampire 2: The Victim (Dependent Personality)

These vampires grate on you with a poor-me attitude and are allergic to taking responsibility for their actions. People are always against them, the reason for their unhappiness. They portray themselves as unfortunates who demand rescuing, and they will make you into their therapist. As a friend, you want to help, but you become overwhelmed by their endless tales of woe: a boyfriend stormed out ... again; a mother doesn't understand; a diva boss was ungrateful. When you suggest how to put an end to the pity party, they'll say, "Yes, but ... ," then launch into more unsolvable gripes. These vampires may be so clingy they stick to you like flypaper.

If you typically get drawn into fixing other people's problems, chances are you've attracted numerous victims into your life. To identify their characteristics, ask yourself the following questions:

QUIZ: AM I IN A RELATIONSHIP WITH A VICTIM?

- Does this person often appear inconsolably oppressed or depressed?
- Are you burned out by her neediness?
- Does she always blame "bad luck" or the unfairness of others for her problems?
- Do you screen your calls or say you're busy in order to dodge her litany of complaints?
- Does her unrelenting negativity compromise your positive attitude?

If you answered yes to one or two questions, it's likely you're dealing with a victim. Responding yes to three or more questions suggests that a victim is violating your emotional freedom.

Conventional psychiatry says dependent personalities have an excessive need to be taken care of, resulting in submissive, victimized behavior. Their approach may stem from childhood feelings of help-lessness or emulating victim-parents. In Energy Psychiatry I've also seen that victims haven't learned to access intuition for inner guidance; they lack a durable spiritual connection from which to garner strength or self-sufficiency. Instead of growing from adversity, the golden rule of emotional freedom, they feel at the mercy of it. These vampires are constantly jonesing for a validation fix, ever in search of a consoling daddy or mommy. With a nursing infant's blind zeal, they lunge for any nipple they can find (a man's or woman's) and will suck as long as you permit.

My just-married patient Jane's new mother-in-law, Bitsy, was the quintessential victim. Bitsy called so often, always bemoaning the injustices in her life, that Jane came to dread picking up the phone. Finally, running scared, she started screening her calls. Faced with conflict, Jane tended to be too nice; she choked on the word *no*. Also, understandably, she wanted to accommodate her new mother-in-law. For months, in lengthy conversations, she sympathized with how Bitsy's ex-husbands, neighbors, and even "an incompetent handyman" slighted her. Eventually Jane couldn't stand another word. She felt resentful, then felt guilty about that. She'd become Bitsy's emotional hostage, turning into a victim herself. Still, she didn't know how to speak up without jeopardizing their relationship. I love what Mahatma Gandhi says: "A 'no' uttered from deepest conviction is better and greater than a 'yes' merely uttered to please, or, what is worse, to avoid trouble." With that in mind, I offered the following suggestions to ward off this species of vampire. You can try them too.

Emotional Action Step

SET LIMITS WITH AN IRON HAND
AND A VELVET GLOVE

Kind but firm limit setting is healthy. People must take responsibility for their own lives. You're not in the business of fixing anyone. Enabling always backfires. Without limits, a relationship isn't on equal ground; no one wins. You might well feel, "I'm sick and tired of your complaints." But instead, using a more measured tone, here's how to address some common situations.

- *With a friend or relative.* Smile and say kindly, "Our relationship is important to me, but it's not helpful to keep feeling sorry for yourself. I can only listen for five minutes unless you're ready to discuss solutions." Get ready to be guilt-tripped. If the victim, irate, comes back with, "What kind of friend are you?" don't succumb to that ploy. Just reply, "I'm a great friend and I love you, but this is all I can offer."

- *With a coworker.* Sincerely respond, "I'm really sorry that's happening to you." Then, after listening briefly, smile and say, "I'll keep good thoughts for things to work out. I hope you understand, I'm on deadline and I must return to work." Simultaneously employ this-isn't-a-good-time body language: crossing your arms, breaking eye contact, or even turning your back. The less you engage this victim, the better. (Studies reveal that most workers can barely focus for eleven minutes without being disturbed by an officemate.)

- *With yourself.* The way I snap out of victim mentality is by remembering how blessed my life is compared with much of our global family. I'm not fighting to survive genocide, poverty, or daily street violence from an insurgent militia. I have the luxury to feel lonely when I'm without a romantic partner or to get irked by some emotional vampire. I have the gift of time to surmount negative emotions. Seeing things this way stops me from wallowing, an imprisoning indulgence. So when you think you're having a bad day, try to keep this kind of perspective.

Emotional Vampire 3: The Controller
(Obsessive-Compulsive Personality)

These vampires obsessively try to control you and have no qualms about dictating what you're supposed to be and feel. They have an opinion about everything; disagree at your peril. Life is either black or white. They'll control you by invalidating your emotions if those don't fit into their rule book. Controllers often start sentences with, "You know what you need?" and then proceed to tell you. They'll sling shots like "Aren't you over that guy already?" or "I'll have dinner with you if you promise to smile." Victims invite these vampires to do their thing. Wavering self-esteem makes controllers bare their incisors. Whether spouting unsolicited advice on how you can lose weight or using anger to put you in your place, their pronouncements from on high can range from irritating to abusive. Controllers are often perfectionists, seeing others as failing to meet their standards. They may feel, "If you want something done right, you have to do it yourself." (Such reluctance to let go is something I've had to grapple with for years, though I'm getting more at ease with delegating.) Controllers are also controlling with themselves. They may fanatically count carbs, become clean freaks, or turn into workaholics. Conventional psychiatry classifies them as rigidly preoccupied with details, rules, lists, and dominating others at the expense of flexibility and openness. What's most infuriating about these vampires is that they usually don't see themselves as controlling—only right.

To determine if you're getting drained by this emotional vampire, ask yourself the following questions. Then you can use the strategies in this section to cope from a more centered place.

QUIZ: AM I IN A RELATIONSHIP WITH A CONTROLLER?

- Does this person keep claiming to know what's best for you?
- Do you typically have to do things his way?
- Is he so domineering you feel suffocated?
- Do you feel like you're held prisoner to this person's rigid sense of order?
- Is this relationship no fun because it lacks spontaneity?

If you answer yes to one or two questions, it's likely you're dealing with a controller. Responding yes to three or more questions suggests that a controller is violating our emotional freedom.

People who feel out of control tend to become controllers. Deep down, they're afraid of falling apart, so they micromanage to bind anxiety. They might have had chaotic childhoods, suffered with alcoholic parents, or experienced early abandonment, making it hard to trust or relinquish control to others or to a higher power. Further, some controllers have a macho drive to be top dog in both business and personal matters—a mask for their feeling of inadequacy and lack of inner power. Body language tells the tale. To assert territorial prowess, they may puff out their chest, slap your back, purse their lips, or get right up in your face when they talk. Even if you take a few steps away, they'll inch forward again into your space. Whatever their motivations, controllers will stifle your emotional freedom with their ongoing impositions.

When you mindfully deal with controllers, you can free yourself from their manipulations. These vampires are predictable. Knowing how they operate will let you choose how to interact with them.

Emotional Action Step

PICK YOUR BATTLES AND ASSERT YOUR NEEDS

Use these methods to deter controllers.

- *The secret to success is never try to control a controller.* Speak up, but don't tell them what to do. Be healthily assertive rather than controlling. Stay confident and refuse to play the victim. Most important, always take a consistent, targeted approach. Controllers are always looking for a power struggle, so try not to sweat the small stuff. Focus on high-priority issues that you really care about rather than bickering about putting the cap on the toothpaste.

- *Try the caring, direct approach.* Use this with good friends or others who're responsive to feedback. For instance, if someone dominates conversations, sensitively say, "I appreciate your comments, but I'd like to express my opinions too." The person may be unaware that he or she is monopolizing the discussion and will gladly change.

- *Set limits.* If an intimate or coworker keeps telling you how to deal with something, politely say, "I value your advice, but I really want to work through this myself." You may need to remind the controller of your position several times, always in a kind, neutral tone. Repetition is key. Don't expect instant miracles. Since controllers rarely give up easily, be patient. Respectfully reiterating your stance over days or weeks will slowly recondition negative communication patterns and redefine the terms of the relationship. If you reach an impasse, agree to disagree. Then make the subject off-limits.

- *Size up the situation.* If your boss is a controlling perfectionist (and you choose to stay), know whom you're dealing with. Don't keep stewing about what a rotten person he or she is or expect that person to change (he or she is sure to pick up on such negative vibes). Then operate within that reality check. For instance, if your boss instructs you how to complete a project but you add a few good ideas of your own, realize this may or may not fly. If you nondefensively offer your reasoning about the additions, you'll be more readily heard. However if your boss responds, "I didn't say to do this. Please remove it," you must defer because of the built-in status difference in the relationship. Putting your foot down—trying to control the controller—will only make work more stressful or get you fired.

Emotional Vampire 4: The Criticizer
(Mixed Personality Disorder)

A close relative of controllers, these vampires feel qualified to judge your alleged merits or demerits. They can spot flaws across a crowded room, then shamelessly suggest how to improve them "for your own good," a phrase I'd hear from my opinionated Jewish mother as she'd eye me from head to toe. She'd say, "If only you'd dress fashionably, you'd be so beautiful." Her justification was "I tell you this because I love you." *Oy vey:* Mother did love me, but she loathed my holey jeans, which I lived in, as much as I canonized them. Criticizers believe it's their God-given right to offer what they deem "constructive criticism," even if it makes you feel horrible. This vampire's comments range from minor critiques to tarring and feathering you. Fascinatingly, *Science* magazine reports that when someone is belittling you, your brain responds as it does to physical pain. Criticism can hurt, whether it comes from another or from within. It impairs emotional freedom by bludgeoning your confidence and making it unsafe to express emotions. Indictments like "You're such a crybaby" or "You're a bad parent because you work part-time" undermine your emotions. If you even half believe such criticisms, well intended or not, they'll linger like a foul odor.

The problem with dealing with criticizers is that many people acclimate to them, feel chronically beaten, or end up emotionally shutting down. To prevent this from happening, begin by asking yourself the following questions to identify these vampires in your life so they don't deplete you. Then you can use the strategies in this section to interact more effectively with them and protect your sensitivity.

QUIZ: AM I IN A RELATIONSHIP WITH A CRITICIZER?

- Do I always end up feeling inadequate in this person's eyes?
- Am I the frequent target of her judgmental zingers?
- Does she spot a flaw in me from across the room, then tell me about it?
- Is she always putting others down?
- Is she harshly self-critical?

If you answer yes to one or two questions, it's likely you're dealing with a criticizer. Responding yes to three or more questions suggests that a criticizer is violating your emotional freedom.

Why do people criticize? Conventional psychiatry says it's a tendency inherent to many personality disorders, especially obsessive-compulsive, borderline, and narcissistic. These vampires typically mimic critical parents and are ruthlessly judgmental of their own "lackings." The self-hatred that goes on in the head of these finger-pointers teeters on masochism. Still, they don't recognize the simple truth that they're hard on you because *they* feel deficient. Also, to these self-designated arbiters of right and wrong, criticizing seems reasonable. "Hey, I'm just being honest," they say, even if the "truth" is a major insult. Yes, sometimes they do intend to be helpful. However, compensating for their insecurities, they may use criticism as one-upsmanship to bolster their own egos and make you feel inferior. Energetically, this can feel like you've absorbed a round of machine gun fire. These vampires get a charge out of emotionally dissecting you. They either don't know about or don't value the spiritual precept of striving for nonjudgment, nor do they give you the option of declining their input. Critical people are like chickens scratching in the coop. You don't want to be at the bottom of their pecking order or throw them any feed.

Try the tactics I suggest to keep criticism in perspective. Being free requires knowing what's true about yourself or not. Criticism can only deflate your mood if you buy into it. As you work through self-doubts, you'll be more able to detach from this vampire's off-the-wall assessments.

Emotional Action Step

HOW TO COPE WITH A CRITICIZER WITHOUT GETTING DEMOLISHED

Use these methods to deter criticizers.

- *Always consider the source.* Criticism is rampant in our world. People have all kinds of opinions about how you "should" feel or be. If someone you respect makes a suggestion, you may want to consider it. Otherwise, don't dwell on a criticism. A good general rule is to try not to take personally even what's meant personally. People say untrue things all the time. Your challenge is to not believe them.

- *Try one of these specific options for dealing with the criticism.*

  ○ *Graciously let the spiky comment pass.* The Dalai Lama suggests, "Sometimes silence is the best answer." If criticizers are peripheral, it may not be worth pursuing. Instead, realize they're off base; keep on moving.

  ○ *Address a misplaced criticism directly.* Start the conversation out positively. In a matter-of-fact, firm tone say, "I can see that you're trying to help. But when you're critical, it's harder for me to hear you. It doesn't feel good when you _____. I'd appreciate it if you'd back off." You might want to make certain topics taboo, such as personal appearance. Also, it's useful to balance such limit setting by giving affirming feedback about other areas of your relationship so these vampires don't feel attacked—for example, acknowledging what a giving friend he or she has been and how much you appreciate being able to communicate openly.

○ *Strike a compromise—don't get defensive.* For instance, if your mate criticizes you for leaving the dishes in the sink, you might want to divide this task up between you. Or if a coworker criticizes you for talking loudly, keep talking, but tone your voice down. Compromise is a sign of respect that goes a long way.

○ *Set off a love bomb.* At times, the best deterrent to these vampires is to be serenely neutral about their criticism and defuse negativity with a massive dose of loving-kindness. No matter what they say, make light of it, and be sweet. Take that, all you criticizers out there! For instance, an old-school surgeon once told me, "We're too sophisticated to teach intuition to medical students in our hospital!" Instead of becoming defensive or angry (which would've gotten me nowhere) I authentically applauded him for his dedicated years of teaching surgical residents and let the comment go. Interestingly, in subsequent conversations, he started asking me about the role of intuition with patients. The love bomb approach softened him up in a way that confrontation could never have done.

○ *Express appreciation for what's useful.* You may want to heed a beneficial criticism, whether it's solicited or not. For instance, my patient's introverted wife would always end up sitting in a corner at a party with a pained expression on her face, then wonder why no one ever talked to her. With all the tact he could muster he said, "Honey, it's not an inviting look. You might want to stick closer to me. I'll introduce you to people you'd enjoy."

My patient's offer was made with such grace, without blame, that
his wife was able to take him up on it. Then parties became more
fun for her. Of course, criticism is harder to digest if delivered in
a cutting tone. Then it's your call to assess its worth.

Emotional Vampire 5: The Splitter (Borderline Personality)

Splitters see people are either good or bad, and they are aficionados
of love-hate relationships. They'll seduce you by placing you on a
pedestal, but you're just being set up for a fall. One minute they ide-
alize their "new best friend"; the next you're evil incarnate if they
feel the slightest bit wronged or abandoned. Then it gets ugly. Once
you're on a splitter's hit list, this vampire is a merciless avenger
who'll lacerate you with anger (this is particularly toxic to empaths).
Splitters are very skilled at being vicious. One of them told his ex-
wife, my patient, "You're a pitiful excuse for a woman." This was in
response to her being vexed about his "accidentally" erasing the only
copy of their son's high school graduation video. At fifty, my newly
divorced patient felt shaky about her femininity. He knew that and
went in for the kill. In addition, he waged an ongoing campaign of
character assassination to turn their son against this good-hearted
woman. *A splitter doesn't play fair and retaliates by impulsively acting
out.* These vampires won't hesitate to sleep with your best friend if
they're mad at you. Or, during an argument they may threaten suicide, slash a wrist, or self-mutilate. As a medical intern, I stitched up
many a splitter's wrist in emergency rooms. Attempting to dodge
these vampires' operatic batterings, you may start walking on eggshells, loath to incite their ire, imprisoned in your own home. Spouses
of splitters often lead lives of quiet desperation, emotionally black-
mailed into submission.

These vampires' wrath doesn't stop with you. It's infectious. They
have a sixth sense for knowing how to pit people against each other,
a trick I was trained to detect working on inpatient psychiatric wards.
Splitters can destroy morale unless staff are united. Trouble is, they're

often so intelligently convincing, they can turn your own mother (or divorce lawyer) against you. Unless you know the games splitters play, they'll poison your interactions and emotional freedom.

To determine if you're dealing with a splitter, answer the following questions. Then you can use the strategies in this section to develop a plan for communicating with them more successfully.

QUIZ: AM I IN A RELATIONSHIP WITH A SPLITTER?

- Do I censor my true feelings because I fear this person's anger?
- Do I go to great pains to keep the peace?
- Does he keep me on an emotional roller coaster?
- Is he adoring when I meet his needs, a rageaholic when I don't?
- Do I frequently feel wrongly accused?

If you answer yes to one or two questions, it's likely that you're dealing with a splitter. Responding yes to three or more questions suggests that a splitter is violating your emotional freedom.

What makes splitters tick? Conventional psychiatry diagnoses them with borderline personality disorder. They are people who feel fundamentally damaged, empty, as if they don't exist. Their relationships are intense, unstable. Borderlines can be personable and giving if you meet their needs. If you don't do so, they feel abandoned, a primal terror that triggers verbal abuse or impulsive acts. Their mixed message is, "I hate you/Don't leave me." They haven't learned to self-nurture by activating their heart energy or making a spiritual connection. Borderlines are hypervigilantly attuned to other people's energy; their intuitive antennae skittishly scan the environment for threats. But because they confuse fear with intuition, their gut feelings aren't reliable. Getting you upset makes them feel alive. They feed on chaotic emotions, because they feel more real when you react.

In my medical practice I now refer borderlines to other psychiatrists—I know my limits. I learned early on that, as an empath, my constitution is too porous to deflect such anger and treat them effectively. It simply takes too much out of me. However, therapists less apt to absorb energy can work better with these patients, enjoy the process, and are able to stick it out for the long haul. Over time, as trust is established, they can help splitters to positively change.

If you have one or more splitters in your life, the following exercise offers a dependable plan for protecting your sensitivity. When you don't go for their bait you can take command of the interaction.

Emotional Action Step

STOP EMOTIONAL BLACKMAIL

Use these methods to deter splitters.

- *Establish boundaries and be solution-oriented.* Splitters respond best to structure and goal setting. For instance, if one launches into an accusatory rant, remove yourself and your kids from the situation. In this state, don't expect a splitter to be reasonable. Tell the person, "I'm leaving until you get calmer. Then we can talk." Or say a splitter relative disparages you to other family members, lobbying for their support. You can do two things. First, from a centered, unemotional place, definitively tell the vampire, "Please don't talk about me to others. It's inappropriate and disrespectful." Then refuse to argue about it, even if egged on. Second, speak with your family privately, not in front of a splitter, to correct their perceptions. Overall, your aim is to modify a splitter's behavior (i.e., stop the person from talking behind your back), not to convince someone to change his or her feelings. Treat a splitter much the same way you'd treat a tantrumming five-year-old—calmly, assertively, with clear rules.

- *Avoid skirmishes.* Don't lash out when provoked, tempting as it may be. Splitters are itching for a fight; that's what feeds them. The more you react, the more their bad behavior escalates. For example, here's how my patient, an actor, dealt with a combative playwright, a classic splitter. Going for the jugular, the playwright told my patient, "I'm thinking of killing off your character in the first act." Thus, my patient's onstage time would be cut in half, his worst fear.

To his credit, he enthused, "What a great acting opportunity. Maybe I'll win a Tony!" Without missing a beat, he stopped the vampire with humor and equanimity. When he got his complete pages he saw that his character made it to the final curtain after all.

- *Refuse to take sides.* Be cautious about accepting a splitter's negative assessment of others or letting his or her venomous opinions destroy your relationships. You might check them out with more reliable sources if there's any truth here to consider.

- *Quickly release negativity.* Break eye contact to stop the transfer of toxic energy. Also, keep breathing out the splitter's anger so it doesn't lodge in your body. Following the interaction, take a bath or shower, or immerse yourself in a hot spring or pool. In addition, drink plenty of water to flush out your system.

- *Visualize a protective shield around you.* If you can't escape, imagine yourself enveloped in a cocoon of white light from head to toe. Picture it as a luminous veil a few inches above your skin, surrounding your body. This buffer zone minimizes exposure to negative emotions. You hear the person's vitriol, but it slides off you and won't go so deep.

THIS CHAPTER HAS given you the nuts and bolts of how to get along with difficult people. Getting along is a great accomplishment, but I also want you to see such people as vehicles for your awakening, not just an annoyance to be overcome. From the standpoint of freedom, vampires are bodhisattvas in disguise, teachers who pester you to develop confidence, emotional resilience, and an integrity of self-care that rarely matures without such an impetus.

Whether you're confronting a drainer or transforming your own negativity, the soul of emotional freedom is empathy. Elevating you to the realm of the heart, empathy allows you to nondefensively understand and even have mercy on antagonizers. Also, you'll better intuit the feelings behind someone's words. If a friend complains that you're being selfish, the deeper meaning could be, "I'm hurt because we're not spending enough time together." With empathy, you're privy to hidden motives. It's crucial to grasp that when people behave shabbily, such as being demeaning or narcissistic, you're butting up against their unconsciousness and suffering, an insight that eludes them. You can be certain that what they do unto others, they also do unto themselves. No one criticizes you unless they're self-critical. Seeing vampires' frailties with compassion doesn't make you a patsy. Though you may not choose to subject yourself to them, you need not hold their suffering against them. Labeling someone "the enemy" is a spiritual wrong turn.

Elegant brain mapping has shown that we're hardwired for empathy. The recent discovery of "mirror neurons" has done for behavioral health what DNA has done for genetics. Mirror neurons are what turn on our empathy. They establish a brain-to-brain bridge that puts you on another person's wavelength. Studies have shown that mirror neurons cause brain cells to "light up" not just when your own finger is pricked with a pin but also when you see someone else's finger being pricked (an explanation for how the empath functions as well as those with less intense sensitivity). The pattern of neurons firing in your brain actually mimics those of the person you're observing. In other words, we can feel each other's pain. What this finding illuminates for me is that our brain's instinct to share another's reaction to pain is the biological mechanism of compassion.

In your life, hold that thought. Endeavor to bring empathy into every relationship. Doing so generates the magic of what I call "the *namaste* effect." *Namaste* is the common greeting in India that means, "I respect the spirit within you." Such honoring of others, including emotional vampires, alters the structure of relationships. It confuses difficult people in a good way, creating a sort of demilitarized zone. Adversaries become less defensive; their hankering to tangle with you diminishes, even though they don't know quite why. The *namaste* effect liberates because it's about harmonizing, not demonizing. Your goal is to see people as they are, then protect your sensitivity accordingly. The *namaste* effect will defang a vampire's bite with empathy. Whether someone changes or not, you're redefining a primal energetic dynamic of the interaction. This shift reverberates beyond the personal, raising the level of compassion in all of us.

Part Two

YOUR TOOLS FOR
LIBERATION

In each of the following chapters, called "transformations," you'll apply the principles of Part One to help you face negative emotions and build positive ones. Even the tiniest move in this direction is impressive. This path to emotional freedom is the hero's journey. Why? Because every choice you make to triumph over negativity, large or small, is about transforming energy. The potent nature of such ongoing transformation makes you stronger, brighter, and more resilient, which in turn acts to illuminate the world.

*As we are liberated from our own fear, our presence
automatically liberates others.*

—NELSON MANDELA

6

THE FIRST TRANSFORMATION:

FACING FEAR, BUILDING COURAGE

RIGHT AFTER I WAS BORN, my mother had a pulmonary embolus. This blood clot to her lungs was nearly fatal. For two weeks she lay bedridden in the hospital. During that time, though I was healthy, my home was a plastic bassinette in the hospital's nursery where premature and sick infants stayed. This bubbled world became my foreground. Nurses in starched caps and white uniforms bottle-fed me sterile formula. Some would coo or make pleasant sounds, what we call words. Others seemed distracted, quiet except for the clacking of their saddle shoes down the tiled corridor leading to my alcove. Aside from short visits with my parents, who held me and gave me my bottle, I was usually alone—a stranger in a very strange land. Something wasn't right. It felt like no one had claimed me. I pulsated with the need for more contact, for safety. How could I have known I wasn't abandoned? This was my primal intuition as a newborn.

The first minutes and weeks of life are exquisitely impressionable; I'd spent mine constantly probing my environment for sustenance that wasn't there. For decades, a fear of abandonment lurked in me, though I couldn't recall the source. I had loving, attentive parents; it didn't add up. This fear crept into my romantic relationships. I'd react with over-the-top anger or hurt to anything that resembled abandonment, such as a boyfriend failing to call or canceling plans. The pain of a breakup could practically do me in.

Then, a few years ago, I participated in a hypnosis session aimed at getting to the origin of my fear. For the first time, in a moment of clarity, I remembered that forlorn nursery and Mother's illness, those weeks long repressed but not forgotten. There are some truths so profound that when you finally encounter them, they resonate and resonate. Grief poured out of me. I wept buckets. Tender tears, my liberators. Now that I'd located where my fear came from, I could begin to learn ways not to be ruled by it. If you don't even know what you're up against, how can you find the courage to overcome it? Painful as this memory was, it provided a gateway to my emotional freedom.

This chapter, which I call "The First Transformation," is devoted to facing fear and building courage, a consecrated undertaking. You're going to track down what scares you, then use courage to transform it.

I begin with fear because it's the mother of all negative emotions from which loneliness, worry, anger, and the rest are spawned. Chinese medicine calls these conditions "clutching disorders." I call them forms of suffering. Fear is such a potent negative emotion because we're genetically cued to associate it with survival. Unchecked fear has no end; its energy will infinitely replicate like cancer if you let it. Understandably, we're easily overwhelmed by fear until we learn to disengage from its suction.

While other negative emotions such as jealousy and frustration are derived from fear, their scope seems more finite since our survival doesn't so directly depend on them. However, they still pack a wallop. In contrast, all positive emotions, such as courage and hope, are born from love. Love is the most encompassing force of all, greater than fear, greater than anything. When going through this book, remember the following schema depicting how emotions differentiate.

Fear → frustration, loneliness, anxiety, worry, depression, jealousy, envy, anger

Love → courage, patience, connection, inner calm, hope, self-esteem, compassion

If you don't make it your business to overcome fear, you better believe it'll try to overcome you. Most people are subservient to this emotion, though they may not know it. I define fear as the emotional response to danger, perceived or real. *What underscores fear in all its permutations is the feeling that you won't be all right.* Fear of aging . . . of rejection . . . of sitting in a sterile room with a paper dress . . . or (fill in the blank) can play interminably in your head, degrading freedom. Dangerously, you may even acclimate to these fears, falling into a kind of hypnotic stupor. As your guide, I intend to help you break fear's spell, align you with the better angels of your nature. So take a big breath and start counting backward. Ten . . . nine . . . eight . . . seven . . . six . . . one. Then open your eyes, feeling powerful, ready to counteract fear with courage.

In Energy Psychiatry, I've learned that conventional methods for treating fear just aren't adequate. As the line in *Jaws* goes, "We're going to need a bigger boat." Thus, I'll describe how to combat fear and build courage by understanding the biology, spirituality, energetic power, and psychology of these emotions. I'll describe how to discern fear from intuition, distinctions you must be clear on. Some fears are external: you're a soldier in combat or airborne in a plane going down. Others are implanted in you: an associate snarks, "You'll botch that account"; a surgeon diagnoses, "You'll always have chronic back pain"; a psychic predicts, "Your husband will cheat on you." Also, fear can be self-induced. You may scare yourself silly by saying, for instance, "I'll always be alone . . . in debt . . . trapped in an abusive marriage because I don't want the kids to suffer"—treacherous rabbit holes to get lost in. Or if you're an empath, as I discussed in Chapter 4, you may unknowingly sponge up people's fears, a tendency you'll learn to spot and curtail.

You can begin to conquer fear by evaluating its present role in your life. It's a tender inquiry, looking within so candidly. To assist you, I'll offer a quiz that provides a baseline of where you currently stand with fear. (In upcoming chapters you'll find a similar self-assessment quiz relevant to the emotion discussed.) As you answer the following questions, realize that this is the start of new growth that you'll build on to alleviate fear. Once you compassionately clarify your relationship to this feeling, you can release it more adeptly as you practice *Emotional Freedom*'s strategies.

FEAR QUIZ: HOW FEARFUL AM I?

Ask yourself:

• Do I typically expect the worst in situations?

• Do fearful thoughts keep me awake at night?

• Am I afraid to speak up or go for what I want?

• Am I afraid I won't meet my own or another's expectations?

• Do other people's fears feel contagious?

• Is it hard to center myself when I'm afraid?

• Do I often feel out of contact with a loving spiritual source?

• Do I tend to catastrophize about the future?

Answering yes to seven or eight questions indicates an extremely high level of fear. Five or six yeses indicate a high level. Three or four yeses indicate a moderate level. One or two yeses indicate a low level. Zero yeses suggest that fear doesn't inhibit how you relate.

Whatever you score on this quiz, keep in mind that courage is the emotional mechanism that overrides fear, imparting the strength, clarity, and spunk to conquer obstacles. It impels you to the light. Try to absorb as much courage from others as possible—if you're an empath, that's a real perk of having sensitivity. Being courageous, though, doesn't necessarily mean you don't have fear, just that it doesn't control you. However, having courage does mean never giving up on yourself, no matter how many fears arise.

Throughout history, people have consistently tried to gain power, personal or political, by instilling fear in others. Sad to say, it's a ploy that predictably works. However, the million-dollar question is, what prevents generations of intelligent people from seeing through this emotional manipulation? Why can't we respond to family, friends, or the government by saying, "Oh, come on, I'm not falling for that one again! Let's try to solve the conflict, whatever it is, without the fearmongering"? As I see it, fear makes us panic and forsake our intuitive good sense. Also, fear is incendiary. My spiritual teacher says, "When two frightened people talk together, it's like passing fire to a scarecrow." Consider how fear spreads via the media to tens of millions of us. You don't have to be an intuitive to feel our nation's jitters. Even so, the good news is that once you're aware of how fear works, you can stop the cycle.

Like everyone, I have my share of fears to confront. What spurs me to be courageous when I'm afraid is how intuitively "off" and unsettling it feels to move in any direction other than toward the light. Plus, it really pisses me off when darkness wins, even for an instant. Therefore, my credo is: I will not give in to fear. I'll offer you the same practical tools I use to live by this stance as well.

The Anatomy of Fear and Courage:
Putting the First Transformation into Action

Prepare to demystify fear so you can face it unafraid. When you learn to recognize and work consciously with its different aspects you won't see it as some haphazard force of nature that can seize you unaware. To achieve such liberation, you'll explore the four components of this transformation's emotions: their biology, spirituality, energetic power, and psychology. This comprehensive approach will allow you to understand the dynamics of how fear operates and gain mastery over it. Study fear closely; allow courage to flow from what you learn.

REPROGRAM THE BIOLOGY OF FEAR
AND COURAGE

Fear, a form of stress, is one of the most extensively researched emotions of the last decade. Science has demonstrated that it has a biological upside and a downside. When you're in imminent danger, fear is a survival instinct that's biologically advantageous. When a thief breaks into your home, a spouse goes on the attack, or any other eat-or-be-eaten scenario occurs, your body's warning systems notify and protect you. Fear is so overpowering because in primeval times, to ignore it was to be dead. Better to be on full alert at the first sign of danger—even if it turned out to be a false alarm—than to be less vigilant and end up as a predator's lunch. Now, fifty thousand years later, that genetic imperative is still in us, though often too tightly wound for the world we live in. Fear works against your biology when it becomes a habitual response to lesser, everyday conflicts. Consistently feeling like a deer in the headlights can make you emotionally twitchy and physically spent.

To review and expand on Chapter 2's explanation of the biology of stress, we'll now focus on what happens to your body when you're afraid. Picture a train coming at you. Your senses register this. In milliseconds they send a signal to your amygdala, the brain's alarm system where fear is centered. (Electrical stimulation of this almond-sized region is enough to elicit fear.) If the threat is deemed sufficiently intense, the amygdala relays impulses to the hypothalamus, which activates a cascade of hormones, including adrenaline, the fight-or-flight hormone. There's a vivid physicality to fear. Your heart rate and blood pressure increase. Muscles tighten. The jaw clenches. Respirations slow. You instinctively hold your breath so you can hear better. Your pupils dilate so you can see better. Your system's cranked to a superalert readiness to fend off danger. *You interpret these physiological responses as fear.* Then you'll know to jump out of the train's way.

Interestingly, lesions in the amygdala block fear. Monkeys with damaged amydalas are no longer frightened by snakes and will brazenly pick them up—not a smart move, considering that boas eat monkeys. All fears aren't created equal. Certain ones can be adaptive, but other kinds, acute or chronic, overtax the body by elevating the stress hormone cortisol, impairing your immune system, and inhibiting the relaxation response that emotionally soothes you.

Want to know why some people love to be scared? You know, the ones who sit rapt in the front row of *The Texas Chainsaw Massacre* watching bloody body parts whirl across the screen, or who seek out dizzying, curlicue roller coasters that make the rest of us want to hurl? (Some theme park rides have giant signs that warn: "Do not enter if you have a heart condition.") The biological answer: they like being aroused by the adrenaline rush in a controlled setting. That, coupled with the subliminal relief of not being eaten or harmed, gives their inner Neanderthal—we all have one—a sense of mastery. Since the DNA of *Homo sapiens sapiens* (us) differs from *Homo sapiens neanderthalis* by only 0.5 percent, it's easier to understand why, primally speaking, fear as entertainment becomes a gratifying experience.

In order to visualize what your body undergoes when afraid, here's a diagram to commit to memory. I recommend that my patients working

Your Body's Fear Response

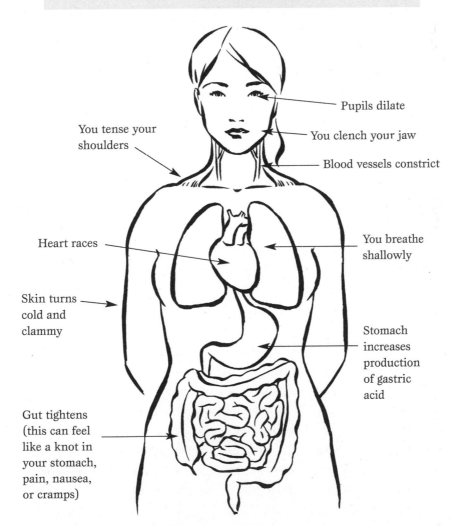

Pupils dilate

You tense your shoulders

You clench your jaw

Blood vessels constrict

Heart races

You breathe shallowly

Skin turns cold and clammy

Stomach increases production of gastric acid

Gut tightens (this can feel like a knot in your stomach, pain, nausea, or cramps)

with fear do this too and carry a copy of it in their wallets. Having something concrete to look at is a sobering reminder to attend to the stress at hand, that your metabolism is being shot into overdrive by vessel-constricting, heart-thumping hormones. (I've read accounts of soldiers who've literally died of fear on the battlefield.) The diagram will also help you make the case to the insecure part of you that you need not succumb to unwanted fears.

As you can see, we're physically programmed to respond to fear and its effects on us can be extreme. But how do we know what to be afraid of? Over centuries, some fears have been encoded in our genes, making us apprehensive about scenarios that threatened our ancestors: fear of heights, bright lights, angry facial expressions, the shadow of a lurking predator. In fact, a lab rat will recoil at the mere odor of a fox even though this rodent has spent his entire life in the laboratory. Also, from birth, infants get frightened when approached suddenly or by loud, abrupt noises. In contrast, other fears are conditioned. You learn to be afraid of particular people, places, or emotions because you associate them with trauma.

Is There a Fear Factor? The Possibility of Designer Emotions

Science can be more bizarre than fiction. Brain researchers are making incredibly controversial advances in bioregulating our experience of fear, reminiscent of Aldous Huxley's futuristic *Brave New World*. A team of neuroscientists, including Nobel laureate Dr. Eric Kandel, have identified a "fear factor" our brains require to generate this emotion. They found that the protein stathmin in the amygdala is necessary to trigger fear. However, when they removed the gene that encoded this protein, mice displayed newfound courage. Unlike their unaltered counterparts who instinctively cower at the edge of an open field—behavior that's undoubtedly helped the species survive—mice without the fear factor boldly explore unprotected environments. Such engineered courage, however, has truly serious implications. I pity the poor mouse who blithely ventures into alien terrain and gets gobbled up by critters higher on the food chain, a pesky detail still to be resolved by researchers. Although the leap from mice to humans is enormous, I've heard rumblings in scholarly journals among neuroscientists about a possible "fear vaccine" for our species, whether it be tweaking our DNA, as Dr. Kandel did with mice, or a pill inhibiting the production of fear signals. One researcher suggests it could supplement, even replace, traditional psychotherapy.

Whatever theoretical fascination such research holds, it's a chilling prelude to the world of designer emotions. Just hearing about the prospect of designer emotions makes me overjoyed to be free to feel what I want, when I want, and work to resolve it in my own good time. I predict that such an option will be available to the public in the next century. Admittedly, I'm way ahead of myself, but I get the creeps envisioning a robotically fearless military or a society of perennially perky Stepford wives. Such a weird, plasticine reality makes me think of what's described by patients with the rare neurological disorder Capgras syndrome, who believe loved ones have been swapped with lifelike doubles. (Still, I'm not against the judicious use of, say, antidepressants; medication is sometimes helpful with debilitating fear, as I'll explain in Chapter 10.) However, I present Dr. Kandel's brainchild and related research with my intuitive forecast about its potential repercussions to consider while you're evaluating the meaning of courage and fear.

In any case, I don't equate the absence of fear with courage if it's the by-product of lobotomized emotions. You're only free when you successfully face your fears in a proactive way. For me, courage is a verb; you seek it or it seeks you. Also, courage requires the presence of adversity. In fact, no fear, no courage. Without something to overcome, there's no biological push to be brave or conquer negativity, true evolutionary milestones. Paradoxically, fear gives our brain that push; it holds the promise of catalyzing courage if we aim for that, the purpose of *Emotional Freedom*'s First Transformation.

As an Energy Psychiatrist, I see biology and psychotherapy as organically entwined. I teach patients courage by helping them become more attuned to their physical response to fear; listening to biological signals is a form of intuition. With this, they can jump on what's making them afraid and consciously neutralize the release of adrenaline to bring the body back to balance. Why is this absolutely essential? *Fear renders intelligent people dumb, so they're not clear-headed or intuitively in sync enough to make brave decisions.*

Take Eve at forty, a Gothic novelist and gifted wordsmith with a devoted cult following. She'd sought me out overwrought by fear that her life was falling apart at a miserable point in her career. I immediately liked Eve, a chicly dressed Vampira in black with an Alabama drawl and pierced eyebrows. She might have emerged from the cobwebs of a medieval castle in one of her quirkily eerie novels. Eve was say-it-like-it-is smart, superintense, a tough cookie impatient with her own vulnerabilities. She always exhorted others and herself to "get over it," but such admonitions weren't helping now. Eve was tormented, hadn't been able to work for days. "Writing feels like chewing through wood," she told me. I empathized when Eve described how her fears uncontrollably inflamed each other. In her head, "I'm so blocked, I'll never publish again" had already metastasized into "I'll end up stone cold broke on skid row when my savings run out." The final nail in the coffin, so to speak, was when her trusted business manager and "friend" (whom she'd had to let go because she couldn't afford him) nastily turned on her, saying, "Your career is over. Nobody wants you anymore." This was a classic, below-the-belt Hollywood line that had badly wounded so many of my actor and writer patients when their careers were floundering. I wasn't surprised that it struck terror even in scrappy Eve. All this, compounded by her four double-shot cappuccinos a day, created the perfect storm to flip Eve's body into fight-or-flight overdrive.

On a purely biological level, my job was to help Eve tone down her adrenalized self to regain her bearings. Psychotherapy wasn't going to work until her body chemistry was less agitated. She had to learn how to unclench her shoulders and breathe in a relaxed way rather than scrunching up into a beaten posture, as if under siege, or grinding the enamel off her molars, as she was doing. Like many of us, Eve was stuck on automatic—protective, defensive. It wasn't that she lacked courage or talent. She just didn't know how to access them while in the biological grip of fear. Nor, as it turned out, was Eve's career anything like over, a malicious smear that had instantly registered as intuitively ludicrous to me. And I told her this, which she appreciated. It was an insight that felt appropriate to share.

So I suggested the following techniques to Eve, which I myself depend on to unkink my body's contractions when fear-based abandonment issues rear up. In conventional psychiatry, the presumption is that you deal first with the psychological manifestations of fear, after which the physical symptoms will be ameliorated. In my practice, however, I begin by addressing and reversing what's going on in the body so that the brain gets the message that the threat has passed. I want to emphasize that with Eve and other patients, this is a starting point, one element in combating fear. Once Eve was more centered, we went on to apply other tools I'll discuss. Our work served to initiate the process of freeing her writing and freeing her from fear itself. To pave the way for such courage, I advise that you too implement these straightforward recommendations.

Emotional Action Step

HARNESS YOUR BIOLOGY TO QUIET FEAR

To short-circuit fear and turn off your flight-or-flight response, you'll need to train your brain to send chemicals to counteract them. Otherwise, fear and its hormones will make you crazed. In contrast, with a calm biology it's easier to find courage by practicing the combined techniques below to quiet your system. (Use these along with the Three-Minute Meditation from Chapter 2.)

To achieve immediate and longer term results:

- Eliminate caffeine, sugar, and other stimulants—these fuel the fight-or-flight response.
- Avoid people who reinforce your fear—they are biological irritants. Stick close to emotional nurturers.
- Stay away from violent newscasts, traffic jams, arguments, or other stress inducers.

When you're in the grip of a fear-driven adrenaline rush, try these quick solutions.

- Use this progressive relaxation technique: In a comfortable position, sitting or lying down, take a few deep breaths while letting your body go as limp as possible. When you're ready, begin by tightening the muscles in your toes. Hold to a count of ten, then relax. Enjoy the relief of tension melting. Do the same with flexing your foot muscles, and move slowly through your entire body: calves, legs, stomach, back, neck, jaw, face, contracting and releasing each area.

- Immerse yourself in hot water to relax muscular tension as soon as possible.

These practical changes, which allow you to take control of your body, can be tremendously effective in restoring calm. You don't have to be passive while battered by fear. The victim mentality takes many forms. It requires courage to assume control, to say, "I'm going to be responsible for my biological self-care." Educating your body how to respond makes you emotionally freer.

UNCOVER THE SPIRITUAL MEANING OF FEAR AND COURAGE

There's an ancient mystical practice in which the teacher tells the student to go to the bottom of a well at midnight and sit there until dawn. What would motivate any sensible person to seek out such strenuous hardship? To face fear and confront the Self. Among certain spiritual traditions, this is the fast track to awakening.

Though my approach is considerably gentler, I'm not the type of therapist who sits week after week listening to your laundry list of fears without also teaching you to counteract them. I view fear as a means to an end, an emotional impetus for spiritual transformation.

What is fear's spiritual role? Simply put, you're given fear so that you can overcome it with courage. This remarkable stretch, this triumph, will embolden your soul and lighten your emotional load. Traditional psychotherapy neglects to frame fear this way, which prevents you from tapping into your full healing potential.

Why is it mandatory to address the spiritual context of fear? Consider these practical reasons:

Reason 1: Courage comes from the belief you have in yourself and the existence of spirit, however you define it, knowing that both are bigger and truer than fear. By joining forces, you'll have a larger capacity to deal even with what seems "too much to bear." When you access spirit, you won't feel alone or embark on the futile exercise of trying to combat fear through willpower alone.

Reason 2: Courage not aligned with a higher good isn't always positive—a burglar can be plenty courageous as he robs you blind.

Reason 3: Fear is a place where the soul is stuck and requires compassionate attention. It isn't simply an uncomfortable symptom to ameliorate.

Let me describe how spirituality helps allay my fear of abandonment. With a fear so large, I've found it invaluable to articulate this unsettling feeling in detail so I can methodically dismantle each aspect that usurps my freedom.

What my fear feels like. Over the years, I've seen how the threat of abandonment can, at vulnerable times, infiltrate my being, shadowing my light, making it appear inaccessible. It may be occasioned by real losses, such as Mother's and Dad's deaths. Or, to a lesser degree, I can still get unnerved if, say, a close friend decides to move out of Los Angeles, or when I anticipate (wrongly) that I'll be alone on the holidays. Fear often erupts without warning, accelerating from zero to sixty in a blink. Suddenly, I can't think straight. I feel panicked and stunned; the ground disintegrates beneath my feet. Most alarming, I forget myself, the strong, loving Judith I've strived to become. Fear cunningly strips me of that memory. No thought, only sensation so painful it makes my hair hurt. My night dreams can mirror my waking fears—recurring ones in which my dog is lost or that a place hasn't been set for me at the family table. To my linear mind, the feeling of abandonment seems like it will last forever.

How I spiritually connect to find courage. At these moments, logic or psychological insights often aren't enough to offset my fear's visceral intensity. To find courage, I need to be rebooted by a spiritual source. I've tutored myself, even as I'm being vacuumed into abandonment's netherworld, to intuitively connect with this source—for me, the energy of love—to move past fear's grandstanding. How? *By inwardly requesting help when I'm swirling: a powerful act that can change my perception and reinstate my spiritual link.* I do this despite my intellect's predictable protests that it'll never work. The analytic mind doesn't mediate spiritual experience—intuition does. Then, I simply stay open to what transpires, not forcing anything. Engaging a spiritual energy larger than the fear, a force I implicitly trust and know is real, plugs me into my heart and a vaster, more accurate sense of what-is. Fear had jammed those circuits. As it abates, static clears within me much like a television set when the picture returns. To my intuition, such spiritual reconnection feels like a coming-to, a veil lifting.

Though fear makes it seem as if that's all there is, a pretty darn convincing illusion, the experience of love exposes that fraud. Once I'm tapped in, fear gets out of my face; the rest of the world returns to focus. With restored perspective, I can see sweet Judith, a newborn, caught in my preverbal terror of being so alone in a medical milieu, without the solace of Mother's arms to soften my entry into life. I can also see that this is not me now. Thus, I can respond to whatever was disturbing me in a more centered way. Over and over again, focusing on the strength and goodness I've achieved as well as spirit's incomparable ability to outmatch negativity lets me realize that I'm so much more than this fear.

If I were a materialist, without any spiritual beliefs, I might have interpreted my formative experience in the hospital nursery completely differently, and I would've missed an incredible chance to transform my fear. I might've felt justified in thinking that it was unfair for an infant to be born with a sick mother who couldn't nurture me instantaneously. I might have become cynical about how this is a dog-eat-dog world, how nobody's watching over us but ourselves. Surely, this take on things could have turned me into a bitter ingrate. Enlisting a spiritual perspective, however, has allowed me to be compassionate but not sentimental. Spirit has no reservations about putting us through our paces so that we might grow. If we're born into adversity, then so be it. Tough, yes; unfair, no. I've come to trust the integrity of what life brings. Most consequential, my fear of abandonment has given me the opportunity to keep finding myself, over and over again, so I don't get lost in fear. Do you realize how monumental that is? When my fear recurs, I can keep learning to free myself from it more deeply. I'm getting the hang of it. Naturally, a part of me is sick and tired of having to deal yet again with anything that resembles abandonment. But it's not the biggest or wisest part. Though this emotional inquiry is rigorous, it's a spiritual strengthening I crave.

Now, I invite you to begin to investigate your fears. We all have them. It takes courage to own up to this. Soft-pedaling fear or deluding yourself that you're immune is more than foolhardy—it's the chicken's way out, a sure U-turn away from freedom. Some fears slowly feast on you like blood-sucking mosquitoes. Others swallow you whole. Both reduce freedom. I suggest focusing on one fear at a time, starting with the lesser ones, viewing each through merciful eyes and a spiritual lens. We grow into a love of ourselves and the world gradually.

Courage or fear is a choice. When a patient starting a catering business said, "I fluctuate between optimism and a sense of impending doom about whether I'll succeed," my response was, "Deciding to be optimistic is your exercise in courage." Freedom comes from making such brave choices. Along the way, if you believe in God, fine. If you don't believe in God, fine. All that's necessary is that you can draw on a positive force of good greater than any negative emotion to regroup when fear shrinks your IQ and intuition. Knowing that this is freeing impels you toward transformation.

Emotional Action Step

HOW TO BE BRAVE

1. *Choose a fear you'd like to be free of.* You can start with less intense ones. For instance, "I'm afraid to say no to a friend . . . to assert myself with a relative . . . to work less obsessively." Later you can go onto larger fears, such as "I'm a failure . . . I'll grow old alone . . . I'll always be in debt."

2. *Identify triggers for the fear.* What sets it off? Be honest. Then record the triggers in a journal. Perhaps seeing a friend's career skyrocketing? Going to a dinner where you're the lone single? Meeting potential love interests who only date supermodels? The more specific, the better. Once you locate common triggers, you won't be taken off guard.

3. *Frame your fear from a spiritual perspective.* Ask yourself, "How can this fear help me develop courage, become freer?" For example, does courage mean cultivating self-love? Building confidence in the talented, fantastic person you are? Persisting in a career goal despite obstacles? Zero in on what kind of courage feels most right. This will help you transform fear rather than feeling victimized by it.

4. *Make a spiritual connection to center yourself.* To deactivate fear, take a few deep breaths to calm down. Close your eyes and repeat this mantra: "I am not just my fear. I am larger." Then inwardly request to connect with a sense of spirit greater than the fear, be it love or whatever feels real. Your soul's about to expand. Go with it. Stay innocent, not cynical. The spiritual world holds magic our rational mind can't comprehend. Keep all intuitive channels open while sensing spirit. Breathe it in; let its well-being infuse you with the courage to be positive. You might also simply ask, "Please take this fear from me." Meanwhile, just remain receptive, without straining. Requesting such intervention brings extraordinary results.

This exercise will help you experience that there is something on the other side of fear worth going for. The principle is to stand in the place where the light is strong and let it saturate you. Where is God? God lives in a corner of the here and now. It's up to you to touch what appears to be invisible but is always there. My spiritual teacher says, "It's not enough to just be strong. We want to have the most luminous light inside." This light in each of us can reverse the stranglehold of fear. Intuition helps you pierce surfaces to find such freedom.

EXPERIENCE THE ENERGETIC POWER
OF FEAR AND COURAGE

A great joy of being an Energy Psychiatrist is that I work on the front lines of inner space. Whatever happens inside you fascinates me, including how you relate to emotional energy. What's your energetic response to fear? To courage? I want to know. I hope you do too so you become adept at taming negativity. Most people motor through life without any consciousness of their subtle energy field—they don't even know they have one. From where I intuitively sit, it's as egregious an oversight as being oblivious to having arms or legs. This energy, however, has a mind of its own, whether you're aware of it or not. Fear and courage radiate from you just as they radiate from me. Anyone with a pulse is affected by these and other emotional energies. How they play out in your own head and in the arena of relationships can either boost or deflate your mood.

To improve your coping skills, I'll train you to sense the energy of fear and courage. I've paired these emotions because I'd like to program you to think about them as point and counterpoint. Remember that negative emotions have a much louder intuitive signal than positive ones. Loudmouthed fear is more likely to lurch out at you, but this doesn't make it credible. Courage often has a quieter charisma, a goodness that increases confidence in yourself and humankind to defeat adversity. Acting courageously is intuition at its finest, listening to what's most nobly on center, whereas fear can elbow out intuition. These are some general qualities of both emotions to observe.

THE ENERGY OF FEAR

- Feels jarring, immobilizing, tiring
- Sucks you under like a riptide
- Makes you intuitively feel unsafe, on guard, shrunken
- Flips you into an alarmist mind-set, out of your heart
- Agitates your mood

THE ENERGY OF COURAGE

- Feels inspiring, expansive, vitalizing
- Uplifts and centers you
- Makes you intuitively feel "in the zone," in touch with greatness
- Opens your heart and increases self-esteem
- Elevates your mood

Getting to know the feel of both emotional energies will enable you to choose courage more consciously. You don't want fear's energy running rampant in your beautiful self, even if you know its root. Whenever you're afraid, invoke courage to transform fear, the formula for freedom. Here's how. Say you're afraid you'll never fall in love again, so you stop looking and hole up in your apartment, miserable. This is fear's handiwork. Courage, alternatively, means exerting the energy to move your bod off the couch and call your friends to let them know you're available to meet people. The energy it took to raise yourself from fear's leaden slump and dial the phone is an example of courage. No act is too trivial to qualify.

A basic law of emotional energy is that we attract who we are. Fear attracts fear. Courage attracts courage. If you want positivity coming at you, you've got to generate it. Lip service won't do it; your energy field transmits invisible messages about where you're really at. You're constantly emitting signals that others on similar frequencies pick up and unconsciously gravitate toward. This influences which people and events keep appearing in your life. If, for instance, you repeatedly magnetize emotional vampires or loser love interests who're petrified of commitment, it's worthwhile to consider if you have insecurities, such as low self-worth, that inadvertently draw them to you. As you heal these, you'll be in a stronger position to attract what you want.

We all ride currents of energy. Sometimes these put you in circumstances that act out your fears. In terms of emotional freedom, these can spotlight areas that need attention. I recently gave a presentation to the National Alliance for the Mentally Ill, an organization for the courageous families of relatives with mental illness. I intuitively read a young woman in the audience and advised her, "Don't let people run over you." My linear mind chimed internally, "Brilliant, Judith. That could probably apply to everyone in this room!" Nevertheless, from the animated expression on her face, this clearly resonated. "People do run over me," she replied. "I'm afraid to stand up for myself. I get paralyzed by fear." Then this woman told a remarkable story. She'd recently been shopping at a farmers' market. Suddenly, an out-of-control Buick driven by an elderly man (later convicted of felony manslaughter) plowed through the crowd, killing ten people and injuring sixty, including her. She asked, "Did I bring this on because I'm such a victim?" My answer: on a conscious level, of course not. No one in her right mind would ever choose such tragedy. But energy moves in mysterious ways. When you're carrying intense unresolved emotions such as fear, you may be prone to situations that compel you to learn about it, as was true for this woman. In her case, the trauma of that day prompted her toward healthy self-examination and emotional change.

If you take these incidents as cues to bravely explore your fears, they're less likely to happen. Though certain things are obviously beyond our control, it's also true that much of life is shaped by our thoughts and behavior. Courage means revoking fear's hold through awareness and mindful responses. This in turn changes your energy field.

Fear isn't an emotion you can mask. Animals and humans can smell it a mile off. Biologist Rupert Sheldrake has documented how people intuitively know they're being stared at, and will check to see if someone's watching them from behind. A female police sergeant at one of my seminars told me that detectives in training are instructed not to stare at suspects' backs because they'll feel a threat and turn around. I get shivers from the description of energy given by poet Stephen Kuusisto, who's been partially blind since birth. He writes in *Eavesdropping,* "When the sighted look you over it feels like you've walked into a ghost in the woods." How often I've felt in others a ghostly tentativeness born of fear, which inhibits their heart force, turning them cold. Such intuitive information can offer lucid emotional insights into people.

I routinely read patients' emotional energy to detect dissonances between what they say and feel. Take Henry, a devoted house-husband who brought in his wife, Joan, a hardworking corporate attorney, to discuss improving their communication. Joan, a Brit who came across as quite proper but dear, was stoic to a fault and had never learned to articulate her emotions. When Henry, a feeler through and through, tried to draw her out, all she'd say was, "I'm fine, really." In our first session, she repeated that phrase ten times—I counted. She didn't seem curt or hostile, just shut down. Truth be told, he wasn't fine, she wasn't fine; their marriage was shaky. Tuning in to Joan, I mainly picked up fear. How? I felt it radiating from her solar plexus into mine (this is the energy center associated with emotions). In Joan and others, I intuit fear as a "something's after me and it's gaining fast" urgency. I also sense it as a droning bass tone compared to anxiety's shrill, high pitch or jealousy's acidic bitterness. (Though all people are a blend of emotions, I'll sense which one stands out.)

My body's intuitive response notified me to gently investigate Joan's fears as I got to know her better. During upcoming months, I helped her speak about the feelings she'd been cut off from, such as being afraid that Henry would reject her if she showed "weakness." Getting the courage to tell him this and other unfounded fears made it safer for Joan to communicate authentically, solidifying their marriage. Compassionately identifying and transforming fear freed energy lodged in her solar plexus, raising it up for her heart to purify, an invigorating shift I could sense.

You too can make this energetic shift. Just because you're afraid of something now doesn't mean you always have to be. The key, though, is to seek out courage by setting your intention and taking action to manifest it. To get a hands-on experience of how this elevates your mood, try the next exercise. It'll help you slow down and witness your responses to fear and courage so you can harness these energies.

Emotional Action Step

ENERGETICALLY TRANSFORM FEAR
WITH COURAGE

Phase 1: Pick one fear and rev that energy up. Really get into a worst-case scenario. Go wild; catastrophize. Let's say you fear failure. That internal monologue might go, "I'll never get a promotion. I'll be stuck in this dead-end job until I die. I'll be unable to pay my son's college tuition." You get the idea. As you hype up that fear, observe how it intuitively feels in your solar plexus, the emotional center, and elsewhere in the body. Is your gut tense? Nauseous? Aching, as if it's been punched? Is your throat constricted? Do you have a tight band around your head? Does fear have a color? Temperature? Texture? Notice all sensations in this area and in your entire body to map the energy of fear.

Phase 2: Make a courageous decision to shift fear. This requires a change of thinking and behavior. Now, instead of catastrophizing, improve the situation. First, set a positive intention, such as, "I'll get a more rewarding, lucrative job where I can advance. My creativity and efforts will be recognized here." Then observe how your body reacts. Notice ways courage feels different from fear. Do you have a release of tension or discomfort in your gut? Newfound strength? An excitement that surges? Also, observe sensations in your heart center in the midchest. Some describe it as a window opening. Or perhaps you feel robustness? Tingles? Heat? Comfort? Let yourself explore the nuances of courage and be emotionally buoyed by it. Get a clear idea how the energy of courage feels.

Phase 3: Take a courageous action to shift fear. Make the action you choose simple and doable. For instance, scour the classifieds or call a headhunter to help you get placed. Take your time. Be patient. If the effort doesn't immediately pay off, don't beat yourself up. Staying optimistic despite fear is a brave turnabout that shifts energy from the solar plexus to the heart. This uplifting feeling and other positive ones you noted in Phase 2 let you know you're moving in the right direction.

Practicing this exercise will reinforce how acting courageously can transform fear, not only in your head but in your subtle energy field. You can't simply cerebrate your way out of fear; it's a visceral life force metamorphosis that you also initiate. With steadiness, courage builds, incrementally lessening fear. I hail the glory of baby steps. May you delight in them too. Your work is to be courageous, to love yourself enough to keep at it. Consciously seeking such freedom will make it your own.

MAP THE PSYCHOLOGY OF FEAR AND COURAGE

Ever wonder what our most common fears are? Statistical surveys show that public speaking tops the list. To many people it is scarier than even death, which comes in a close second. Comedian Jerry Seinfeld once said most of us would prefer being in the casket to delivering the eulogy. Other frequent fears include getting fat or sick, being financially insecure, and flying—very different from survival-oriented threats such as a fire breaking out in your home. Psychologically, fear arises from how we're programmed by family and society, including exposure to abuse, violence, or other trauma. These fears can always be conquered when you're motivated despite what you've endured. I'm reminded of a joke: How many psychiatrists does it take to change a lightbulb? One, but it has to really want to change.

I applaud my patients when they come to me sick of being afraid, willing to do whatever it takes to free themselves. If you're at or near that point, I'm excited for you. It's cause to be excited for yourself too.

My psychological approach to fear has two stages. First, take stock of what makes you afraid, and distinguish irrational fears from legitimate intuitions. Second, take appropriate steps to heed protective fears and transform the others with courage. At times you may foresee real danger, but more frequently unproductive fears clobber you. Therefore as a general rule, train yourself to question fears tied to low self-esteem; we're all worthy of what's extraordinary. For example, it's right to question the fear that you're too emotionally damaged to love; even the severely wounded can have their hearts opened again. True intuitions will never put you down or support destructive attitudes or behavior. Here are some guidelines for distinguishing legitimate fears from irrational ones.

How to Tell Fear from Intuition

SIGNS OF A RELIABLE INTUITION

- Conveys information neutrally, unemotionally
- Feels right in your gut
- Has a compassionate, affirming tone
- Gives crisp, clear impressions that are "seen" first, then felt
- Conveys a detached sensation, like you're in a theater watching a movie

SIGNS OF AN IRRATIONAL FEAR

- Is highly emotionally charged
- Has cruel, demeaning, or delusional content
- Conveys no gut-centered confirmation or on-target feeling
- Reflects past psychological wounds
- Diminishes centeredness and perspective

For comparison's sake, I'll share radically different examples of how I use the above criteria. One morning I got two calls from frightened patients who both claimed to be hearing voices. Truly a typical day in my office! The first came from Bill, a schizophrenic who'd been skimping on his meds. Bill's inner "voice" kept haranguing him, insisting he was a bad person, that his food was poisoned, that his son was being raped again by the grandmotherly babysitter. Believing these delusions (false beliefs unsubstantiated by fact), he was absolutely unhinged. So Bill kept calling the cops, who sent a squad car out twice but found no threat. Tolerant but tiring of this, the officers warned that if he contacted them again, they'd haul him off to a psychiatric hospital. My other patient, Jean, had been coping with despair about her brother suffering from end-stage AIDS. Jean's inner "voice" said to immediately fly to New York to join him, though he'd recently been stable. True of authentic intuitions, it came through clear as a bell and oddly matter-of-fact, and it followed the typical progression of being "seen first," then felt.

Both patients asked me, "What should I do?" I urged Bill to take his meds and offered reassurance about his safety, a tack that had lessened his fear many times in our decade of working together. Jean, however, I supported in buying a plane ticket because her intuition felt so imminent, so right. Fortunately, she did, despite the expense and inconvenience to her job. That week her brother took a sudden turn for the worse, slipped into a coma, and died within hours. Heartbreaking as witnessing his death was for Jean, she was able to be at her brother's side in those precious last moments.

Try to separate unhealthy fears from intuition. Though Bill's case was extreme, you may also have some fears that belittle you or cause you to misinterpret danger. Perhaps in a fit of anger your ex-wife called you "useless" and you believed it. This is not intuition. Nor is being frightened of having cancer whenever a brown spot appears on your skin. Also, be skeptical of long-standing fears, such as of heights; these are typically not premonitions.

If you're an emotional empath, it can be especially tricky to ascertain which fears are authentic, helpful intuitions. Because you tend to absorb other people's emotions, you may pick up their fear and think it's your own. To avoid this, always ask yourself, "Is the fear mine or someone else's?" One dependable way to find out is to distance yourself from the source. Move at least twenty feet away. If you experience relief, it's likely you're perceiving another's fear. Although it's fine to absorb courage and all positive emotions from others because they'll strengthen you, you don't want to absorb negativity. Move away, and keep releasing extraneous fear by exhaling it until the feeling passes.

While some apprehensions may be empathically linked to another's feelings or, like Jean's, are distinct intuitive warnings, the more garden-variety ones reflect ingrained negative psychological patterns. To resolve these, you must know where they come from and do what's necessary to loosen their hold.

To get started, I suggest asking yourself four simple questions. They'll provide a structure to launch the psychological transformation from fear to courage. Permit what you uncover to percolate and evolve. My spiritual teacher says, "No work is ever wasted. Don't walk ahead of yourself." Appreciate that there's a growth curve. Over time, chronicle your responses to these questions in a journal; notice how they change. Keep an updated log of new insights.

Emotional Action Step

FOUR QUESTIONS TO TRANSFORM FEAR

1. *"What are my top five fears?"* Name what scares you. Clarify what you're dealing with so you're not taken by surprise or misread these signals as intuition. (I advise limiting yourself to five fears to avoid getting overwhelmed by the process.) For instance, one that's high on my list is ending up drooling alone in a nursing home. Come clean about your fears too. No shame in this admission, only liberation. Also rank your reactivity to the fear to understand the degree to which each knocks you off center (most reactive ranks first, least reactive ranks fifth). Since it's often harder to resolve a fear that's more entrenched, I recommend building confidence by

tackling the lower-ranking ones first. Then you can have appropriate strategies in place to cope effectively.

2. *"Where do these fears originate?"* Fears don't just spring out of nowhere. Review your life to find their initial stimulus. Perhaps, as a child, watching your mother weaken from heart disease made you afraid of illness. Or being betrayed by your first love made you wary of trusting romantic partners. Knowing these origins lends perspective to your reactions today. Weigh the information to see how a prior unresolved trauma may be negatively affecting your current relationships.

3. *"What people or situations set off a fear?"* Know what pushes your buttons so you're not lured into the same negative reactions. If you fear illness, is it visiting a sick relative? If you fear aging, is it seeing a gorgeous young coworker? If you fear being alone, is it a friend gushing about a man she just met? Isolating the triggers gives you a choice to respond in a non-fear-based way using the strategies below.

4. *"What change can I make to be freer?"* Now's your chance to do things differently. Say to your fear, "Thank you for sharing," then compassionately reframe it. Here's how:

- It's okay to admit, "I have insecurities. I've been hurt. I've seen things that have frightened me. I've been given harmful messages about myself." Cry about it. Talk to a friend or therapist. Rail at God.

- Then gather the courage to replace fear with a positive alternative. For instance, affirm, "Even though I link illness with my mother, I can be loving with a sick friend." Or "I will be taken care of, not abandoned, when I grow old." This mental turnabout counters fear with a positive truth; it will alter your perception of yourself and others.

- Take the pressure off by setting boundaries. Be kind to yourself. If you fear illness, it's okay to limit the time you spend visiting a sick relative. Or, with a good friend, share your fear of being alone so she tempers her gushing about her new man out of respect. These actions can make you more comfortable as you proceed to heal your fears.

The purpose of these questions is to shake up your emotions. Notice what fears surface when awake and asleep; they'll give you a clearer idea of what you need to face and transform. Pay particular attention to dreams, the scarier the better. Your subconscious generously provides a stage to dramatize your worst fears so that you may heal them. These dreams can be unsettling—*you can't explore fear without discomfort*—but capitalize on the information to break free.

My patient Cher, at thirty a librarian, feared she was a "pathetic geek," a label her two Beavis and Butt-head older brothers had continually taunted her with since adolescence, and even now at family gatherings. Being repeatedly called a "pathetic geek" had become a self-fulfilling prophecy. Cher dressed to suit the role: horn-rimmed glasses and nunnish cotton dresses. When addressing the four questions, she dreamed:

> *I'm looking at a pair of tight satin pants in a store. A pimply-faced teenager is admiring them too. I ask, "Do you like them?" He says, "Yes, they're great for a young, thin, beautiful girl, but not for you." I stay calm but am very upset. I lie, saying, "I'm a size 4." He shakes his head and says, "No way."*

Cher woke up angry—a healthy response. She recognized the teenager in the dream as a stand-in for her brothers with their cruel teasing. She was mad at them for being so crudely vicious and at herself for allowing them to dictate her self-image. She was also humiliated by opting to lie about her pant size. This psychological dream helped change what Cher projected and felt. She didn't want to be that frightened person in the store. For the first time, she bravely began setting boundaries with her Animal House brothers: she declared comments about her appearance off-limits and waged a campaign of self-love, which included a wardrobe makeover. As Cher's therapist, I was enormously pleased to see all this.

Similarly, see how the four questions can elicit dreams that flush out your fearmongers. If you dream that a purple-eyed people-eater is chasing or dissing you, find its identity. When awake, ask yourself, "Who or what in my life fits this description?" Is it a person, past or present? Evaluate family, friends, colleagues, authority figures. Or is the fear self-propagated? Regardless, follow the dream's lead to expose fear instead of reinforcing warped perceptions. It takes guts to stop the fear cycle, a success to commend.

WHEN WE REMAIN UNCONSCIOUS about the source of our fears, we become puppets whose strings are pulled by this emotion; we suffer physically, emotionally, and spiritually as a result. Let this chapter's First Transformation help you step up to fear and use courage to rebuke this negative behemoth. Take the challenge on. The "tools for liberation" presented in this book will give you power. Practice them, not just today but always. Fear will never win if you stay aware and keep picking yourself up when you fall—we're all brought to our knees sometimes. So, together, let's gather the courage to topple fear by using both our brains and our hearts. I want you to draw on knowledge about your biology, spirituality, energetic power, and psychology to outthink fear, intuitively outmaneuver it, and know that overcoming it is a valiant feat. Our visions of courage are what poet Sarah Teasdale describes as "holy thoughts that star the night."

Meditation on Freedom

Awakening Courage

In a relaxed, quiet state, focus on a time when you were courageous. Perhaps you spoke up for yourself or took the road less traveled despite what others said. Or you fought injustice or helped someone in need. Maybe you just got yourself out of bed in the morning when you felt down. All acts of courage matter. Try not to judge one as better than another. For a few minutes, bask in the feeling of courage, letting it infuse you.

Have patience with all things, but chiefly have patience with yourself.

—SAINT FRANCIS DE SALES

7

THE SECOND TRANSFORMATION: FACING FRUSTRATION AND DISAPPOINTMENT, BUILDING PATIENCE

WE NEED A new bumper sticker: FRUSTRATION HAPPENS. Every morning, noon, and night there are plenty of good reasons to be vexed. Another long line. Telemarketers. A goal isn't materializing fast enough. People don't do what they're supposed to. Rejection. Disappointment. How to deal with it all? You can drive yourself crazy, behave irritably, feel victimized, or try to force an outcome—all self-defeating reactions that alienate others and bring out the worst in them. Or you can learn to transform frustration with patience.

Patience doesn't mean passivity or resignation, but power. It's a kick-ass, emotionally freeing practice of waiting, watching, and knowing when to act. In this chapter, I want to give patience a twenty-first-century makeover so you'll appreciate its worth. Patience has gotten a bad rap for the wrong reasons. To many people, when you say, "Have patience," it feels unreasonable and inhibiting, an unfair stalling of aspirations, some Victorian hang-up or hangover. Is this what you're thinking? Well, reconsider. I'm presenting patience as a form of compassion, a reattuning to intuition, a way to emotionally redeem your center in a world filled with frustration.

To frustrate means "to obstruct or make ineffectual." Frustration is a feeling of agitation and intolerance triggered when your needs aren't met; it's tied to an inability to delay gratification. At our own risk, we've become too used to immediate results. E-mails zip across the globe in seconds. Parents text-message their kids to come in for dinner instead of yelling from the front porch. You can get the temperature in Kuala Lumpur or the Malibu Beach surf report with a click of a mouse. Despite the digital age's marvels, it has propagated an emotional zeitgeist with a low tolerance for frustration—not just when you accidentally delete a computer file, but also in terms of how you approach relationships and yourself. Without patience, you turn into your own worst taskmaster. You treat your spouse and friends as disposable instead of devoting the necessary time to nurture love. But with patience, you're able to step back and regroup instead of aggressively reacting or hastily giving up on someone who's frustrating you. You're able to invest meaningful time in a relationship without giving up or giving in. In fact, patience gives you the liberating breath you've always longed to take.

Frustration prevents emotional freedom. My spiritual teacher says, "It's not the key to any door." Expressing frustrations in an effort to resolve them is healthy, but it must be done from a nonirritable, nonhostile place. If not, you'll put others on the defensive. Wallowing in frustration leads to endless dissatisfaction, placing us at odds with life. This emotion makes us tense and kills our sense of humor. It also leads to procrastination: we put things off to avoid the annoyances involved. Conquering frustration will revive your emotional life by making it your choice how you handle daily hassles and stresses. It's a skill I'll help you learn.

Disappointment is a form of frustration that occurs when our expectations are dashed. I'll offer a plan for dealing with it so you can quickly bounce back. Naturally, no one wants disappointments. Still, I'd like you to consider that some aren't the catastrophes they're cracked up to be. As you'll see, perhaps in hindsight, at times it's better not to get what you want. Also, people frequently fail to realize that freedom isn't about always having your needs instantaneously met, the infant's fixation. My position is that patiently coping with disappointments without crumbling or leaving a trail of carnage can be a greater emotional victory than simply getting your desires fulfilled. Why is conceptualizing frustration in this way so pertinent? Because we'll all lose sometimes—marriages, jobs, friends. But how we manage these situations, what we learn about that elusive state of feeling okay even when we don't get what we want, is the difference between being emotionally free or not. Practicing patience when faced with disappointments can help you achieve this.

I'm defining patience as an active state, a choice to hold tight until intuition says, "Make your move." It means waiting your turn, knowing your turn will come. Once you've gone all out toward a goal, it entails trusting the flow, knowing when to let the soup boil. With patience, you're able to delay gratification, but doing so will make sense and feel right. Why? *Intuition intelligently informs patience. It'll convey when to have it and if something is worth working on or waiting for.* As a psychiatrist, I'm besotted with patience because it's intimately intuitive, all about perfect timing, the key to making breakthroughs with patients. I can have the sharpest intuitions or psychological insights, but if I don't share them at the right moment, they can do damage or else go in one ear and out the other. With regard to this, I strive for enormous patience; anything less would impede healing.

I'm also struck by the fact that every world religion sees patience as a way to know God—an incentive for me to practice it, and perhaps for you too. Whereas frustration focuses on externals, patience is a drawing inward toward a greater wisdom. Lastly, patience doesn't make you a doormat or unable to set boundaries with people. Rather, it lets you intuit the situation to get a larger, more loving view to determine right action. Patience, a gift when given or received, moves within reach when you can read someone's deeper motives.

In twenty years of studying with my spiritual teacher, I've never seen him impatient. At times, we students have asked some ridiculous, long-winded questions, detailing our frustrations as others in the group fidget and squirm: "How can I find a girlfriend?" "Why can't

I sell my screenplay?" And, my favorite, "Am I making my dog de-pressed?" Our teacher isn't a psychologist or a psychic. Nor does he indulge our need for him to tell us what to do or infantilize us. But still, sometimes we just can't help this impulse to be dependent, though we know better. During hundreds of classes, I've scrutinized my teacher's face for cringes, frowns, some tiny twitch of irritation. I've vigilantly listened for a terse tone. Truly, not a single sign of impa-tience has ever manifested itself. Instead, I've watched him display boundless compassion and good humor, adeptly addressing the suf-fering or meaning behind a question rather than getting annoyed by the question itself. What a phenomenal role model he's been for me! Always, I aim for patience, a perspective that lets me honor others as well as the impeccability of how my own life is timed.

To tame frustration, begin by evaluating its present role in your life and how much it limits your capacity to be happy. The following quiz will let you know where you are now so you can grow freer by devel-oping patience.

FRUSTRATION QUIZ: HOW FRUSTRATED AM I?

To gauge your success at coping with this emotion, ask yourself:

- Am I often frustrated and irritable?
- Do I typically respond to frustration by snapping at or blaming others?
- Do I self-medicate letdowns with junk food, drugs, or alcohol?
- Do my reactions hurt other people's feelings?
- When the frustration has passed, do I usually feel misunderstood?
- During a hard day at work, do I tend to lose my cool?
- When I'm disappointed, do I often feel unworthy or like giving up?

Answering yes to between five and seven questions indicates an extremely high level of frustration. Three to six yeses indicate a high level. Two yeses indicate a moderate level. One yes indicates a low level. Zero yeses suggest you're dealing successfully with this emotion.

Even if your frustrations are off the charts, patience is the cure. You'll have ample opportunities to cultivate this invaluable skill. Life teaches patience if you let it. Bear in mind that your patience will always be tested, often when you're in a rush. Once, late for work, stuck in traffic, I honked (a rarity for me) at the SUV in front of me, which appeared to be holding things up. Then, to my abject horror, I realized the driver was a patient. Mortified, I sank down in my seat, hoping against hope he wouldn't recognize me. Whew—he didn't. He never knew I was that frustrated, all-too-human honker. My close call was another reminder of the value of patience. Like it or not, traffic is an ideal place to practice. Might as well: Americans spend an average of six months over their lifetimes waiting at red lights. In this vein, stay aware of what everyday holdups can teach you. The way you handle smaller irritants forms the template for approaching larger ones.

The Second Transformation trains you to dependably overcome frustration with patience. To actualize this process you'll examine emotion's biology, spirituality, energetic power, and psychology and come away with very practical tools. How will your life change? Needling annoyances or infuriating people won't ravage your equanimity. Letdowns or rejections won't demolish you. You'll become more tolerant of your own and others' shortcomings, better able to love. No longer will frustrations, minor or major, be able to undermine your joy.

The Anatomy of Frustration, Disappointment, and Patience: Putting the Second Transformation into Action

To reorient how you perceive frustration, I'd like you to view it as an impetus to cultivate patience. Since there's no way to escape this emotion, you'll have numerous opportunities to do this. Setting that intent, try to embrace frustrating incidents rather than only considering them hassles. Let patience reveal its grace to you.

REPROGRAM THE BIOLOGY OF FRUSTRATION, DISAPPOINTMENT, AND PATIENCE

Patience supports our well-being and best interests. To appreciate its biological advantages, consider: what makes a dieter able to forgo an alluring scoop of ice cream, or a compulsive shopper to resist a blowout sale? The ability to delay gratification helps attain a greater long-term goal. Patience is a victory of the reasoning brain over the impulsive one, an emotional coping mechanism with an evolutionary rationale.

Throughout millions of years as our brain has developed, we've come to require a more sophisticated kind of patience. When early human behavior increased in complexity, the neocortex in the front grew larger to comprise most of the brain; it's responsible for planning ahead, judgment, and intellect. Patience was adaptive for our ancestors—it aided stalking prey, hunting with a slingshot, tool making, and creating intricate cave paintings. Our present-day superenlarged neocortex also encompasses a more expanded role for patience in relationships and to counter stress.

Using a shrewdly simple experiment, Princeton University researchers identified the neocortex as a region in the brain associated with patience. They presented student volunteers with various problems to solve, including several in which they'd have to decide whether to spend money now or save it for later. The researchers scanned the volunteers' brains with MRI machines while they made their choices. The results were consistent: when the volunteers chose immediate rewards, the emotional center of their brain was activated, while opting for future rewards lit up the neocortex. Two entirely different anatomical structures were operating. What's most practically relevant about this finding is that patience seems to be more a function of reasoning than of emotion. Whereas the emotional brain may have a harder time imagining the future, the logical brain can foresee consequences and be more patient about waiting for positive results.

How does this relate to your emotional freedom? Delaying gratification is a master skill that lets you harness your brain. The idea isn't to become overcontrolled or stifle your spontaneity, but to develop patience as a success strategy. We've all experienced how impulsive choices made by our emotional brain can so easily win out over reason, and we've paid for it. The message to take away: when it comes to patience, don't leave it up to emotions. Get in sync with your neocortex by using the gift of reason. Patience doesn't just materialize. You must mindfully plot it out. *Realize: when up against frustration, you must decide to be patient, a choice not based on emotion.* I'll also describe how to consult intuition in concert with this decision to underscore the rightness of this choice (remember, intuition is neutral information), an example of mind and instinct working harmoniously.

Why are some of us more patient than others? What causes a low tolerance for frustration? Researchers have discovered that some people who are less prone to frustration have larger regions in the neocortex, which are associated with feeling this emotion. Also, temperament is germane. From infancy on, some of us are more easily frustrated than others. Children with a low tolerance for frustration tend to give up quickly; those able to withstand deterrents continue despite obstacles and resist leaving a task unfinished. Notably, an inability to tolerate frustration is linked to later substance abuse, addictions, and eating disorders. What contributes to temperament? Your mother's health and its influence on you in the womb. For instance, crack babies have a predictably low tolerance for frustration. Other factors include genetics, illness, and your body's baseline threshold for arousal and stimulation. Children with attention deficit disorder (ADD) have a lower threshold, as do many children with chronic disease. Also, upbringing molds your proclivity for patience. A neglected or abused child often becomes aggressive and more easily frustrated. Alternatively, parents who are healthy role models for dealing with frustration and disappointment have kids who are more likely to cope well with those emotions.

It's traditional wisdom that patience is important to teach children, but you may not realize how important. A classic experiment conducted at Stanford University proves the point. Picture the setup: four-year-olds are individually invited into a room with no distractions, where a researcher offers them a choice: "You can eat one marshmallow now, or wait for me to come back from an errand and receive two." Some children grab the treat the instant he leaves. Others take a few minutes before giving in. But some are determined to wait. They put their heads down, cover their eyes, even sing to themselves. When the researcher returns, they receive the hard-earned marshmallows. What's even more eye-opening is the follow-up data about these kids in high school. Those who held out for the second marshmallow grew up to be more well-adjusted, popular, adventurous, dependable teenagers. Also, they scored a staggering 210 points higher on their SATs! In contrast, the children who gave in to temptation were lonelier, more easily frustrated, broke down under stress, and recoiled from challenges. Thus, our propensity for patience as children—a product of biology, temperament, and parenting—has a gigantic impact on our success as adults.

However, all is not lost if, like many of us, you didn't experience the great fortune of having a patient temperament or patient parents. Starting today, you can begin developing patience. From a biological standpoint, this is a brilliant medical move: it'll help reverse the effects of frustration on your body. When you're disappointed or hit roadblocks, patience can make the difference between an inflammatory response that physiologically burns you out and a relaxation response that stabilizes blood glucose, blood pressure, and mood, and increases longevity.

Making a more deliberate choice to delay instant gratification and cultivate patience will help you achieve emotional freedom. And the more often you make such a mindful choice, the more biologically evolved you'll become. Why? Because you'll reprogram your neuronal circuits to function more efficiently. In turn, this enhances the plasticity of your brain—its amazing capacity to make new cells and connections, one of the most astonishing discoveries in recent neuroscience. Similarly, enlisting new emotional skills helps your brain restructure itself instead of lazily relying on old circuitry. Therefore, when you refuse to be stuck on autopilot and begin to change frustrated thinking and behavior, your brain actually rewires itself, staying younger and more fit.

If you want an instant lift from the Second Transformation, try the following exercise. It'll heighten your awareness about the physical benefits of patience versus frustration, a biological perk you can enjoy in everyday life.

Emotional Action Step

TAKE THIS CHALLENGE:
PRACTICE PATIENCE IN A LONG LINE

To turn the tables on frustration, find a long, slow-moving line to wait in—perhaps in the grocery store, bank, or post office, or if you're renewing your driver's license, dare to take on the mother of all lines in the DMV. But here's the switch: instead of getting irritated or pushy, which taxes your system with a rush of stress hormones, take a breath. Tell yourself, "I'm going to wait peacefully and enjoy the pause." Meanwhile, try to empathize with the overwrought cashier or government employee. Smile and say a few nice words to the other beleaguered people in line. Use the time to daydream; take a vacation from work or other obligations. Notice the stress release you feel, how your body relaxes. Lines are an excellent testing ground for patience. To strengthen this asset, I highly recommend standing in as many as possible.

Frustration is a relic from the dark ages of how many of our parents communicated. It makes no biological sense. Patience, on the other hand, allows you to be happier, healthier, more at ease. Keep practicing it. But don't expect others to be patient first. You must be the path forger who sets the tone for reducing exasperation. Give yourself a pep talk: "I'm going to behave in a new way because the old way isn't working." Patience is attractive and contagious. When you manifest it, others will too. Subsequently, patience becomes more widespread. It's a progressive approach that reflects a vibrant biology.

UNCOVER THE SPIRITUAL MEANING
OF FRUSTRATION, DISAPPOINTMENT,
AND PATIENCE

If you're fed up with letting frustrations get the best of you, consider what every major world religion has to say about patience. Despite fiery disagreements about who or what God is and how to make contact, all these religions agree that patience is the essence of spirituality and thus grants great strength. Judaism says, "A patient man is better than a warrior." In Buddhism, bodhisattvas train in this practice to become enlightened. Christianity and Islam deem it a sacred virtue. Patience endows you with faith in yourself and your destiny, an illuminated capacity to deal with frustration and disappointments.

Viewed through a purely materialistic lens, success means getting what you want when you want it. If you don't, your impatience feels warranted. But from a spiritual standpoint, success means acquiring patience, feeling okay about yourself whether or not you get what you want. Everything is about right attitude. Knowing that your spiritual challenge is to transcend frustration permits you to reframe and resolve the natural, bruised feelings of being let down or derailed. From this, you gain a new understanding. Interestingly, the real purpose of frustration isn't just to frustrate you. It's to prompt you to align with your larger self.

The paradigm shift here is to realize that disappointments aren't necessarily failures or bad. The Dalai Lama believes, "When you lose, don't lose the lesson." Of course, the lesson of surmounting frustrations takes considerable patience; that's the point. I want you to fight for your dreams but also, if you're thwarted, to be able to land on your feet, resilient, centered. Then you're always a winner. Here's the heart of the matter: what if you don't have (or will never achieve) the perfect relationship, perfect job, or perfect health? Rather than getting bitter or losing hope, you can make peace with what is. *That* is true emancipation from suffering.

Having patience isn't always easy, but it lets us interact with more composure and compassion. There's a wonderful story of two people standing before God. God asks them about their goals in life. One person states, "I'd like to be a saint." God responds, "That's very nice." When the other person says, "I'm just trying to be a good human being," God replies, "You are very ambitious." Patience is a worthy ambition in our relationships and lets us become our finest selves.

To authentically live the power of patience, confer with your intuition. It's easy to say "Have patience," but this state of being must make gut-centered sense. Otherwise the dictum seems arbitrary, facile, what you're "supposed to do." You'll attempt it grudgingly, without genuine optimism. When faced with frustration, expect to hear two opposing voices about how to respond. The nonmindful part of you feels entitled to remain distraught, but the mindful part will enlist intuition to locate the greater teaching. The next action step offers specific spiritual strategies to do this.

Emotional Action Step

APPROACHING FOUR COMMON FRUSTRATIONS WITH PATIENCE

COMMON FRUSTRATION 1: THINGS AREN'T HAPPENING FAST ENOUGH

When something you've slaved over and hoped for isn't moving as quickly as you'd like—a universal gripe—realize that there's your timetable and there's spirit's timetable. Timing is tricky. Though we may prefer quick results, my spiritual teacher reminds me, "A plant flourishing in a small pot will die if prematurely planted into a larger one." Patience isn't a limitation; it primes us for flowering when the time is right. Trusting flow—a larger-than-Self intelligence that carries us through life—means pacing ourselves, optimizing what we've got. This is more appealing than overstriving or pressuring others (turn-offs that make us look desperate). When you've swum against

a mighty ocean current, you know how exhausted you become.
Same when you fight the flow of life.

How can intuition facilitate being patient? It can help you
attune to flow. Complementing logical considerations, it will
clarify whether a goal is achievable and at what speed. For
insight into these or other issues related to flow, first get
yourself into a quiet meditative state, breathe deeply to relax,
then use these techniques.

- *Ask a question and wait for your intuition's response.* You can
  confer with intuition about any frustration. Say you need to pin
  your boss down on vacation dates. Though he keeps promising to
  get back to you, he doesn't. You loathe being pushy but need to
  know. So inwardly ask, "Shall I remind him again?" Then hold
  the question lightly in your awareness until you get an intuitive
  "yes" or "no." Try to set irritation aside so that you are coming
  from a neutral place. Note what you pick up. "Yes" often feels
  like an acceleration, excited but smooth sailing. "No" may feel
  like inertia, a fizzle, as if you're hitting a wall. This is your
  intuitive answer. Heeding it will keep you in the flow.

  Still, intuition doesn't always tell what you want to hear. One
  of my patients was alarmed that her sister wouldn't leave a
  verbally abusive husband who refused to get help. Acting out of
  frustration, my patient did everything battered women's support
  groups warn against. She nagged, pushed, cajoled: nothing
  worked. When consulting intuition, she got a definite sense that
  her sister wasn't ready to leave. Difficult as this was to accept, it
  motivated my patient to get counseling to better deal with her
  own feelings and her sister. In your own life, if your intuitive
  answers aren't what you'd wished, try to listen anyway. Doing so
  deepens patience and understanding in all situations.

- *Consult a dream.* To shed light on frustration, request a guidance
  dream. Before sleep, formulate one question. In the morning
  record your dream in a journal. Note if you received an answer.

Then try it out. Since dreams bypass your "figuring-out" mind, they offer a fresh spin on overcoming emotional impasses. Do this every night for a week until a breakthrough comes.

This technique set me straight during a stage when my writing was agonizingly slow and I was becoming impatient. Despite knowing it was futile, I kept bearing down, pushing, but nothing much came out. In the midst of my struggles, I asked for a dream to guide me. After doing this, I had one in which I was given a phone number. Half asleep, in the dead of night, I blearily jotted down each and every digit. In the morning, without hesitation, I dialed the number. I'm bold in this particular way, having had life-changing experiences with dream phone numbers before. An officious, hurried male voice answered, "Hello, UCLA Labor and Delivery Room." I had to laugh—I could hardly believe my ears. My dream had led me right to the very section of the hospital where babies are born, and for sure, there's a whole lotta pushin' goin' on there. Babies. Birthing. Books. *Hello,* indeed! I'm so fortunate my dreams have the kind of humor that just cracks me up and puts me back on track. I was also being given the message that babies come completely on their own schedule, but they do indeed come—not to worry. Afterward, I could take myself less seriously and relax with the birthing of this book. A labor that takes years can blossom only with patience.

COMMON FRUSTRATION 2: YOU DON'T GET WHAT YOU WANT

To roll gracefully with life, try to accept that sometimes you get what you want and sometimes you don't. However, one unshakable truth is that, spiritually speaking, you'll always get what you need. This is great news—even if your small self isn't overly consoled. Though I'm convinced that holding positive visions of your aspirations will help attract good things, it's also true you may give your all but not attain success, or at least not the success you'd pictured. If this should happen, conceive of it this way:

- *Disappointments build patience and self-compassion.* To further spiritual growth, begin to deal with disappointments in a freeing, patient way, without berating yourself. Instead console yourself with loving-kindness by saying, "Honey, I know you're crushed. You did your best. Though this one thing fell through, it'll be okay." Also, it's cathartic to vent frustrations with friends, family, or a therapist, but keep moving beyond defeat. Make disappointments a path to inner power. Singer Leonard Cohen tells us, "Didn't get the girl. Didn't get rich. Follow me."

- *Disappointments may actually be blessings in disguise.* From my medical practice and personally, I understand the impulse to interpret disappointment as failure. I also know how easy it is to confuse what you want with what you need. One patient, a commercial developer, fantasized for decades about making millions and did—but it broke up his marriage and he's miserable. On the other hand, I've seen how some disappointments ultimately improve life. Another patient's crazy, one-sided, unrequited love in fact saved her from a man who later proved to be a rampant philanderer. Disappointments aren't always what they seem. In the bigger picture, some desires are better left unmanifested. To register this in your gut, intuitively tune in to the situation. From a quiet, calm place, see if there's even the tiniest recognition within that you got spared, an inexplicable relief that may be coupled with the disappointment. Apart from your desires, connect with what makes you breathe easier in the grander scheme.

COMMON FRUSTRATION 3: YOU'RE REJECTED

The feeling of rejection, of being unaccepted or discarded, can be the most painful version of not getting what you want. People fear rejection, anticipate and avoid it, and have nightmares about it. You can be rejected for a variety of reasons, fair or not. Some rejections are bigger than others. They can range from a simple no to a snub or a betrayal. Rejection is a bear, but you need to get a grip on it so you're not devastated. One way to address it is from a spiritual angle (later I'll describe a psychological one). As I advise patients and have seen proven time and again myself: *think of rejection as God's protection.* This applies to everything. Frustrating and dispiriting as rejections can be, try to find their meaning in a wider context.

A particular experience made this vivid for me. Years ago, in the heat of a steamy romance, I got this bright idea for a book called *Psychic Sex.* It graphically detailed my partner and my sensual intimacies from an intuitive point of view. Looking back, I can see that I was hormonally blinded by passion and in a rebellious bad-girl mode. Undaunted by what anybody might think, I was utterly possessed to write. And I did, almost one hundred pages. When the manuscript was sent to prospective publishers, it was rejected everywhere, not benignly but with ire. "It's embarrassing," one editor commented. "Crude and disgusting," said another. Still, with every rejection, I prayed harder for this project to happen. Only more rejections ensued. For weeks, I felt decimated by disappointment, and I began to have painful doubts about myself as a writer and teacher. However, with the luxury of hindsight, I thank the sweet Lord for this rejection, that the book wasn't published. In the end, I would have overstepped my comfort level and my partner's about revealing these very private experiences, which, to be kind, belonged under the category of "too much information" for anyone else but us. Though I couldn't see it then, something wiser was looking out for me.

How do you know that this attitude isn't just a convenient rationalization? First, life will validate the protective reason for the rejection if you patiently watch how it plays out. Second, search your intuition for the truth of this validation too. As I've suggested for other disappointments, in quiet moments try to sense if you dodged a bullet, which was true for me.

Nevertheless, if your intuition keeps saying to go for it, don't let this one rejection stop you. Positively frame obstacles, as Thomas Edison described in his quest to perfect the incandescent light-bulb: "I have not failed 10,000 times. I have successfully found 10,000 ways that will not work." Me, I always root for the underdog. I say, be scrappy. Investigate alternatives. When one door closes, another one opens if something is meant to be.

COMMON FRUSTRATION 4: OTHERS DISAPPOINT YOU

Sooner or later, even in the most loving relationships, you'll get disappointed, and you'll disappoint others. It's part of the terri-tory of intimacy. I've had patients come to me with the cock-eyed expectation that in healthy relationships—especially with a "soul mate"—you won't be disappointed. Not so. There will *always* be disappointments; mindfully dealing with them is what counts. Though some people never recover from the blow of disappointment, emotional freedom means bouncing back better than before. How? From a spiritual perspective, try to practice tolerance, patience, and forgiveness (discussed in Chapter 12). Remember, no one is perfect, including you.

With all disappointments, weigh how grievous they are. In rare cases the breach is so extreme (e.g., your spouse sleeps with your best friend) that you may opt for a divorce from him and her, then patiently devote yourself to healing. But with lesser disappointments, try to work through them. When a relative habitually cancels plans at the last minute, address the issue. Talk it out so the behavior can change. Sometimes, though, it's the better part of love to accept a person's limitations if change is unlikely. Say a colleague doesn't go to bat for you because he's not secure enough to speak up even for himself. Or a friend disappears during your parent's illness because she's too afraid to deal with it. Naturally you feel hurt, but being tolerant of their shortcomings can be a stellar spiritual feat. Specifically, what does that entail? You might not like an aspect of someone, but you're able to accept it without forfeiting a worthwhile relationship. Often, like all of us, people are just doing the best they can, which needn't warrant dropping them or closing your heart. How much do you gain by bolting whenever someone lets you down? Without a reserve of patience, love can turn to hate if people don't give you what you want. Avoid this grim fate by aiming for patience when you or another falls short.

Refuse to let frustrations interfere with your capacity to love. Want to experience God? Go for it. You be the one to have the biggest, most patient heart in the room. Don't give up on others too quickly, and above all, *never* give up on yourself. My teacher says, "The most important quality on a spiritual path is endurance." (The word *patient* comes from the Latin meaning "to endure," whether it refers to one who's seeking healing or the character trait.) Without patience, forget about enduring anything. Patience fortifies you against frustrations, a necessity because emotional freedom requires time and dedication. Let's support one another in becoming as patient as fishermen, a steady effort that's transformative.

EXPERIENCE THE ENERGETIC POWER OF FRUSTRATION, DISAPPOINTMENT, AND PATIENCE

My medical office building's security guard, Charles, is my "patience guru." Day after day, he sits at the heavily traveled entrance, the first person patients see. Charles is swamped with questions: from the infirm, elderly, mentally ill, and demanding yuppies. I've eavesdropped, and I know these people can ramble on, complain, or act superior or crotchety; sometimes they're hallucinating or have dementia, so Charles has to endlessly repeat himself. No matter: Charles treats everyone like gods and goddesses, respectfully addressing them as "sir" or "sweetheart" no matter how frustrating or long-winded they are. He creates a bubble of friendliness at his station, a healing energy of patience for these patients—and for me. I'm in awe. I'm so lucky to learn from watching him. Charles is the kind of person I want to be.

In the practice of medicine, patience is crucial, but even veteran physicians sometimes don't have it. As I've experienced and perhaps you have too, it's the worst feeling when your doctor gets impatient with you. (Research has shown that doctors tend to interrupt twenty-two seconds after a patient begins to talk.) There you are, in need of healing, but your doctor is hurriedly checking his or her watch, taking phone calls, or irked if you ask too many questions. Impatience and frustration aren't just attitudes; they also transmit subtle energies that your body assimilates. They create an aura of dismissiveness that's counterproductive to wellness. Reflect on how unpleasant impatience feels as a reminder to embody something more. When discerning the energetic differences between frustration and patience, watch for these common qualities.

HOW THE ENERGY OF FRUSTRATION FEELS

- Tense, prickly, like you're spinning your wheels
- Frayed at the edges
- Deadly serious, restless, tiring
- Like the lead balloon of disappointment
- Trapped in your head, not intuitive

HOW THE ENERGY OF PATIENCE FEELS

- Respectful, appreciative
- Generous, conveying "there's enough time" for someone
- Like a big, slow exhale
- Soft, embracing
- Intuitively and spiritually on center

To energetically experience the huge difference between the Second Transformation's emotions, try this experiment with daily frustrations.

First, rev up frustration. For example, if you're being ignored by a salesperson, don't even attempt to be patient. Unleash your full wrath. Be overbearing. Roll your eyes. Sigh. Grunt. Chide the salesperson, "I'm in a rush. You're keeping me waiting!" Then observe what happens. How does frustration feel physically? How does the other person react? What are the vibes between the two of you? Register this, so you remember. Then, in another frustrating situation, do the reverse: be patient. If, say, a mechanic declares your car must be in the shop for a week, don't erupt. Convey thanks for his attention to your car, but also mention, "If it's ready earlier, it would mean a lot to me." Get him on your side instead of antagonizing him with irritation. Beam out all the patience you can muster. Then compare how that energy feels to frustration: in your body, in your relationship, and in the results.

Patience Is a Beauty Secret

Of all the great reasons to be patient, vanity can be particularly motivating. I've seen chronic frustration and impatience permanently scrawled on my patients' features, unforgivably aging them. Their faces become sour-looking: pursed, tense, with frown lines. Their body language is unflatteringly bullish and aggressive, as is their energy. Next time you're around someone impatient, decide for yourself how appealing such testiness looks and feels. Do you want to be like that? Not me. Now, here's a real beauty secret: patience makes your appearance and energy more radiant, soft, approachable. How? By shifting you out of the frustrated churning in your solar plexus—the emotional energy center—to the beguiling energy of the heart. The more patient you are, the more attractive you'll be. Patience keeps us young and spares us from the stressed-out look of perennially trying too hard and fighting the flow. It lets us be a friend to others and to ourselves, energetically charismatic and nurturing.

Patience Honors Life's Energy Flow; Frustration Goes Against It

Frustration is an emotion that subverts flow. Personally, I've seen how it may cheat you out of incredible experiences, especially in situations you'd prefer not to be in. One day, after everything that could go wrong did, I was supposed to attend a fancy dinner party with my

boyfriend at that time. It was thrown by the trustees of the Chautauqua Institution in rural New York, where he'd been invited to speak.
We'd been staying at Chautauqua, partaking of the rich cultural community established in 1874. Franklin D. Roosevelt delivered his "I
Hate War" speech there, and the institution has presented luminaries
such as George Gershwin and Ralph Waldo Emerson. Thousands arrive
each summer to hear their symphony orchestra, poets, and thinkers.

Ordinarily, the dinner would have been fine, albeit a little too white-
bread and proper for my taste, but I was very tired, cranky, and not up
for it. The setting for the dinner was idyllic: the backyard of a Victorian home by a lake, handsomely dressed and coiffed silver-haired
people mingling, crystal champagne goblets. I was planning to make
the best of it—that is, until I checked the place cards and realized that
my boyfriend and I had been seated at separate tables. The hostess had
put me at the other end of the gathering with some very conservative-
looking couples. Having to make small talk with strangers for hours
would be torture. My boyfriend politely asked the hostess if we could
sit together. Just as politely, she said no.

"That's it," I thought, "I'm leaving." My boyfriend was truly okay
with this. So I told the hostess, "I'm not feeling great. Please excuse
me. I have to go." But as I started walking away, she grabbed my arm
with an iron hand. In a tone befitting a seasoned dominatrix, she said,
"You're not going anywhere. Sit down there." Her freshly manicured,
bloodred fingernail pointed to my assigned seat. I couldn't believe she'd
grabbed me. I was fuming with frustration. I'm a peaceful person, but
I wanted to smack her one. Fortunately, at that moment, my more
enlightened side kicked in, advising, "Just go with the flow and stay.
Don't do or say anything you'd regret." Hearing this, I knew it was
correct. I dutifully went to my seat and prepared for a long evening.

Attempting to be social, I struck up a conversation with the man on
my right. "What kind of work are you in?" He said, "I'm a doctor. I discovered Lyme disease." I was so relieved we had grounds for a conversation. We discussed the disease and its cause. It was fascinating. He
educated me, which was very generous of him. Then I turned to the
man on my left and casually said, "Hi, how are you?" Not having overheard my conversation with the doctor, he proceeded to reveal that he

was painfully recovering from Lyme disease. Now, that's quite a synchronicity! What are the odds? I live for such moments of inspired coincidence. Exuberant, I told this man, "Guess what? I have someone to introduce you to!" Thus I linked the patient up with the very expert who could most help him. No doubt about it—an intuitive bull's-eye.

What did I learn from this about emotional energy? Had I let frustration possess me, I could've done damage, generating bad feelings and bad energy at that party. Despite being frustrated and longing for my bed and a hot bath, the flow was for me to stay. Sensing and surrendering to this, I became the messenger for a synchronicity to occur. At times I feel a current running through me. I'm a connector of people, which gives me great pleasure. That summer evening in New York State and always, I'm proud of not caving in to the temptation of frustration—and it *is* tempting at times. But life's flow has intriguing things in store when we say no to that negative energy. If I'd just bailed when I was frustrated, without heeding my intuition, I would've missed this synchronicity and facilitating a magical interchange.

I want to share some practical techniques to transform the energy of frustration. They're especially handy if you're stuck somewhere you don't want to be with people you don't want to talk to. Rather than just staying miserable, counting the minutes until it's over—which projects negativity and makes you tense—better to slyly sidestep this emotion.

Emotional Action Step

TAKE CHARGE OF A FRUSTRATING SITUATION

To reset the energetic tone of your interactions, try one or more of these options.

- *Use humor.* Laughter is a quick way to break the spell of frustration and become more patient with what is. Emotionally, laughter raises your spirits, softens defenses, and spreads positive vibes. My patient Wes, an acting coach and jokester, was stuck in a long supermarket line. He was in a rush, but the pace was glacial. The harassed checker dropped a carton of milk, which spilled on the floor and required a lengthy cleanup; a woman forgot her credit card. Wes thought, "I've had it." Next thing he knew, the coach in him declared to the checker and the weary people in line, "Hey everyone, listen up! Take a deep breath and focus!" "At first they just stared at me incredulously," Wes said. "Then they all began laughing. I must have sounded absurd. Even I was shocked by my outburst!" But afterward, the line started moving faster. Getting people laughing woke them out of their energetic stupor.

Like Wes, use laughter to counter frustration. How? Don't just grit your teeth. Bring levity to a conversation. Ask others about themselves; respond with lightness and humor. Joke around, laugh easily. Also, scan the place for a frustrated comrade with whom you can commiserate. They're often the silent ones who look out of place or who take refuge on the balcony or in a bathroom. As I've found, being stuck together at a tedious event can be material for a bunker kind of hilarity. Putting a humorous spin on a trying situation tempers frustration.

• *Focus on the positive.* Changing your attitude changes your energy. In any situation, there's always something positive if you look for it. Perhaps it was the ethereal light in the room, a delicious meal, or the one person you did connect with at an otherwise disappointing meeting.

I was tickled to read an article about a pastor who challenged his congregation to stop bemoaning their frustrations for three weeks. A good-natured, beloved leader, he was fed up with their litany of complaints, including about the choice of worship music, their spouses, and their kids' behavior. He was urging his flock to look at the bright side, not to become overly chirpy. Though only 18 of 250 members succeeded for the entire time (three weeks was asking a lot), everyone started thinking more positively, which uplifted the congregation's energy.

As a policy for living, place your attention on what's working, not on what's frustrating or disappointing. With practice, you can train your thinking to do this.

- *Go with the flow.* When there's no escape from frustration, don't fight what is. The more you resist the flow, the unhappier you'll feel. Accept that, temporarily, you're meant to be there. Relax into it. Practice patience with the circumstances and yourself instead of simply feeling like a restless horse in a stall. Also, stay open to discovering surprises and unexpected connections. Try to feel the perfection of even this moment.

This action step builds patience by behaviorally and energetically raising the bar on how you deal with frustration. Frustrations can proliferate like ant armies; just when you think they're gone, they're everywhere. Still, regardless of numbers, as this emotion's energy becomes less seductive—and it will—your tendency to succumb becomes history.

MAP THE PSYCHOLOGY OF FRUSTRATION, DISAPPOINTMENT, AND PATIENCE

During our medical training, we residents weren't always exemplars of patience. No wonder. Throughout those years we were perpetually sleep-deprived from being on call every third night, so pressured we sometimes couldn't even go to the bathroom without our pager beeping. I remember that back then I read *The House of God* by Samuel Shem (a pseudonym to protect the resident's identity and medical career). This tell-all exposé of the darker side of hospital training was unnervingly accurate. I still wince to think of his description of nursing home "gomers"—an acronym for "get out of my emergency room." These, the most mentally and physically deteriorated patients, with a scorecard of fatal diagnoses, were frequently treated as nonbeings by the hospital staff. We often felt just too rushed to be kind. All we could think about was expediently "turfing" cases to appropriate facilities to release a bed for emergencies.

Medical school teaches that a good doctor is patient. But little is said about how to have patience when you're stressed out at 3:00 A.M. evaluating an obnoxious drunk in the ER who vomits on you—or how it applies to the art of psychotherapy. Patience was more of a nebulous goal than an in-the-trenches practice. This is unacceptable. Our health care practitioners must be specifically trained for patience. Being spread too thin is an explanation for impatience, not an excuse. I believe that classes on patience belong in the core curriculum of training programs. Then, methodically, we can both draw on it and teach it to those we treat.

In traditional diagnostic terminology, frustration and irritability are clumped with depression and anxiety. Also, in the extreme, they're associated with bipolar disorder, cyclic mood swings from mania to depression. Manics can be terrifyingly irritable with no impulse control, and I mean none. One manic patient I saw in the ER had been arguing with a bank teller who wouldn't cash her check. When the teller made the great mistake of pointing his index finger at her for emphasis, quick as a cobra, she bit it, hard. Bank security handcuffed her. The police brought her in. When the symptom of frustration is that severe, it may need to be medicated. Also, this emotion is grist for psychotherapy, though learning patience is not typically a central issue that doctors discuss with patients. Regrettably, most psychiatrists haven't integrated patience into their vocabulary or treatment regimens, though it must be for any hope of curing frustration.

I admire the work of psychologist Albert Ellis, who in the 1950s introduced the concept of low tolerance for frustration, which he equated with an obsession with instant gratification. Ellis's therapeutic techniques are still used to help patients increase their tolerance levels by teaching them how to make concrete changes in their beliefs and behavior, which increases their patience and flexibility. For example, instead of feeling justified in chomping at the bit until frustrations at work improve, see what kind of rewarding exchanges you can have in the meantime with coworkers. Substitute a positive approach to a difficult situation for a negative one. Unfortunately, Ellis's practical "cognitive" method was just skimmed over in our residency program, as were most psychological theories that didn't relate behavior to body chemistry or the use of medications. How I wish I'd learned more then about strategies for transforming frustration! Like Ellis, I believe that emotional suffering largely comes from how you perceive an event, not just from the event itself. The psychological path to freedom involves adopting a new skill set to counter frustration and communicate constructively.

I'd like to offer some basic rules for interacting with frustrating people. Using this template for communication, you won't be thrown off center. Stay aware that there are two levels of reacting to frustration. The first is to vent your feelings to supportive others, not usually the source. Here, don't worry too much about being politically correct. "I've had it with my bossy in-laws and they're driving me insane" is cathartic. You've got to get it out of your system to be able to focus on solutions. Sometimes just venting is sufficient. But if you need to take action in addition, move on to the second level of reaction, following these rules for addressing and resolving the issue.

Dealing with Frustrating People: Four Rules for Communicating with Patience

When someone frustrates you, always take a breath first before you react. Decide if you want to talk now or wait to calm down. If you're highly reactive and upset, have the discussion later, when you're grounded. Then you'll be more persuasive and less threatening. At that time, use this approach:

Rule 1: *Focus on a specific issue—don't escalate or mount a personal attack.* For instance, "I feel frustrated when you promise to do something but there isn't follow-through." No resorting to threats or insults. In an even, nonblaming tone, lead with how the behavior makes you feel rather than how you think the other person is wrong.

Rule 2: *Listen nondefensively without reacting or interrupting.* It's a sign of respect to listen to a person's point of view, even if you disagree. Avoid an aggressive tone or body language. Try not to squirm with discomfort or to judge.

Rule 3: Intuit the feelings behind the words. When you can appreciate someone's motivation, it's easier to be patient. Try to sense if this person is frightened, insecure, or up against a negative part of themselves they've never confronted. If so, realize this can be painful. See what change they're open to.

Rule 4: Respond with clarity and compassion. This attitude takes others off the defensive, so they're more comfortable admitting their part in causing frustration. Describe everything in terms of remedies to a specific problem, rather than generalizing. State your needs. For instance, "I'd really appreciate you not shouting at me even if I disappoint you." If the person is willing to try, show how pleased you are. Validate their efforts: "Thanks for not yelling at me. I really value your understanding." See if the behavior improves. If not, you may have to minimize contact and/or expectations.

In communication, patience is valuable emotional currency. As you're more able to tolerate the discomfort of frustration and not blow it by acting out, your relationships will function on a higher level. In any interchange, always define what you're after. Is it to resolve a specific frustrating behavior? To say no to participating in a dead-end pattern? Or simply to convey your feelings without expectation of change? Even if the frustration is irresolvable, patience sets the right tone to treat others and yourself respectfully.

In addition to these general rules for communicating, here are some specific tips for patiently addressing two frustrating situations you'll frequently encounter.

How to Respond When Someone Makes a Mistake

If a person makes a mistake that directly affects you, whether minor or horrendous, it's natural to feel frustrated and disappointed. Most people, though, don't respond to others' mistakes or their own very well. The old paradigm is to get mad, blame, demean, punish, even abruptly cut the other person out of your life. The new paradigm of emotional freedom requires a more mindful, patient approach.

Consider: what is a mistake? It's a blunder, a blooper, an unintentional oversight or faulty decision due to lack of knowledge or inattention. Remember, mistakes aren't done on purpose, unlike vindictive acts. Worst-case scenario: someone didn't put the time in to get it right or has appalling judgment, in rare cases unforgivable. More often, though, people make mistakes that fall under the category of "nobody's perfect" and deserve at least a second chance.

Once I had to face up to the fallout of how I impatiently mishandled a mistake by a loyal associate with whom I'd worked on many projects. This time she was helping me organize a large lecture I was giving. On the night of the event, she came down with a horrible flu and was uncharacteristically miserable, negative, and curt. Still, she showed up, for which I was grateful. I knew she belonged in bed but, not wanting to let me down, had pushed herself to get there. To my great chagrin, however, she took off an hour early without warning me, leaving me in the lurch. After speaking to eight hundred people, now I was alone with a massive crowd, plus I had to manage the cleanup and lug many heavy cartons of books and supplies to my car with no help. I don't play the diva, but this was too much. As she well knew, I'd depended on her assistance, not just for practical matters, but to buffer me from getting overwhelmed and exhausted in large groups— issues I've had to consistently struggle with as do other empaths. Wonderful people were coming at me from every direction with good questions and comments, but still I felt abandoned, beset. The next day, she called to apologize for her mood and for leaving. I responded with an obviously frustrated tone, which she then heatedly told me felt "disrespectful." Next, she announced she was quitting. Tit for tat, I shot back, "Fine. It's best we don't work together anymore"—a bullet in my own foot. She replied, "Fine." *Click.* We both hung up.

A few days passed. I huffed and puffed with friends and tried to feel good about the parting, but couldn't. Then my spiritual teacher said, "When people make a mistake, don't just squash them. You lift them up!" This had the force of revelation: I knew he was right. Shouldn't I have known this? But I didn't. Despite feeling justified, I was crazy to sacrifice a close, long-term relationship over one mistake and some unfortunate communication around it. Swept up in my frustration about being overwhelmed and stranded, I'd lost sight of compassion for how dreadful she must have felt to have fled so abruptly. Nor had I conveyed appreciation for her prompt apology. I must admit, it wasn't easy to pick up the phone to apologize for my mistake of not treating her with more kindness and respect, for not sympathizing with how ill she was. Also, I conveyed that I was grateful for her unstinting support for the past several years, and that I treasured our relationship. I wasn't just making nice. I greatly cared for her and respected her expertise. I badly wanted us to reconcile. The beauty of this incident was that I owned my part in the mistake, and she owned hers. Now we've resumed working together; our relationship is better than ever.

Discussing a mistake can be touchy because people quickly become guarded. Even if they're not doing a job properly or are downright incompetent, it won't serve you to act frustrated or to chastise. You may be "right," but that won't suffice if you want to maintain the relationship. I'm not saying mistakes grant permission for repeated carelessness, but they can be a catalyst for getting things right. One of my patients hired a contractor to remodel her bathroom. He turned out to be slow and cut corners. When she impatiently brought up his negligence and mistakes, he responded, "Are you calling me lazy?" Then he got even slower. Halfway through the job, she realized she had a choice: either the hassle of firing him or shifting her attitude. She opted for the latter. Why? She and I went through the Four Rules for Communicating with Patience listed above. Using them, she adopted a "we're in this together" attitude and described specific improvements she wanted without characterizing him as wrong. The contractor *was* wrong, but that wasn't the issue. Getting the results she wanted required letting go of frustration to bring out the best in him.

Mistakes are inevitable. You'll make them. Others will too. We're only human. To be free means giving yourself a lot of room for growth. Rather than punishing people for where they falter, support them in being better to see if they can. Also set your ego aside and apologize if you reacted poorly, hard as it is. Doing so makes people melt and lets them more readily see their part in an error. Communication is a learning curve. Try not to let frustration control you. Patiently help another and yourself through mistakes. Honoring the desire to change permits positive professional and personal relationships.

How to Survive Rejection

Rejection can come at you from many directions: family, work, friends, romance. On the most fundamental level, it's a turning down of a request, a refusal of something you're hoping for. Someone you're interested in isn't interested in you. A project doesn't go. You're overlooked for a raise. Feeling rejected can be as mild as a twinge of frustration or as sharp as a dagger in the gut. It can rip you apart even if it's done considerately. *Being free means surviving rejections, major and minor, without turning on yourself or allowing them to define you.* Rejection shines an exposing spotlight on all your self-doubts. "Am I good enough? Does anybody like me? Am I creating anything of value?" If you had rejecting parents or a difficult childhood that didn't instill self-esteem, you may be ultrasensitive to rejection. All the more reason to be loving with yourself as you utilize these suggestions to face rejection.

- *Change what you tell yourself about it.* The story you tell yourself can change your emotion. There are a thousand different narratives to describe what happened; choose one that focuses on and affirms your strengths and assets. Instead of going right to "I'm an inadequate, useless loser," substitute that negativity with "It just wasn't a good match for the situation, but I'm glad I put myself out there; that took guts," a more accurate assessment. Express the hurt. Then dust yourself off and start making a dream come true in another way.
- *To lessen embittering rejection, do your best not to take other people's opinions personally.* Strive to make your self-worth independent of anyone's approval. It's difficult to do, but something we all have to work toward. Realize that reasons for rejection are always subjective, not based on the "truth," and can be unfair. However, if you do find some validity in the criticism, try to learn from it.
- *Let friendships and romances develop slowly.* This cultivates trust

instead of prematurely giving your heart away. You'll get a more reliable sense of whether the other person reciprocates your feelings, which makes you less of a target for rejection.

• *Turn to loving friends.* They can mirror the beautiful person you are when you're shot down.

My treatment of rejection differs from that of traditional psychology, which focuses on alleviating pain. I don't deem feelings of rejection "bad." My focus isn't on getting rid of them, but rather on exploring and transforming them. How? First recognize what's going on: "I feel rejected." Then patiently, as neutrally as possible, witness the feelings. Recognize they're not all of who you are. "I'm crippled by my mother's rejection" is a self-limiting way of perceiving the experience, an endgame statement. Instead, begin to view rejection from a larger, wiser aspect of yourself, using the above techniques and the spiritually oriented ones I've discussed. To enhance psychological insight, ask yourself, "Is the current rejection opening old wounds, say, with my mother?" If so, you can appreciate how this history would magnify your current pain. Pinpointing the emotional dynamic enables you to distinguish past from present. Rejections are hard enough to face without old suffering compounding them. Witnessing your reactions, instead of getting lost in the pain, lets you minimize this. Though traditional therapies don't emphasize or teach the logistics of such nonattachment, I believe this healthy objectivity makes you freer.

Whatever frustrations arise, use this section's psychological strategies. Your challenge will also be to make frustrations short-lived. Do what's necessary to confront the issue, but don't linger there. Frustrations often come in bursts: something happens, and you react. The secret to not prolonging the misery of this emotion is to adopt the attitude I recommend in the next exercise.

Emotional Action Step

DON'T TURN A FRUSTRATING TEN MINUTES INTO A FRUSTRATING DAY

When something aggravates you, *choose* not to give it running room. The old way is to brood on it and let it infest your waking moments, which can taint an otherwise lovely day. The new way is to tackle the incident to the best of your ability but not let it ruin the wondrous moments that follow. For instance, if you get a flat tire on the way to work, which prevents you from attending an important meeting, feel the frustration. Express it to a friend. But cut it short by not staying focused on it. You be the one to decide how you feel the rest of the day. Sure, you could keep mulling over the frustration. But why? Instead, concentrate on the hilarious joke a colleague shared or the afternoon meetings that did go well. Emotional mastery comes from opting for happiness.

Practicing this exercise puts you in the right psychological frame of mind to take the edge off life's annoyances. Make patience a pillar of your approach. More and more, you'll be the patient one when others are contorted with irritation. Psychic pain becomes incendiary when it has no controls. Monitoring your frustrations gives you the emotional chops to take charge of your feelings.

THE SECOND TRANSFORMATION lets you enjoy a lightness of being that isn't accessible to the chronically frustrated. I'm ecstatic when I can walk around unpressured, neither on other people's backs all the time nor on my own. I endorse patience as a way to reequilibrate your pace and philosophy, putting you in sync with your natural rhythms. It requires slowing down, mindfully scoping out a situation, seeing beyond a momentary upset to a greater emotional good. Then frustrations won't be able to consume your attention, nor will life flit by in a blur. We're incessantly told to go faster and achieve more, which lambastes our mental and physical health. But patience promotes moderation and well-being, not nervous breakdowns or heart attacks.

Patience is balance. A fear some patients have when we first start working together is "If I stop pushing, I'll lose my edge or motivation," as if it's an all-or-nothing toss-up between being frantic or sluggish. I'm saying that you can determine the gradations of how fast or slow you go in any situation. Tortoises inch along achingly slowly in the desert but often reach an age of 150. It would be one heck of a long haul if they all went around grumbling about their lack of velocity! In Far Eastern lore, the turtle symbolizes patience, quiet strength, and unwavering vitality—not flashy traits, but ones that bring happiness, a youthful sparkle, and longevity. You can't rush your way to emotional freedom. When you're patient, you have time to live richly, to see fully.

Meditation on Freedom

Experience the Grace of Patience

Declare today a holiday from being frustrated with yourself or others, a special time to bathe in patience and compassion. If you're frustrated or disappointed, take the pressure off. Sweet words only. Say, "I've done my best. Honey, it'll be all right." No recriminations. Treat yourself like a precious child who's admirably learning self-nurturing.

To connect. Only connect.

—E. M. FORSTER

8

THE THIRD TRANSFORMATION: FACING LONELINESS, BUILDING CONNECTION

IMAGINE HAVING AN abundance of nurturing relationships, a warmth of belonging quelling the oceanic ache of loneliness. You're about to embrace that caliber of emotional freedom. Loneliness is a dis-ease of disconnection that keeps you emotionally isolated when you don't want to be. If your loneliness is severe, you may feel like the last survivor of your tribe, chronically homesick for a kindred community. But this will soon change. I'll describe ways to bridge the distances that separate you from people and from yourself.

My patient Kim, thirty-eight and an architect, came to me because she'd been lonely for as long as she could recall. Kim loved her work, even more than the men she'd met so far, and had several close friends, but she'd never married, though she longed to. She'd had relationships lasting a year or two, but each ended. One man proved to be a compulsive gambler, always scheming to get something for nothing—to her chagrin, he even snuck into movies without paying. Another wasn't ready to commit. Still, like many people, she believed that meeting the right mate would cure her loneliness. She joined a cyberdating service; online introductions appealed since she worked long hours. This service promised to match couples up by compatibility according to personality tests, which sounded reasonable to Kim. But the computer made some choices that were, at best, comical. First, out of five million members, it fixed Kim up with her full-of-himself neighbor, a baby food mogul, for whom she'd never felt an ounce of chemistry. Bad start. The next "perfect match," a Hollywood director, stated, "What I most want to share with my partner is tantric sex," and, he added, "she must have advanced lovemaking skills." Understandably, Kim didn't find these expectations an aphrodisiac. Another prospect, an accountant, asked her to call him promptly at 3:00 P.M. She did, but he wasn't there, and never got back to her. Although in hindsight Kim could see a bit of humor in these real-life *Seinfeld* episodes, she "felt like a loser," lonelier than ever. Painful and true, but in therapy we utilized this loneliness as a starting point for Kim's emotional growth and transformation. The wound was now exposed and ready to mend using the techniques that you'll learn too.

Years of hearing patients voice their loneliness and feeling my own have taught me that there's more to this emotion than what's traditionally believed. "I'm lonely because I don't have a boyfriend" is usually only one aspect of what's missing. The unstated message I hear is "I don't have full access to a whole place in myself or to a sense of spirit." Investigating these layers ensures that connectedness starts from within. Otherwise, you may find yourself in a relationship and still lonely, a miserable feeling. Although being single intensified Kim's loneliness, through our work together over the next year she learned some unexpected remedies as her depth and range of connections grew. Then when she met a caring man, a fellow architect, Kim was able to enter this relationship more empowered, and she's been seeing him for months.

This chapter examines the anatomy of loneliness and offers strategies to build meaningful emotional connections. To highlight solutions, I'm presenting the biology, spirituality, energetic power, and psychology of how to actualize the Third Transformation. You'll need this data so you aren't blindsided by misguided mass assumptions— for example, the media-hyped edict that finding Mr. or Ms. Right will eradicate loneliness, that an all-powerful "other half" will make you whole. Although I'm a romantic, a die-hard believer in love, this notion is absurd. Why? Let me break it to you gently: *You don't have another half because you're already whole.* Always have been. Just as you can't be a little pregnant, you can't be a little whole. Your job is to become aware of your many sides and integrate them, the agenda of emotional freedom. No one else can do this for you. It's a slippery slope to anoint someone as completing you: if they're gone, your sense of self is blown. However, with awareness, your wholeness gradually takes form, an amazing feeling of a jigsaw puzzle with all pieces fitting into place.

I know it seems logical to see being single as solely responsible for your loneliness. I'm a veteran at spending long stretches of time on my own. However, it's a belief that limits you because it derails your capacity to be happy as is. Though I periodically bemoan to my spiritual teacher, "I'm lonely without a relationship," he rarely indulges this counterproductive thinking, responding only, "Be patient. Enjoy your wonderful life." Recently he added, "Get a dog." Miserably, I thought, "Oh great! No man, but a canine." Then I realized that actually I'd wanted one forever, though I'd talked myself out of it because I travel so much. I'm still considering it, though, and I'm close to making the leap. My teacher wasn't saying I'd never meet someone, but his consistent message is not to hinge well-being on externals. Don't get me wrong—certainly, a compatible partner may soothe loneliness. Also, the right two people can be better together than alone, helping to keep each other sane, well-loved, and secure. *Nevertheless, here's where we've got it backward. A loving relationship can never make us whole. Rather, it allows us to better experience our own wholeness.* Only from this perspective can we can realize ourselves emotionally.

My approach to loneliness differs from the conventional because I believe it's a disruption of the tripartite link between self, spirit, and others. Freedom comes from establishing a viable intuitive connection with all three, though everyone needs a varying degree of each. Then, when you have more resources to deal with loneliness, your equanimity won't rely exclusively on who is or isn't in your life.

I've long been fascinated by loneliness, being a writer and part loner myself. I see it as an inherent part of the human condition that can deepen us. I'll present this emotion's upside and downside. I'll also differentiate loneliness from voluntary solitude, which furthers introspection, a state that replenishes me and perhaps also does you. Without enough time alone, I start getting homesick for myself. It's a fine balance, people versus solitude, a changing need I must keep intuiting. We'll discuss this topic so you too can find the right measure of each.

I'm defining loneliness as a feeling of separation from a nurturing source, from an inner and/or outer sense of home. It's being a pea without a pod, unable to find a "right fit" in life. Though it might overlap with depression, loneliness typically reflects a discontent with the quality of your relationships, whereas depression spills over into many other areas of life. To identify where this emotion comes from within you, consider the following origins.

COMMON CAUSES OF LONELINESS

1. *Lack of positive human contact or community.* You've lost a friend or spouse, or you feel alienated from family. Perhaps you want a romantic partner. Or you've just relocated to a new city and simply need a little company. Though some loneliness is transient, easily solved by quality time with others, it often becomes chronic. Forty million Americans suffer from this, and these are only the brave souls who admit it. The most malignant strain is social isolation, when there's no one with whom to share private feelings or close contact. Research indicates that social isolation threatens mortality as much as high cholesterol or obesity does.

2. *Lack of spiritual connection.* Irreplaceable as supportive human interactions are, I'm also presenting loneliness as a distancing from spirit, a feeling of home that, as I do, you may not experience completely on the material plane. Whether you're lonely alone or with people, connecting to spirit is a return to wholeness, a place where all is truly well. The more you intuitively tap in to this, along with a deeper bond to yourself and others, the more belonging you'll feel.

3. *Temperament.* We seem to be born with a predilection for certain emotions. Some babies look lonely when they're born, just as

some nursery school children always choose to sit in the corner. (At times an innate need for personal space can lead to isolation.) Our temperament colors our tendency to experience loneliness.

4. *Acceptance that we are alone.* This kind of loneliness represents embracing an honest, rich part of ourselves. From an existential standpoint, we are fundamentally alone, despite the presence of those we may love. This doesn't preclude our ongoing connection with a higher power. Rather, it speaks to the autonomous nature of our development: we arrive and leave this life alone; we're responsible for ourselves and our growth, no matter how powerfully our lives interconnect with others. Part of emotional freedom is learning to accept the naturalness of such loneliness—not in morbid resignation, but as a liberating feeling: "I'm alone but I'm grounded." You don't need to remove this loneliness, merely appreciate it as a tincture of your soul that instills depth and moves you toward creativity and empathy. Psychiatrist Carl Jung, who spent much of his childhood alone in his attic, writes that his loneliness is what initially opened him to dreams and a spiritual life. Throughout the ages, mystics, artists, and seers have tapped this emotional impetus for more extensive access to themselves, their work, and the universe. You can too.

To make headway with the Third Transformation, you need to evaluate your present level of loneliness. Take the following quiz to get a baseline for gauging progress as you expand your connections. These ten questions may reflect ways you often feel, though not necessarily all the time. As usual, have compassion for where you're at and prepare to grow freer. Even if you're lonely now, know that everybody has been there too and that change is possible.

LONELINESS QUIZ: HOW LONELY AM I?

Ask yourself:

• Do I feel on the outside looking in?

• Do I feel invisible or excluded?

• Do I hunger for friendships or close family to open up to?

• Is it painful to be alone?

• Do I spend more time on the Internet than with people?

• Do I feel that no one understands me?

• Am I missing a nourishing sense of spirituality?

• Am I out of contact with my intuition and my heart's desires?

• Is it hard to ask for emotional support?

• Do I feel easily rejected in social situations?

Answering yes to all ten questions indicates an extremely high level of loneliness. Five to nine yeses indicate a high level. Three or four yeses indicate a moderate level. One or two yeses indicate a low level. Zero yeses suggest you have ample nurturing.

The Third Transformation counters loneliness by exalting nourishing connections that further a sense of belonging. I'm defining connection as the ability to make contact with sustaining alliances of many kinds. Perhaps it's a friend or colleague with whom you feel "seen," an enlivening summer thunderstorm or sitting in the hollow of a grandmother oak, which allows you communion with nature, or cuddling on the couch with your cat. (Animals and trees make the finest companions.) Experiment with innovative connections. Whether you're a loner or a people person, the quality, not quantity, is what counts.

Henceforth, I suggest you go in pursuit of loneliness instead of fleeing or trying to anesthetize it with busyness, workaholism, overeating, or shopping. Your purpose is to understand and undo its constraints by exploring its biology, spirituality, energetic power, and psychology, not to languish there. Inevitably, transforming this emotion involves a reckoning with the self, establishing an inner home base. You'll also gain a fresh take on forging outer connections. As part of your emotional freedom, I want to help you feel more in touch and less alone. You're on the cusp of that discovery.

The Anatomy of Loneliness and Connection: Putting the Third Transformation into Action

In American culture there's an unspoken cult of loneliness. All three hundred million of us have experienced this emotion, though it's rarely talked about, let alone in an open, nonjudgmental manner. Typically, we feel sorry for lonely people, as if they're stricken with some virus. Nonsense: if you're human, you feel it. When you explore this emotion, simply evaluate what is, looking inside yourself. Don't be blue if you find a well of loneliness in there. With an attitude of truth or bust, see what needs to be seen. Transform what needs to be transformed. There are plenty of nourishing connections waiting to fulfill you.

REPROGRAM THE BIOLOGY OF LONELINESS AND CONNECTION

For as long as we've existed, loneliness has been part of the human condition. From the outset, the emotion conferred a distinct evolutionary advantage, since the desire to avoid loneliness drove the solitary Neolithic hunter back to the fold, where the group shared supplies and survived. Without such a longing for companionship, his less lonely counterpart was more likely to continue hunting alone, and thus succumb to predators and inhospitable conditions. During prehistory, belonging to a community meant survival; exclusion was a death sentence. Loneliness goaded our ancestors toward the comfort of companionship and furthered procreation. Since ancient times, our primal need to be cared for and to share has relieved stress and calmed our biochemistry.

Flash forward to the twenty-first century. Now loneliness has become epidemic, with its health hazards outweighing its adaptive role. By 2010 over thirty million Americans will live alone, nearly double the figures from 1980. Many are at risk for loneliness, particularly the elderly and socially isolated. Lonely people have been shown to sleep poorly, to have more depression, infections, heart disease, and to have greater risk of premature death. Moreover, research indicates that when we're chronically lonely, our brains hypervigilantly and selectively see the negative in social situations. Case in point: because they fear rejection, the lonely conjure the worst possible interpretation of cocktail party interactions. They misconstrue someone crossing his or her arms or frowning as a snub, which then activates the brain's pain center. This skewed perception undermines socializing and reinforces isolation, a lose-lose response.

On the flip side, there's scientific consensus about the many benefits of caring relationships. People who have them enjoy increased immunity, display greater emotional resilience, and live longer, happier lives. There's only good news about how your biology responds to nurturing.

You might never have thought about loneliness and connection in terms of how your brain works, but understanding this aspect of your biology allows you to fine-tune your choice of relationships. I'll present two concepts, which I've simplified, that you can apply to daily life.

Concept 1: Engage Your Mirror Neurons

The brain is no fool when it comes to emotions. It reacts to the effects of both loneliness and nurturing. A seminal advance in neuroscience is the identification of mirror neurons, distinct brain cells that register emotional interchanges (a topic I introduced in Chapter 4's discussion of empathy). Not much gets by them. If you're with a friend in pain, these neurons trigger the pain centers in your brain. Same with compassion or other emotions. For better or worse, humans resonate on a feeling level, which may impact their emotional type, particularly if they're empaths.

As an Energy Psychiatrist, I'm intrigued by our capacity for biological empathy, a cellular form of intuition that synchronizes us with the moods of others. Emotions are catchy. A recent brain mapping study demonstrated that when women were about to receive an electric shock, they felt calmer and their brain circuitry quieted when their spouses calmly held their hands. Realize that loving presences have a profound biological impact, and start harnessing this brain-to-brain link to become emotionally freer. How? By seeking relationships that nullify your stress response. Think about how your mirror neurons are reacting to others, for better or for worse. Make this a part of your everyday consciousness.

Concept 2: Activate Oxytocin, the Elixir of Friendship

I find friendships to be miraculously healing on many levels. Like many of us, I turn to friends when I'm lonely—people I can speak my truth to, no matter how untidy it is, and not be judged. Through thick and thin, friends have come to my emotional rescue and I've come to theirs. The time they take to listen, to share support, leaves me comforted and brings me back to myself. Scientists have established that this emotional effect has a biological base: friendships boost the hormone oxytocin, a balm for loneliness.

Though friendships clearly enhance the health of both sexes, women typically turn to them more than men. Why? Scientists hypothesize that it's partly because women tend to cope with stress by reaching out and self-disclosing, whereas men more frequently have the "fight-or-flight" reaction of aggression or withdrawal. Researchers have also found that women produce more oxytocin. It spikes during orgasm, labor, childbirth, and nursing. At these times, when oxytocin interacts with estrogen, it spurs women toward the sanctuary of friends, which further boosts oxytocin, eliciting a warm, fuzzy "wash of love" effect, a mechanism thus far not clearly documented in males. Studies of people with autism, a disorder that affects the ability to relate to others, show that they have lower levels of oxytocin. When oxytocin levels are high, whether because of nature or if given by injection, you're less prone to the ravages of stress, which may explain why women tend to live longer than men.

In the following exercise, you can harness your oxytocin to combat loneliness by seeking nourishing interactions. If you're a woman, you've got the oxytocin factor in your favor. If you're a man, reach out anyway. Hormones are just one element in the mystery of relationships.

Emotional Action Step

INCREASE OXYTOCIN, THE "LOVE HORMONE," WITH THESE STRATEGIES

When you're lonely, don't isolate yourself. Be proactive about enhancing oxytocin. Leave the house instead of marinating in negative thoughts. Even a warm exchange with a store clerk can take the edge off loneliness. Also, call friends instead of waiting for the phone to ring. Invite them to tea or a movie so you don't have to do things alone. Or volunteer in a soup kitchen or participate in any other kind of community service. Even if you resist this, still try it. Making the effort despite feeling down will lift you over the hump of your discomfort. Human contact is the crux of boosting oxytocin. Quality time with others lessens loneliness.

Loneliness is an emotion that can quickly abate in the right circumstances. The more connectivity you have with others, the less lonely you'll feel. Start exploring now. Forget whom you're "supposed" to like. Discover friends you're on the same wavelength with. The existential loneliness that's inherent to being human doesn't preclude this. So throughout your life, nurture others and let others nurture you, which takes heavy-duty stress off your biology.

UNCOVER THE SPIRITUAL MEANING OF LONELINESS AND CONNECTION

I practice a faith that's been long abandoned,
Ain't no altars on this long, lonesome road.
—BOB DYLAN

During childhood, I always felt "different," that I didn't fit in. Many nights I'd gaze at the stars and fantasize that a spaceship would land on our front lawn to take me back to where I came from. I felt like an alien who'd landed in an unfamiliar world that wasn't my own. I'm sure that being so alone with my early premonitions contributed to this feeling of being an outsider, as did my mother's illness when I was born. Still, it was more than that. I had a clear sense I didn't belong here, lonely for my true home.

Now, as a physician and personally, I realize that loneliness has a spiritual dimension that can explicate this emotion. "Where do we come from?" and "Where do we belong in this universe?" are fundamental human concerns. In my workshops I've met so many people who carry a loneliness they can't understand, similar to what I felt as a child. This spiritual loneliness has more to do with where we ultimately call home than with our existing social network. Here's a piece of information that most haven't considered. *Being in physical form can seem lonely and claustrophobic compared to the vastness in which our spirits originated.* This feeling is completely natural, but it isn't usually acknowledged in child rearing and traditional psychotherapy, although it should be. It takes adjustment to be in a body, which, compared to spirit, is a more bounded form. Sad to say, we're not taught how to acclimate to this separation while growing up, which can be especially detrimental to intuitively sensitive children. Thus, we may never feel totally at home in our own skin or in the world but not know why.

We shouldn't too quickly conclude that this is a "mental health issue" or related to a deep, dark psychological wound. The solution to spiritual loneliness is to connect with your heart and the Divine, to regularly draw on that succor. Home *can* be of this world: a sense of nationality, family, community, your physical abode. But home also can be spiritual, and I'll teach you how to get there as well.

For me, realizing that the material world itself cannot totally assuage my loneliness made an enormous difference. Appreciating loneliness from a spiritual sensibility has helped me turn a corner in my own life. I'm an only child, single with no children. After my father passed, five years after my mother, relatives tried to make me feel better, but their anxieties intervened. "You're alone, you're alone," one uncle reminded me. Others kept using the word *orphan.*

True, my parents were gone. But at the very core of things, I had an enduring relationship with Spirit. Intuiting this on deeper and deeper levels has been an ongoing meditation. Of course, loneliness sometimes has its say: "Who's going to take care of me?" my inner child asks, trembling. The answer? Spirit will (in part by giving me loved ones like a cousin who reassures me, "As long as I'm breathing, you'll never be alone"). Spirit can manifest in so many ways, each of them transforming loneliness.

Consider this real-life story. My friend and colleague Harriet, a social worker who never minces words, told me she would have "offed" herself from loneliness if it weren't for her spirituality. She said, "Years ago I used to make men up so I could relate to them. When a romance fell apart, I was crushed because it didn't match my fantasy. I was completely lonely. I didn't feel connected to myself— not to friends, family, anything." In that bleak mood, she left social work to pursue a get-rich-quick scheme selling real estate seminars. Loneliness drove Harriet to see a counselor. Though she had no spiritual leanings, she did believe that she could learn to change her negative thinking. "I was ready for a miracle. And this counselor, a practitioner of a school of thought called Science of Mind, billed herself as the 'Expect a Miracle Lady,' which was the group's philosophy. That's why I went there. The counselor asked me, 'What changes do you want?' And I said, 'I don't know.' The counselor replied, 'Okay, then I'll pray that you find your rightful work. Meanwhile, see what presents itself.' "

Harriet was more than a little baffled. She'd come there to cure her loneliness, not to change jobs. A part of her thought this was complete baloney, but, desperate, she agreed to give the plan a try. A week later, Harriet was dutifully going through job listings in the *Los Angeles Times*. A notice for a social worker to run an addiction recovery center for criminal offenders caught her eye. "I got major goose bumps. The hair stood up on my arms," Harriet said. "I'd never considered this option, but I suddenly *knew* this was my rightful work. Could the counselor's prayer have worked?" Harriet applied for the job and got it. Helping ex-con substance abusers and others stay clean and sober has been her passionate spiritual calling for more than twenty years.

The counselor was far wiser than Harriet knew: her loneliness was transformed on many levels. Connections lead to connections. A year later Harriet met her husband, Mark, through her work—he was one of the inmates. Mark was doing time for embezzling and drug dealing. As Harriet tells the story: "It was hardly love at first sight. Mark was a loud, arrogant, aggressive know-it-all." But still, with her program shorthanded and poorly funded, Harriet issued him a challenge: "If you're so smart, when you ever get out of here, why don't you help me with my program?" She never expected that he'd show up four months later. Destiny is a mysterious thing. Harriet had issued the same challenge to numerous inmates, but Mark was the only taker. After a few months they fell in love. And as colleagues, they had a bond of joint purpose. Harriet and Mark soon married. Now, over two decades later, their program, House of the Return, is one of the most successful addiction recovery centers in Los Angeles.

Though Harriet wasn't looking for spirituality, loneliness was her entry into it. As she put it, "Once I found my work, life so improved from just being open to prayer. I then decided to believe a greater force exists." What difference has this made to her emotional freedom? Harriet said, "Instead of pitying myself for being so lonely when relationships collapse, I have a belief system that tells me not to give up, that there are better times ahead. Before, it used to be 'I'm a born loser. What's the point?' "

Harriet is one of those people who restore my faith in humanity. With no pretension or phoniness, she's a mix of street smarts, academic smarts, and heart. Harriet has learned from loneliness. She believes every life is worth fighting for, that every person, no matter how lonely, can change. In her work and emotional growth she says, "I just keep on plugging." To me, that's true greatness. Such persistence to liberate ourselves and be of service to others ensures emotional transformation.

Spirituality is on call for you at any moment. It resides in a corner of the here and now. I say, turn to it when you're lonely, get filled by its ever-flowing compassion. Some claim: "When you talk to God, you're spiritual, but when God talks to you, you're psychotic." If this were universally true, I would've been locked up long ago.

Dialoguing with God is the point: talking and listening to the Divine is one of the sanest and wisest things you'll ever do. Get this repartee going. Then you'll know where to turn when the panic of "I'm going to be lonely forever" keeps you awake at night. Intuiting that a higher power is always there releases tension and lets you see that the fear of being spiritually alone is just a figment of the mind. You can take a big breath, knowing that you matter and will be cared for.

The next action step will help combat loneliness. It'll teach you how to find a sense of spiritual home and enlist other strategies to feel more connected. All of these techniques are practical and fast-working.

Emotional Action Step

TRANSFORM LONELINESS WITH THESE SPIRITUAL SOLUTIONS

Instead of obsessing about how lonely you are:

1. *Meditate on home.* Spend at least a few minutes communing with Spirit, your ultimate home. It's the place you came from and where you'll return. Visualizing the details of this home will solidify a connection to a loving force greater than yourself and your inner divinity.

   Here's how to do it. Before starting your busy day or while on a break, close your eyes. Take a few deep breaths to get settled. Then inwardly ask, "Let me experience my spiritual home." See what intuitive knowings come. What does home feel like? Perhaps warm. Safe. Somewhere you truly belong. Or maybe it's a sense of being unconditionally loved or understood. Also note any images you equate with home, no matter how stereotypical. A toasty hearth. Family. Laughter. Candles. A meadow of golden daffodils. These common associations will permit glimpses into the ecstasy of your spiritual home. Fantasize away. Don't worry about "making things up." The bliss of returning home exceeds your wildest imaginings. Regularly meditate on this. Do as Dorothy did in *The Wizard of Oz* when she conjured herself back to Kansas by repeating, "There's no place like home." Meditating on home lets you freshly access your spiritual self by remembering its origins.

2. *Listen to your intuition.* If you have a question about loneliness, pose it to Spirit. You can do this as a waking exercise or consult a dream. In a centered state, begin the conversation. For instance, ask, "How can I reconcile with my mother? I miss her." Then listen for what intuitions or dreams come. Some possibilities: You might get an image or dream of simply picking up the phone to call her. Or a lightbulb goes off within when you feel the rightness of getting beyond your anger. Whatever the answer, pay attention and act on it. Observe how this lessens loneliness.

3. *Practice gratitude.* Focus on people you care about and who care about you. Take time to cherish these relationships. Also, keep a gratitude journal so you can write down the beautiful things about your life, say, your morning walk, your health, a friend who listened to you when you were hurting. Then allow at least a few minutes to revel in the glory of that appreciation.

4. *Help others.* Being of service gets you beyond the "I" to the "thouness" of the world, a spiritual teaching of theologian Martin Buber. Helping others puts you back in the circuit of human connection, rather than feeling like a reject on the periphery. Making life a little easier for someone is therapeutic for your loneliness and also theirs. Meditate on how you might volunteer or reach out to someone else. Notice which possibilities move you.

The Third Transformation's formula for addressing loneliness—connecting to self, Spirit, and others—lets you strike a necessary balance. Without this, you may be in tiptop spiritual shape, yet still feel utterly lonely. Find love from many sources. My teacher says,

"The spiritual journey is always alone, but it doesn't have to be lonely."
Our search is for home, a need so fundamental that wars have been
fought over it for eons. Our crucible moments of connection can bring
us there.

EXPERIENCE THE ENERGETIC POWER
OF LONELINESS AND CONNECTION

When I intuitively read patients, their loneliness is obvious even if
they try to camouflage it. This emotion smacks of an "adrift at sea but
don't want to be" feeling, an unrequited yearning for something sim-
patico. Energetically, I sense it as a pale violet vapor effusing from
their pores. It feels achingly fragile. Many people go through contor-
tions to mask loneliness; they become excessively perky or extroverted,
or they cram their schedules so they don't have room to breathe, let
alone feel. But on an intuitive level, none of that matters: the energy
of loneliness can't be hidden.

Think of loneliness and connection as energetic opposites. Of all
the difficult emotions, loneliness can have the quickest turnaround;
it's acutely responsive to loving interactions. That's what it's screaming for. That's what it needs. Therefore, it makes sense to cater to
loneliness in this way so it ebbs rather than flows. For a head start on
counteracting this emotion, become accustomed to how its energy
intuitively feels in contrast with that of connection. Here are some
general qualities to observe:

HOW THE ENERGY OF LONELINESS CAN FEEL

- A hollow ache
- A melancholy vapor
- Emptiness or a hurting heart
- A sense of being homeless, lost, detached
- Like you're invisible, not emotionally seen or heard

HOW THE ENERGY OF CONNECTION CAN FEEL

- A warm sun or electric
- Nourishment
- Being cocooned, embraced
- A heartful linkage to others or the world
- Being on the same intuitive wavelength with someone

When sensing emotional energy, notice how your body uniquely responds. It's exciting to experiment. Say you wake up feeling lonely. Instead of concluding "What a bummer" and trying to push through it, examine how that energy feels, every niggling nuance. You want to get loneliness's number. Then set your intention to transform it by initiating a positive connection. Go to dinner with a friend instead of watching another *Law and Order* rerun. Have fun with your children instead of working until midnight. Romp with a pet. Tend to a plant. Paint. Marvel at the clouds. Anything that turns on your life force reverses loneliness. Then notice the changes. Your actions transform energy, an irrefutable law of emotional freedom. Rather than pegging loneliness as the enemy, use it as a springboard for connection.

Why Energy-Sensitive People May Stay Lonely or Alone

Loneliness gets to some more than others. But why it hangs on isn't always apparent when read by traditional medical eyes. Understanding subtle energy helps free you from this emotion by revealing another side of it. In my practice and workshops I've been struck by how many sensitive, empathic people come to me lonely, wanting a romantic partner, yet remaining single for years. Or else they're in relationships but feel constantly fatigued and overwhelmed. The reason isn't simply that "there aren't enough emotionally available people out there," nor is their burnout "neurotic." Personally and professionally, I've discovered that something more is going on.

Energy-sensitive people are a species unto themselves. Whereas others may thrive on the togetherness of being a couple, for empaths like me, too much togetherness can be hard to take and may even cause us to bolt. Why? We tend to intuit and absorb our partner's energy and become overloaded, anxious, or exhausted when we don't have time to decompress in our own space. We're superresponders; our sensory experience of relationship is the equivalent of feeling objects with fifty fingers instead of five. A revelation of Energy Psychiatry is this: *Energetically sensitive people unknowingly avoid romantic partnerships because deep down they're afraid of getting engulfed. Or else they feel engulfed when coupled, a nerve-wracking, constrictive way to live.* If this isn't understood, empaths can stay perpetually lonely; we want companionship but, paradoxically, it doesn't feel safe. One empath patient told me, "It helps explain why at thirty-two I've only had two serious relationships, each lasting less than a year." Working with her, I was able to guide her toward a solution. Once we empaths learn to set boundaries and negotiate our energetic preferences, intimacy becomes possible.

For energy-sensitive people to be at ease in a relationship, the traditional paradigm for coupling must be redefined. Most of all, this means asserting your personal space needs—the physical and time limits you set with someone so you don't feel they're on top of you. Energy-sensitive people can't fully experience emotional freedom with another until they do this. Your space needs can vary with your situation, upbringing, and culture. For instance, my ideal distance to keep in public is at least an arm's length. In doctors' waiting rooms I'll pile my purse and folders on the seats beside me to keep others away. With friends it's about half that. With a mate it's variable. Sometimes it's rapture being wrapped in his arms; later I may need to be in a room of my own, shut away. One boyfriend who truly grasped the concept got me a KEEP OUT sign for my study door. For me, this was a sign of true love. All of us have a subtle, invisible energetic border that sets a comfort level. Identifying and communicating yours will prevent you from being bled dry by what feels like the voraciousness of those near and dear to you. Then intimacy can flourish, even if you've felt suffocated before. Prospective mates or family members may seem like emotional vampires when you don't know how to broach the issue of personal space. Once you get this down, you're able to build progressive relationships.

If you're energy-sensitive, or if the ordinary expectations of couple-dom don't jibe with you, I'll help you picture what a doable relationship might look like. This requires thinking out of the box, not conforming to social pressures about what's usually done. There's no need to feel chronically lonely, especially when making new rules about time and space management can prevent this. So rev your intuition; design a life in sync with your energy preferences. You may need to educate your mate or family; make clear that this isn't about not loving them, but get the discussion going.

The following action step lets you address different aspects of personal space requirements that often arise in relationships. Its strategies have greatly assisted me and my energy-sensitive patients. Don't feel guilty about using them. You're not being a prima donna or demanding too much. Emotional freedom comes from communicating your comfort zone.

Emotional Action Step

MAKE NEW RELATIONSHIP RULES: DEFINE YOUR PERSONAL SPACE

Here are some tips for energy-sensitive people to feel at ease in a relationship.

Tip 1: What to say to a potential mate. As you're getting to know someone, share that you're a sensitive person, that you periodically need quiet time. The right partner will be understanding, supportive; the wrong person will put you down for being "overly sensitive" and won't respect your need.

Tip 2: Clarify your preferred sleep style. Traditionally, partners sleep in the same bed. However, some energy-sensitive people

never get used to this, no matter how caring a mate. Nothing
personal; they just like their own sleep space. Speak up about
your preferences. Feeling trapped in bed with someone, never
getting a really good night's rest, is torture. Energy fields blend
during sleep, which can overstimulate sensitives. So, brainstorm
with your mate about options: separate beds, separate rooms,
sleeping together a few nights a week. Because non-energy-
sensitive people may feel lonely sleeping alone, make good-faith
compromises when possible.

Tip 3: Negotiate your square footage needs. You may wax rhap-
sodic about your beloved until you live together. Experiment
with creative living conditions so your home isn't a prison.
Breathing room is mandatory; know your requirements. What
space arrangements are optimal? Having an area to retreat to,
even if it's a closet? A room divider? Separate bathrooms?
Separate houses? What's worked for me is to have my own
bedroom/office where I can't hear a peep out of a commingler.
I also can see the beauty of separate wings or adjacent houses if
affordable. Here's why: conversations, scents, coughing, movement, and the energy field of another overlapping mine can feel
intrusive. Though my partner's vibes may be sublime, sometimes I'd rather not sense them even if they're only hovering
near me. I'm not just being finicky; it's about maintaining
well-being if I live with someone.

Along similar lines, the *New York Times* recently reported a
burgeoning trend in long-term two-home couples—a completely
new demographic researchers call "living apart together" (LAT)
relationships. Married or not, these couples reside in separate
homes. (Woody Allen and Mia Farrow defied convention by
doing this even after starting a family.) The arrangement's
appeal for these mates: they share quality time but also can be
alone, and they aren't in each other's way, a gift from the gods
for energy-sensitive people.

Tip 4: Travel wisely. Traveling with someone, you may want to have separate space too. Whether my companion is romantic or not, I'll always have adjoining rooms with my own bathroom. If sharing a room is the only option, hanging a sheet as a room divider will help. "Out of sight" may make the heart grow fonder. Knowing you won't be stuck in tight quarters, traveling becomes a joy.

Tip 5: Take regular mini-breaks. Energy-sensitive people require private downtime to regroup. Even a brief escape prevents emotional overload. Retreat for five minutes into the bathroom with the door shut so the kids can't intrude. Take a stroll around the block. Read in a separate room if your beloved's frustrations are weighing on you. One patient told her boyfriend, "I need to disappear into a quiet room for ten minutes at a party, even if I'm having fun," a form of self-care that he supports. Inform your intimates how crucial mini-breaks are. Taking them allows you to be more present with others.

In my practice, I've seen this creative approach to relationships save marriages and make ongoing intimacies feel safe, even for energy-sensitive people (of all ages) who've been lonely and haven't had a long-term partner before. Once you're free to articulate your needs, horizons open. One such patient, single for decades, had a prescient dream:

I'm on a sailboat alone on a sunny, windswept ocean. It's exhilarating but lonely. No one as far as the eye can see! Then, from far away, I spot another lone sailboat peeking through the white crests of waves as they swell and subside. It's heading toward me.

Soon after, she met her mate of five years, someone who has no problem with her need for alone time—the spacious feeling she experienced on the water—but who can come together too. I find their mutual respect and communication beautiful. I advocate new paradigms for loving. It's unreasonable to attempt to squash our differing sensibilities into a one-size-fits-all relationship model. No wonder more than half of married couples divorce. What I'm suggesting is a new kind of conversation. Initially it may feel awkward or risky to raise these topics. But, if you do so tactfully—not making your partner wrong, just expressing your energetic needs—you'll have a chance at building an extraordinary relationship.

MAP THE PSYCHOLOGY OF LONELINESS AND CONNECTION

One truth that all current psychotherapeutic modalities agree on, despite their often contentious rivalries, is the healing power of meaningful connections. The sense that you're seen, heard, and appreciated is fundamental to mental health. Such rapport between us—the part of me that connects with a part of you and vice versa—allays loneliness. Whether it lasts a moment or a lifetime, these exchanges add up to feeling like a part of humanity and the world. Freudians believe loneliness stems from an infant's unresolved separation anxiety from the mother; behaviorists believe it's conditioned; Jung says it's "being unable to communicate the things that seem important to oneself." But for every therapist, regardless of philosophy, our credo is to guide patients in attaining satisfying bonds with others, to give and receive love.

The need for nurturing seems so basic, but if you read a child care manual seventy years ago, you'd be appalled at what passed for conventional psychological wisdom. In the 1940s John Watson, president of the American Psychological Association, warned, "When you're tempted to pet your child, remember that mother love is a dangerous instrument." He also suggested that mothers put their kids to bed with a proper handshake. Such behaviorists believed that anything more than minimal affection would produce a weepy, dependent child and that rocking an infant was a "vicious practice." Therefore mothers needn't breast-feed or frequently visit hospitalized infants; a nurse with a bottle would suffice. Watson even proposed a future where babies would be removed from parents at birth and raised on farms away from corrupting maternal influence.

Enter psychologist Harry Harlow, who revolutionized his field by showing the value of nurturing. In his world-famous experiment, studied by every Psych 101 student, he raised baby monkeys who had the choice of a warm, soft, terrycloth-padded surrogate mother versus a forbidding, cold, wire counterpart. The babies always chose the cloth mother, even when the wire mother was holding the bottle. In fact, they ran to it when frightened for reassurance and love. Harlow's experiment overturned the barbaric dogma of the day that anything beyond a modicum of affection was unhealthy. It showed how a sense of nurturing (we're not even talking about a live mother monkey here) influenced a baby's well-being and maternal attachment even more than getting its caloric needs met.

So, psychologically speaking, everybody needs a little tenderness. Even if your parents might have resembled those spiky, ungiving wire monkeys, a reason to feel lonely and deprived while growing up, this needn't stop you from finding rich human contact now. However, I urge you to take a close look into your emotional upbringing—what you got, what you didn't get—lest you inadvertently recapitulate detrimental patterns. Loneliness is inherited only if we allow it to be.

You must revisit the past to psychologically free yourself from negative emotions, but it's natural to resist doing so. With loneliness, in particular, I periodically hit a wall. There's a hermetic and sometimes lonely side of me that's much like my dad. (A doctor, he was a radiologist, a specialty not known for its people skills.) This feeling can make me terribly vulnerable and raw; it hurts. Throughout his life, Dad mostly kept to himself, much as I often do as a writer. My mother practically had to harass him to socialize. But she did, and despite protests of "Maxine, leave me alone!" I think he enjoyed that push into the world. But when Mother died, Dad's life shrank; he did nothing to stop it. Especially in his final days of having Parkinson's disease, he isolated himself, not wanting whatever friends he had left to see him in such dire straits: diapered, unable to dress himself or walk unassisted. My tendency to be solitary like him sometimes scares me because it can so easily blur into excessive reclusion. To understand and avoid this, I want to understand my dad so I don't emotionally mimic what need not be my own. Also, in my strongest and clearest moments, I know not to overidentify with him because there were always major differences between us. I'm a great lover of relationships, whereas they were more of a bother to Dad except at the level of "How's your golf game?" I'm aware of and work with my emotions; he was out of touch with his, and hated it when I tried to get him to express them. For me, transforming the downside of loneliness (not the variety that deepens creativity) is an emotional work in progress. I try to be gentle with my resistance. During one of such periods, I dreamed:

> I'm in a sunlit little apartment. My father's things are strewn over every inch of the floor. I'm overwhelmed at the prospect of going through them. Some objects I recognize, like the eight-foot wood carving of flying horses I gave him when I was ten: "A big gift from a pipsqueak like you," he said with pride and love. But there's lots I haven't seen. While I glumly ponder the situation, in walks a jovial woman bus driver who identifies herself as God. I instantly perk up, delighted to see her. Smiling, she tells me, "To get your refund check for the cleaning fee, you need to clear out everything!"

I awoke knowing She was right. To be free, I had to survey every item that unreasonably bound my loneliness to my father's. And what better messenger than God, the ultimate bus driver? My dreams so cleverly know how to bypass my resistance and make a point. Lord knows I want my final refund check, everything cleaned up, when I leave this sunny little apartment I call my material life on earth. I want to exit with work complete, aimed in other directions. But in the meantime, the psychological roots of my loneliness can point me there. I endeavor to proceed with a light heart. I'm intent on learning everything that will liberate me from the pain of this emotion and foster soul connections with people and the natural world, true consolations on the sometimes lonesome road.

To get a psychological grip on loneliness, it's time to figure out what messages, implicit or explicit, your parents gave you (and may continue to give you) about this emotion. Delving into the past, tread lightly to soften the natural resistance that may arise. Children aren't oblivious. Their eyes and ears are open. They know what loneliness looks and feels like, even before hearing the word. Also, children are emotionally porous. When parents are lonely, we may take on their loneliness, or fear that we'll be that way too. Turn back time to see how this emotion registered on you. Then you can more easily disengage from it as an adult. Note these common ways one or both parents may have unhealthily modeled this emotion:

- Leading lives of quiet desperation
- Feeling victimized, as from a bitter divorce, and blaming others for their loneliness
- Workaholism, shopaholism, substance abuse
- Isolation (for example, retreating into television or cyberaddiction)
- Feeling alone and overburdened but too independent to ask for help
- Remaining in a marriage with no communication

See if you've adopted these habits of dealing with loneliness. As with the parent, so with the child. It's no surprise that their coping styles may have rubbed off on you. Emotional freedom becomes possible when you shed their personas and find your own. It's the worst feeling to keep parroting what you didn't like about a parent but not know how to stop. Like many of my patients, you may have solemnly vowed, "I'll never be like them," and yet, horror of horrors, in certain dismal moments, you're their clone. But, with psychological insight, this can change. How? You compassionately identify behaviors and make a conscious choice to alter them. For instance, if you're addicted to the Internet just as your father was addicted to the TV, seek out some human contact. Or if, like your mother, you consider loneliness a cross to silently bear, give up the martyr mentality. Start expressing your loneliness to a friend or therapist in an effort to resolve it.

Cutting the emotional umbilical cord with parents is an emancipating, necessary separation. Although, inevitably, you'll share likenesses with them—some good, some bad—your karma is not the same and who you are is different, as is your desire to transform negativity. Get clear about these differences. Parents don't always know best about emotions. With consciousness, you won't have to react like them or take their loneliness on.

I've devised the next action step to replace defeating styles of coping with loneliness with more freeing ones. The Third Transformation is accomplished by building nourishing links of many kinds, including with yourself. Sometimes people get stalled in therapy by concentrating only on why they're lonely and not doing anything about it. Psychological insights alone, no matter how right on, can't liberate unless they transform behavior.

Emotional Action Step

ATTRACT NURTURING CONNECTIONS: FIVE CURES FOR LONELINESS

Use these strategies to prevent and reverse loneliness.

Cure 1: Make a relationship wish list. To attract people who do your heart good, ask yourself, "What qualities are most important to me?" Then list them in a journal. For instance:

- The ability to let you speak your truth without judging you
- A sense of humor
- Behavior that matches words
- Being open to spirituality and intuition
- Being loving, kind

Clarifying your priorities helps you hold the vision of what you need. I don't want you to simply go through the motions of socializing and hope for the best. I want you to specifically visualize and pursue others with desirable traits.

Cure 2: Practice reaching out: look for similarities in people, not differences. When you're lonely, it may feel hard to reach out, but here's a tip that will make it easier. A key to connecting is to focus on what you have in common with others, not on what you don't. I find this especially useful at parties, where I'm apt to end up in a corner feeling lonely, just talking to the friend I came with. Since I'm basically shy, I find it hard to break the ice with new people. To me, they look like they're in cliques. I don't want to intrude where I don't belong. Such thinking only fosters loneliness and paints an unfriendly world. Instead, I remember my teacher's words: "We're all basically the same, though we may act differently." Then, feeling more in common with my fellow partygoers, I can smile and say hi rather than stay in my corner. The roots of our division come from not seeing similarities. In your interactions, look for them rather than harping on differences.

Cure 3: Connect with yourself; take time for solitude. Solving loneliness involves connecting to yourself as well as others. That's why it's vital to find your own right rhythm of worldly involvement and solitude. Periodically step away from phones, paperwork, and small talk to seek inner stillness. As you'll see, solitude and loneliness can be very different. Inform intimates that this is a restorative break for you so they can honor it. Tell yourself, "I am with someone wonderful. I am with myself!" Whether walking in a forest or meditating, keep sensing your own beauty. This is your inner self, and you're excellent company. If you regularly tune in to who you really are from the inside, you'll never be alone.

Cure 4: Consult your dreams. When you're lonely, ask a dream for a solution. Before you go to sleep, pose a question. Then in the morning record your dream in a journal. Look for the answer. Try this every night for a week. For instance, one of my stridently self-sufficient patients asked, "How can I be less lonely?" She dreamed:

> *It's the dead of winter. I'm in a cozy house with a warm fire and friends. There is a dangerous snowstorm outside. I leave*

everyone to drive miles in the storm, braving empty roads
alone. I don't ask anyone to accompany me on this lonely,
frightening trip.

The message my patient took away was that emotional support was available (the warmth of friends) if only she'd ask. She
didn't have to brave everything solo. Like many independent
people, she'd become resigned to loneliness, not realizing it was
self-inflicted. This dream's guidance showed her how to change,
and she listened. Similarly, you can benefit from your dreams.

Cure 5: Acknowledge your current connections. It's important to
realize the value of the nurturing bonds you've already made,
though they may not always be with people. For instance, your
love of nature, animals, or music and your cozy home all speak
to your intimate capacity for connection and bode well for your
ongoing quest for supportive friends and community.

Practicing the above psychologically oriented strategies is a way out
of the lonely mind. No matter what your head says, no matter how
terminal this emotion may feel, there is always relief. The art of the
Third Transformation is to keep balancing your need for connection
with others and with yourself, for interdependence and independence.
The poet Rilke writes, "I am too alone in the world, and not alone
enough to make every moment holy." Many of us well know this predicament, the vertiginous disequilibrium of never getting it quite right.
Understanding your psychology moves you toward achieving balance
and the peace that comes from it.

THIS CHAPTER PRESENTS a forward path through lone-
liness to touch a greater whole. Your small self may feel diminished by
this emotion. But your large self sees that no matter how intense the
loneliness, you are more expansive than it is. That is emotional freedom. As always, you feel but transform the negative.

Practicing the Third Transformation, appreciate that the logical mind isn't sufficient to resolve loneliness. You also need intuition, which helps you cultivate what the ancients called "a sympathy for all things." On an intuitive level, there's no such thing as a stranger; a bond exists between everyone and everything on earth. Consider the phenomenon of fish swimming in schools. One fish isn't saying to another, "Turn left" or "Turn right." There's an inborn interconnection. The same is true with humans, though it's harder for our overintellectualized selves to grasp. Feeling lonely is quelled by realizing we're all one family, regardless of race, country, or ideology. Imagine living your life in a way that reflects that certainty. Imagine everyone knowing that no matter what happens, we all have one another. Such emotional freedom would irrevocably change our perception of loneliness.

Meditation on Freedom

Experience the Comfort of Connection

Take a few minutes to lovingly focus on something or someone you feel connected to. Perhaps it is your mate, your child, a parent, a close friend. Or it could be a cherished pet, a tree, a poem, or a song. Whatever your choice, close your eyes and relish the comforting security of your bond. Let yourself blend together as one, being understood and understanding. Adore that link. Heart open, see how freeing the connection feels.

Do not anticipate trouble or worry about what may never happen.
Keep in the sunlight.

—BENJAMIN FRANKLIN

9

THE FOURTH TRANSFORMATION:
FACING ANXIETY AND WORRY,
BUILDING INNER CALM

PICTURE THIS: You're in a traffic jam, but you feel triumphantly calm. Your boss is in a vile mood, but you don't let it faze you. You're behind on a project, so you put a few more hours in without tying yourself into knots. Emotional freedom entails building an increasing sense of inner calm, the opposite of anxiety. Calm is in you, in everyone. Lamentably, many of us don't have the faintest idea how to find it. No one ever showed us. Now you'll learn. Being calm doesn't mean numbing your feelings or becoming boring or airy-fairy. It's an empowering state of centered quietude and composure that you can access in any situation.

The Fourth Transformation explores the multitentacled emotions of anxiety and worry and offers strategies to transform them with inner calm. Our Age of Anxiety barrages us with so much so fast: violence, crime, job cuts, poverty, global unrest, natural disasters. Every day we're pummeled with new off-the-scale tensions. Compound them with personal concerns about everything from family to health to aging, and it's no wonder that forty million Americans are diagnosed with chronic anxiety disorders. Four million regularly use tranquilizers. (Valium is proudly touted as the biggest-selling drug in the history of medicine, a dubious honor.) And nearly half of us report worrying every day. No argument there: sometimes reality *does* bite. Still, how you deal with it is your choice. *Inner calm gives you the resilience to respond without panicking.* You may be justifiably anxious about something, but that needn't condemn you to a jaw-clenching, tossing-and-turning existence. From the standpoint of emotional freedom, anxiety doesn't preclude equanimity. In fact, our mega-tense world is the ideal laboratory to cultivate inner calm. Just think of the opportunities you'll have!

You can discover how to remain calm despite the most jarring circumstances or lurking worries. Causes of anxiety will vary; depend on it. But you'll develop an inner calm that stays tried and true in any situation if you make honing it a priority.

In Energy Psychiatry, I consider anxiety an intensified emotional response to fear, whether or not it's based in reality. Think of it as fear plus an added level of agitation. Whether acute or chronic, it's a highstrung, rats-in-the-attic apprehensiveness about your well-being. (In this it differs from depression, whose signature is sadness.) Though anxiety may keep you mentally and physically alert, it can lead to burnout. *A large part of this emotion is about anticipating danger: "What will happen if _____?" rather than living in the Now. Anxiety keeps you mentally a few steps ahead of yourself, anticipating the worst.* It has a spectrum of manifestations, from picking your cuticles to nervousness about a job interview to full-blown panic attacks. How do you know if you're overanxious? According to the American Psychiatric Association, you qualify if you tend to worry a lot; are restless, irritable, and a perfectionist; have difficulty concentrating; and sleep poorly. Does the shoe fit? Or you may be obsessive-compulsive, warding off anxiety with excessive neatness, hand washing, list making, or repeated visits to doctors. Also, you may experience agoraphobia, dread about being in places where escape is difficult, so you put strict limits on socializing or don't go out of the house.

Common causes of anxiety include situational stressors and/or a biochemical imbalance. Though fears are usually specific and identifiable—for example, "I'm afraid of poisonous snakes"—anxiety can be free-floating. You may be a little or a lot anxious but not know why; it's all too easy to acclimate to this state. "It's just the way I am," you might conclude. But don't. There are better alternatives. The *Diagnostic and Statistical Manual of Mental Disorders, Fourth Edition (DSM-IV),* a prodigiously exhaustive compendium of psychiatric diagnoses, has no category for "fear disorders." It lumps fearful symptoms under the category of "anxiety," which casts a wide net to include phobias, panic, and obsessive-compulsive symptoms. I, however, find it far more useful to differentiate fear from anxiety in the service of taming each.

After my mother died, I learned firsthand that anxiety could be mercilessly tumultuous. In one swift movement the earth vaporized beneath me. I lost my footing. I felt alone, abandoned—my biggest fear—and was hurtling out of control. For decades, my energy had been locked up in the struggle to make peace with Mother. We were both headstrong, in an emotional tug-of-war. She browbeat me to lead a traditional life, to be married to a Jewish doctor with all that "security." Even so, I just had to meander on the road less traveled—my intuitive path in both medicine and my personal life—preferring the electric green moss adorning a pebble to eternities at country club fund-raisers. In the end, though, mutual respect and love prevailed over our differences. After her death, all I could think was, "How am I going to survive without this woman?" I'd always had something to butt up against emotionally, for better or for worse. When that was gone, I was left in free fall, like an astronaut cut loose from the mother ship and cast into the void. I was shocked by the degree to which my center depended on Mother, by how much our umbilical bond was still such a stabilizing force. Unbelievably, my intuition was nonetheless partially intact, relaying that this was an important passage, that I'd be okay. But calm felt beyond me. In the past, when I'd been upset, I'd depended on finding calm in meditation. But now, in such a vertiginous spin, I couldn't contact it.

I didn't want to be anxious, but this emotion, compounded by my fear of abandonment, just took hold: I was quaking inside, lying awake in bed at night watching the clock, restless like a dog unable to settle into the right position. I remember walking on the jetty by the ocean near my condo one afternoon, trying to calm down, but feeling so jittery I wasn't even sure I could make it home. Weird things come to mind in that state. I recalled how, as children, my friends and I used to ask ourselves impossible questions such as "Would you rather be deaf or blind?" We had to decide which was the lesser of two torments. Although nobody asked me now, I decided I'd rather be depressed than anxious. Then, I figured, at least I'd be slowed down, which would be preferable to the feeling of wanting to jump out of my skin. Even imagining I had a choice, which I didn't, was oddly reassuring. Nevertheless, that day I realized I couldn't get through this by myself, or even with friends' support. Fortunately, I found the right therapist, who became my north star. Working together over the next few months, I felt gradual relief as my anxiety quieted down. What helped was expressing it; realizing that though I'd lost Mother, she hadn't abandoned me; and beginning to find my place in the universe and in myself without her. I also became a connoisseur of techniques to find inner calm that I could use along with others I'd already practiced such as meditation and energy balancing. I'm eager to share these with you.

This experience left me with a God-fearing respect for anxiety. Wrenching as it was, I evolved emotionally and gained greater compassion for others going through anxiety—gifts of getting to the other side of darkness. My curious nature is drawn to the deep end of living and finding my way back toward the light. "Stretch my soul and make me free" is my stance for coping with emotions in a world where most people avoid pain like the plague. I came away with a more profound grasp of the value of consistently developing inner calm, rather than scrambling for it during an emergency. Inner calm is a grounding, intuitive center within each of us. No matter how far away it feels or what's emotionally coming down, you can learn to find it.

The Fourth Transformation also focuses on relieving worry with inner calm. Worry (the word is from the Latin for "to constrict") is anxiety directed at a specific target. For instance, you may worry about money, aging, work, or your children. I love the bumper sticker NORMAL PEOPLE WORRY ME. Also, you may worry that if you don't worry, bad things will happen—a form of superstition. Whether you're a chronic worrier or an occasional ruminator, this emotion is an attempt to gain control and overcome a sense of helplessness about the future. Though this emotion may motivate you to solve problems, avoid errors, or be prepared (say, for an exam), there are healthier, more enjoyable coping mechanisms. Clearly, legitimate concerns arise in life that require productive action, but *worry takes concern into the realm of suffering.* My spiritual teacher has said, "If you're climbing a mountain and worrying about tomorrow, it will be a very difficult climb." I'll show you how not to be enslaved by this negative emotion. For starters, consider the following questions.

WORRY QUIZ: AM I A WORRIER?

To determine how much of a worrier you are, ask yourself:

- Do I worry about many things every day?
- Do I make problems larger, not smaller?
- Do I worry about things that no one around me worries about?
- Do I worry even during happy times?
- Do I find I can't stop worrying, though I try?
- When one worry is solved, do I immediately focus on another?

If you answered yes to all six questions, worry plays a very large role in your life. Four or five yeses indicate a large role. Two or three yeses indicate a moderate role. One yes indicates a low level. Zero yeses suggest that you're more warrior than worrier.

Worry and anxiety are often resistant to change when treated using a traditional psychiatric paradigm. The usual mainstream treatments, including antianxiety medications, psychotherapy, and behavioral interventions, may be useful, but they're not sufficient. My approach to these emotions involves a joint understanding of their biology, spirituality, energetic power, and psychology. If one of these elements is missing, there's a huge gap. For instance, if you're dealing with worry and aren't aware that it's a form of spiritual disengagement or don't know what to do about that, you won't get very far. And if you're unsure how to find inner calm, being anxious is a tenuous emotional position. In the clutches of this feeling, the last thing you want to do is act, a counterintuitive mistake. I'll explain how to master the methods behind this transformation so you'll be ready when you need them.

The Anatomy of Anxiety, Worry, and Inner Calm: Putting the Fourth Transformation into Action

Achieving inner calm involves intellectually grasping the principles behind it and intuitively knowing how to get there. Inner calm isn't an amorphous concept, nor is it a single entity. Biological, spiritual, energetic, and psychological calm can feel distinctly different and are often attained through different techniques. In upcoming sections, we'll explore all these so you can enjoy synchronized calm in every area. With this information, you'll be able to outmaneuver the Fourth Transformation's negative emotions to find your center point.

REPROGRAM THE BIOLOGY OF ANXIETY, WORRY, AND INNER CALM

When anxiety escalates in the body, it can make fear's state of hyper-arousal seem lightweight in comparison.

Let's go straight to this emotion's worst-case scenario: the full-blown panic attack. What happens biologically? Adrenaline floods your system. Blood pressure, pulse, breathing, and the stress hormone cortisol surge. Hydrochloric acid—yes, acid—pours into your esophagus, where it's not supposed to be, and burns it. Your bronchioles spasm. Your chest tightens. You're short of breath. You hyperventilate, which expels too much carbon dioxide from your system: you're dizzy, numb, and have pins and needles in your fingers and toes. You're trembly and feel out of control, like you're going to pass out— or die. (Many people with panic episodes feel like they're having a heart attack.) The immediate, short-term solution? You breathe slowly into a paper bag, which restores carbon dioxide balance, breaking the panic cycle.

To appreciate the biological effects of less intense forms of anxiety, simply take the panic symptoms described above down a few notches. For instance, worry, which creates a steady biological hum of anxiety, might not grab your attention as fast or dramatically, but it's chronically grating. How? Impaired resistance to viruses, added risk of heart disease, ulcers, asthma, irritable bowel, and migraines. Anyone with these illnesses can testify to their agony. I emphasize this not to make you panic but so you don't slip into denial about the health risks of anxiety. Instead, do all you can to reduce the daily levels of this emotion.

Let me tell you about a wake-up call I had when I personally experienced the biology of anxiety. My closest friend, Berenice, a fellow psychotherapist, was to receive chemotherapy for melanoma. For decades we'd been there for each other: I was at her daughter's wedding; she was with me through the illness and death of each of my parents. We're also professional colleagues and have the same spiritual teacher. Not surprisingly, then, I was extremely anxious about seeing her suffer, or, God forbid, losing her. A few weeks before her chemotherapy, I developed irregular heartbeats. At first I thought it was nothing, but then they became more frequent and stronger. It felt like a hiccupping of the heart, an alarming sensation. I went to a cardiologist, who suggested hooking me up to a Holter monitor to record my cardiac rhythm for twenty-four hours. The scheduled day coincided with the start of Berenice's treatment, which would continue for several months. As a physician, I've sat with many patients undergoing chemo, but watching my beloved Berenice, at seventy-four, connected to multiple monster IVs in that dingy, medicinal hospital room nearly undid me. I purposely wore baggy clothes to hide this big black box of the Holter monitor fastened on my belt and the maze of wired electrodes stuck to my chest. Though I always tell Berenice everything about myself, I withheld this; she had more than enough to deal with. Later that week, when the Holter was interpreted, it showed my irregular beats tripled during the few hours I was at Berenice's bedside. I was, however, greatly relieved to learn that the cause for all my heart symptoms turned out to be anxiety. (Berenice has since been in remission a few years and, at seventy-nine, recently attended a tantric sex workshop.)

This synchronicity branded in my memory how anxiety and worry register in us physically. Learning may come at the most unexpected times. Stressful experiences, such as mine with Berenice, are common triggers for these emotions. So is heredity; scientific evidence suggests that anxiety runs in families through either conditioning or genetics. Also, brain chemistry plays a role, since anxiety is linked to a deficiency in three main neurotransmitters, chemicals that enhance communication between brain cells. They are:

- *Gamma-aminobutyric acid (GABA).* This neurotransmitter is a natural tranquilizer that slows down brain signals and keeps you calm. People with panic disorders may have abnormally low levels.
- *Dopamine.* This neurotransmitter blocks pain and is linked to the brain's pleasure centers and feelings of enjoyment. Cocaine is so addictive because it increases dopamine.
- *Serotonin.* This neurotransmitter is a mood regulator for anxiety, anger, and depression. Without enough it's harder to self-soothe. Chocolate increases serotonin!

Knowing these biological basics helps you visualize what's physically going on and proactively remedy what's off. Finding calm via this chapter's interventions gives you a role in balancing your own brain chemistry instead of passively being on the receiving end of these emotions.

Conventional antianxiety medications work by regulating the above neurotransmitters. During my UCLA psychiatric training, I was taught that such drugs were the "big guns" of anxiety treatment. If you consult a mainstream doctor, you may be offered these. Now, I rarely prescribe them, and when I do, it's in conjunction with spiritual, energetic, and psychological strategies to find inner calm. However, when used judiciously in the short term, these medications may break a painful anxiety cycle, offering transient relief. If a patient and I decide on this route, we both carefully monitor how his or her body responds. My gripe is that these medications are overprescribed (without even psychotherapy) when the Fourth Transformation's approaches are less toxic and often more effective. Here is a summary of the risks and benefits of these drugs.

A Brief Guide to Common Antianxiety Medications

1. *Beta-blockers.* Typically prescribed for hypertension, these medications, such as Inderal, also reduce stage fright. By decreasing the fight-or-flight response, they induce relaxation. Beta-blockers last only about three hours and have relatively few side effects.

2. *Benzodiazepines.* By elevating levels of GABA, these calm and relax muscles. I prefer Ativan; it lasts twelve hours compared to fourteen hours with Xanax and thirty-two hours with Valium. While these medications improve sleep and allow anxious people to function, they have the potential for addiction, depression, confusion, memory loss, and impaired ability to remember dreams.

3. *Selective serotonin reuptake inhibitors (SSRIs).* Of this group, also prescribed for depression, Celexa and Lexapro can ease insomnia and anxiety. They boost serotonin and dopamine, plus Celexa has an antihistamine calming effect. Possible hazards include weight gain, blunted emotions, memory problems, blurred vision, sexual dysfunction, and difficulty remembering dreams.

With patients, I try always to tune in to the most appropriate option for them, without bias. I also help them intuit the best choice for their bodies. If you have intense anxiety, a discerning use of a medication may be warranted. There's no shame in this, but remember to keep intuiting how the medication feels in you. To minimize side effects, use the smallest possible dose for the shortest possible time. To further balance your biochemistry and help lower or eliminate the need for medication, practice the following strategies and others in the chapter.

Emotional Action Step

FOUR WAYS TO FIND CALM AND CURE ANXIETY

1. *Try these natural remedies.* Consult your physician before trying these supplements, especially if you're combining them with traditional antianxiety medications. Also realize that in your health food store you'll find many natural antianxiety options, some of which are unproven. "Natural" doesn't always mean harmless. In addition, dosage guidelines are very important; never take more than what's advised.

   • *5-HTP (5-hydroxytryptophan).* This plant extract, which converts into serotonin in the brain, gently reduces anxiety and improves sleep. Infrequent side effects include nausea, headache, loose stools, and decreased libido. Standard dosage is 50–150 mg daily.
   • *Kava-kava.* Taken from the root of a plant that grows in the South Pacific, it promotes relaxation, improves sleep, and relieves muscle tension. Potential side effects include loss of balance, disorientation, nausea, and (rarely) liver damage. Standard dosage is 150–300 mg one to three times daily.
   • *Calcium/magnesium.* These essential minerals, which can be depleted by stress, are calming and improve sleep. This combination minimizes constipation that may come from calcium alone. Standard dosage for adults nineteen to fifty years old is 1,000 mg calcium/400 mg magnesium daily. For adults above fifty, it's 1,200 mg calcium/400 mg magnesium daily. Consuming more calcium than recommended can cause kidney stones.

2. *Quiet your system.* Avoid caffeine and other stimulants, excessive sugar, and violent newscasts and films—these make you jumpy and increase the startle response. (Be aware that in addition to the usual sources, such as coffee and tea, caffeine can be in cold remedies, premenstrual syndrome formulations, green tea, and some citrus sodas; read the labels.) Also, excessive noise can be

agitating, raise blood pressure, and increase the inflammatory response throughout the body. Try to gravitate toward quiet places. In loud settings, I suggest earplugs, noise-canceling headphones, or listening to serene music with a headset. Being extremely sound-sensitive myself, I know what Florence Nightingale meant when she said, "Unnecessary noise is the most cruel abuse to be inflicted on the sick or the well."

3. *Practice belly breathing.* When anxious or worried, you tend to breathe more quickly and shallowly from the upper chest instead of the belly. This makes you hyperventilate, which aggravates anxiety. Belly breathing helps stop the cycle before anxiety builds. Use it many times a day.

   - While sitting comfortably or lying on your back, place one hand on your chest, the other on your abdomen. As you take a deep breath, the hand on the abdomen should rise higher than the other.
   - Take a slow, deep breath in through your nose to a count of eight while allowing your lungs and belly to fully expand.
   - Slowly exhale through your mouth to a count of eight. At the end of the breath, tightly contract your abdomen to expel the remaining air from your lungs. You deepen breathing not by inhaling more air, but by exhaling completely. Generally, exhalation should be twice as long as inhalation.
   - Repeat this pattern of breathing at least five times for each sitting.

4. *Do aerobic exercise.* Regular aerobic exercise such as walking or running markedly reduces anxiety by upping serotonin and dopamine, the calming neurotransmitters. It also boosts feel-good endorphins, natural painkillers responsible for the "runner's high." Even exercising just ten minutes a day improves mood and sleep. One patient, who wakes up with "a million anxious thoughts," exercises in the morning to start the day calm. He says, "I never trust a thought I haven't run on!" When I was a child, I galloped

around open fields to relieve my antsiness during long car trips; my parents called this "letting off steam." As the old rhyme goes, "When in worry or in doubt, run in circles, scream and shout." Exercise expels pent-up and anxious energy and helps you find inner calm. Combining it with stretching or yoga is ideal.

The above strategies are based either on using natural supplements or on softening around anxiety and worry; neither involves clamping down. These emotions wield some commanding neurochemicals, but don't be intimidated. Our challenge is to counteract them, not be bull-dozed. You can do it.

UNCOVER THE SPIRITUAL MEANING OF ANXIETY, WORRY, AND INNER CALM

As an Energy Psychiatrist, I always present anxiety and worry as opportunities for your soul to expand. These emotions can test you to your breaking point, but they're worthy teachers nonetheless, driving you to find calm from within and to link yourself to something greater. Being in the material world, apart from your spiritual home, can be a legitimate reason to feel separation anxiety, though you might not have realized that's an aspect of this emotion. Calm means more than not being stressed out. It's a reunion with something spiritual inside that resides beneath the outer layer of troubled thoughts and whirling mind. Contacting it for seconds, minutes, and longer eman-cipates you more and more from daily anxieties and worries.

On the other hand, people who don't believe in a divine context for emotions or life may see the world as a series of random, chaotic, frequently punishing events. They don't have faith in a higher power or sacredness of the Self. They can find nothing redeeming about anxiety. It just makes them feel helpless, victimized and weak. Their sole agenda is to get rid of it with a quick fix—such as medication or bailing on that "demanding" partner—and going right on with their lives. If it works for them, fine, I suppose, but what if relief doesn't happen fast enough or at all? What if high anxiety subsides but they're still nail-biting worrywarts? What if difficult partner A is immediately replaced by difficult partner B? No peace there.

I'd like you to think of anxiety and worry as symptoms of spiritual disengagement, and also as prompts to reengage. What can we gain from dealing with these emotions in this way?

- We can learn to trust in the integrity of what life brings, the impeccable spiritual impulse behind it—especially when things get painful or go wrong.
- We can stop projecting our anxieties into the future, instead staying in the Now.
- We can appreciate how anxiety ratchets up our tendency to over-control, instead of knowing when to wait and let divine flow happen.
- We can see how we've been conditioned to believe that nothing positive can come from failure, roadblocks, or messes.
- We can see that worrisome events are junctures for love and grace to enter our lives.

Of course, being human, we're prone to spiritually disengaging when anxious. Be prepared: it'll happen over and over again. But don't let that deter you or use it as an excuse to beat up on yourself. Simply try to catch the lapse more quickly. I love that the Buddhist teacher Sylvia Boorstein calls herself "a recovering worrier." She cops to being someone who habitually makes up negative scenarios about what might happen. Who can't relate to that? But Sylvia, a meditator who knows the value of inner calm, uses all her knowledge not to fuel worry. So must you. Transforming anxiety and worry is a process of recognizing when you spiritually disengage and taking steps to reconnect.

There's a reason that in the Sermon on the Mount, Jesus passionately told his followers, "Do not worry." There's a reason why the Buddha said that the secret to health isn't to worry about the future but to live in the present. And the Talmud tells us to follow our own path and not worry about the darkness. This is of particular interest to me because worry was so hyperbolic in my Jewish family; sometimes we were straight out of a Woody Allen film. *"Oy vey,"* a Yiddish version of "Woe is me," was a regular part of our vocabulary. (I hear that Bobby McFerrin, who wrote "Don't Worry, Be Happy," has a Jewish wife.) Nevertheless, no one has a monopoly on worry; it's something all *Homo sapiens* do, whether we let it all hang out or are stoic.

Worry dilutes your light by removing you from the moment. It scatters your attention and convinces you that you're in an unsafe world without spiritual recourse. Plus, the bulk of what you worry about doesn't occur. (Will Rogers said, "I must be the best worrier in the world. Nothing I worry about ever happens.") Most of the time you did turn off the stove and people weren't thinking horrible things about you. Let this observation penetrate. To be free, attempt to see through the smoke and mirrors of worry. Try not to jump to conclusions or always assume the worst.

I'm not suggesting that there aren't real issues that are disturbing. Naturally, it's appropriate, say, for a mother to be concerned about her sick child, but worry turns legitimate concern into suffering. Always, I'd help that mother fight for her child's health. But I'd also urge her to be kinder to herself, to ease her worry. Constructive action is one thing, constant anxiety another. What a spiritual perspective adds to even excruciating events is that you can use them as chances for your heart to grow, a hard-won but liberating way to conceptualize pain. Though sometimes it seems impossible, we must strive to accept life on its own terms and do everything possible to locate inner calm.

Spirituality can shrink worries, large and small. Take aging, something my fifty-four-year-old patient Darlene used to obsess about, despite being attractive and knowing her husband of twenty years was still wild about her. Darlene had come to me for innumerable anxieties. Would her interior design business go under? Would her son the Goth ever find himself? Spastic colon, hot flashes . . . the list went on. When I first met Darlene, she had the attention span of a hummingbird on speed, but aging was an ever-present worry in her

mind. Each morning she'd examine her face with a magnifying mirror for new sags and wrinkles (such torture devices are categorically
blacklisted in women's magazines). She came to the most frenzied
conclusions. "My neck looks like a turkey wattle," she told me. I'd hear
about her crow's-feet, sagging eyelids, brown spots, creviced naso-
labial folds. The more "defects" she noticed, the more she wanted to
take control and erase them, a refusal of aging that was doomed to fail.
Darlene practically took up residence in the dermatologist's office getting Botox injections and wrinkle fillers. Never fully satisfied, she was
considering a face-lift. Intuitively glimpsing Darlene's future, I saw
that none of this could really make her happy. Her worrying would
become viral. With each passing year, she'd get more desperate and
self-critical, imprisoned in an unkind mind, missing out on the power
that aging can bring.

Granted, in the warped "young and thin" Hollywood culture in
Los Angeles, Darlene's behavior wasn't unusual. Some of my other
patients, particularly "older" actresses—those over forty—were victims of brutal ageism and pressure to look preternaturally young.
The only parts they could hope for were grandmother, mother, or
drab older sister. (Goldie Hawn famously said that actresses have
three ages: "babe, district attorney, and *Driving Miss Daisy*.") As a
woman, I too wrestle with aging issues. I confess that more than
once when there's no one around, in front of the mirror I've put my
index finger on each cheek and lifted up the skin on my neck and
face. Why? To imagine myself without anything drooping or dropping. I've also had anxiety dreams about getting older. I remember
one in which Jack Nicholson, all crocodile smiles, says in a rascally,
knowing tone about my appearance, "Hmm, I see time's finally getting the best of you." I awoke in dread that my bell had tolled—
which wasn't, however, the correct interpretation of my dream. This
is: though I admire Jack Nicholson's acting, he's a womanizer who
dates starlets half—a third?—his age, hardly a poster boy for evolving consciousness. The "Jack" part of me was what I needed to address. I needed to re-form my attitudes about aging, honor my beauty,
and not allow myself to be brought down by the bourgeois, backward

"Thou shalt not age" cultural prejudice. Otherwise, I'd have no hope of emotional freedom.

For many of my patients, including Darlene, and for myself, spirituality has helped us claim the power that accompanies aging. To be liberated from this or any worry, ask yourself, "What is the spiritual teaching of the emotion?" This vantage point will change your thinking and behavior. For instance, a crucial lesson for Darlene was to value more dimensions of herself rather than being tortured by the external. So, in sessions, we focused on accessing her inner light. In Goddess lore, the priestesses called this evoking their "glamour," more dazzling than any nip or tuck. I also shared with her Audrey Hepburn's sage beauty tips, which were read at her funeral: "For attractive lips speak words of kindness. For lovely eyes seek out the good in people. For poise walk with the knowledge you will never walk alone."

In therapy, I continued to work with Darlene to make peace with getting older. I'm not against cosmetic assistance in moderation as long as it isn't an unwinnable denial of aging, as it was for Darlene. Denial isn't liberating; you're just locked in illusion. Instead, Darlene proved to be open to discovering that spirituality involves striving to harmonize with life's cycles—a developing wisdom, and a different kind of allure. There's loss, but there are also gains. Further, sexiness doesn't have an age limit; you can exude it to your final breath, as Peter O'Toole so sensuously demonstrated in the film *Venus*. Thus, Darlene started to think of aging more positively, far preferable to going on the warpath with time. As baseball great Satchel Paige said, "Age is just mind over matter—if you don't mind, it don't matter." Darlene could hear me because I wasn't telling her not to look good or not to pursue a healthy, fit lifestyle. My message was simply to balance the outer with the inner so she wouldn't worry so much, could better savor her charms, and would have a more serene, pleasurable passage as she aged.

The next action step, which Darlene uses, summarizes how to spiritually frame and reverse any kind of worry. If you practice it methodically, the endpoint is always more inner calm.

Emotional Action Step

SPIRITUAL STRATEGIES TO LIFT
ANXIETY AND WORRY

1. *Change your thinking.* Ask yourself, "What is the spiritual teaching of my anxiety or worry?" Then write your response in a journal. Be specific. For instance, "I'm worried that I won't get financing for my business" may be a lesson in believing in your dream, not giving up. Or "I'm worried my daughter will always be depressed" may be a lesson in doing everything you can to help, then learning the power of prayer and letting go. Whatever your worry, search for its greater meaning. Ponder how it can further your spiritual growth.

2. *Be in the Now.* When anxious thoughts project you into the future, bring your attention back to the Now. Say to yourself, "Just for today I can be happy. Just for today I'll do what I can to move forward—that will be enough. Just for today I will be loving with myself and appreciate what's beautiful, what I have to be grateful for."

3. *Say a prayer.* Sometimes worry grips you and just won't let go. You know it's overkill but you just can't stop. At these junctures, ask for help from whatever you conceive of as Spirit. Say a prayer from your heart. It could simply be, "Please take this worry from me." You can improvise. One surgeon says this prayer to become calm before he operates: "Dear God, these are your hands. Don't embarrass yourself!" Or here's a 2,500-year-old Buddhist loving-kindness practice I suggest repeating.

> *May I be free of worry*
> *May I be well*
> *May I feel safe and at ease*
> *May I be at peace.*

When worry sets in, keep praying: while taking a test, in your boss's office, before a speech. In any situation, let your bond with the Divine melt worry away. Requesting such intervention will keep you calm.

4. *Meditate on the deep calm within.* No matter how anxious you feel, calm is your deepest center. *Think of contacting it as a spiritual experience to treasure.* Anxiety and worry are limited to the mind, an outer layer of awareness. Finding calm means going further within. To get there, whether you're walking or sitting, start by taking a few deep, slow breaths to release tension and relax. Then visualize yourself dropping deeper and deeper into the core of your being, to a place of total peace and safety. There is still water in each of us. Without straining, try to intuitively sense this stillness so you can return there, to that sublime feeling. The more you focus on it, the more it will grow.

For both my patients and for me, it's reassuring to have spiritual options to offset anxiety. It's been said that worry looks around, sorry looks back, and faith looks up. Having faith that you're partnered with a higher power gives you more confidence to be calm. Sometimes, though, you might notice, as I do, that you feel anxious and calm simultaneously. It's a strange mixture, but the states can coexist, especially as your reserve of stillness is just building. The dexterity of emotional freedom is to choose calm rather than angst. This moves the emotional tipping point toward serenity.

EXPERIENCE THE ENERGETIC POWER OF ANXIETY, WORRY, AND INNER CALM

No one can empty a room faster than an anxious person. Anxiety is highly contagious, an ants-in-your-pants vibe that even the most thick-skinned people want to flee from. You can sense anxiety in the air. People intuit it like dogs hearing a whistle pitched beyond the range of the human ear. Interacting with someone who's anxious can make you anxious too. Inner calm does the reverse. It's comforting, attracts others, puts them at ease.

Working with anxious patients, I always anchor the session, at the beginning and throughout, by generating inner calm. I do this by connecting with the stillness inside of me, actively beaming it into the room. I've learned to set aside personal problems so I can mobilize the stillness. You can't fake inner calm—a cool veneer is meaningless. Embodied calm is transmitted, an energy others read and respond to. It ripens through meditation, spiritual practice, and other methods of becoming tranquil—alas, not a priority for most mainstream physicians. To patients riding the bucking bronco of anxiety, calm is manna from heaven. They instantly intuit if it's real or not, and if it's real, they ingest it the way the starving ravenously eat food. My job is to hold a calm energy until they can do so for themselves. (An anxious therapist treating an anxious patient—not a rare thing—can be pure torture for both.)

I'd like you to become acquainted with the subtle energy of the Fourth Transformation's emotions. The key to averting anxiety and worry is to swiftly recognize them, then switch gears to become calm. Intuiting the nuances of energy subdues worry and anxiety before they're full-blown—it's similar to attending to a twinge of pain before your back goes into spasm. As an investigation, I suggest amping up each emotion for a few minutes. Why? To compare their effects and learn to mindfully shift emotional states. First, picture what makes you anxious. Think extreme, perhaps losing every last penny of your life savings or your trusted mate. Then picture what brings calm: financial security or romping in the womb-warm Caribbean with your beloved. In each case, observe the energetic variations in your body. The following are common qualities of both emotions to note.

HOW THE ENERGY OF ANXIETY CAN FEEL

- Restless, fidgety
- Speeded up, agitated, irritable

- Clenched

- Like a siren in your head warning "danger"

- Louder than intuition

HOW THE ENERGY OF CALM CAN FEEL

- Smooth as silk

- Spacious, flowing, relaxed

- Settling, grounding

- Vitalizing, as if your system has been rebooted

- Conducive to hearing intuition and the heart

Once you get a sense of each, stretch yourself. Practice switching between anxiety and calm a few times, a kind of fast-paced emotional relay race—a few minutes anxious, a few minutes calm. Such flexibility programs you to choose your mood instead of remaining anxious by default. *For more freedom, always work negativity down.* This means minimizing problems rather than accentuating them. Detachment helps: if you think of anxiety and calm as pure energy rather than personalizing them, liberating yourself comes down to choosing one frequency over another. Experiment with seeing emotional transformation with that much neutral dispassion.

To be happy, really happy, you must recognize and discharge difficult emotions because their energy may get lodged in your body. Positive emotions can accumulate too, though these augment well-being. As an Energy Psychiatrist, I don't view past traumas and anxieties as simply memories. I acknowledge their propensity to coalesce as energetic scar tissue that restricts health and joy. However, breaking up encased emotions dissolves these scars so that energy can flow once more.

Gifted neuroscientist Candace Pert, who discovered the brain's opiate receptors, offers an elegant explanation for this. She believes our bodies' cells—all one hundred trillion of them—have the capacity to store memories and emotions in strings of amino acids called neuropeptides. (She calls them "molecules of emotion" in her book of the

same name.) These migrate through your system and attach to receptors in different physical locations. Muscles are havens for clogged
angst. The anxiety you felt about being fired a decade ago lives on in
your shoulders or back. So when a massage therapist starts working
on these muscles, you're suddenly flooded with flashbacks. What's
happening? Memories lodged in muscles are activated. During massages I've had the wildest emotional recollections—arguing with an
ex, a traffic jam in Greece, taking a pre-med calculus exam. These
were all anxieties I hadn't thought of for ages, yet there they were.
Hands-on attention in the right area brings memories and emotions to
the surface by firing cells that encode them. Some are simply blasts
from the past without particular significance. Others are supercharged
feelings that need to be released. After a massage, I feel lighter, as if
I've been dug out of an avalanche or freed from hiding. Depending on
the anxiety's source, you may require a few bodywork sessions. Sometimes psychotherapy can also help.

In *The Heart's Code*, psychologist Paul Pearsall chronicles arresting
accounts of our body's cellular emotional intelligence. He tells of
Claire Sylvia, the famous heart-lung transplant recipient who suddenly began craving new kinds of food—chicken nuggets and beer—
as well as experiencing unfamiliar emotions. But why? Stunningly, in
dreams, she had conversations with her donor (whose identity had
been kept anonymous, standard hospital policy), which allowed her to
locate his parents. They confirmed that her new tastes and feelings
were those their son had too.

Pearsall also describes an eight-year-old girl who received the heart
of a murdered child. After the transplant, the girl started having nightmares about the man who had killed her donor. Her mother then took
her to a therapist. Details she reported in therapy sessions were so pre-
cise—time, weapon, the murderer's clothes, crime scene—that they
notified the police. Astonishingly, the girl's information led police to
the murderer.

Understanding Pert's research and Pearsall's real-life examples can
enhance your emotional freedom. Realize that anxiety resides both in
the mind and in the actual structure of the body. Overcoming it may
require more than talk therapy. Sometimes you need hands-on energy

techniques to dislodge what's emotionally imbedded on a physical level, whether by literally kneading it out or by using acupuncture and energy-oriented methods. Verbalizing may not get to these places, but the following methods will. I routinely recommend them to patients; they complement our psychotherapeutic work by reaching the subtle energetic nooks and crannies of emotions. Try each. See what's most effective.

Emotional Action Step

USE THESE ENERGY THERAPIES TO RELIEVE ANXIETY AND INCREASE INNER CALM

1. *Massage.* A good massage quiets the mind, unkinks muscles, and removes physical pockets of anxiety. If emotions arise, don't inhibit them. Healing proceeds by letting it all come through. Just take deep breaths to keep the body relaxed. I recommend weekly massages, not just when anxiety peaks. It's best to find a practitioner who works with subtle energy, though some with a loving touch do so naturally without knowing it. Types of massage range from the gentle Swedish variety to Rolfing's deep tissue work.

2. *Acupuncture.* This ancient technique consists of inserting tiny needles along pathways called meridians to promote energy flow. (Brain scans demonstrate that when a needle is placed in a foot meridian associated with vision, the brain's visual cortex lights up.) Double-blind clinical trials have also confirmed acupuncture's efficacy. Practitioners aim to restore the balance of *chi,* the vital life force, among the seven energy centers, or chakras, that run from the base of the spine to the top of the head. Anxiety is considered an imbalance of *chi,* an indication that a chakra is "blocked" and energy needs to be released so it can flow properly along the body's meridians. By rebalancing energy, anxiety-related symptoms improve. How? Acupuncture seems to pacify the exact part of the brain linked to our emotional response to pain.

3. *Energy healing.* This is a gentle, powerful modality in which a
   practitioner sends subtle energy through his or her hands to
   promote physical and emotional balance. It's wonderful for
   maintaining well-being and for dissipating acute or chronic
   anxiety. Types of energy healers include therapeutic touch
   practitioners and Reiki masters. I appreciate energy healing
   because it's in sync with my sensitive system. Plus it gets you
   calm fast. I also employ it with patients and teach them the
   techniques. Here's an exercise I suggest.

Soothe Yourself with Heart Energy

At the first signs of panic or anxiety, place the palm of one
hand over your heart chakra, the energy center for unconditional love located in the midchest. Simultaneously visualize someone or something you love. Breathing slowly,
keep your hand there for a few minutes. Notice sensations
of warmth and comfort. Also watch for images. Once,
focusing on my father, I saw the most touching vision of
him, with his hands in the prayer position, meditating
within me. Be soothed by these impressions. Whether
you're wound up by a tense business meeting, arguing with
your spouse, or battling the claustrophobia of being in an
MRI scanner, the heart is able to calm anxiety.

4. *T'ai chi ch'uan.* This exercise, consisting of very slow, graceful
   motions synchronized with rhythmic breathing, leads to inner
   stillness. A twelfth-century Daoist monk who closely studied five
   animals concluded that snakes and cranes were best able to over-
   power fierce opponents. From his observations, he developed t'ai
   chi ch'uan, a series of "forms" based on the movement of these
   creatures. The modern-day opponents of stress and anxiety can
   be disabled by practicing it. Besides increasing the flow of blood
   and oxygen to the brain, strengthening muscles, and enhancing
   immunity, t'ai chi ch'uan balances your subtle energies, restoring
   physical and emotional vibrancy.

Along with reducing anxiety, these energy therapies may put you in the most divine altered state. As the linear mind relaxes, intuition sharpens. During a massage or acupuncture treatment you may experience sudden insights that prompt emotional breakthroughs. Physically armoring yourself with muscle tension to guard against anxiety obscures such vital intuitions. When you employ energy therapy, the body becomes less defended, energetic channels reopen, and clarity returns.

MAP THE PSYCHOLOGY OF ANXIETY, WORRY, AND INNER CALM

A seminal study in *Psychological Science* recently reported that you can worry yourself into an early grave. The good news is that if you learn to worry less, you'll live longer, a life-altering shift on the order of lowering cholesterol if you have heart disease. In terms of longevity, worry is something to be worried about.

As with all emotions, there are multiple theories about causes and cures. Psychoanalysts believe anxiety is relieved by working through unconscious childhood conflicts and traumas. Psychiatrist Carl Jung called it a "complex" that binds energy until released; emotional calm flows from balancing a rich inner and outer life. Behaviorists say anxiety is learned but can be unlearned through desensitization techniques (you're gradually exposed to threatening situations under relaxed conditions to alter your response). So who's right? My take: there may be truth in each, depending on your circumstances.

The psychological approach I take to anxiety integrates tools from the above disciplines and more, but with two major differences. First, I don't perceive anxiety as merely an emotion to be understood and eliminated. I always pair it with the capacity to develop inner calm so that it can be emotionally transformed. Second, I'm guided by intuition, not formulaic prescriptions from a particular therapeutic gospel. I don't favor any one method; doing so would be a disservice to my patients. What's crucial is that a treatment effectively harmonizes with each individual. As a therapist, I try not to assume anything. Whether we're sitting together the first time or the hundredth, intuition lets me freshly see where you're at.

Nonetheless, there are basic psychological dynamics I always go over with anxious patients to assist them in reversing sabotaging emotional patterns. These include examining the ripple effect of anxious mothers, being tyrannized by an inner slave driver, and perfectionism. If you're wrestling with this transformation's emotions, consider how these dynamics apply to you.

Dynamic 1: Anxious Mothers Can Create Anxious Children

More than fathers or other relatives, a mother's anxiety forcefully influences children. Think back: You were in your mother's womb for nine months. When you were born, she fed and diapered you, held you, put you to sleep. Since a mother is typically the primary caregiver, she emotionally models how to view the world, whether you feel safe or not. Ask yourself: "Was my mother basically anxious or calm? How did that rub off on me?" Perhaps she was calm and you're calm too. But if she was anxious, it's likely you took some of that on, especially if you're an empath. The solution is to grasp this psychological dynamic, set your intention to disengage, and develop a healthier mode of coping.

Take my patient Phil, who'd suffered from health anxiety most of his twenty-five years, though he was fundamentally well. He told me, "My mother had every symptom under the sun. She was always sick with something, constantly running to doctors. Indigestion, palpitations, rashes. Her medicine cabinet was jammed with ointments, elixirs, and pills. She brought all these medical manuals home about various diseases, which I avidly read. But then I began getting nervous about being sick too, a worry I still periodically grapple with. Lately, it's gotten worse. I'm losing days at a time and wonderful moments worrying about what illness might be lurking in my body."

Phil's health anxieties struck an all-too-intimate familial chord in me. My physician-mother, dynamo that she was, had countless illnesses, some serious and some not, some real and some not. Between experiencing a pulmonary embolus when I was born, a heart attack at forty, and chronic lymphoma for twenty years, my mother did endure a lot. But she was hardly a stoic or calm personality. From early child-hood on, I heard melodramatic play-by-plays about every ache and pain. I'd see her retreat alone to the bedroom, drawing the blackout shades so tight they seemed to suck all the oxygen from the air. "Judith dear, sit here and hold my hand," she'd often request in a tiny voice, then pat the space on the blanket beside her. Honestly, I didn't want to, but how could I have said no? I loved my mother, but watch-ing her physical discomfort, seeing such vulnerability and her anxiety about it, made my world precarious. Holding hands in that stuffy, tomb-like darkness, I sensed her emotions penetrating me, invaders I didn't know how to turn away. But Mother didn't usually stay down much longer than a day. She'd rise like a phoenix from the ashes when she felt better. These about-faces were weirdly abrupt. Suddenly she'd morph into superwoman, superdoctor, and life of the party—not in a manic way, but more with a proud, hard-ass "nothing's going to stop me" attitude. Always, I'd breathe easier when her blue terrycloth bathrobe returned to the closet and she'd resume strutting her trade-mark Chanel. But Mother's health anxiety wasn't restricted to herself. She was irrationally apprehensive that I'd get ill too. Growing up, if I had a cold, she'd treat me like I was at death's door. Taking my tem-perature every few hours, forcing fluids, installing a vaporizer by my bed to clear my sinuses, she was an overwrought Jewish mother on overdrive. Understandably, I've had to do quite a bit of work to stay on top of my own nervousness about health so I'm not imprisoned by the panic my mother taught me.

Sharing what I had to learn personally in addition to my medical training, I taught Phil ways to liberate himself from constant health anxieties and build inner calm. *Worrying about symptoms, minor or major, only makes them worse.* Phil's starting place, though, was under-standing that anxious mothers can create anxious children. It made Phil aware that he was unconsciously parroting his mother. Wanting to relieve her anxiety, he'd inadvertently shouldered it, something he also did with friends. Realizing this, along with discovering the differ-ence between listening to his body's signals and being hyperfocused on every sensation, enabled him to be calmer. Always, emotional free-dom involves choosing where you put your attention.

Dynamic 2: Your Inner Slave Driver Can Tyrannize You

Worried, anxious people typically have an inner slave driver who won't quit: the part of you that's addicted to workaholism, rushing, and going nonstop until you drop. If you don't put in a ten-hour day, you get anxious. Also, you feel guilty relaxing, taking time off from work, or solving emotional problems. In your mind, to feel calm is to feel guilt, a linkage you must first notice and then reprogram. The inner slave driver shows no mercy. Unchecked, it'll whip you into an anxious state of physical and emotional collapse. To transform anxiety, rein in your slave driver by treating yourself with more compassion, turning down the tension, and regularly planning stress-free interludes. Once, during an anxious period when my inner slave driver took over, I dreamed that a ceramic mug I loved, with the words DANCE-SING-PLAY written on it, cracked. This upset me because I couldn't drink tea from it anymore. Upon awakening, I got the message: to have more fun and put less pressure on myself so that I didn't crack. Similarly, oversee your inner slave driver. Staying mindful of this voice and saying an emphatic no to it preserves calm.

With patients, I focus on helping them break the connection between workaholism and self-worth. In our society we haven't been taught to see slowing down and practicing self-care as a virtue; however, this is what I propose in Energy Psychiatry. Also, if my patients' inner slave driver tendency comes from parents or other early role models, it's important to discover this so that they don't keep acting out negative conditioning. I emphasize to patients, and to you, that emotional freedom is predicated on finding self-worth through love—whether that means honoring your energy needs, not working an all-nighter, or telling your family you require downtime. Such self-care is a way of honoring yourself and quieting the inner slave driver.

Dynamic 3: You're a Perfectionist Who Can't Tolerate Mistakes

Kissing cousins of inner slave drivers, perfectionists are easy marks for anxiety. They hold themselves to impossible standards, beat themselves bloody over mistakes, and are unforgiving when others make them. Perfectionism can spur you toward accomplishments, but these are often hard to enjoy because in your own eyes they never seem good enough. You aggravate anxiety with all-or-nothing thinking, a list of "shoulds" about how life must be led, and fear of not measuring up. See if you find something of yourself in any of these traits.

SIGNS OF PERFECTIONISM

- You believe you must always be perfect to be considered likeable or worthy.

- You find it hard to compromise or tolerate shortcomings, yours or others'.

- You keep your home spotless in case a neighbor drops by.

- Your outfit and makeup must be flawless even if you're only going to the car wash.

- You get a B on a test or a performance review and see yourself as a failure.

- You say or do something you regret and can neither make amends nor pardon yourself.

Emotional freedom involves refocusing on your positive traits and what you have to be grateful for, not becoming a perfection gestapo. I say shoot for excellence but show a little lenience toward yourself and others. With patients, I work with perfectionism in two basic ways. First, I advise that they take the pressure off themselves by setting realistic goals and affirming those successes. For instance, with a patient who was chronically anxious because she couldn't complete her never-ending to-do list, I suggested aiming for only two tasks per day, then telling herself what a great job she'd done. This is a behavioral way to scale down excessive expectations and practice positive self-talk. Second, I help patients discover what's motivating the anxiety of perfectionism so that it can be reprogrammed. Did their parents equate success with perfectionism? Were their teachers intolerant of mistakes? Did they lack role models for self-compassion? Knowing these answers helps patients pinpoint where their anxiety began so that it can be replaced with new beliefs and behavior. Unless you are aware of these psychological influences, it's easy to click into automatic with perfectionism. Then setting realistic goals to combat workaholism or other overly conscientious habits may feel intolerable. Instead, try to catch perfectionism by seeing what motivates it and showing yourself compassion so that real change is possible. We're all imperfect; that's part of the beauty of being human. I'd like you to try to see it this way. Learning tolerance and self-acceptance, particularly when confronting limitations, fosters calm.

INTUITION: A CALMING TOOL TO COMBAT ANXIETY AND WORRY

To overcome negative emotions, consulting intuition is always useful. How can it guide you? During nervous periods, it offers a more centered alternative to agitation. Intuition is a neutral form of information that allows you to soberly gauge the validity of your worries. If you tune in and find out they're unfounded, you'll be relieved. If they are founded, you can develop a strategy to deal with them. In both cases, you'll have a gut-centered game plan for success.

My colleague Jan, a spiritual psychologist, is convinced that listening to intuition instead of anxiety was lifesaving. He'd been on a vision quest with a group in the Alaskan wilderness, an intensive period of fasting, dreaming, and communing with nature. For three days, they'd each gone off on their own, setting up camps miles from one another. When it came time to return to the group, Jan, who'd spent days without food or water, was disoriented and soon realized he was lost. Panic welled up. Where in God's name was he? Would he ever find the others? Would he live or die? But before panic completely claimed him, he fought to gather his wits, pause, breathe, and confer with intuition. "What should I do?" he inwardly asked. For a few minutes, he stayed as still as he possibly could, listening. It seemed like an eternity. Then, after this apparent forever, an inner voice responded, "Follow the quacking of the ducks." "What?" Jan thought, bewildered. He didn't even know if ducks lived in the tundra; he hadn't seen or heard a single one. But still, no novice at trusting intuition, he started walking, ears attuned like giant radio receivers. After fifteen minutes of clock time, which felt like it took eons to elapse, to his enormous relief he discerned one lone quack in the distance, then another, then a chorus. Jumping for joy, Jan followed these guiding sounds back to the safety of the group's camp.

Take a cue from the quackers: in the midst of anxiety, remember to tune in. There's a still, small voice inside that knows how to outmaneuver this emotion. Intuition resides in the calm part of you, something we all have but need to summon. Expect to be thrown off by anxiety's turbulence; plan ahead. Tell yourself, "When I feel this emotion, I'll take a breath, pause, and center myself. The world might be crumbling, but I'll ask my intuition what to do." It feels like a miracle when, during chaos, the answer comes. But to me, the even greater miracle is trusting yourself enough to ask, then to act on what you receive. A flash, a vision, a voice, a knowing—whatever form your intuition takes, test it out. See if the advice works. Begin with lesser anxieties, than build up to others. It's the best way to develop validated confidence in this wisdom.

On occasion it may be difficult to discern whether you're being anxious or intuitive. Here are some clues. Generally, intuition is conveyed in an impartial tone, even if the content or your reaction to it is emotionally charged. It feels correct in your gut. The message is clear and calm, and it pops out at you. On the other hand, anxiety feels like an emotional twister. It reflects areas where you've been hurt or your insecurities. To avoid misconstruing these as intuitions, you must know your tender points, the ones that trigger anxiety. Also, as you practice acting on your intuitions, it's important to get feedback about whether they were accurate or not.

My patient Julie had a high-anxiety dream about her thirty-year-old son Ben, about whom she had no particular cause to worry. She dreamed that he was being savagely attacked by swarms of insects and was gasping for air. Oddly, in the dream, Julie was observing the scene nonreactively. However, the minute her eyes opened and the dream registered, she became flushed with anxiety. Though Julie wasn't the overprotective type, she decided to contact Ben to see if he was okay. He wasn't. Minutes before, the police had called: his girlfriend had just been killed by a drunk driver on the way to work. In shock, barely able to hold it together, he told her, "Mom, I'm so upset I can't breathe." Mother's intuition: in the dream, anxiety was its messenger, a premonitory emotion that alerted Julie to call her son. Though Julie hadn't been sure what this anxiety dream meant, she followed through to find out. Doing so furthered love and allowed her to support Ben during this tragedy.

Since psychology is the comprehensive study of mind and behavior, my philosophy as a physician necessitates bringing intuition into the mix. Were I a by-the-book conventional therapist, I'd have focused on exploring Julie's anxieties about her son, certainly worth investigation. I wouldn't have framed her dream as an emotional premonition since that wasn't part of my training or belief system. But Julie's dream was a call to action. There was no time for conventional therapeutic talk. I never forget that we are complex psychological/intuitive beings with gut instinct elegantly informing our behavior. Working with patients, I make room for anxiety's multiple creative dimensions. Then I can see each person fully and prescribe treatments unique to his or her needs.

For some, intuition is the make-or-break factor. Over a few years I saw a patient with obsessive-compulsive disorder (OCD) who told me: "As a child, I had frightening intuitions about bad things happening to others that came true: illness, accidents, getting fired. No one could explain them to me. I thought that if I washed my hands over and over again until they bled, the intuition wouldn't happen, or if I touched the doorknob a hundred times in the 'right' way, the person would be okay. I thought that if I controlled everything, they'd stop." Lowering this patient's anxiety involved helping him make peace with his intuitive abilities, understand that negative emotional events are simply easier to pick up, and learn to differentiate authentic intuition from anxiety. Also, I taught him how to sense what's positive too about intuition, a more nurturing aspect of tuning in. In the final tally, what benefited his OCD the most? He said, "You didn't call me crazy and you worked with my intuitive experiences on their own terms." Over the years, each of my patients has amplified my reverence for the inventive inner forces that shape feelings and behavior. Freedom comes from respecting every element of our wholeness.

While mastering the Fourth Transformation's emotions, use this combination of psychological and intuitive strategies. They'll work. Make them your own.

Emotional Action Step

PRACTICE EVERYDAY TECHNIQUES TO REVERSE ANXIETY AND CREATE INNER CALM

1. *Catch early warning signs.* Watch for telling personal behaviors that give away these emotions. Common ones include rushing, forcing an issue, and becoming demanding or impatient. When I'm anxious, I huffily insist on talking to people's supervisors if I perceive my needs aren't being met (for example, while getting my car serviced or being kept interminably on the phone with computer tech support). Identifying these behaviors lets you take charge of them so anxiety doesn't destroy your people skills or equanimity.

2. *Pause when agitated.* Make this vow: "I will never have a conversation with someone, send an e-mail, or make a decision when gripped by anxiety." No matter what the upset is, do not act until you have gained calm and composure.

3. *Evaluate the anxiety.* Thoughtfully consider if a real threat exists or if you're blowing things out of proportion. For instance, if you get anxious every summer before your daughter goes to camp and she's always been okay, your concern is likely unrealistic. When you suspect a legitimate threat, try this. If, say, you think a coworker is really trying to steal your job, check for proof, then tell yourself, "I can handle this," and formulate a coping plan. For further clarification, also intuitively tune in: sit quietly, fully inhale and exhale a few times to get calmer and more neutral, then inwardly ask, "Is my concern justified? How can the worry be resolved?" Stay open to gut feelings, flashes, or knowings. Factor these into your assessment of the situation.

4. *Work the anxiety down.* Train yourself not to turn life into one big emergency. Instead, make your anxieties smaller. In Hasidism there's a practice of not worrying, of making "something into

nothing." You can try it too. For instance, if you have a financial setback, see it as a problem with a solution, not the end of the world. If you have an argument with your mate, don't immediately assume "he's leaving me"; rather, find a compromise to resolve the issue. Even in a severe crisis, working anxiety down lets you face it more serenely.

5. *Meditate to calm yourself.* A relaxing meditation to practice is to focus on the middle distance. Eyes open or closed, imagine a point in the distance at the center of your visual field. It may help to picture a road disappearing from the foreground into an area about halfway to the horizon line. For a few minutes, gently place your awareness on that convergence point, a potent focus that, according to mystical traditions, brings balance and peace.

These strategies prevent anxiety from putting a wedge between you and tranquility. Set out to cultivate calm. Recently I stayed in a hotel whose do-not-disturb sign said: SHH. I'M FINDING MY INNER SELF. What a right-on practice for everyone to adopt! Make time to do it. In life, there are millions of things we could be anxious about. Without a method for handling all this, you may never find peacefulness. Better by far to stand up to anxiety and worry, and be free.

TRUST ME, I know how hard calm is to hold on to. But as this higher state of consciousness builds, it's self-sustaining and real. A workshop participant once told me that when she worked at Disneyland in the 1970s, employees were told to put on a "Disneyland smile." She said that if you didn't smile, they'd remind you. More than three reminders was grounds for dismissal. Such feigning of happiness and the calm it purports to represent is abhorrent to me. Authentic calm is earned, a dynamic stillness that emerges from conquering anxiety and worry.

Transforming these difficult emotions puts you in the passionate center of everyday tasks and pleasures. Don't run from life, run into it; consider cultivating inner calm as an emotional art form whatever you encounter. Poet Gwendolyn Brooks speaks for me when she writes, "Conduct your blooming in the noise and whip of the whirlwind." That's what emotional freedom is about: your blooming. Let that take precedence. Staying positive by using the tools I've presented in this chapter and the rest of this book will provide you with exactly what to do and when.

Meditation on Freedom

Savor the Ecstasy of Calm

For a few glorious minutes, immerse yourself in knowing that all is completely well. There's nothing to change, nothing to do. Everything—I mean everything—is in perfect order. Though life has ups and downs, that's perfect too. No worries or pressures, only total relaxation. Soften around it. Allow yourself to melt into that feeling of ecstasy.

Everything that is done in the world is done by hope.
—DR. MARTIN LUTHER KING JR.

10

THE FIFTH TRANSFORMATION:

FACING DEPRESSION,

BUILDING HOPE

CONQUERING DEPRESSION is possible. You're entitled to enjoy life without being hounded by despondency. Even if depression has bedeviled you, now's your chance to deal with it differently. Emotional freedom offers a path to hope, compassion, and relief of suffering.

As a psychiatrist, I've been privy to hearing courageously honest patients pour out their despair in the healing process, but it still boggles my mind how many of us are consistently gloomy. In America, one in five report being depressed or unhappy; depression is the leading cause of workplace disability; someone attempts suicide every sixteen minutes. What makes depression so prevalent, so insidious? It's been called the "invisible disease," since many of us are so darn good at hiding it, suffer silently, and may be ashamed of our feelings when others often *appear* fine. Meanwhile, you put on a brave face to mask misery, or become resigned to going through the motions of life without much pleasure. Perhaps you instinctively self-medicate with excessive caffeine, sugar, alcohol, or other substances just to be able to function in a decent mood. If you've done any of these, you know the strain of having to keep up a chirpy appearance and smile when you're hurting inside. You don't want to have to labor so hard to keep it together. Nor do you wish to become acclimated to depression, even if it's mild. This chapter's methods will make feeling good come more easily.

The Fifth Transformation presents answers to depression. Applying these will lift this emotion's inertia and oppressive grayness, lending light and hope to any situation. We'll explore the spectrum of depression, from what the American Psychiatric Association calls dysthymia—having the blues you can't shake—to the dark despair of major depression.

What is depression? We all have low periods, but depression is a *persistent* sense of feeling down, pessimistic, and self-critical, whether minimal or consuming. Compared to sadness, which you may also feel when depressed (though sadness often stands alone and is more transient), intense depression has profound physical effects. You may have disturbed sleep, brain fog, no sex drive, fatigue, heightened sensitivity to pain, or a hopelessness that can make life seem not worth living. During a major depression, sadness clings to you, in contrast to passing sadness about a painful event. In this state, even a rose can seem to have no beauty. Sometimes it may be hard to get yourself moving. As an empath, I've also experienced how depression manifests in my body: lingering stomach ailments or back pain alert me that this emotion may have physically burrowed into vulnerable spots.

Depression is a blunting of power, a separation from heart, spirit, and intuition. You'll learn its causes, which include decreased serotonin, stress, and low self-esteem, and how to remedy them. Fear also instigates depression. One patient, terrified of nearly everything, disclosed in tears, "I'm afraid to wake up. I'm afraid of the morning. Depression is like a wolf at my door," an angst I'd like to spare you. Similar to fear, depression may falsely appear to have no exit. Don't be fooled. Using my methods, which go beyond the traditional, there is a way out, and also hard-earned yet liberating wisdom.

Though I'm against coddling depression, this emotion is more than a bad mood to "snap out of"—an erroneous notion lacking empathy and knowledge, often cavalierly held by those who've rarely been depressed. To tell a depressed person to "pull yourself together" is like telling a snail to go faster. Transforming depression requires a more compassionate understanding of this emotion's symptoms.

Depression's lesson is always hope, the belief in your capacity to rise above darkness, inner or outer, even when it pervades—to not give up. We must fight to find hope, especially when it feels beyond us. I've been in that abyss; maybe you have too. In the framework of emotional freedom, hope is a heartfelt wish to better your situation, another's, or the world's—never a desire to see someone stumble and "get what he deserves." It holds the potential for good things to happen and for trouble to pass. Hope is a key ingredient for achieving success, whether in a new job, a marriage, or medical treatment. Imagine starting these ventures feeling doomed . . . not a constructive attitude. Uniquely, hope is more concerned with the future than the other emotions are. (In Hebrew, the word *hope* is interpreted as a line into the future.) When you hope for depression to lift, for health, for peace, you're making an appeal to the future, intuitively partnering with what hasn't yet materialized. Hope may be supported by hard data, but it doesn't always need to make sense. Being hopeful can be an intuitive call, what feels right to do in service of loving or beating the odds. About surmounting depression, my spiritual teacher says, "Hope when there is no hope. Have faith in yourself and in goodness." Hope is often rooted in a spiritual philosophy that allows for divine intervention in turbulent times and also sustains you no matter what happens. Still, hope doesn't have to be linked to anything spiritual. Even so, you've got to be able to tap the strength to remain positive and not become embittered if things don't go your way, admittedly very big ifs!

Personally and in my medical practice, I've seen that hope usually comes from a series of mini-transformations. It's a developing power rather than a single epiphany. A friend's faith in you lets you have faith in yourself. Your depression lessens when you take a step to improve your life. Hope is not blind optimism; it's based on intuition, love, and the gumption to reach the other side of depression more awakened.

As a physician, I'm a stalwart bearer of hope. About this, I once had a striking dream. Many boats were becalmed at sea; their supplies were waning. In the midst of the crews' desperation, a sudden glorious wind came out of nowhere to fill their sails and carry them safely to harbor. My dream showed that, like the wind, hope can be a redemptive, intervening force. When my patients are becalmed in the darkness, I do everything to summon hope for a bright future, hold hope for them until they can hold it for themselves. Here's my stand: no matter how far down you've gone, there is always hope to recover from depression. *Sometimes you have to chip away at this bleak emotion, but a better time will come. Hope is about waiting to behold a happier day.* It sets the tone for change. However, in situations where there is no turning back, I don't encourage false hope which contradicts intuition and the facts. One patient's husband was in hospice care, obviously dying of brain cancer. My job was to gently help her accept this and then grieve, rather than enforce her denial about his condition. In such cases, it's healthy to give up hope about a wished-for outcome— painful though this may be—but never to give up hope in the integrity of life's flow, even in the face of great loss. To this end, I'll show you how intuition imparts a clearer sense of what is and isn't possible so hope becomes well informed.

Some of my patients fear that if they delve into depression, they'll get more depressed, so they want to skirt the topic. Here's what I advise them and you: go at your own pace and treat yourself with compassion. But do it. Otherwise this emotion just sits there like an elephant in the living room that you foolishly attempt to ignore. Don't let depression take up residence in your psyche. Establish this emotion's current role in your life by reviewing the following signs. Not to worry if you check them all off. You're at a threshold where change is imminent.

DEPRESSION QUIZ: AM I DEPRESSED?

Ask yourself:

- Do I feel down in the dumps more days than not?
- Am I usually negative, tired, or bored?
- Is everything an effort, as if I'm going uphill?
- Do I have a poor appetite or overeat?

- Do I have insomnia or want to sleep a lot?

- Do I regularly turn to drugs and alcohol to alter my mood?

- Am I dependent on caffeine or excessive sugar to function?

- Is it hard to experience pleasure?

- Is it difficult to make decisions or concentrate?

- Do I feel worthless, hopeless, or frequently beat myself up?

Answering yes to all ten questions suggests a high amount of depression. Six to nine yeses indicate a moderate amount, three to five yeses a lesser amount. One or two yeses suggest mild depression. No yeses mean you're doing fine—have a fantastic day!

This chapter takes on highly charged topics: despair, sadness, thoughts of suicide, grief (which radically differs from depression). Let's address them all to reconceive our attitudes so they're congruent with emotional freedom. I champion the Fifth Transformation because my medication-based training in psychiatry overlooked the spiritual and energetic relevance of an emotion plaguing most of my patients. I'll share my knowledge of medications, pros and cons, and other psychological interventions. You'll learn when these can be valuable, but emotional freedom goes much further. It's an activist, multifaceted set of solutions to transform depression with hope. I'll also frame depression more cosmically, as a rugged journey of consciousness expansion. Without that vantage point, despair can feel like a friend to no one. I understand how this *émotion noir* wears you down. Still, I want to insist on depression's greater purpose, as a tough-love teacher of the heart, and thus a friend. Hope is a thicket of brilliance in a dark wood. Finding it brings liberation.

The Anatomy of Depression and Hope: Putting the Fifth Transformation into Action

Whether you've experienced big-time depression or just a taste of it, you're in the company of many well-known, accomplished people:

Florence Nightingale, Theodore Roosevelt, Princess Diana, Anthony Hopkins, Marilyn Monroe, Marlon Brando. Winston Churchill, the great inspirer, called this emotion, from which he suffered terrible bouts, the "black dog." Depression is not evidence of weakness or anything to be ashamed of. It's a human feeling many of us face. This chapter presents you with numerous options to transform depression as you explore its biology, spirituality, energetic power, and psychology. Choose the ones that feel right to you.

REPROGRAM THE BIOLOGY OF DEPRESSION AND HOPE

Depressed? You're lucky to be born at a time where science has made significant progress. Historically, the treatment of serious depression has been barbaric. Our ancient ancestors are believed to have seen any mental aberration as possession by evil forces; they made large holes in the skull to expel them, a horrific process called trepanning. In the seventh century, demonology was the psychiatry of the day; the Devil was the culprit for "deviant behavior." The severely depressed, who could be mute, agitated, or uncontrollably weeping, were rounded up in witch hunts along with psychotics and seers to be burned at the stake. During medieval times and later, insane asylums were the dumping ground for society's "undesirables." The mentally ill were chained in rat-infested cells, exhibited to the public like zoo animals. Psychology didn't emerge as a field until the late 1800s. Thus, we can appreciate why Freud's psychodynamic approach to depression, analyzing its unconscious causes, was such a humane revelation at the turn of the twentieth century. Even so, until the 1950s, lobotomies, electroshock (sometimes still used successfully with seriously depressed patients who're unresponsive to other treatments), and insulin therapy were standard interventions for extreme cases. Depression was often confused with schizophrenia—two completely different maladies, we now know. It was in this same period that antidepressants entered the scene. Along with them came lithium, which stabilized the manic mood swings of bipolar disorder, formerly called manic-depression—an illness for which prescriptions have recently doubled.

The Role of Traditional Antidepressants in Emotional Freedom

What are antidepressants? How did they come to be? Today it's clear that major depression and often some lesser kinds are caused by a decrease in neurotransmitters, brain chemicals that contribute to hope and optimism. Antidepressants raise the levels of serotonin, norepinephrine, and dopamine, which get depleted by emotional and physical stress. Biochemical imbalances may also be genetic; they can run in families. Interestingly, profound stress as well as alcohol and substance abuse may actually activate a dormant gene linked with depression. Our environment is crucial in shaping the way our genes are expressed.

A reveler in synchronicities, I appreciate the story of how the first antidepressant was discovered, even though, strangely, no one was looking for one. In 1958, a drug for tuberculosis was found to make patients "inappropriately happy," and thereafter became approved for depression. This fluke revolutionized treatment methods, ushering in what proved to be the controversial era of psychopharmacology. To reduce dismaying side effects, tricyclic antidepressants such as Elavil were developed—then thirty years later, Prozac took the world by storm. Such serotonin-enhancing drugs are currently the most commonly prescribed antidepressants.

I often get asked, "Should I take antidepressants? How do I know?" Make this a collaboration between you and your doctor. These medications can be lifesavers for some, wrong for others. Initially, I always rule out physical problems that can mimic depression such as low thyroid, anemia, and chronic fatigue syndrome. If these aren't present, the answer may be more clear-cut. Suppose you've had a biochemical depression before and you're in one now. You can't sleep, can't function, can't find a glimmer of light anywhere. You painfully obsess on what's negative; you want to stop but are unable to. If antidepressants have worked for you before, use them now. Or suppose you've never considered medication. You're too fuzzy to focus or tune into your intuition. Your doctor recommends medication. You have faith in her.

Here, following her advice makes sense. Preferably, though, you're given information and your intuition affirms if it feels right to proceed. Finally, should you and your doctor agree that medication isn't necessary, you'll gain by examining your feelings and riding the depression through. It's important to recognize periods when your own resources are sufficient.

Grieving can be one of those periods. Grief is an emotional response to loss, which generally lessens in intensity with time. As the feelings are dealt with, acceptance of loss becomes easier. If you're mourning the death of a loved one, I'm reluctant to prescribe medication, even though your serotonin levels may be temporarily sapped by the stress of loss. Grief is an organic recuperative process. Of course, it is depressing, but it typically works its way toward a healing alchemy. Acute or sudden grief, though, can shock the body. Our systems become overtaxed as the orderly plans we have for our lives shatter under the weight of the unexpected. In fact, the death of someone dear (or an abrupt romantic severing) can be so traumatic it mimics a heart attack. The *New England Journal of Medicine* terms this "broken heart syndrome." Sufferers have mega-levels of stress hormones in their systems, specifically adrenaline, three times higher than in heart attack victims. But after the initial jolt of this syndrome, in the course of processing the grief, most people recover their health. (I'll discuss healing grief in greater depth later in the chapter.)

Sometimes, though, antidepressants open the door to emotional freedom. Take my patient Todd, at twenty-eight a scuba diver and avid surfer who'd won international competitions. His "church" was the ocean. When he needed to think, he'd put on scuba gear, descend to the sea floor, and just lie there looking up at the mirror of the surface, gazing at waving kelp and schools of fish. But now Todd couldn't muster the energy to even go into the water. Depression had left him too listless to engage the ocean. Todd came in rail-thin with sunken cheeks, circles around his eyes dark as a raccoon's. "This is my second depression," he said. "Nothing in particular set it off. But for two months, I've been up most of the night. I can't think straight. My mood is black." In this funk, unable to work as a Web site designer, Todd had started hanging out at the beach with lowlifes of the Zuma

surf scene: "robo-trippers" who abused cough medicine and speed—
nothing he'd yet tried, but bonds with these "dudes" only augured bad
things. Though Todd liked the camaraderie—it got him out of the
house and killed time—I smelled a rat. His judgment was too clouded
to see what he was in for. Depression is a setup for substance abuse,
and substance abuse, depleting neurotransmitters, causes depression.
If that happened, he'd become a two-time loser. At our first session, I
felt the full weight of Todd's leaden despair; his pretty-boy face was
drawn with a sadness all its own. Like many people immersed in
depression, he appeared remote, flat, in the bubble of a monochrome
world. This "I'm here but I'm not" quality wasn't purposeful; he'd
just drifted far away from his center and needed retrieving. Though
Todd had surfed professionally since age ten with much public exposure, he was actually more bonded with his iPod than with people.
Depression amplified that isolation, a disconnect from others that
always made him feel "slightly broken."

Todd's classic biochemical depression differed from less crippling
kinds triggered by specific events—bankruptcy, divorce, being fired,
or other arduous transitions often best negotiated without medication. In such situational depressions, by drawing on inner strength
you can emerge stronger. A biochemical depression, however, isn't
just a rough patch, it's a descent into hell. Todd wasn't likely to rally
until his neurotransmitters were replenished. Once this happens,
recovering from depression can feel like waking from the dead. Over
the next six weeks, on Prozac, Todd gradually came to and was much
more present to participate in therapy. Then we began uncovering
and transforming patterns related to depression, including how to
form nurturing relationships. Among the amazing moments that
stand out in my years as a therapist, I will never forget Todd's exuber-
ance when he shared, "Yesterday, I picked up my board and surfed in
the light again." *To surf in the light again.* Todd's depression had lifted;
he had come home.

Nonetheless, I want to emphasize that taking any medication is a
start, not the whole answer. Physicians want to avoid running prescription mills—fifteen-minute sessions, a pill dispensed, then out the
door. As with Todd, not only do I recommend psychotherapy, but I

always encourage patients to meditate and develop a spiritual practice in conjunction with the Fifth Transformation's other strategies. Why? Body and spirit are always conjoined. In Energy Psychiatry I've seen how solidifying the connection between the two builds up neurochemicals and speeds recovery. The result? Many of my patients have been able to lower a medication's dose and reduce side effects. Others have discontinued it completely. Miracles happen when mind and body are harmonious.

I wince at the generalizations that people make about medications, positive or negative. Some frequent misperceptions include "I feel like a weakling because I can't do this on my own" or "I've failed spiritually if I take a pill." These are valid considerations, but I believe that God is in the laboratory when medications, from aspirin to Prozac, are discovered. God is present everywhere. Taking medications is in itself neither spiritual nor unspiritual. The crucial issue is that you employ a spiritual and intuitive point of view about whatever treatment you choose. For instance, even someone who meditates and has a strong spiritual connection may suffer deep depression if his or her body's biochemistry goes awry. As with diabetes or heart disease, medications rectifying biochemical imbalances can be caring, intuitively viable solutions. In such cases, courage lies in being willing to use them.

If you decide on an antidepressant, always notice how your body responds. Some are more calming, such as Celexa; Prozac is more stimulating. As with my patient Todd, the neurotransmitter lift from antidepressants can feel like a rebirth, but there may be side effects: weight gain, working overtime for even a modest orgasm, not feeling sexual or in touch with emotions, spirituality, or dreams. Paradoxically, even deeper feelings of depression or suicidal thoughts may occur. If you experience any of these, consult your doctor to calibrate the dosage or try a different medication.

In Energy Psychiatry, I'm acutely aware that many highly sensitive, empathic people can be blown away by even small amounts of medication, and they may require a fraction of what's usually recommended. This is where I differ from mainstream physicians. Why? Personal experience. When I have to take Tylenol, a quarter of a tablet suffices. Over the years, doctors have adamantly tried to prescribe larger doses of medications than my body tolerates or needs. They just don't get it. I've learned to insist on simply taking the amounts that feel right. Similarly, when empaths who're depressed come to me, I've successfully treated them with slivers of Prozac. Taking more only overloads their system. A fair question to ask is, how do I know their reaction isn't just a placebo effect? Well, they show the same benefits and lesser side effects than when using standard doses. Also, certain people are quick responders. Medication kicks in far more rapidly than the expected time, which is two to six weeks. I've seen relief happen overnight. If this is you, trust your experience. Work with a health care practitioner who honors your body's intuition about proper dosage and respects your option to reduce the amount or taper off if it feels right. (Always consult your doctor before reducing or discontinuing any medication.)

Alternatives to Traditional Antidepressants

In addition to medications such as Prozac, there are other prospects to consider that can tune up your biology. For mild to moderate depression, I often suggest 5-HTP, a natural precursor to serotonin available in health food stores. It's a gentle way of supplementing serotonin if your system is lacking. Another treatment is St. John's wort, an herb that's been used for centuries for depression and pain. I've seen it help some patients and not others; its potential side effects include increased dizziness, digestive upset, sexual side effects, sensitivity to light, headaches, and impairment of your liver's breakdown of other drugs such as birth control pills or heart medications. Also, a number of my depressed patients have benefited from SAM-e, an amino acid available over the counter that has minimal side effects, which may include nausea and constipation. It's expensive, however, and, from what I've seen, improvement can be subtle. Again, talk with your health care provider before combining these options with traditional medications. Also, realize that even "natural" antidepressants may have side effects.

Coffee as an Antidepressant: Its Pros and Cons

In America, we consume over four hundred million cups of coffee every day. Ever wonder why so many of us make such a lustful beeline for our caffeine? Could it be the oodles of antioxidants it contains? Or that science has revealed its health benefits, including lowered risk of diabetes, Parkinson's disease, gallstones, and colon cancer? I don't think that even these unquestionable virtues are what make coffee the highlight of your day. Then what does? The mood- and energy-enhancing effects of caffeine. Caffeine stimulates the central nervous system and acts as an antidepressant by elevating serotonin and dopamine—it's even been shown in the *Archives of Internal Medicine* to lower suicide rates. Some experience the mood boost more than others. Unknowingly, many people self-medicate depression with caffeine. How to know if you're doing this versus just getting a beneficial pick-me-up? Some tip-offs: you consume more than four caffeinated beverages daily, including teas and diet sodas, or you keep increasing your caffeine intake to feel less depressed, but it's losing its effectiveness. I'm all for making the most of coffee's therapeutic perks to allay low-level depression, but sometimes you may need other approaches when this emotion still persists. To find out if you're self-medicating depression, you can stop your caffeine intake. After a month (most withdrawal symptoms, which include headache and fatigue, will be over by then) notice if you're notably more depressed without caffeine, not always an easy experiment. Should you discover that you are self-medicating, also consider the numerous therapies discussed in this chapter to augment coffee or to replace it. However, mild depressions can respond well to simply drinking up to three cups daily. (Try spacing them out; caffeine remains in the system four to six hours.) More than this increases side effects and raises the chances of tolerance and addiction: you consume greater quantities but don't get the lift. Always consider caffeine's pluses and minuses. Reduce your intake if you have insomnia, heartburn, palpitations, headaches, or nervousness. Moreover, if you're being treated for heart disease, hypertension, gastrointestinal problems, or other chronic illnesses, consult your physician before you ingest caffeine in any form.

The Biological Healing Power of Hope

Whatever treatment for depression you choose, hope amplifies it by fortifying your neurotransmitters. How? Hope actually reprograms your biology and keeps you positive. Being positive increases serotonin and reduces levels of stress hormones. With less stress, you'll feel happier and generally function better. Studies have shown that hope improves the performance of athletes, and that students with great hope of doing well on a test achieve higher scores. Hope is only good for your health. If you've had surgery or a heart attack, hope accelerates recovery; depression retards it. Hope helps you stay mentally fit as you age, whereas depression increases chances of dementia. Your autonomic nervous system, which regulates breathing, circulation, and digestion, is particularly responsive to positivity. Hope acts as a natural stress reducer, relaxing your gut, blood vessels, and bronchioles. Your system is peaceful, not constricted or tense. Plus, science suggests that hope lessens pain by increasing levels of endorphins, the feel-good biochemicals.

In the spirit of hope, I advise practicing the suggestions in the next exercise to improve your emotional state and transform depression. Use them with all the Fifth Transformation's other techniques.

Emotional Action Step

TRAIN YOUR MIND, CHANGE YOUR BIOLOGY

1. *Exercise, don't ruminate!* Rather than staying home with a head full of negative thoughts, get your body moving. There's something magical about just putting one foot in front of the other. Besides sending yourself a message that you're going forward, it increases serotonin and energy, enhances self-image, and improves sleep. Start with gentle walking. Don't think you're going too slow or doing too little. Even ten minutes daily gets your body used to the idea that it's coming alive again. When you're ready, you can walk longer or expand your exercise routine.

2. *Get sufficient sunlight.* Evolutionarily speaking, we weren't designed for a sedentary, indoor lifestyle. Don't hole up in your office or home. Exposure to sunlight elevates your mood by stimulating your brain to produce serotonin. It also helps relieve seasonal affective disorder (SAD), depression that occurs during

the fall and winter months. Aside from natural sunlight, photo-
therapy can also treat SAD. It involves sitting across from a
special box that emits full-spectrum light for forty-five minutes
each day. If you're prone to depression, remember to maximize
the natural antidepressant effect of sunlight.

3. *Laughter is good medicine.* Laughter is emotional freedom. It raises
   your spirits, increases levels of endorphins, relieves pressure, and
   reverses learned seriousness. Researchers have found that after
   people viewed funny videos they were significantly more hopeful
   and less depressed than those who didn't watch them. Humor
   seems to compete with negative thoughts by inserting positive
   ones. Try to surround yourself with humorous, upbeat people.
   Also, watch hilarious movies, listen to comedy routines, or read
   books that make you smile. Laughter will take the bite out of
   depression.

When you're feeling low, now you know what steps to take to gal-
vanize your biology with hope. I have a friend, a nanotechnologist,
who has the instruments in his lab to track the gossamer movements
of atoms; he can actually see and hear them. If I'm depressed, I like to
remember what he has observed: that each cell has a song. It makes
me happy that such minute particles in us are serenading life at all
times. If I'm dejectedly slogging along, to imagine the music of our
being inspires me to do what's necessary to rise from the muck. It's
enormously empowering when you can intervene to reverse a physical turn toward depression. Often, even a little tweak here or there
makes a big difference to your mood.

UNCOVER THE SPIRITUAL MEANING OF
DEPRESSION AND HOPE

According to Greek mythology, Pandora, the first woman on earth, suc-
cumbed to temptation by opening a forbidden container. An onslaught

of emotional curses were unleashed into the world—depression, envy, revenge, fear. She struggled to close the lid, but by then the entire contents had escaped except for one blessing: hope, our ability to see beyond darkness to a place of freedom.

In Energy Psychiatry, I help patients realize that from a spiritual perspective, there is more to their depression than they think, and that hope comes from connecting to something larger. Certainly, it's the pits to be depressed. Your poor worn-out self says, "I'm miserable. I hate this. There's nothing to be hopeful about." I hear you. However, this isn't depression's whole story. Keep searching for this emotion's deeper purpose, which may seem elusive until you construe it in spiritual terms. What is being asked of you? To access dimensions of love and hope more powerful than depression. This emotion's rigorous teaching is to make such mood-elevating leaps attainable in everyday life.

Mainstream medical thinking has a limited capacity to address such apparently impossible realities as hopelessness and suicide. My outlook goes further: we urgently need a different take on utter despondence to make sense of what can never make sense to our linear minds. As torturous as some feeling states can be, as self-destructive as some acts are, a realm exists beyond the material that lets us see their larger context.

Depression as a Spiritual Transformation

Transforming depression is sacred work. My blood runs cold when I hear of people entering conventional psychotherapy for this emotion without a peep of spirituality mentioned as part of healing. Why is this such a damaging form of neglect? You deserve to have an illuminated appreciation of depression to justly dignify it. Otherwise you'll lack appropriate awe for what you're going through. I believe, as do many spiritual traditions, that depression is the dark night of the soul, a term used by mystic priest Saint John of the Cross, describing his journey through despair to fuller holiness. Seeing depression this way reframes it. *The "dark night" speaks to your soul's development. It's not just about a biochemical imbalance or a neglectful mother, though these may be the provokers. It's a releasing of your ego's grasp on the psyche, permitting positive change that can prompt redefinition of the self.* Since the period is profoundly unsettling, it's commonly perceived as "darkness." Mystics consider the dark night of depression not as a negative but as a test of faith, an occasion for transformation.

The dark night varies in intensity for each of us. It may last weeks or longer. Sometimes your depression may be all-encompassing, or it can be less extreme. Whatever your experience of the dark night, it's invaluable to find a therapist or wise guide familiar with the divine nature of this terrain (see the Resources section). Then you won't be at the mercy of some well-meaning but spiritually clueless practitioner who pathologizes your experience according to a dogmatic medical model. I stick close to my patients who're undergoing the dark night. I want to lend a supportive, dependable voice. I want them to know they're not alone, to show that depression leads to awakening. When patients say, "I'm questioning everything. I don't know what's important anymore," I say, "Yes, to reevaluate is often excruciating, but it's healthy." When they say, "I feel too disconnected to meditate," I say, "Don't try to force yourself. You'll get back to it again. To feel separate and adrift is a phase of depression." My patient Pat lost her husband, the love of her life, when he suffered a fatal heart attack while being mugged. She asked me, "What kind of God would let this happen? How can I ever believe in one again?" I honored her anguish as it was. I responded, "Of course you can't. There's no need to." Trying to make a case otherwise in the initial aftermath of such seemingly senseless, inconceivable loss would've been misguided and disrespectful.

I'm no Pollyanna, but what I've learned about the dark night is that it can organically incubate something wondrously unexpected—and good—if you have the proper support. The emphatic "I can'ts" often evolve into surprising ways of viewing yourself and spirit even when everything in you argues against such possibility. After a year of grueling therapy, Pat bravely confronted her grief and depression, an ongoing pursuit. Having survived the very worst, she was now in a different place. Though she no longer defines God as a force outside herself, or indeed even uses the word, Pat now volunteers helping victims of violent crimes. Giving back is how she's redefined spirituality in this stage of our work together. Just as Pat sought my help to emerge from torment, not embittered but more whole, it's imperative not to pass through the dark night alone. I wouldn't wish that isolation on anyone. The danger of not reaching out is that you may stay painfully lost for a long time. During depression, you've got to look into eyes you trust. You've got to receive consistent, reliable counsel to keep moving ahead. Whenever I've been depressed, you'd better believe I've sought a spiritually canny guide to be there for me.

Oddly, the path to emotional freedom can sometimes wind in directions that may seem like the wrong way. I cherish Buddhist nun Pema Chödrön's position on the dark night: "In the process of discovering our true nature, the journey goes down, not up, as if the mountain pointed toward the earth instead of the sky. We move down and down and down, and with us move millions of others, our companions in awakening. . . . Right there we discover a love that will not die." During depression, let this expanded awareness sanctify your passage and bring hope. Hope that depression will end. Hope that you'll ascend from the depths brighter, more openhearted. Hope that you'll gain deeper compassion for yourself and others.

Suicide: A Perspective Beyond Time and Space

The dark night of all dark nights is the hopelessness of wanting to die. In this state, you can see no promised land beyond depression.

Over the years, several of my patients have attempted suicide. One did die: a heavy-metal rocker with a sapphire-blue Mohawk and a sensitive soul. But superstardom could never allay his depression or the persistent back pain for which none of the many specialists he consulted could locate a medical cause. Legions of fans revered him, but he didn't revere himself. He felt happy and pain-free only onstage, immersed in his music and adulation. When he killed himself, we hadn't met for many months, but I was deeply saddened. I'd been his safe place for two years; we'd been very close. I'd done everything I could think of to help him, but he was on a runaway course. Plus, he was surrounded by shark-like managers who urged him to go on tour despite his precarious condition. Intellectually, I realized all this, but still I lamented my inability to save his life. I'll always miss him. I'll always recall those days I'd visited him after a previous suicide attempt. He was on a locked psychiatric ward along with others who were psychotic and homicidal. To me, it's a crime to put someone who's depressed in with that mix. I wish I could've sent him to a peaceful retreat with sunlit porches and hammocks to dream on. But our mental health system isn't organized like that. All those needing intensive care go to the same hellish ward in traditional hospitals. So I saw him there until he was no longer suicidal. Against my advice, he went back on the road too soon. I was greatly afraid for him. Then, four months later, I got the call: he was found dead in his London hotel room after slashing his wrists.

Most suicides are preventable with skilled interventions. I know people—including those on a spiritual path—who at dark times have considered taking their lives. (Suicide is the eleventh leading cause of death among Americans.) If you've had these thoughts, they're nothing to be ashamed of. But I also know that suicide isn't the answer. Freedom comes when you persist in searching for the light until it's visible again.

In service to our growth, life asks an extraordinary amount of us. That used to anger me. Some situations seemed unendurable. Watching my ebullient, talented mother waste away from cancer, struggling to find strength to be there for her without disintegrating, I'd inwardly protest, "I can't do it. I don't have it in me." But I did—and had to see that. So must you. Try to keep reaching beyond pain toward a greater power within. My spiritual teacher says, "Heaven is not a dead-end road." With hope and the proper support, you will find it.

For years I believed suicide was an option we had the right to choose if things got rotten enough. I no longer feel this way except, possibly, with terminally ill patients in constant physical agony. From deepening my intuition, I came to realize that holding on to suicide as an out separated me from the essence of living. A commitment to staying in my body through it all was mandatory for being fully alive. Thus, to be more present, I've vowed to follow the wisdom of whatever life brings.

Weigh this critical point: leaving your body doesn't make emotional

challenges disappear because the soul's work continues. What I intuitively sense about its destinations is that who you are here is who
you'll be there too, albeit without the physical form you're accustomed to identifying with. I don't mean this punitively. I'm simply
saying you'll eventually have to face your demons. Personally, I'd
rather do it now than drag out the ordeal. I prefer to go on to other
things. For those who believe in past lives, facing the self is unavoidable. Whether now or in distant eons, you must do it. This is good.
This is purifying.

I've had an ex-boyfriend and some acquaintances commit suicide
when depression became unbearable—two by overdosing, one with a
gun. Though I wasn't in regular contact with these people at the time
they took their lives, I was notified by mutual friends the day each suicide happened. While I was shaken by these losses and the terrible
desperation that must have occasioned them, I was also curious about
where these people had gone and their subsequent state of being. So I
tuned in, simultaneously inquisitive and anticipatorily weary about
the kinds of pain I'd encounter. What did I find? None of them was in
a place I'd ever want to be, and each felt utterly lost. Always there was
severe confusion, a swirling-through-limbo vertigo that made me nau-
seated. Where they were at felt like the alarming, abrupt plummeting
of an airplane during turbulence—but cube that by the speed of light
and picture if it didn't let up. Still, despite the dire straits they were all
clearly in, I also intuited a beneficent force surrounding them, though
it didn't seem as if they recognized it. They felt totally alone. When
tuning in to the lawyer who'd shot herself in the head, I found her disorientation so jolting I could barely stay with it. This panicked woman
had had no idea where she was. Dizzying, disjointed memories of her
life were bombarding her at such speed that *overwhelmed* didn't begin
to describe her condition. I suspect it took a while to find her bearings
and proceed to a calmer place. From what I could intuit, the violence
of her suicide made the transition even more chaotic. Once I got the
gist of her experience, I wanted out of that vision so I didn't risk absorbing such angst.

I share my perceptions with you to offer what I sensed about suicide. As you can see, it may not be a way out of anything, as many depression sufferers envision. Though the pain in question may be temporarily put on the back burner, suicide seems to create another set of problems and a tumultuous journey. Even so, I'm certain that the soul eventually finds clarity and gets all the chances it needs to master emotional obstacles.

My duty as physician and healer is to talk people out of suicide. I'm fortunate to have had many successes: patients, friends, even a young man who was about to throw himself overboard on a "New Age" Caribbean cruise on which I was a speaker. It was a harrowing situation. With one leg dangling over the railing, he kept wailing, "I'm nothing inside. I'm worthless. I want to die." For what seemed like an eternity, I kept talking him down, gently repeating, "No one is nothing inside. I understand you feel terrible. But we'll get you help. You'll find yourself again. Please take my hand." You can imagine our collective sigh of relief when he finally reached out to me. Then a group of us stayed with him until he was helicoptered to a mainland hospital for treatment. People on board asked how I was able to get through to him. To begin with, my emergency room training has brought me into contact with all kinds of human disaster; it's not alien to me. Also, I can be effective with potential suicides because I absolutely know there's hope for everyone and that depression is a distortion. It swallows the light, making misery seem like the only truth. But it is not. You must remember that. If ever suicide starts looking good, stop, regroup, and fight to find hope. Reach out for help. Don't be seduced by the voice of despair or misconstrue it as reality.

In the next exercise, I'm presenting prayer as a treasured aid for traversing the dark night, especially if hope is waning. What is prayer? It's an intuitive reaching out to something larger than yourself to rekindle your forgotten power. You can't just pray with your intellect. You must open to the tenderness of being touched, of sorrow being soothed; these heart openings catalyze hope. Prayer works whether you believe in God, in angels, or that your grandfather is watching over you. (Mine is.) Whomever you pray to, let yourself be infused with that unconditional love.

Emotional Action Step

FIND HOPE THROUGH PRAYER

Take a breath. Close your eyes. Know that there's another world
the linear mind cannot comprehend. With sincerity, say a prayer
such as "Please remove my depression so I can feel happy again."
Then stay open to the sense that your burdens are lightening.
Praying with humility, not insisting on results but remaining
receptive, makes you exquisitely vulnerable to its benefits.

I recommend trying other forms of prayer too. Sometimes
reading poetry or hearing music is a prayer for me. I can't listen to
Leonard Cohen's "If It Be Your Will" without becoming uplifted.
I always weep when I hear his gravelly, lonesome baritone begin,
"If it be your will let a voice be true / From this broken place let
me sing to you." When I pray, I want to weep with abandon. This
dissolves the barrier that keeps me from my tenderness, my faith.
Similarly, expose yourself to whatever kinds of art instill hope
and move you past depression.

If you're depressed, don't consider this an unspiritual place to be.
Philosopher Martin Buber writes about "holy despair," viewing depression as a route to wholeness. Prayer is a friend that can ease your way
through the thorns and rubble. From Judaism to Buddhism, numerous
mystical traditions have recognized the holy role of arduous feeling
states. We must too. My passion is to reinstate this hopeful wisdom into
mainstream mental health, to consecrate all our emotional pilgrimages.

EXPERIENCE THE ENERGETIC POWER
OF DEPRESSION AND HOPE

I'm continually drawn to study the energy of depression and hope in
patients and in myself. What I've observed is that depression is a veer-
ing of vectors away from the light. It dims our spark, enthusiasm, and

intuition. Flow is disrupted; even simple tasks can feel like an effort. In contrast, hope's energy is brightening, a rekindling of possibilities and flow's momentum.

I'm grateful that my own feelings of depression have greatly diminished over the years; if they arise, they rarely linger. What used to trigger them were power struggles with my mother, which continued through my thirties. By then, I'd gotten stronger through meditation, therapy, and the techniques I'll describe—and she'd become more accepting because she wanted our relationship to work. This was a vast improvement in how we communicated. Before, when we'd fight—and we had some knock-down drag-outs—I'd vehemently defend my identity if she'd pressure me "for my own good" to be different than I was. "Why not wear elegant clothes to show off your looks? Why date men twice your age? Can't you be more social?" I'd rebel, assert the reasons for my choices, proclaim, "You have no right to interfere!" Truth was, however, I cared way too much about the opinions of this woman who had so tenderly sung me to sleep with lullabies as a child. I wanted Mother's approval but couldn't betray myself. These battles left us both emotionally bloodied with festering wounds. In me, this manifested as depression. For days, sometimes weeks afterward, I suffered these energetic consequences: my vibrance eroded, a leadenness descended—even my eyelashes felt heavy. In the pit of my solar plexus, the emotional energy center, I had a hopeless "why try?" feeling about Mother. This spilled over into the rest of my life. I felt brittle, sluggish; sometimes it was even hard to recall people's names. Instead of holding my center point, I'd drift into the energetic fog of depression. Learning to maintain emotional balance, regardless of people's opinions about me, has been an essential and gratifying accomplishment.

To be able to access hope quickly, I'd like you to become familiar with sensing what its energy feels like compared to depression. Then you'll know specific qualities to focus on if darkness comes.

HOW THE ENERGY OF DEPRESSION CAN FEEL

- Flat, apathetic, disconnected from people and yourself
- As if you're moving through molasses

- Like a sinking in the pit of your stomach

- Tight; you take shallow breaths, sigh frequently to inhale more oxygen

- Heavy, making you cower and slump

HOW THE ENERGY OF HOPE CAN FEEL

- Like a quickening, a perking up

- As if a veil has parted; you can see, hear, taste, and smell better

- Like you're opening your arms to a bouquet

- Comforting; melancholy dissipates

- Like you're physically lighter; you sit more upright, breathe easier

Sensing energy takes you beyond mental assumptions about depression, revealing its subtler manifestations in your body. As I've seen with patients, recognizing energetic warnings that precede depression gives you a chance to divert it. The form these take can vary. Identify your unique cues and act on them. Swift intervention prevents depression from gaining momentum.

Energy work often goes where the mind can't by speaking to difficult emotions more convincingly than logic. There are times when you're unable to talk yourself out of depression, despite valiant efforts at staying positive. "My life is too good for me to feel so miserable" might be logically true but might not do a dang to budge depression. If logic doesn't console, energy work touches the deepest parts of you. The principle is this: the way to transform depression is to ignite the energy of hope, similar to lighting a stove's pilot; once this is done, your body senses the flame, and genuine optimism will follow. Being able to feel hope, even a little, inspires it to grow. Realize that a change in energy can precede a change in attitude. To start this process, I recommend the following strategy. First, select the energetic quality of hope that most resonates for you (refer to those I've listed above or others you've found). Then visualize it for a few minutes several times a day for a week or longer. Let's say you relate to hope as opening your arms to a bouquet. Picture yourself doing this. How does holding the bouquet feel? What kinds of flowers are in it? What are their colors? Their scents? These images and sensations can energetically catalyze hope, which in turn allows you to think more positively.

Are Depression and Hope Contagious? How to Stop Absorbing Other People's Negative Moods

Since depression and hope are both energies, you can potentially "catch" them from people without realizing it. If you're an empath, it's vital to know how to avoid taking on an individual's depression or the free-floating kind in crowds. Another twist is that depression can turn people who aren't normally empaths into emotional sponges by wearing down their defenses. Suddenly they become hyperattuned to others, especially those with similar pain. That's how empathy works; we zero in on hot-button issues that are unresolved in ourselves. From an energetic standpoint, depression can originate from several sources. What you're feeling may be your own; it may be someone else's; or it may be a combination. I'll explain how to tell the difference and strategically bolster hope so you don't shoulder depression that doesn't belong to you.

Take my patient Nell, a streetwise "broad" with a contrarian streak, but more empathic than you'd ever guess. For years, she'd fought depression. In the 1970s, as a New York cop, she worked in "war zones with drug lords, ghetto violence, and organized crime day in and day out, a domestic Viet Nam." With a defiant growl she said, "The Mafia once put a hit out on me, but I'm still here." (I'm deleting her avalanche of expletives about these people.) You couldn't help but admire her attitude: "Nobody's going to get me." It would be beneficial in overcoming depression, too. I saw the warrior in Nell's eyes, but also the pain that comes from bearing long-term darkness. Despite having no shortage of bravado, Nell was a self-described "pain absorber." She'd get terribly depressed by the incessant physical and emotional brutality of the streets—a reaction she faulted as "spineless" and didn't risk confiding to her fellow officers. Nell told me, "Some nights I'd just go home weeping," particularly after child abuse cases. She recognized there was reason to be sad, but her agony was incited by another source. Nell herself had been a victim of child abuse, which made her more vulnerable to absorbing such hurt. Once, as a sick joke, her father and his drunken buddies threw her, at four years old, into a pool before she could swim. They howled with laughter as she flailed her arms, gasping for air. Her father did pull her out, but the terror of that experience and others he perpetrated made sensitive Nell a prime candidate for depression.

Five years ago, for self-preservation, Nell left the police force to run a small security business. This was a wise move, sparing her the constant desperation she'd witnessed as a cop. Things were better, but still she was prone to depression. In therapy, we explored various aspects of this emotion, but discovering she was an empath and how to protect her energy was of the greatest significance. It had never crossed Nell's mind that she could absorb depression from others. Realizing this, she was able to make changes. Nell's responses weren't about being "spineless." Now she had options for coping with her sensitivity without taking on the suffering around her. Enlisting the following strategies (along with those in Chapter 5 to prevent emotional drain), she was able to stay more centered, deflect negativity, and surround herself with hopeful people and situations. You can too.

Emotional Action Step

ATTRACT HOPE, RELEASE DEPRESSION

To detach from depression:

- *First, ask yourself: "Is the feeling mine or someone else's?"* It could be both. If the depression is yours, gently confront what's causing it on your own or with professional help. If not, try to pinpoint the obvious generator. For instance, if you've just watched a comedy, yet you came home from the movie theater feeling blue, you may have incorporated the depression of the people sitting beside you; in close proximity, energy fields overlap. The same is true with going to a mall or packed concert.

- *When possible, distance yourself from the suspected source.* Move at least twenty feet away; see if you feel relief. Don't err on the side of not wanting to offend strangers. In a public place, don't hesitate to change seats if you feel a sense of depression imposing on you.

- *For a few minutes, center yourself by concentrating on your breath.* This connects you to your essence. Keep exhaling depression and inhaling calm; practice the grounding and breathing meditations you've already learned. Visualize depression as a gray fog lifting from your body, and hope as golden light entering. This can yield quick results.

- *Shift the energy.* Depression frequently lodges in your emotional center at the solar plexus. Place your palm on your solar plexus as you keep sending loving-kindness to that area to flush depression out. For long-standing depression, use this method daily to strengthen this center. It's comforting and builds a sense of safety and optimism.

- *Look for hopeful people and situations.* Call a friend who sees the good in others. Spend time with a colleague who affirms the bright side of things. Listen to hopeful people. Hear the faith they have in themselves and others. Also relish hopeful words, songs, and art forms. Hope is contagious; it will lift your mood.

The Power of Tears

The energy of depression is begging for release. Along with the above suggestions, I strongly recommend doing some crying. It's the body's way of purging stress and unhappiness—yours or what you've assimilated from another. Crying makes you feel better, even when a problem persists. Like the ocean, tears are salt water. Protectively they lubricate your eyes, remove irritants, reduce stress hormones, and contain antibodies that fight pathogenic microbes. You don't want to hold tears back. Patients sometimes say, "Please excuse me for crying. I was trying hard not to." My heart breaks when I hear this. I know where that sentiment comes from: parents who were uncomfortable around tears, a society that tells us we're weak for crying. I implore you to get rid of these false conceptions. It is good to cry. It is healthy to cry. This helps resolve depression. When a friend apologized for curling up in the fetal position on my floor, weeping, depressed over a failing romance, I told her, "Your tears blessed my floor. There is nothing to apologize for." I've been this enthusiastic about crying for years. In fact, during my psychiatric residency when supervisors and I watched videos of me with patients, they'd point out that I'd smile when a patient cried. "That's inappropriate," they'd say. I disagreed then; still do. I wasn't smiling because my patients were depressed. I was smiling because they were courageously healing depression with tears. I was happy for their breakthrough. In my life, too, I love to cry. I cry whenever I can. I wish I could cry more. Thank God our bodies have this capacity. I hope you too can relish the experience. Let your tears flow to purify depression and negativity.

Releasing the energy of depression makes room for hope. Igniting hope releases depression. Practicing each refreshes your system instead of letting despair accumulate. I still recall what a prison inmate once told me: "I can really relate to the importance of transforming energy. Being where I am, one must make the best out of nothing every day not to give up. Hope's the only way to get by." We can all learn from him. Hope sustains. Free and openhearted, we can transform depression.

MAP THE PSYCHOLOGY OF DEPRESSION AND HOPE

Want a guaranteed strategy to loosen depression's hold? Become aware of your psychological risk factors so you can counteract them. The *American Journal of Psychiatry* reports the top instigators are early sexual or emotional abuse, poor formative relationships with parents, family discord, financial stress, and lack of social support. Also, major transitions can set off depression: moving, switching jobs, retiring, divorce, becoming a new parent, caring for an ailing parent. These changes of routine, often fraught with fear and uncertainty, can jar your emotional comfort level by activating self-doubt. Knowing your risk factors highlights areas in need of healing and cautions you to take special care during stressful times.

Working with patients to discover the psychological origins of depression is compelling to me because of the sure prospect of finding light. I know it's there, though my patients may have to take that on faith. When we start our work together, I feel I'm witnessing a great ocean liner about to leave port on its maiden voyage. Initially, where we're headed is often a big unknown, but only temporarily. Together, we investigate the whys of depression from birth onward and identify unconscious motives. This psychodynamically oriented approach lets us track depression's beginnings and clear its stubborn echoes. As usual, I use intuition to ascertain the timing of what issues to address. If, say, parental abandonment predisposes someone to depression, I wait until my patient has built up enough emotional resources to begin the complex, difficult inquiry into what it feels like to be nobody's child, a frequent perception in such cases. I always prefer going slow in therapy, allowing us to secure the bonds of our relationship. In addition, I'll use cognitive behavioral methods to help patients develop specific action-oriented goals to overcome depression. For instance, I treated a socially isolated insurance saleswoman who worked at home and said her only company was a cricket. But she loved reading and, at my suggestion, joined a weekly book club, a first step toward more human connection. Learning to respond healthily to what predictably prolongs depression instills hope that things can be different.

Psychiatrist Viktor Frankl, one of my heroes, has profoundly shaped my thinking about hope and overcoming even the most savage precipitants of depression. Frankl speaks of our freedom to transcend suffering and find purpose, regardless of how negative our conditions. In *Man's Search for Meaning,* he portrays the years he spent as a prisoner in Auschwitz.

> *Even the helpless victim of a hopeless situation, facing a fate he cannot change, may rise above himself, and by doing so change himself. . . . The salvation of man is through love and in love.*

In our lives, we can use Frankl's principles to reconceptualize depression as a form of potential strengthening and expansion. *Sometimes pain is unavoidable, but your response is what determines how much you suffer.* Having faith in yourself and the power of goodness are attitudes that bring hope to the most unredeemable circumstances. Suffering can quicken your capacity to awaken, and so to heal. Remember this as you delve into what's precipitated depression in your history.

To be free, it's crucial to locate depression's origins because these affect your relationships, ability to communicate, and quality of happiness now. Even if you've blocked out or prefer to forget a parent's vicious temper or neglect, such traumas can psychologically position you to be depressed. Denying them can make you the inadvertent auteur of your own misery by imprisoning you in the past. It's hard to be hopeful if this happens. I know these memories are difficult—and I emphasize once again that I'm not suggesting you fixate on your childhood. Still, you can't afford to have such a monkey on your back, particularly one you can't see. The emotional cost is that you're chronically depressed but don't know why.

Let me tell you about Professor Angel, so nicknamed by his fourth-grade students. This big bear of a man with his signature red bow tie was beloved by them, and also, as far as I could tell, by everyone else in his life, especially his wife of three decades. He was the kind of person who passed on every kiss to others that he promised to give. Still, he came to me after many months of a low drone of depression, perplexed by growing apathy, grumpiness, and lack of joy. Both he and his wife agreed this wasn't like him. I'm not easily charmed, but Professor Angel charmed me. He was humble, caring, and gracious, someone who seemed always to have been grateful for the bounty of small things.

So where was his depression coming from? During our first session, he recounted a recurring, deeply disturbing nightmare: "I keep dreaming of a blind owl without eyes." Hearing this, my body was all chills. Intuitively, I knew this numinous image would get to the root of his depression's psychology. How articulate dreams are—a wise creature who couldn't see was a perfect image for Professor Angel's puzzlement about his despondence. I asked, "What aren't you seeing?" In an apparent non sequitur, he immediately began describing his mother. Three months before, at eighty-five, she'd entered a nursing home following a partial stroke. Every afternoon after school, he'd visit her. Observing his ordinarily strong-as-a-horse mother in such a physically vulnerable state shook him to his core. Worse, she was just plain mean to him. She'd criticize and complain; nothing he did was right. She scolded him for bringing chicken soup instead of tomato, for dandruff on his suit, for not coming earlier. Professor Angel said, resigned, "It's okay. I'm used to it. Mother always treats me like this. She doesn't know better." Okay? I didn't think so. This was going to need attending to. Throughout his childhood, the more his mother disparaged him, the more loving he'd become. To sidestep her ire, he avoided conflict by becoming too kind, though he was by nature a considerate person. Any negative feelings he had about such shabby treatment were submerged. I wholeheartedly believe in being good to one's mother, but we'd found an emotional pattern clearly linked to his depression.

For Professor Angel, the stress of witnessing his mother's deterioration stirred feelings toward her he didn't know he had. Anger at being unjustly criticized. Shame that he didn't speak up. Fear of losing her. Sadness for the maternal nurturing he never had. Cumulatively, these emotions underlay the onset of Professor Angel's depression, which coincided with his mother's illness. Behaving too nicely when negative feelings lurk within squelches emotional freedom. Our sessions provided an outlet for him to express at his own pace what he'd previously kept to himself, especially anger—directed at her or anything else, past and present. This was a practical cathartic skill he'd never developed. With this emotional release, he gradually started feeling better. He just needed to define and address his feelings in a balanced way. Recently, he dreamed he'd been lost in a dense forest but then found a path out that led to a pristine clearing—an indication of his newly found direction. Though he chose not to confront his mother and remained as tolerant a son as ever, he felt more honest about his own emotions and at peace with their relationship.

The next exercise describes how to transform psychological patterns enabling your depression by taking an inventory. As you do this, also note relevant dreams that inform the process. Here's how to structure the inventory. Using a journal or notebook, divide a blank page into three columns. In the first column, list up to five sources you believe have contributed to your depression. That will be more than enough to start with. Later you can add to the list, but you don't want to get overloaded as you begin the exercise. In the second column, list a dead-end emotional pattern you've developed as a response. In the third column, list a new, positive behavior you can practice to replace the unproductive pattern. (Merely knowing your depression's origins won't free you unless you alter your response to them.) You can do this inventory on your own or work on it with your therapist. What you learn from it can augment psychotherapy or other approaches to depression you've chosen. Use the following sample's format.

Emotional Action Step

TAKE THIS INVENTORY TO LIFT DEPRESSION

Source of Depression	Old Dead-end Pattern	New Hopeful Behavior
1. Hypercritical parents	I emphasize the negative in myself	I'll affirm my attributes
2. A rageaholic mate	I withdraw emotionally	I'll begin healthy limit setting
3. Financial stress	I catastrophize the future	I'll focus on making positive changes in the Now
4. Romantic betrayal	I avoid intimate relationships	I'll take baby steps toward trusting a friend
5. Verbal or physical abuse	I'm afraid to express my needs	I'll practice speaking up with safe, supportive people

Completing this inventory lets you clarify what's depressing and squashing your spirit. Hope comes from functioning in more expansive ways. Begin by focusing on one emotional pattern you've identified. Then, over the next few months, practice substituting it with a freeing behavior. When you've achieved a level of success you're comfortable with, you can begin shifting another pattern. No rush. Give each one as much time as you need to make progress. Developing new behaviors reconditions your psychological response to depression.

HEALING LOSS: THE DIFFERENCE BETWEEN GRIEF AND DEPRESSION

Depression is an emotion to be consciously transformed; grief is a reaction to loss that can transform you. Loss comes in many forms: the death of a loved one, the death of a pet, the loss of a job, the end of a relationship. It's a stripping away of a potent connection, leaving an aching emptiness inside. Despite grief's agony, try to let it flow rather than attempting to change it or get it over with. Unlike depression's emotional inertia, grief has an inherent healing trajectory that seeks to resolve itself. Choking grief off inhibits this forward motion and leads to depression. As I can attest, if we don't shut down, grief can ultimately open the heart.

On January 24, 1982, I learned that my uncle Sidney had been murdered. A stoned teenage punk robbed him, then shot him point-blank in the head, right after Sidney handed over the money in his business's cash register. For over thirty years, Sidney and his brother Jerry had run I. Orloff and Sons Furniture. It was started in 1920 by my grandfather in South Philadelphia, an area that had disintegrated into a crime-infested ghetto. Uncle Sidney was a Humphrey Bogart look-alike who got into the role, calling his kids, wife, and me "schweet-heart." He was a modest, kind man. Everyone in the neighborhood adored him. When I moved to Philadelphia for medical school, Sidney helped me furnish my tiny one-room brownstone apartment overlooking the art museum. I remember watching him proudly lug a brand-new plaid couch from his store up five flights of stairs, an act of utter devotion. Uncle Sidney's caring eased my waves of homesickness for California. He'd sometimes just look at me and beam, saying, "My niece, the doctor!" When I later finished medical school at USC, he wrote me, "Your graduation announcement holds a place of honor on my den table. What a pleasure to renew our lives when you arrived with your companion Pipe [my dog] in Philadelphia. Please thank your mother and my brother for raising such a precious human being." Three years later, my father, pale as I'd never seen him, broke the news: "Sidney has been murdered." In the next moments of numbing silence, I staggered with disbelief. How could this be? Dear Sidney, who'd never wished anyone harm. Why would a complete stranger want to kill him?

My grief at the death of my uncle set off a torrent of feelings in me with a momentum of their own. Shock. Rage. Anxiety. Sadness. Losing someone who loved me so much, and whom I loved so deeply, was unthinkable. It took a while for this brutal reality to sink in. I yearned to talk to Uncle Sidney, hug him, eat dinner at his house. But none of these everyday intimacies that you think will always be there was possible anymore. Even now, over twenty years later, though I've accepted Sidney's death, I still miss him. Some grief you never fully get over. To this day, pangs of grief continue to resonate through me, not as a burden, but as a widening portal into the compassion of what enduring love means.

In psychiatrist Elisabeth Kübler-Ross's iconic book *On Death and Dying,* she presents common stages of grief. Denial: "This can't be happening!" Anger: "I'm furious about the loss or at everything." Bargaining: "I promise I'll be a better person if only you bring him back." Depression: "I don't care anymore. Life is too unfair. Why try at all?" Acceptance: "I'm coming to terms with what-is. I'm devastated but I can continue to keep loving." We each have our own time frame with these stages. Over the year following Sidney's murder, I experienced every one. Sometimes I wanted to grieve alone. Sometimes I wanted to talk about it. Always I kept looking to the night sky for answers, as I have since childhood. Its spacious splendor offered consolation by embracing me in a oneness that reunites all love and lovers. The stars had Sidney in them: I felt them shimmering through me, bringing niece and uncle into communion again. I'm thankful for the support of my family, friends, therapist, and the heavens that cradled me through this anguished period.

Depression can be a healthy stage of grieving, but people can get stuck there. What complicates grief is when it taps into early traumas or losses that contributed to depression, such as a chronically ill parent, a volatile divorce, or the death of a close relative or friend. Your current grief is compounded by depressions that preceded it. One tip-off that this is happening is that grief becomes mired in depression rather than evolving or resolving. Another tip-off is that old traumatic memories intrude on the present; you can't get them out of your mind. In such cases, it's imperative to obtain psychological assistance so you don't become lost in the limbo of these feelings. Beyond this, stay aware of ingrained, depression-related negative beliefs that may get reactivated by the current loss. For instance, my brave cousin candidly said about an initial phase of his mourning, "My dad's death reinforced the fatalistic views I used to have, how you can try and try but something can always be ripped away from you. I stayed angry and depressed a long time until I was ready to open my heart again and be grateful for each day." I know how easy it is to become cynical or hopeless, particularly after the tragic loss of an innocent. But emotional freedom necessitates fighting not to give up. When you lose irreplaceable relationships, there will be gaping holes in your life. True, some things may never be the same. However, your future holds the promise for other rich bonds with other amazing people. Your dear ones who've gone don't want you to stop loving. During grief, if old beliefs associated with depression surface, be kind to yourself, but seek the help you need to combat hopelessness.

In many patients and friends, I've seen grief catalyze an intuitive opening. Coping with death, in particular, tunes you in to instinctual knowledge organically tied to the passage. Even if you've never considered the possibility of an afterlife before now, that question may become eminently relevant. Loss stimulates a part of you that may long to know. When grieving, notice any intuitions that lend insight. Pay special attention to dreams. After the passing of loved ones, it's been commonly reported that they appear in dreams to assure us they're all right. They know how much we worry. What's striking is that the departed look younger, healthier, happier, no longer sick or in pain. Recently, I had one such dream following the death of Jim, the psychiatrist I described in Chapter 1 who'd been my savior as a teenager. He'd been suffering from cancer for months, which finally claimed him. I was moved that his wife invited me to the memorial service. Afterward, I dreamed:

> *I'm in Jim's home with his family. Jim is there too, but I'm the only one who can see him. He looks like himself, not at all a haunting specter. I ask: "Jim, are you dead?" He just smiles and says, "I don't really see it that way!"*

I awoke smiling too. Dreams about death are often conveyed with the lightness of cosmic humor to allay our worries. Intuitively, they enable us to see that despite death's physical finality, the spirit endures. Knowing this is enormously therapeutic when dealing with grief and in continuing a meaningful life. It may not console the part of you that needs a hug from those you've lost, but it's feedback that they're fine. We all die with our music in us and keep making it as we move on—an incredibly hopeful certainty. Swami Muktananda said, "The only thing you lose when you die is your fear of death." We, the grievers, have it much harder. Still, accepting loss as part of life's cycles eases your struggle with it. Unavoidably, there's one appointment we all must keep. Once we can accept death, our own and others', it puts the true nature of things into perspective, letting us savor every moment of our intimacies now. We can also more appropriately revere those who've passed, without morbidness or trepidation. (In this spirit, some enlightened medical schools instruct students to consider the cadaver they dissected in anatomy class as a "guiding hand" to remember throughout their careers as healers.) Acceptance of loss doesn't mean we like the idea of this sacrifice. But it does impart equanimity about such letting go and a hopefulness about the longevity of love throughout time. Love never dies. It's what animates the light throughout infinity.

When facing loss, try to keep breathing deeply and trust the process as grief transforms itself and you. I picture grieving as riding the tail of a comet on its orbit; this is different from the downward arc of depression's stubborn gravity. Meanwhile, addressing old issues related to depression, as well as listening to intuition, enables you to psychologically work through grief and accept loss more easily.

THE FIFTH TRANSFORMATION offers secrets to enduring happiness by presenting ever-ready tools to overcome depression. Why are these so necessary? Scientific research suggests that we have a biologically determined set point for our emotional range. It's been found, for instance, that both people who win the lottery and those paralyzed in auto accidents feel roughly the same within a year as before these fortunate or tragic events. Their emotional set point wasn't significantly altered. However, Harvard University studies show that mindfulness meditation techniques can tip the emotional set point toward happiness. How? By teaching people to monitor depression or other feelings and detach from recurring triggers that make them spin out of control. Utilizing a similar principle, the Fifth Transformation's methods let you stay centered and clear. The vital issue here is that happiness can't be sustained by anything that happens externally; it comes from within.

There's a part of us untouched by suffering, a witness place that lets us see that we're more than the sum of our thoughts or feelings. Hope comes from knowing that. Once I spoke to an auditorium of thousands of cancer survivors who'd been to hell and back in their healing journey. I'll never forget the outrageously palpable hope that permeated that atmosphere, an experience of higher consciousness that this luminous group shared with me. My spiritual teacher, who emphasizes service, describes hope this way:

H Helping
O Other
P People get
E Enlightened

Realize that hope is enlightening, whether we hold it for others or for ourselves. Enlightenment is the acquiring of wisdom enabling clarity of perception, the height of spiritual attainment. Aim to steadily cultivate hope and the mounting emotional freedom it brings.

One night, feeling depressed, I was driving on the Pacific Coast Highway during a January storm. Just as the rain let up, I made a wrong turn into the parking lot at the Santa Monica pier. As I wound my way toward the exit, around gigantic celestial-white tents housing a photo exhibit, my car was suddenly enveloped in a sea of bubbles. They were everywhere, bouncing on my windshield, countless micro-universes glistening with rainbows. I was rapt with astonishment. Then I saw a homeless man sitting on the curb who seemed to have materialized out of nowhere. I stopped, rolled down my window, and asked, "Where are these all coming from?" Without speaking, grinning like the Cheshire cat in *Alice in Wonderland*, he pointed to a shoe box–sized bubble machine he'd set up a few feet away. I looked around. No one was in sight but the two of us. What enchantment: bubbles, the sound of surf breaking, the pier's Ferris wheel twinkling like jewels in a crown. The man said, "I'm glad the bubbles made you smile." An amazing grace it truly was to come upon something like this when I was so down. I watched an explosion of bubbles floating, spectrum after spectrum of color, lifting skyward, lifting my spirits. Hope was on the rise.

Meditation on Freedom

Embracing Hope

When you're feeling low, devote a few minutes to meditating on these marvels of existence to rally hope. Our galaxy is made up of over a hundred billion stars. The sun and all the stars you can see are moving at a hundred million miles a day. Every moment, the universe keeps expanding, bringing more light everywhere. Miracles abound. Whatever you're going through, there's always hope for a new day.

My wife's jealousy is getting ridiculous. The other day she looked
at my calendar and wanted to know who May was.

—RODNEY DANGERFIELD

11

THE SIXTH TRANSFORMATION:

FACING JEALOUSY AND ENVY,

BUILDING SELF-ESTEEM

DO YOU EVER find yourself green with envy at another's good fortune? Do you sometimes feel you don't measure up or get your due? Are you addicted to comparing yourself to others? Perhaps it's your husband's office assistant who has impossibly long legs. A friend who's got an inheritance while you're working triple overtime. A coworker with a close-knit family when yours is certifiable. Though you may want to be happy for others, sometimes you just can't.

This chapter explores the very human emotions of jealousy and envy, and how to transform them with self-esteem, an authentic sense of worth and clarity about who you are and where you're at. What is jealousy, aptly called in Shakespeare's *Othello* "the green-eyed monster"? It's a type of insecurity, being freaked out that something will be taken from you. For instance, you're jealous of that leggy office assistant, afraid she'll steal your husband, which reflects a lack of confidence in yourself and him. Envy, however, one of the seven "deadly sins," means wanting what the Joneses have that you don't, and idealizing their lives. If you're single, you might envy apparently contentedly married friends in a way that leaves you painfully diminished.

Though you wished them all the happiness in the world at the wedding, you might secretly hope their relationship fails. Envy renders us unable to rejoice in others' successes, though we're never envious of their struggles.

Jealousy and envy may be hard to cop to because they're the antithesis of goodwill and are politically incorrect emotions for "spiritual" people to have. It's difficult to admit—to ourselves or others—that we don't want the best for others, because their attributes, assets, or accomplishments make us feel small, or to acknowledge the depth of our self-doubt about our own value. Nevertheless, to be emotionally free, we must do both. Repeatedly, I've seen how sanitizing or denying these feelings can make my patients passive-aggressively hostile: they unconsciously respond by putting others down to defend against a shaky self-image. Although envy and jealousy can be high-octane motivators that goad you to excel more than merely admiring someone would, plainly put, they're signs of low self-esteem. These emotions become chronic causes of suffering unless we consciously address them.

Envy has been an important teacher for me. I've never felt envious of most people, but for years I'd turn acidic when a peer, "deserving" or not, got on the *New York Times* bestseller list—a milestone I haven't yet achieved. I felt "less than," overlooked, invisible. This horrible burning feeling seared into me. I wanted to salute their achievement but couldn't. In this regard, I can relate to author Gore Vidal's frank admission: "When a friend succeeds, a little part of me dies." I never envied other writers personally, nor was the seduction monetary. What I envied was the recognition accorded their work. All along I was aware enough to realize that envy stemmed from my own feelings of inadequacy; it was an obstacle that stunted my spiritual and emotional growth. Thus, I've been determined to overcome it, and I've made strides using the techniques I'll share with you. Also, I must confess, I'm a pushover. When someone I envy is nice to me or appreciates my writing, suddenly it becomes a lot easier to be happy for them. Though feeling valued does wonders to appease my envy (a dynamic children learn in any school yard sandbox), it doesn't resolve this emotion, which is what I'm after. Now I feel triumphant whenever I'm pleased for another's accolades without feeling slighted. As my self-esteem has grown, my envy has faded, a reward of emotional freedom.

The Sixth Transformation will get you off the hamster wheel of jealousy and envy, of feeling inferior to others, so you're able to be magnanimous. The fact is, you are not inferior. No one is better than you, despite their moments of glory. To help you register these truths, this chapter will analyze the causes and cures for these emotions.

The following quiz will offer insight into how jealous or envious you are. Having these feelings, even a little, can work against you. But try to be honest without judging yourself. We all possess these tendencies to a varying extent at different times. Be brave: identify areas where you need to grow. Using the techniques I'll suggest, you'll soon progress as you solidify self-esteem.

JEALOUSY AND ENVY QUIZ: HOW JEALOUS OR ENVIOUS AM I?

Ask yourself:

- Do I sometimes get satisfaction from putting people down?
- Would I feel relieved if a colleague didn't get promoted, even though I may like him or her?
- Do I often think that others are better off than me?
- Do I resent people who seem to have everything?
- Do I feel diminished by someone's beauty, brains, or accomplishments?
- Am I afraid of people trying to outdo me?
- Am I threatened by my mate's past?
- Am I bent out of shape when my mate looks at someone else?
- Do I see my mate's friends as rivals for my attention or affection?

Answering yes to six or more questions indicates a significant amount of jealousy or envy, three to five yeses a moderate amount, one or two yeses a small amount, zero yeses probably very little (or you're kidding yourself). Be aware that even one affirmative response gives you an opportunity to clear these emotions.

Self-esteem is the solution to jealousy and envy. I'm presenting it as a living, breathing positive force that expands from within, not as some abstract concept or psychobabble from pop culture. Rather, self-esteem is a heart-centered sense of worth you steadily develop, a belief in yourself and your spiritual unfolding. It isn't based on egotism or believing you're better than anyone else. Self-esteem can become dangerous if it makes you smug, superior, or blind to your shortcomings. Bullies often think highly of themselves, as do racists and serial killers.

To endure, self-esteem can't be solely predicated on anything external—that's a house of cards that too easily collapses. Though it naturally reflects pride in, say, your career or children, it's not dependent on these. Self-esteem based only on externals is illusory. As a psychoanalyst friend says, "You're just renting it." Predictably, when many celebrities' careers crash, they feel like nothing without the public's adulation, an agonizing fall from grace I've watched several patients experience. Still, I know how tempting it is to believe that something outside—a great job, meeting Mr. or Ms. Right, winning the lottery—can make you feel okay and mollify envy. For a while these may seem to work, but an outer fix alone, no matter how gratifying, can't sustain self-esteem. It only neutralizes feelings of inadequacy temporarily, until another outbreak occurs. True self-esteem is more consistent and fluctuates less from outer influences. It lets you count on the person you've become in both good and rough times. It's not a Band-Aid for envy and jealousy; it's a cure. Therefore, in terms of emotional freedom, these negative emotions can only be transformed by strengthening how you internally perceive yourself.

Recently, I had a dream where I saw a man frantically trying to climb up a ladder. From below I kept whispering, "Pssst, pssst," but couldn't get his attention. I called up to him, "You know, there isn't anything up there!" No matter how often I kept trying to tell him, he wouldn't listen, and kept up his frenetic scrambling. Now, here's wisdom I need to be reminded of as much as anyone: climbing the ladder of endless desire won't make us free, isn't the source of happiness that we may imagine. What if, instead, we could value our acts of goodness above worldly striving and applause? Though it's laudable to have dreams and seek excellence—and it's fine to want what someone you admire has—you must garner self-esteem from the love you create. Then no one can put it in jeopardy.

The upcoming overview of jealousy, envy, and self-esteem will assist you in mastering these emotions by understanding their biology, spirituality, energetic power, and psychology. From Oedipal complexes to the guarding of sperm, you'll discover from whence primal impulses stir. The methods I'll offer to build self-esteem can liberate you from denigrating feelings of being "less than" or from a fractured ability to trust. I guarantee that such relief is possible. My spiritual teacher says, "A superior person works systematically to become a better human being. Not that he or she is better than anyone else." On your journey, remember this intention. Aim high. As one of my patients put it, "My goal is to be the person my dog thinks I am!"

The Anatomy of Jealousy, Envy, and Self-Esteem: Putting the Sixth Transformation into Action

Freeing yourself from this transformation's negative emotions starts with inviting them in to reveal parts of you that may be hidden. Then you can observe these feelings neutrally, like a naturalist studying flocks of pink flamingos in the wild. You're a fascinating subject, so get into it. Be both the witness and experiencer of your reactions. This gives you the detachment to determine areas in need of healing with self-esteem.

REPROGRAM THE BIOLOGY OF JEALOUSY, ENVY, AND SELF-ESTEEM

Since the dawn of time, jealously has been related to mating, a high-stakes, high-drama ritual that evokes deadly territorial responses in

humans and other animals. Why? Researchers say that evolution cleverly designed jealousy so that we would vigorously defend our sexual
turf; when this domain is violated, it threatens our sense of domi-
nance and security. Thus, from a purely primal view, a man becomes
jealous because he wants to fight off other suitors and ensure that his
mate carries only his sperm to produce offspring. A woman becomes
jealous because she wants to drive off rivals and ensure the male will
be there to assist in child rearing. In short, jealousy flares when repro-
ductive success is endangered. Procreate or perish is as primal an
imperative as you can get.

For our cave-dwelling ancestors, and for us too, even twinges of
jealousy can elicit what biologists term "mate-guarding" behavior.
Some is benign. For instance, your husband puts his arm around you
when a handsome or esteemed peer approaches. Or in the presence of
an attractive or accomplished woman, you may do this with your husband. Problem is, jealousy can crazily escalate to threats of violence,
stalking, beating, or homicide. (Male sexual jealousy motivates more
than half of spousal murders; jealous women also kill their husbands,
though less frequently.) I once read a shocking newspaper account of
a man who patted the rear end of a woman in a bar. She called her
boyfriend, who charged over to this guy and demanded an apology.
When the man just laughed in his face, the boyfriend followed him
home and bludgeoned him to death with a baseball bat.

If you're jealous or know someone who is, watch for specific mate-
guarding behaviors that have been proven to forecast violence. The
top three include verbal denigration, isolating a mate from friends and
family, and monopolizing a mate's time. Also, men and women tend
to vary in styles of expressing jealousy, though these are generalizations. A male might yell at his partner for talking to another man,
whereas a woman might threaten her mate with a breakup. A man's
blood tends to boil over if his mate commits physical infidelity,
whereas a woman is often more disturbed by the emotional intimacy
of her mate's affair.

Mindlessly acting out Neanderthal jealousies can be detrimental in
our post-hunter-gatherer age. It hurts other people to be that brutish.
It also stresses your biology and theirs by overstimulating cortisol and

adrenaline, instigators of premature aging and disease. To be free necessitates taming this emotion, a choice with biological clout. I want you to understand that jealousy, like fear, can take two very different paths in your brain. It can take a slower route through the cerebral cortex, the locus of reason. Or it can leap onto the fast track to the most primitive part of your gray matter, the amygdala, to sound an immediate alarm. *You control which way jealousy goes by taking command of your brain.* How? By recognizing what scientists call "territorial flash points," predictable triggers that make you crazed—for instance, if your partner is late but doesn't call, or if at a party he or she is flirtatious. When you consciously pause to consider these triggers, you'll put yourself on the slower brain path so you're not some loose cannon who jealously defends your mate as if your life depended on it. Rather than retaliating thoughtlessly, you can ask yourself from a more measured place, "Is this a real threat or am I being reactive because someone set off my insecurities and low self-esteem?" Establishing what's motivating you lets you respond more wisely and find productive solutions.

High school is a spicy setting for witnessing the biology of jealousy and envy in vitro. Jealousy and envy are endemic in high school, a petri dish for these emotional microbes. Adolescence is a hormonally intoxicated state of near-insanity that amplifies these emotions. When girls gushing with newly flowing estrogen, producing fertilizable eggs each month, meet desperate boys crazed with testosterone, nature's procreative agenda kicks in like gangbusters. These drives, albeit unconscious, are at the crux of teenage catfights and male competition.

In my high school culture, self-esteem was often linked to being in a twosome, a bump up in social status compared to the unattached "rejects." I'd never been part of the in-crowd who hung out at lunch on the quad's Upper Patio. My hippie friends and I snuck cigarettes by the auditorium across the hinterland of the athletic field. Despite my pride in being a rebel, it nonetheless felt like a disgrace to be "unpopular," a stigma I just had to bear. I envied those golden ones who seemed to effortlessly have it all. Like many female classmates, I envied girls with boyfriends. Or when I had one, I was jealous of femme fatales who could steal him away; this kind of thing happened all the time. Then, for two years, I had a boyfriend who meant the moon and stars to me. But, fickle as teenagers often are, he dropped me for a blond-haired, blue-eyed cheerleader because he wanted to be "popular." Losing him nearly ripped my heart out, and it dealt a blow to the intuitive part of me that had trusted so fully with an all-you-need-is-love innocence. This hurt shadowed my romantic relationships for a long time, making it hard to trust and love with surrender.

Biologically, it makes sense for sex hormones to up the ante for jealousy and envy in adolescence and later on: the body's mission is for our species to propagate. However, your mission, as freedom is evolving, isn't simply to be impelled by your most primitive impulses but to draw on other aspects of your character and of human potential.

Though envy has been studied less than jealousy, research by Oxford economists provides surprising insight into how much people hate a winner because they're envious. The researchers designed an experiment played with real cash in which subjects could decide to "burn away" other people's money, but only at the price of expending their own. Despite large, real financial cost to these subjects, the majority chose to annihilate another's wealth instead of building up their own reserve of cash. Ruefully, these researchers concluded that their experiment documented the darker, envious side of human nature.

The alternative to this emotional low road is to develop self-esteem so that insecurity doesn't turn you into your darker self. Science touts the health benefits of self-esteem. It's been shown to buffer stress, elevate endorphins, and support emotional and physical well-being. It follows that when you feel positive about yourself, your physical body is more content. Conversely, low self-esteem increases the risk of depression, eating disorders, suicide, and chronic physical symptoms such as fatigue or back pain. Some people with low self-esteem are prone to floccinaucinihilipilification, the habit of deeming everything worthless. (It's one of the longest words in the *Oxford English Dictionary.* I dare you to pronounce it.) Those afflicted are not only down on themselves; they're negative all the time. One comedian who was a patient of mine swore she had to be that miserable to maintain a comic edge, a conviction that kept a cap on how far our therapy could go. Low self-esteem isn't a biological benefit and doesn't lead to health, happiness, or any semblance of emotional freedom.

The next exercise will increase your sense of self-esteem and help you strengthen shaky areas. On a purely biological level, simply trying out new thoughts and behaviors can generate neurochemicals of well-being that will set that process in motion.

Emotional Action Step

BOLSTER SELF-ESTEEM, OPTIMIZE YOUR BIOLOGY

1. *Review this self-esteem checklist.* See if you possess these traits. Great if you do. No sweat if you don't or relate to just a few. First evaluate where you're at, then begin to make changes.

   - You generally have a positive attitude
   - You value yourself highly
   - You're comfortable asserting your emotional needs
   - You see yourself as competent, in control of your life
   - You take people's opinions of you in stride
   - You aren't threatened by other's successes

2. *Focus on one area of self-esteem to strengthen.* Identify one issue in the checklist that needs a boost. Then do an experiment for a week. Let's say you want to feel more competent at work. Choose a doable goal. Tell yourself that you can achieve it rather than indulging in negativity. That starts the biological shift. Then take a small step forward. Finish one report that's due. Take pride in that accomplishment. Remind yourself of the virtues of completing the task; show yourself some love. Replace recriminating attitudes with self-affirmations. Then listen to your body. Notice how these efforts invigorate well-being. Continue retraining your attitudes and concentrate on new areas when you feel ready. No task is too small. It's your positive attitude about it that supports emotional and physical health.

Practicing this action step lets you partner with your biology and enjoy all the endorphins that flow from enhanced self-esteem. Aspire to connect the dots between a positive body and a positive mind. Make no mistake: jealousy and envy will preclude that blissful synchrony. Remember, in biological terms, the stress of such negativity is costly.

UNCOVER THE SPIRITUAL MEANING OF JEALOUSY, ENVY, AND SELF-ESTEEM

When patients come to me jealous or envious, intuitively this is what I perceive: there's a vast sky all around them, yet they're locked in a windowless cage filled with noxious fumes, so close to but so far from the surrounding expanse. As an Energy Psychiatrist, my job is to help them and you connect with something larger than the myopia of negativity—a sense of spirit that dissolves toxins.

The difference between us and our early ancestors is that, mercifully, our brains have evolved so that we can opt to transform these emotions instead of merely reacting to them. It's taken more than three and a half million years, the time that hominids are believed to have been on earth, to get to this point—a long time coming. Part of this adaptive turnabout involves grasping the spiritual meaning of jealousy and envy, how they can prod us to cultivate self-esteem. I see a spiritual approach as particularly pertinent to overcoming these emotions. Why? Self-esteem doesn't just arise from the material world. It also means finding worth in your intuitive bond to a higher power, the growth of your goodness, and the deepening of your soul. It's being spiritually mature enough to know the merit of vanquishing negativity with love, which makes tenderness possible between us. That's where true self-esteem must come from. If you stay stuck in your small self by colluding with jealousy or envy, you'll be the biggest loser by selling out your power. To avoid this, utilize a mantra my spiritual teacher suggests: "I am superior to anything small within me." As I do, regularly repeat this to stay cued in to how large you really are.

Throughout the Bible and sacred literature, jealousy and envy abound. Recall Cain, the first murderer, who slaughters his brother after the Old Testament God announces that Abel's gift to him is more pleasing. In Genesis, God banishes Cain from Eden to become "a fugitive and vagabond on Earth." Or how about Dante's *Inferno*, in which the envious have their eyes sewn shut with wire because of the "sinful" pleasure they got from bringing others low? Judging so punitively, however, isn't the answer to liberating these emotions in anyone. I see jealousy and envy as having their own inherent consequences simply by virtue of their burden on freedom. It's awfully hard to expand spiritually if you're that emotionally constricted.

The Spiritual Backbone of Self-Esteem

Perceiving the symbiosis of spirituality and self-esteem requires an about-face from our society's obsession with externals: "If only I'd get _____, I'd be fine." For some who're addictively chasing that pipe dream, even instant gratification isn't fast enough, and it dissipates quickly. With patients and personally, I've found two principles for fostering an evergreen sense of worth and dignity:

1. Practice radical humility instead of egotism.
2. Thou shalt not compare.

Being jealous and envious consumes tremendous energy. Why not redirect it to solidify your spiritual core? At first glance, the principles I'll present may seem counterintuitive to the Western notion of self-esteem because they don't propose inflating your ego and outdoing others as the solution. I'm pleased to offer another way to be.

First Principle: Practice Radical Humility Instead of Egotism

The most spiritually credible people I know are humble and soft-spoken. They don't strut around like peacocks, enchanted by how wonderful they are. My heroes are the Dalai Lama, Nelson Mandela, and Rosa Parks—gentle persuaders to a more noble path, not power-hungry egomaniacs. Don't get me wrong. I advocate a healthy ego. It's our conscious sense of self, the "I" of the human equation. However, egotism is having an inflated identity, a strain of negativity that infects spirituality and the liberation it brings. To me, egotists seem bloated, flatulent. They watch out for number one, peer down their noses at you, and tend to be jealous or envious. (Still, egotists usually have varying capacities for empathy and love compared to narcissists, who're typically more incapacitated in these areas.) *Egotism is not a sign of self-esteem. It masks feelings of inferiority, which is why these Mr. Bigs denigrate others and often have unquenchable ambition.* Like everyone, I've met plenty of egotists, but my friend's boss, a Fortune 500 CEO, takes the cake. Poised in his Bel Air mansion's entryway is a ten-foot, three-hundred-pound statue of Julius Caesar, someone to whom he frequently compares himself. At the annual Christmas party, beholding his host's marble alter ego, my startled friend was tempted to salute. Like all good centurions, egotists want to be hailed.

My spiritual teacher describes a person with a big ego as "a feather pretending to be an arrow." Intuitively, this rings so true. When I tune in to patients who are egotists, their self-esteem feels frail and wobbly, but it steadies once they discover a sounder sense of worth and connection to Spirit. Forget about how impressive egotists might look on the outside or how others kowtow to them. They are grand pretenders, even to themselves, with underdeveloped hearts. Egotists parade what they've got: possessions, social status, or even the "high spiritual plane" they believe they're residing on compared to us mortals.

Small ego, large soul: that's emotional freedom. One way there is through humility, a spiritual prophylaxis for egotism. Nonetheless, in high-achiever circles, humility is wrongly associated with weakness, being a pansy, getting walked on because you lack gumption. The typical alpha male and female our culture so idolizes are the opposite of humble; they're rabid go-getters and proud of it. About humility, let me set the record straight. Here are some qualities that constitute this inner power. Possessing them will help break the stranglehold of jealousy and envy.

Humility is:

• Having awe for being a speck in an infinite universe rather than seeing yourself as the center of it.

- Realizing we're all on equal ground; no one is on a pedestal.

- Seeing spirit in everyone you meet, even those you don't like.

- Knowing your gifts (but not flaunting them) and your limitations.

- Being able to laugh at your foibles.

- Trying your best to surmount self-doubts, even if someone gets what you deserve or outdoes you.

- The consistent practice of being simple and valuing simple things. For example, appreciating the beauty of a flower, a loving interchange, the grace of ordinary moments—not being addicted to material extravagance to define self-esteem.

In Energy Psychiatry, I encourage these qualities of humility in my patients. They're secret weapons for guarding self-esteem because they redefine what constitutes worth. As the Zen saying goes, "After ecstasy, the laundry," a healthy balance I prescribe in therapy. Traditional psychiatry, however, doesn't usually discuss humility as a therapeutic goal. Rather, it addresses the state of rage at being humiliated, a concept more related to shame. To me, humility is a crucial attitude with which to approach jealousy and envy, as it addresses them from both cosmic and material slants. It can feel exhausting being the center of the universe; conversely, it can be a relief to take yourself less seriously. When self-esteem becomes more about who you are than winning an endless series of competitions, freedom reigns.

A book I keep by my bed is *The Practice of the Presence of God* by Brother Lawrence, who joined the "barefoot" Carmelites in Paris in 1666. He had one desire: communion with God, which he found as much in kitchen duties as in his cathedral. Little is known about this humble brother except for his work in the kitchen, and that he was a great awkward fellow who broke everything. Brother Lawrence's calling was seeing the holy in the commonplace. Through his lifetime, this was where he found meaning.

Similarly, practice humility as a way of life. Find self-esteem in the sacredness of small, mindful acts and in the love you make to the world. Don't hold your breath waiting for big things to happen to instill worth. Brother Lawrence writes, "Fame and greatness are often a delusion and a snare. Perhaps the greatest of all men are those who don't seek greatness at all." Still, humble people have egos; they're just not out of control. Nor are they into the vanity of false humility, using apparent modesty or self-deprecation as masks for egotism, a hazard for everyone, including "spiritual people." Whether you're flipping burgers or running a country, humility is an equalizing attitude of respect toward yourself and others.

Recently, at a conference where I'd given an intuition workshop, an attendee spotted me in a T-shirt and yoga pants in an elevator and said, "Wow, you're a regular person!" I took it as a compliment and beamed back. A woman nearby overheard this and said, "Oh, I'd hate to be called a regular person. I want to be extraordinary!" As she walked away I felt, in contrast, that it was the best thing anyone could've called me. Like us all, I have my moments of vanity; I don't claim to be a perpetual beacon of humility. But I genuinely appreciate how spectacular the ordinary is. I'm enriched and consoled by every human-to-human connection, the fellowship we all share. Humility gifts you with the freedom to be natural, without pretense or something to prove. In your life, practice humility. Be a flower among flowers—and, as poet Mary Oliver puts it, "a weed among weeds." Great liberation comes from this.

Second Principle: Thou Shalt Not Compare

Comparing is a natural tendency we all have. It can be absolutely neutral, as when you merely evaluate similarities and differences. Such comparison is essential for astute reasoning. It's also productive if you're inspired to emulate another's impressive traits. However, it becomes dysfunctional when it stirs envy and jealousy, if you judge yourself as better or less than others. Think about it: without comparisons, jealousy and envy couldn't exist. (Interestingly, it's more common to feel inferior to those with "more" than to feel grateful compared to those with "less.")

We're a society of comparison junkies. It starts from day one. Babies are compared to each other. Who's smarter, cuter, more precocious? Then comes grammar school. I remember a hideous game some of my king-of-the-hill classmates would play. They'd pick a target, usually the shy, insecure one. Then, in an unapologetically malevolent tone they'd singsong in unison, "There's a fungus among us. Her name is (<u>fill in the blank</u>) fungus," until the poor kid, totally humiliated, slunk away. So at school, there were basically the funguses and the non-funguses. Not so different from the breakdown of our comparisons in later life, interpersonally and politically. Shiites and Sunnis. White supremacists versus Jews and blacks. Protestants and Catholics in Belfast. Comparing yourself to others can preclude a bond of common fellowship and is a barrier to finding true worth. Either you'll end up with the short end of the stick or, if you deign to put yourself in a stratosphere above anyone, you're nowhere. Self-esteem must come from simply being you.

In a spiritual sense, comparing your path to another's is comparing apples and oranges. Your life is explicitly designed for your soul's growth. Intuition helps you know this. When you tune in, try to intuit the grace of both the hurdles and the joys you've been given. These are life's legacy to you. Self-esteem comes from embracing this, working with what each day brings. How you spend your time here is up to you. Why squander it by comparing? Realistically, you'll probably still do it. We all will. Even so, let's persist in keeping our eyes on ourselves to build self-esteem; let it forge freedom.

My patient Joe, a no-hype marketing executive who's the opposite of slick, struggles with envy when his firm's shark-toothed associates are assigned the most prestigious clients. Joe asks, "How come the ruthless one always score so big?" Not that he'd compromise his ethics, but in comparison, he deems himself less successful, bemoaning that "these sleazes" look so self-satisfied. To me, it was natural for Joe to feel distraught when he was marginalized. But the treacherousness of low self-esteem is that it condemns you to that impotent place. Thus, I wanted to support him in becoming more assertive and urged him to brainstorm with management about securing clients he desired. I also helped Joe adopt a spiritually oriented take on the situation. Though the laws of physics dictate that every action has an equal and opposite reaction, the freedom that power-mongers sacrifice isn't always evident. From working with such patients, I know that ruthlessness is a tapeworm that consumes your vital force. Chronic pain, depression, a crippled capacity for intimacy: others may not see these sequelae of ruthlessness, but I do. I was right with Joe as he went on about how unfair life can be, a sobering fact to grasp at times. But I also insisted that he not stop there, as most people do. Beyond asserting himself or getting another job, Joe's spiritual imperative, and ours, is to keep refocusing on what we have rather than what we lack, not letting comparisons eclipse our worth or our contributions to the world.

The following exercise will allow you to experience the emotional benefits of the two spiritual principles I've discussed. They'll recondition how you deal with jealousy and envy. As these emotions arise, instead of being consumed, you can say, "Fie, O ruthless ones!" Then ask for a little help from Spirit and apply the techniques I suggest to change direction.

Emotional Action Step

LET SPIRITUALITY BOOST YOUR SELF-ESTEEM

1. *Choose a person you feel jealousy or envy toward.* Perhaps it's a coworker your supervisor favors, or a cocky, well-off relative. Make this person your test case before you go on to transforming these emotions with others.

2. *Behave differently.* Practice dealing with jealousy and envy by mindfully using humility and avoiding comparisons, even if the person irritates you. For instance, rather than automatically bristling or shrinking down a few inches in your seat when your supervisor praises this coworker, second her good ideas in a collegial gesture. Try not to feed into feeling "less than." Instead, as an empowered equal, add your own good ideas, not letting the rapport between your boss and coworker or your wobbly self-esteem deter you. Although you have the right to be upset about your supervisor's favoritism, a humble but confident approach

will begin to improve things. In that instance and the situation with your well-off relative, practice the commandment "I shall not compare." Shift your mind-set to concentrate on what you do have, on what makes you happy. Let that be the tenor of your interaction.

3. *Praise yourself.* Gain self-esteem from your efforts to deal with these emotions positively. Showing humility and avoiding comparisons binds you to a growing goodness within and without, a spiritual essence. It fosters a loving posture in relationships instead of a defensive one.

Enlisting these methods sets a precedent for emotional liberation. "You're doing well," I proudly tell myself every time I stand up to jealousy and envy, whether I totally overcome them or not. The consistent message I want to give to negativity is, "You won't win. I'll never stop trying to overturn you." Commit yourself to this too. Once you take a definitive position about these emotions, something upstairs hears and aligns with your intent. It doesn't do the job for you, but it'll confer the moxie to pursue victory.

EXPERIENCE THE ENERGETIC POWER OF JEALOUSY, ENVY, AND SELF-ESTEEM

A centerpiece for emotional freedom is learning how positive and negative feelings intuitively affect your body. Each emotion has distinguishing characteristics. To energetically map jealousy, envy, and self-esteem in your system, I suggest a three-pronged approach.

1. Sense the Energy of Emotions

On a subtle energetic level, I liken jealousy and envy to the regurgitating burn of acid reflux disease. These emotions fry my insides and give me hot flashes—a jittery, vitality-sapping state. Jealousy and

Judith Orloff, M.D.

envy will singe both body and spirit if you permit it. On the other hand, self-esteem feels like I'm being filled with the most luscious warm honey, a restorative balm for jealousy and envy's inflammation. I intuitively track these energies in my body as a first line of defense against negativity.

While exploring the Sixth Transformation's emotions, notice their physical effects on you. Go for it: conjure someone who incites jealousy or envy. Just spit it out; don't judge yourself. It could be a Nobel laureate or a supermodel, depending on what sets off your insecurities. Rile up these emotions while simultaneously noting your body's responses. Next, conjure someone who enhances your self-esteem—a teacher, a lover. Observe how different this feels. Here are some common qualities of both emotions to watch for.

HOW THE ENERGY OF JEALOUSY AND ENVY FEEL

- Like feverish waves of heat
- Acidic, burning, inflamed
- Obsessive, pressured
- Like it boomerangs to sap you
- Oppressive; it makes you shrink down into your seat

HOW THE ENERGY OF SELF-ESTEEM FEELS

- Straight like an arrow
- As if you've grown taller
- Soothingly warm, strengthening
- Calm, invigorating, peaceful
- Supportive of good posture and eye contact

Appreciating how jealousy and envy register internally sets you on course to transform them instead of letting these energies dominate you. Also, recognizing the energetic hallmarks of self-esteem makes it easier to summon, but the above list is just a starting point; see how these emotions uniquely manifest in your body. Acting swiftly and decisively to champion the positive is the way of the emotional warrior.

2. Watch for Emotional Synchronicities

Being attuned to energy makes you more sensitive to how grace can intervene to clear negative emotions. Once you're aware that life is about flow, that our energy fields are constantly overlapping, you'll have a fuller openness to synchronicities, a form of grace. These "inspired coincidences" are moments of perfect timing when things fall into place with startling precision. The emotions you're working with will shape the synchronicities you experience. Perhaps when your self-esteem needs a lift, a person you've just met offers you the perfect job. Or you can't stop thinking of a friend who senses your envy about his becoming engaged, and he lovingly calls to talk things through. The intellect may chalk these events up to mere chance, which is an ignorant underestimation. Such auspicious intersections are bona fide intuitive moments when energetic forces align via synchronicities to assist you emotionally.

A gift-from-the-gods synchronicity helped my friend Tess with a job applicant. Good-natured Tess always gives people the benefit of the doubt; this time, it came back to bite her. Tess wanted to expand her graphic design firm and was interviewing potential partners. She met with Ellen, an apparently ideal candidate, smart and talented—though she did seem a bit grumpy and made a snide comment about the office's "passé" bubble gum pop décor. "She's probably just having a bad day," Tess figured. Later, about to offer Ellen a contract, she called her cell phone. What a connection—Tess could hear Ellen talking to someone else, and the subject was her. Tess repeatedly said she was on the line, but couldn't be heard. So, for a few interminable minutes, she listened in shock to Ellen's envious dissing of everything from her "pseudo-hip furnishings" to her "foo-foo" designing awards. "Who does Tess think she is?" Ellen's envy was an earful, but it was information Tess needed. She credits this synchronous technological snafu with protecting her from a partner from hell. Also, it wised her up to the necessity of heeding intuitive warning signs about people instead of assuming the best when they haven't earned it.

As Tess did, notice what synchronicities can teach you. Transformation doesn't just take place in your therapist's office. You've got more help than that. The universe conspires to provide clues if you're creative enough to look. Keep your third eye open along with your other two for whatever informs jealousy, envy, and self-esteem: newspapers, television, conversations with friends or strangers, messages in dreams. Synchronicities happen when you least expect them.

One came to my rescue when my confidence was wounded after a series of disappointments. One night, while doing research on the Internet, I typed in the title of my first book, *Second Sight,* to find new references on intuition. What popped up was a link to a 1972 *Bonanza* TV episode (remember ol' Hoss Cartwright and the Ponderosa) called "Second Sight." Uncannily, its plot was about a psychic named Judith struggling with intuitive powers her pastor-fiancé didn't want her to use. I did a quadruple take. Could it be? That was the very story of my life I told some twenty-five years later in my book, right down to that Orthodox boyfriend I mentioned here in Chapter 4, whose rabbi broke us up by calling me a witch for talking about my premonitions. It's been said that synchronicities are God winking at you. For me, this was a dose of wonder reinforcing that my self-doubts were smaller in scale than the larger mystery of life. There was an order at work more compelling than whatever got me down. Someone simply telling me this wouldn't have had nearly the same oomph. Further, synchronicities have always excited me and cheered me up. When I turned off my computer that night, I was feeling much better about myself and life in general.

Freedom requires being a detective, coordinating many sources of information about emotions. Don't get too fixated on how change will occur. Energy has its own wisdom about the way new insights transpire. Mastering emotional energy means grasping that how you got there is as important as what you've attained. The process, always the process—synchronicities are part of that richness.

3. Transform Emotional Energy
The key to shifting the negative energy of jealousy and envy is to identify when they surface, then replace them with what's positive. How? Using the techniques that follow, try to wish the best for someone.

This can be really tough. Your ego isn't apt to be thrilled about the idea; it's too riddled with insecurity. Override it by coming from a higher place—something you very well may resist, but attempt it anyway. As against your instincts as this exercise may seem, it'll take these emotions by surprise, confusing them and stopping them in their tracks.

Emotional Action Step

RELEASE JEALOUSY AND ENVY

Phase 1: Debrief your feelings. Share them with someone safe. No editing. Let it all out. Burst the boil. This emotional expression must happen to ready you for the next phase of release.

Phase 2: Practice these energy-transforming strategies.

- *Root for a rival's happiness.* Fat chance, you might think. But doing this changes the wavelength of negativity. Begin with an attitude change, though it may take a while to fully mean it. Say to yourself, "I want my rival to be happy." This points you in a more positive direction. Then, as you get more comfortable with this attitude, try going further. Tell someone you envy, "You're doing a fantastic job." (Psychoanalyst Melanie Klein offers this suggestion in her classic book *Gratitude and Envy.*) In addition, pray for the person—and not just that God removes his or her countless faults! Get it right. Pray for his or her happiness and prosperity. This constructive intent will gather a momentum of its own.

- *Give to others what you most desire for yourself.* If you want your work to be valued, value others' work. If you want love, give love. If you want a successful career, help another's career to flourish. What goes around comes around, an energetic dynamic you can mobilize.

- *See people as teachers.* Put the names or photos of people you're jealous of next to a bouquet of flowers, or, if you have them, statues of Buddha or Quan Yin. Consider these people teachers

who can help you transcend negativity. There won't be any
shortage of instructors!

- *Learn from a rival's positive points.* Get your mind off what you
  perceive you lack and toward self-improvement. Yoko Ono says,
  "Transform jealousy to admiration, and what you admire will
  become part of your life"—an inspiring credo to live by.

Practicing this action step builds self-esteem by giving you the confidence and satisfaction of becoming a bigger person. It reinforces the
cosmic law that when you support others and wish them well, it helps
you too. Realizing that jealousy and envy cause suffering gives you
the motivation to get past them. Sure, sometimes change goes against
the grain. Expect that. There's an old joke: "What's the definition of
a Buddhist vacuum cleaner?" The answer: "No attachments!" This
speaks to negative emotional habits as well.

MAP THE PSYCHOLOGY OF JEALOUSY, ENVY, AND SELF-ESTEEM

Self-esteem sometimes comes in tiny packages. While visiting the his-
toric Peabody Hotel in Memphis, I had the thrill of watching the
March of the Peabody Ducks, a tradition since the 1930s in which
five mallard ducks march to and from the posh Grand Lobby. At
11:00 A.M. and 5:00 P.M., the red carpet is rolled out and these noble
ducks march down it to John Philip Sousa's "King Cotton March." All
of us guests waited in rapt anticipation for them to arrive from their
rooftop home, called "the palace." You could hear a pin drop. Then the
elevator opened. There they were, quacking with a joy of celebrity
that would've made Elvis proud as they waddled together toward the
travertine marble fountain where they'd spend the day. We all applauded. I was tempted to stand up and cheer. Those ducks' ebullient
confidence continues to warm me, modeling possibilities for life.

Psychologist William James coined the term *self-esteem* in 1890, defining it as "feeling good about yourself and your accomplishments." These are some factors that contribute to the psychology of self-esteem.

1. The quality of your womb experience, whether it was nurturing or not. Nine months of having a sick or stressed-out mother can test your assuredness before you even enter the world.
2. Our innate temperament and biochemistry. Some of us may pop out of the womb like little Buddhas, whereas others are more insecure.
3. Your parents' attitudes and acceptance of you. Research shows that this impacts your self-esteem more than their wealth, education, and job. As you mature, friends, teachers, mates, and colleagues affect self-esteem too.
4. Interestingly, studies indicate that confidence in your appearance comes more from how you perceive yourself than from some socially accepted standard of good looks. Charmingly, a balding friend with ample self-esteem says, "When I look in the mirror, I see a full head of hair"—a testament to ways positive thoughts construct our attitudes.

These are some factors that contribute to the psychology of jealousy and envy.

1. You feel these emotions after a younger sibling is born, forcing you to share your parents' attention, an important but often painful start to realizing that the universe doesn't revolve around you. (Being an only child, I never learned such sharing, which I'm sure colored my envy later on.)
2. Freudians famously espouse the Oedipal and Electra complexes, when at age five, you want to jealously possess the parent of the opposite sex. How do these impulses resolve? In this theory, fear of being castrated by your father (for boys) or fear of losing your mother's love (for girls) compels you to refocus on other objects of desire. This passage is facilitated by healthy bonding with your mother. It is also aided by seeing healthy bonding between your parents, a resounding message that Mom belongs to Dad and vice

versa. According to Freudians, when such bonding is missing, Oedipal desires linger. Jealousy and envy may haunt your adult relationships, sometimes to a destructively obsessive degree. You'll keep trying to possess lovers, as you'd wanted to do with your parents, behavior that suffocates intimacy.

3. Research reveals that low self-esteem is related to damaged upbringing, such as coming from an abusive home, or from early romantic traumas, such as betrayal by a lover. These make you more prone to envy, jealousy, and mistrusting a mate.

4. Children raised with high self-esteem have proven to be more capable of overcoming these emotions as adults.

In Energy Psychiatry, I help patients trace the psychological roots of jealousy, envy, and self-esteem to gain insight and alter their behavior. As my patients do, ask yourself, "Where did these emotions come from?" and "How do I release myself from them?" But jealousy and envy may have different remedies. For example, envy always requires identifying and healing your insecurities while concurrently building self-esteem. The problem is never the envied person. With jealousy, though, it's critical to differentiate "normal" from "delusional," two distinct species of this emotion that I will clarify.

Personally, I was amazed to find that a survey of marriage counselors indicated that jealousy is a problem in a third of couples seeking therapy. Normal jealousy, sparked by a real threat to a relationship, is more amenable to concrete solutions. Perhaps your husband's leggy office assistant really *is* trying to steal him away. In that case, don't sit on your feelings. You're entitled to be upset and concerned, but stay calm. Jealous rage won't further your cause. Openly, honestly communicate your feelings to him. Then collaborate on fixing the situation— perhaps hiring someone else or having him tell this woman loud and clear he's not available because he's in love with you. Jointly working on a resolution forges mutual trust and commitment. However, normal jealousy may also arise from something less extreme, say, a waiter flirting with your wife. If she doesn't reciprocate, it's still fine to mention (not belabor) your discomfort about the flirting. Also explore how this incident triggered your feelings of low self-esteem, such as feeling less virile or desirable. However, if your wife is a flirt and it makes you jealous and uneasy, you must broach the subject with her either alone or with a therapist. This enables her to be aware of its effect on you, so she can stop it. To build strong relationships, clarifying which behaviors each of you can and cannot tolerate ensures you're on the same page.

Warning: When you're dealing with jealousy, the risk is that you become so skittishly reactive that you misread signals or have over-the-top responses to smaller infractions. Your mate's flirtatious toss of the hair or smile can hurt as if you've been truly betrayed. To keep a balanced perspective, notice your reactivity. Routinely inquire: "Is my response appropriate or have old wounds fueled this fire?" If your father always chose your sister over you, realize you may be supersensitive to jealousy in situations that involve favoritism today. When you become a more conscious witness and interpreter of your emotions, you can choose to modulate the intensity of your response.

On the other hand, delusional jealousy (aka the Othello syndrome) is a tougher case to crack. It's a rigid, persistent belief, with no basis in reality, that one's partner is unfaithful. Conventional psychiatry categorizes such jealousy as a paranoid delusional disorder. Curiously, sufferers might seem fine in every other way but are utterly convinced they're being betrayed. Thus, they batter their mates with accusations of infidelity, attempt to control where they go and who they see, may hire private detectives, or resort to violence, even murder. These fascistically jealous people make their partners dread even being seen with anyone who could be construed as a threat. Paranoia lurks in every corner, corrupting the emotional freedom of both perpetrator and recipient.

Once I had a boyfriend with this kind of jealousy. He was an otherwise endearing, brilliant, socially conscious environmentalist. At first I thought he was kidding when he'd say, "You really like that guy, don't you?" after I'd chat casually with someone at a party. He'd express jealousy of my past relationships and would get agitated if I talked on the phone to a former boyfriend. I'm as loyal as you can get, completely, unconflictedly monogamous. Nevertheless, my boyfriend didn't believe me, nor was he kidding. Over the next few years, his jealousy ratcheted up to such a crescendo that I got too spooked to wear white T-shirts, lest my nipples show, or to touch other men, let alone hug them hello. Walking on eggshells, I started having nightmares about macabre men-monsters stalking me, a clear sign both that I was feeling persecuted and that I was stepping into the unsavory role of victim. I loved my boyfriend, but no reassurance or reasoning mitigated his jealousy. Most disturbing was how fast it escalated. There was a thin membrane between his smiling amicability and the grimace of a madman. Though jealousy caused him enormous pain, he "didn't believe in psychology" and wasn't willing to see a therapist—except once, to pacify me. "What did she say?" I asked all too eagerly. His interpretation of her recommendation about the situation was that he needed to think long and hard about being with "a woman like that." Whether he'd convinced her of his delusion or heard only what he wanted to hear, the therapist couldn't sway him.

The thing about this type of jealousy is that the sufferer will twist any situation to fit his or her paranoid notions and win over others. Fittingly, my spiritual teacher said, "You know you're not doing anything wrong. Why let his accusations get to you?" This was in no way facile or thoughtless advice. As was his style, he was reminding me to believe in myself, stay calm, and let others' opinions go. To my credit, I persisted in that spiritual practice and made steady progress in becoming more centered. Still, there was a niggling, unsure part of me that said, "Maybe I *am* doing something provocative." And I wanted the relationship to work. So I continued trying to modify my wardrobe and limit physical contact with men, hoping against hope this would solve the problem. There was so much incredible about this man, I didn't want to lose him. I struggled with the questions "How much do you work on a relationship? And when is enough enough?" But finally, predictably, his relentless suspicions destroyed us. They prevented him from trusting me enough to fully commit. Also, I was plum tuckered out from being treated like Othello's Desdemona, a woman who was falsely accused. So, with great anguish, we parted.

It took a long time for my heart to recover. Well-meaning friends came to my rescue, saying things like "What a shame he wouldn't go into couples therapy" and "How sad he couldn't deal with his jealousy." For me, it was certainly a shame and sad. But now, having had time to reflect, I believe, more than ever, that everyone has the inalienable right to deal with dark emotions, or not. At this stage in his life, apparently, it wasn't this man's path. To him, it wasn't sad at all that he didn't face his dark side. As an environmentalist, he felt he had other worthy work to which he was devoted. Still, I got a good chuckle when my friend Berenice, a psychotherapist, and I joked: "In his next life, poor guy, he'll be reincarnated as a therapist. Then he'll have to deal with emotions!" Maybe so. Still, I see jealousy as shackling his heart. This relationship taught me more about jealousy than I'd ever thought I'd learn. Grueling as it was, the fact is, I'm grateful for what I experienced and was able to take from it.

Even for the most ingenious mental health practitioner, delusional jealousy is difficult to treat. Patients must want to change—rare because, like all card-carrying delusionals, they believe their perceptions are valid. But even if they desire help, it's still hard. The problem, as I see it, is that this kind of jealousy is largely based on a disowned projection rather than solely low self-esteem: sufferers project onto mates what they themselves want to do, such as being flirtatious or promiscuous. Because they either have a basic inability to be self-aware or find owning the projection too painful, their delusion holds on. Treatments with partial success include antidepressants, antipsychotics, psychoanalysis, and behavioral therapies to reprogram responses to jealousy. (The next emotional action step will be beneficial too.) In my practice, I've sometimes seen that the caring and acceptance they experience in long-term psychotherapy can make it safer to explore this issue. With perseverance, such jealousy can decrease, becoming less in the forefront of consciousness, which improves the serenity of all parties involved.

To psychologically purge jealousy and envy, you'll need a sense of purpose and a plan. Once you've decided these feelings have outlived their usefulness, you can go after freedom. Aside from being able to set limits in situations involving normal jealousy, as I've mentioned, the idea here is to define areas you need to strengthen in yourself rather than obsessing about anything external.

TAKE YOUR EYES OFF OTHER PEOPLE
AND AFFIRM YOUR SELF-ESTEEM

Instead of feeding envy and jealousy, try these techniques.

1. *Journal about your feelings.*
   - *Identify the object of your negative emotions.* For instance, "I'm jealous of my sister because she gets all our family's attention." Or "I envy a friend because she's thin."
   - *Frankly admit what insecurity got stirred in you.* For instance: "I don't deserve my family's attention since I'm not as interesting as my sister." Or "I'll always be overweight."
   - *Look further.* Track down when you first felt jealousy or envy. Perhaps while growing up, your dominating sister never let you get a word in edgewise. Or at school, classmates were stick-thin while you've always battled weight. Remember how these scenarios made you feel. Did you lose confidence? Was that when you began labeling yourself as unworthy, unattractive, or uninteresting? Record the details of your experience.

2. *Substitute negative messages with affirmations.* Observe your insecurities, but reel them in. Also challenge them to see if they have any basis in fact. Is it true you don't deserve attention or are forever condemned to being overweight? Collect facts to confirm or deny these beliefs. Reorient your focus to reinforce self-esteem. If you're jealous or envious, say, "Okay, I know what's happening. I can turn this around." For instance, tell yourself, "I'm interesting and deserve to be close with my family." Or "I'm beautiful, regardless of weight. Besides, I can always become thinner if I set my mind to it." Then behave accordingly. Be more assertive at family gatherings, not letting your sister steal the show. Or start a weight loss regimen that feels right to you. By constructively channeling your energy, you won't waste it on jealousy or envy.

3. *Seek professional guidance.* Working with a psychotherapist you
click with can help remove blocks to self-esteem and hasten the
transformation of negative emotions.

The freedom you'll gain by practicing these skills is that you won't
keep cogitating in the emotional mind-set of what I call "Your Majesty
the Baby." We all know how that "wah-wah" attitude goes: "I want
what I want when I want it. If I don't get it, I'm frustrated and I'll
envy anyone who does have it." The baby believes, "You're the one
who makes me feel bad," and doesn't take responsibility for his or her
emotions. You can't be a baby and be free. I hope you're as tired as I
am of that infantile mode of relating. Self-esteem provides a refuge
from envy and jealousy, and imparts an accountability for emotions
so you don't falsely believe your mood is at the mercy of others. It'll
grow when you keep replacing dilapidated psychological patterns
with enlightened ones.

WE ALL COME INTO LIFE with different emotional hot
buttons. Some of us have more jealousy and envy to contend with
than others. The Sixth Transformation offers the chance to relinquish
what you've got and broaden your self-esteem. This is a tribute to our
brain's plasticity, the ability to change as the result of new learning,
both linear and intuitive. The heightened consciousness that follows
will enliven your life. However, I agree with Sherlock Holmes when
he says, "Our brain can only hold so much. It's of the highest importance, therefore, not to have useless facts elbowing out useful
ones . . . to keep a clear mind and open space around you." Removing
negative emotions enables your soul to fully spread its wings. That
gorgeousness happens when self-esteem phases out jealousy and envy,
a calculated evolution of emotional freedom.

I love this Buddhist precept: "My happiness is your happiness.
There is no greater happiness in the world." Experiencing such

magnanimity, even for a few moments, lets you see the fellowship that's possible between us. Wishing each other well augments collective abundance and circulates that good energy back to you. This intuitively substantiated position is emotional light-years ahead of feeling constantly belittled by others' assets. The Sixth Transformation's jewel is self-esteem, accepting your true beauty and value, a reality-shaping recognition. Whenever I lose track of this, I like to remember that we all have a little stardust in us.

Meditation on Freedom

Celebrate Self-Esteem

In a relaxed, quiet state, dedicate at least five minutes to reveling in what you're most proud of about yourself. Make this a negativity-free zone: only positive thoughts allowed. Tell yourself, "I feel great about _____," then fill in the blank. For instance, "I feel great that I exercised today . . . that I'm being kinder to myself . . . that I'm a hard worker . . . that I'm treating myself with more kindness." Don't be shy. You deserve credit. Saying "yes" to your attributes celebrates self-esteem.

*Holding on to anger is like grasping a hot coal with the intent of
throwing it at someone else; you are the one who gets burned.*

—THE BUDDHA

12

THE SEVENTH TRANSFORMATION:

FACING ANGER, BUILDING

COMPASSION

WHO SAYS PEOPLE can't change? Listen to what happened
to my colleague and friend Mark Borovitz, whose progression from
gangster/con man to rabbi exemplifies how anger can be transformed
by compassion.

After the death of his father when he was fourteen, Mark was
enraged by this "senseless, irreparable loss." He viewed the world as
unfair and hypocritical. His response was to cop an attitude of "Who
cares? I'll get mine." He wrote bad checks, ran stolen goods for the
mob, became an alcoholic. A stint in prison only increased his rage at
the world. After decades of scamming, he once again landed behind
bars, where this time his life changed. He started attending Alcoholics
Anonymous meetings. Then, with the guidance of a chaplain, he
began reading Torah, trying to figure out the relationship of his confused life to the teachings of this sacred text. Also, he met Harriet, a
social worker, who helped him and other inmates get sober (I described
her spiritual journey and work in Chapter 8). When Mark was released
from prison, he became a resident at the halfway house she ran on the
outskirts of the Tenderloin, a Los Angeles barrio, where helicopters

with loudspeakers and spotlights chasing gang members were daily occurrences. Harriet soon asked him to join the staff. They subsequently married, though many doubters didn't think it could last. Twenty years later, their marriage is strong and they continue to run "House of the Return" together, a shared dream. But despite their great success with ex-cons, Mark knew that many mental health professionals didn't take him seriously because he lacked formal credentials. As he moved deeper into his spiritual quest, Mark felt a calling and went to Israel for rabbinical school. Now a rabbi and back in Los Angeles, he's spiritual director of the program he and Harriet have made their life's work.

Today, Mark is red-bearded and robust, still true to his wild spirit, but utterly dependable. He exudes a quietness of being that complements his passionate intensity. How did the emotional turnabout happen? Entering both individual psychotherapy and couples therapy with Harriet, he began to look within to address the loss of his father and other areas where he'd felt wronged so he wouldn't stay imprisoned in resentments. This helped him transform rage-fueled behavior and to take the risk of love and trust. In the course of healing, he went from seeing everything as "all about me" and playing the bitter victim who blamed the world and wanted to "get back" at everyone and everything to taking responsibility for his feelings and actions. As a result, he gained more compassion for others and himself. Further, as a rabbi, his ever-growing spiritual connection and dedication to serving others continues to take him beyond self-centeredness to emotional freedom. Full of hope as Mark's story is, however, it's not a fairy tale with a pat ending. At times he still has to confront the many layers of his anger so that he can keep growing—an impressive commitment to transforming this emotion.

The Seventh Transformation explores the dynamics of anger and offers numerous tactics to overcome it with compassion. You'll learn to identify anger, then work through and release the feeling without being possessed by it, becoming a loose cannon, or alienating people. This will empower you and improve your relationships. In my psychiatric practice, I've seen how expressing anger positively can be liberating on a personal level and enhance communication. I've also witnessed anger's destructive force, whether directed toward others or oneself. Anger is toxic to your system and damaging to relationships *unless it's healthily communicated,* a skill set most people lack. It can eat you alive, close your heart, and make you unable to think straight. Of all the negative emotions, it's most apt to erupt into physical or verbal aggression. I'm determined to deal with (not suppress or spew) this potentially incendiary emotion in my life as quickly as possible so it doesn't make me anxious or sick or needlessly wound anyone. Over the years, I've had to hold on to my seat and my center during many a couples therapy session where spouses venomously accosted each other until they learned to relate with more compassion. Spitefully calling a mate an "unfit mother" or "rotten lover" cuts deep. Some words are nearly impossible to take back. Though anger is very human, I'll describe how you can rule it rather than being its slave.

WHAT MAKES YOU ANGRY?

I'm defining anger (from the Latin *angere,* "to strangle") as a strong sense of displeasure and antagonism that arises when a need isn't met or an expectation isn't fulfilled. What commonly gets us angry? Being treated unfairly, manipulatively, or with disrespect, especially if it's intentional. Also feeling unappreciated, feeling threatened, or having our emotional or physical borders infringed upon. Studies document that couples most frequently fight about sex, money, children, and chores. For my part, I get most angry when someone presumes to dictate how I should feel or be. Given my makeup, such trespassing never works. Do you hear me up there, Mother?

Anger can arise from a range of situations. It results from everyday irritants: your teenager's messy room, an officemate's loud voice. Anger can also have more serious provocations: your spouse has an affair, a friend goes after your job. Or, beyond the personal, you can be incensed at travesties such as racism or pollution. Or you can be angry at God for whatever seems unfair, from war to poor health to being alone. Depending on the circumstances, anger may range from getting mildly peeved to homicidal rage.

In fact, our twenty-first-century lives are so rage-filled we've given various types of outbursts different names. Road rage. Plane rage. Desk rage. Cell phone rage. Grocery store rage. Standing in line at my market, I once saw a woman unleash her fury at an express-lane violator by spraying him with a can of whipped cream. Many people have so much pent-up, unexamined anger simmering beneath the surface that minor provocations can make it blow. They're more likely to erupt at a waiter if their soup is lukewarm, or at their mate for leaving laundry on the floor. Sometimes the results can be tragic. Take the horrendous example of the enraged dad who killed his son's hockey team coach at a practice game because he disagreed with how the coach was training the team. Such out-of-control rage can have devastating physical and emotional consequences.

The Seventh Transformation offers solutions for addressing anger, whether justified or not, and how to cope without feeling destroyed if someone is angry at you. You can begin by honestly evaluating this emotion's current role in your life—an important step because you can't stuff anger without consequences. It's a shape-shifter. If internalized, anger can turn into depression and other painful emotions as well as cause gross stress-related outbreaks and purgations ranging from acid regurgitation to rashes to diarrhea. Or it'll manifest as unconscious passive aggression—belittling others, withholding emotionally, nastiness, or gossiping. Blind to the fact that your anger is being displaced, you may snipe at or denigrate people, which won't endear you to anyone. To avoid such a fate, take the following quiz to clarify this emotion's hold on you.

ANGER QUIZ: HOW ANGRY AM I?

- When I'm hurt, do I want to hurt the other person?
- Do little things make me mad?
- Am I frequently irritable, bossy, or argumentative?
- Is my anger hard to control?
- Do I say things during a conflict that I regret later?
- Do I make judgmental or cutting remarks?

- Does my anger hurt loved ones?
- Do I hold onto resentments?
- Do I lose my temper in traffic jams or lines?

Answering yes to between seven and nine questions indicates a high level of anger, far more than is good for you or anybody else. Four to six yeses indicate a moderate level, something to work on. One to three yeses indicate a minimal level. Zero yeses indicate you're in a peaceful zone.

Even if you're carrying around some heavy anger now, compassion can help alter lifelong patterns so you can respond more effectively. I'm defining compassion as the humane capacity of empathizing with your own or another's suffering, shortcomings, and aspirations, which may spur you to help others in need. It's a form of *unconditional* love so sweet it can melt the anger within. You can also feel compassion when you simply witness something touching, such as a momma bird feeding a baby bird or a hardworking friend achieving her career dream. *Compassion is necessary to transform every negative emotion, but it's particularly central to anger. Why? It enables you to mercifully uncover and heal the hurt underlying this emotion. Otherwise, you'll remain oblivious to your anger's deeper causes, which puts you at risk for becoming self-righteous or aggressive.* When you develop compassion, you'll be less reactive. If people get angry at you, you won't slip into what my spiritual teacher calls "the old response of yelling, punishing, or picking up a stick to chase them." This doesn't excuse others' harmful behavior, but compassion gives you more insight into it so you can wisely respond and aim toward forgiveness, a liberating practice I'll elaborate on.

The Seventh Transformation asks you to radically redefine anger through the eyes of compassion. You'll accomplish this by examining the biology, spirituality, energetic power, and psychology of these emotions. Then you'll have more inspired options than just baring your claws, shutting down, or turning your anger inward. You'll also learn how to deal with bullies and gossips, and recognize the ruinous effects of revenge and spite. However, being compassionate doesn't

mean you'll never get angry or that you'll be a doormat. It's appropriate to feel anger when you've been wronged, or at injustices. It's
appropriate to set clear limits on hurtful behavior or remove yourself
from unhealthy situations. But anger turns to suffering if it consumes
you. I unreservedly agree with Krishnamurti: "To end violence we
must relentlessly keep freeing ourselves from the violence within."
That's the purpose of this chapter's techniques.

The Anatomy of Anger and Compassion: Putting the Seventh Transformation into Action

What I greatly value about this transformation is that it'll prepare you
to contact compassion more swiftly in the face of anger. Over the
decades of my medical practice, I've realized that most patients aren't
trying *not* to be compassionate; they simply don't think to go there
when they're angry or pause long enough in heated moments to summon this state. Compassion is often a sleeping giant within that needs
to be awakened with awareness. In the next sections you'll learn to
recognize anger's earliest signals and compassionately handle the situation that instigated it.

REPROGRAM THE BIOLOGY OF ANGER AND COMPASSION

Anger is intensely, primally physical. Consider what it does to your
body. Let's say a colleague double-crosses you in a business deal. You
feel angry. Your amygdala stimulates adrenaline. You get an energy
rush that rallies you to fight. Blood flows to your hands, making it easier to grasp a weapon. Your heart pumps faster. You breathe harder.
Your pupils dilate. You sweat. In the red-hotness of this hyperadrena-
lized state, aggression mounts. You may raise your voice, point accus-
ingly, stare him down, grimace, flail your arms, verbally intimidate,
barge into his personal space. Taken to an extreme, you could be

driven to knock him out or beat him up. In a pure survival-oriented sense, you want to dominate and retaliate to protect yourself and prevent further exploitation. (Alternatively, when you're the object of anger, you may have the instinct to fight or else take flight, depending on your coping style and the situation.) Anger is one of the hardest impulses to control because of its evolutionary value in priming us to defend against danger.

What biological variables have been shown to make us more susceptible to anger? One is an accumulation of built-up stresses. That's why your temper can flare more easily after a long, frustrating day in the office. The second is letting anger and resentments smolder. When anger becomes chronic, cortisol, the stress hormone, contributes to its slow burn. Remaining in this condition makes you edgy, quick to snap. Research has proven that anger feeds on itself. The effect is cumulative: each angry episode builds on the hormonal momentum of the time before. For example, even the most devoted, loving mothers may be horrified to find themselves screaming at their kids if they haven't learned to constructively defuse a backlog of irritations. Therefore, the powerful lesson our biology teaches us is the necessity of breaking the hostility cycle early on, and that brooding on the past is hazardous to well-being.

For optimal health, you must address your anger. But the idea isn't to keep blowing up when something flips you out; rather, it's to develop body-friendly strategies to express this emotion. Otherwise, you'll be set up for illnesses such as migraines, irritable bowel syndrome, or chronic pain, which all can be exacerbated by tension. Or you'll keep jacking up your blood pressure and constricting your blood vessels, which compromises flow to the heart. Underscoring this, a Johns Hopkins Medical Center study reports that young men who habitually react to stress with anger are significantly more likely than their calmer counterparts to have an early heart attack, even without a family history of heart disease. Further, other studies have shown that hostile couples who hurl insults and roll their eyes when arguing physically heal more slowly than less antagonistic partners who have a "we're in this together" attitude. Still, repressing anger isn't the answer either. Research also reveals that those who keep silent during marital disputes have a greater chance of dying from heart disease or suffering stress-related ailments than those who speak their minds. In contrast, studies have shown that religious people have better health because they're more compassionate.

So what's the solution? Cultivating compassion can both improve your health and biologically reprogram your approach to anger by training you to view this emotion differently. Sure, you can act spitefully or dump anger on others. You may even feel a brief catharsis, but it won't do anything good for your health, immune system, longevity, or relationships. Compassion, on the other hand, lets you say to yourself in a fight with a friend, "This is a painful situation. I'm furious. She's furious. Still, how can I be kind to myself and not react vindictively?" This quantum leap of consciousness subdues the fight-or-flight response, calms your system, and assuages the killer instinct that only wants to do damage by striking back. Then you can try to get your needs met more peacefully. This doesn't mean you can't express your feelings. It just colors the tone and energy with which you do this, and it lets you have more empathy for the hurt underlying your own and another's anger.

My patients Cody and Sara, in their twenties and just married, were crazy in love, yet they fought constantly. Two artists living in a downtown Los Angeles loft, these intense, bright-eyed idealists indulged their anger in the name of passion. But like many people, they hadn't a clue how to appropriately get angry, let alone with compassion. They came to me because they were tired of fighting—about money, bossy in-laws, even taking out the trash. Since they both lacked positive role models for dealing with anger, they automatically mimicked their parents' dysfunctional behavior. Typically, when anger arose, Cody would wage World War III and Sara would try to contain her feelings for an hour or two until she'd break down weeping. They'd have toxic explosions, then passionate makeups. This was a roller-coaster ride for their neurotransmitters, which taxed their bodies and required a recovery period to regain an even keel.

I was glad Cody and Sara came to me so soon in their marriage. I've seen many couples remain entrenched in similarly angry struggles for decades, addicted to the fight. But not this pair. Cody and Sara were still in the blush of new romance. Studies suggest that the brain in this phase is much like a brain on drugs. MRI scans illustrate that the same area lights up when an addict gets a fix of cocaine as when a lovesick person is in the midst of that rapture. This biological fact could benefit Cody and Sara because they were so eager to please each other and communicate better. However, neuroscience indicates that what makes a relationship last is compassionate love, which goes beyond honeymoon chemistry. It's the kind of love and mutual respect you feel after years of arguments, celebrations, and tragedies. Don't get me wrong. I didn't want to take away one iota of this couple's passion. But I did want to introduce an early dose of compassion into their handling of anger so that they could have any hope of living happily ever after.

How and when anger gets expressed in a relationship is as intimate a consideration as making love. We all have biological and other preferences that must be honored. In couples therapy, I helped Sara and Cody become aware of their own needs as well as to have compassion for each other's. Over a six-month period, I guided them through all aspects of the Seventh Transformation, but discovering anger's impact on the body let them make headway in a critical area. For example, following a bout of anger, Cody would turn into a junkyard dog; if you didn't rile him for a while, he'd become sweet again. But Sara hadn't grasped this biological fact about Cody's makeup, nor had he perceived this need in himself. Sara's style of dealing with anger was different. She wanted to talk through their differences right away. When Cody didn't reciprocate, she'd crank up the pressure, which only got him madder. Then she'd feel rejected, whimper, "You don't love me," and cry so hard her body heaved and quaked. Seeing Sara in such distress would tear Cody apart. He'd comfort her, profess undying devotion. They'd snuggle, kiss, and often have sex, which would temporarily break the tension, but the pattern around anger wasn't resolved. A few days later, they'd fight again about something else.

The couple realized that Cody needed to be left alone after an argument until his neurotransmitters cooled down. Sara has started to give Cody more biological breathing room, and he's doing his best to discuss the conflict in question within a day so that Sara doesn't become anxious. Further, they're both trying to promptly pinpoint and clear

areas of contention to prevent these physically and emotionally draining explosions. It's one thing to love someone and another to have
compassion for that person's needs, especially when it comes to anger.
But watching this young couple's willingness to change their behavior,
their ongoing dedication to creating a compassionate relationship—
which included persevering when they didn't succeed—was inspiring.

The following exercises will reprogram the biology of your anger
with compassion. These simple, commonsense techniques will help
calm all inflammatory interactions, whether you're on the giving or
receiving end of anger.

Emotional Action Step

FOUR EVERYDAY TIPS TO DEFUSE ANGER
AND NURTURE COMPASSION

1. *When you're upset, pause and slowly count to ten.* To offset the
   adrenaline surge of anger, train yourself not to lash back impulsively. No matter how vile someone is being, wait before you
   speak. Take a few deep breaths and *very* slowly, silently, count to
   ten (or to fifty if necessary). Use the lull of these moments to
   regroup before you decide what to do. To relax, repeat inwardly,
   "Calm is beautiful." Exhibiting such mindful constraint gives
   you command of the interaction and spares you untoward
   repercussions.

2. *Take a cooling-off period.* To further quiet your neurotransmitters,
   take a longer time-out, hours or more. When you're steaming or
   after an altercation, retreat to a calm setting to lower your stress
   level. Reduce external stimulation. Dim the lights. Listen to
   soothing music. Meditate. Do some aerobic exercise or yoga to
   expel anger from your system and wind down. The first scientific
   study on anger, conducted in 1899, and many since have
   documented the importance of a cooling-off period to center
   yourself before taking stock of the anger's cause.

3. *Don't try to address your anger when you're rushed.* Make sure you have adequate time to address what's made you angry. Research on the neuroscience of the Good Samaritan phenomenon reveals that being in a rush poses a major obstacle to our natural compassion. A Princeton study found that even after theology students heard a lecture on the Good Samaritan, they didn't stop to help a distressed person on the street when they thought they'd be late for their next class. The moral: allotting unhurried time to resolve the conflict lets you tap in to your most compassionate response.

4. *Don't try to address your anger when you're tired or before sleep.* Since anger revs up your system, it can interfere with restful sleep and cause insomnia. The mind grinds. Better to examine your anger earlier in the day so your adrenaline can simmer down. Also, being well rested makes you less prone to reacting with irritation and allows you to stay balanced.

Taking these biological precautions saves you from being bashed by anger's biochemicals. You'll have the lucidity and forbearance to model a more compassionate kind of being, a testament to how our brains have evolved. As I've previously described in reference to empathy, our mirror neurons can facilitate this heartfelt shift by providing a brain-to-brain bridge designed to help us connect intimately with others. If you're with someone who's angry or serene, these emotions will reverberate in you too. Therefore, we must embody compassion in the face of anger to advance beyond a Neanderthal kill-or-be-killed mentality. You can practice this now. Start with your own relationships. As Gandhi said, we must be the change we want to see.

UNCOVER THE SPIRITUAL MEANING OF ANGER AND COMPASSION

Compassion is a radical form of spiritual activism that lets you see deeper into anger than you've ever seen before. It requires observing this emotion from the top of the mountain instead of at its own level. We can come up with so many good reasons why we shouldn't feel compassion: Someone doesn't deserve it. They got what was coming to them. They're beyond forgiveness. These usual, limited ways of reacting to anger, however, are yesterday's news once we access our spirituality to counteract this emotional crippler.

Here's an example of what I mean. A woman once traveled to Dharamsala, India, to interview the Dalai Lama. On the street she saw a man viciously beating a dog. She asked the Dalai Lama about it. He said, "Compassion means being sorry for the man as well as the dog." Needless to say, we're justified in being appalled by the despicable louse who'd beat an innocent dog or anyone else. But if we take a spiritual perspective, we can't stop there. We've also got to recognize the suffering in the perpetrator that would prompt him to such brutality—not condoning the act but accurately perceiving the pain motivating all angry acts. In terms of emotional freedom, this understanding will lead us to transform anger in ourselves and infuse compassion into how we deal with anger in others. I know this may be hard to wrap your mind around. But until we can stare anger in the eye and react differently, we haven't gotten very far.

Transforming anger involves authentic, often hard-earned compassion, not the faux variety where you're compassionate only when people are looking or if it's politically correct. Also stay aware that extravagant acts of kindness don't eclipse the value of their less showy cousin, human decency. Anger can be a bear to transform. Even when you're diligently working with this emotion, it's still easy to get your buttons pushed or lapse into behavior you're not proud of.

In this regard, I was in stitches watching the film *Anger Management*. Following a series of flukes, the emotionally repressed character played by Adam Sandler uncharacteristically flies into multiple rages in public and lands in anger rehab, where Jack Nicholson plays his court-appointed "anger therapist." Nicholson is supposed to be teaching him how to express anger positively but really may be after his girlfriend. As part of "therapy," Nicholson takes him to meet his boyhood nemesis, Arnie Shankman, a bully who'd humiliated and beat him up throughout school. They track down Arnie in a Zen monastery. He'd become a monk! They find Arnie in saffron robes, head shaved, meditating, and humming *"om"* under a tree. But Arnie's monkhood didn't stop Nicholson. He prods Sandler, "Aren't you ashamed you never stood up to Shankman? Confront him or you're going to prison." Sandler can hardly get it out and stutters: "Arnie, when we were kids, you bullied me." Then, as the momentum of his brewing rage from adolescence builds, he proceeds to list the litany of tortures Arnie put him through. The reformed Arnie calmly apologizes, explains he's on a spiritual path now, and has seen the error of his ways: "I'm a changed man," he sincerely declares. But Sandler keeps needling him, trying to get under Arnie's skin. Nothing works, until he blurts out, "In high school I slept with your sister to get back at you!" Suddenly, Arnie's serene veneer finally cracks; red as a beet, he furiously begins whaling on Sandler, reverting to true bully form. Sandler starts punching him. They roll on the ground fighting. A fellow gardener-monk comes to Arnie's rescue, going at Sandler with a rake. Then a gleeful Nicholson pulls out a gun, aims it at the growing crowd of about thirty monks, and threatens to shoot. They all think it's real. But when Nicholson pulls the trigger, it sprays the crowd with water. Fists raised and yelling bloody murder, dozens of monks chase the two of them off the grounds as they run for their car.

Ah, anger. How deep it can run, how quickly incited. Expect it. But whether or not you're wearing saffron robes, strive to enlist your highest self in all aspects of life, especially when it's most difficult. This can be confusing because Western culture has a split view of anger: it denounces extreme versions but tends to view subtler ones as necessary strengths that allow you to be aggressive and "get ahead." Offering another perspective, scholar Robert Thurman says in his book *Anger* that Buddhists consider anger a root addiction similar to desire, born of a delusion that leads to suffering. Here are four spiritually based guidelines to help you cultivate the compassion that can transform anger in daily life. This will give you a stronger center of gravity when contending with anger and help you feel good about how you respond.

Guideline 1: Set Your Intention to Release Resentments

A resentment is a grievance or grudge that you harbor after you've felt mistreated. It's easy to hold on to all the incidents that angered you, from a gossiping hairdresser to a two-timing ex-boyfriend. And if you took a poll, you'd probably get a lot of people on your side about your right to stay resentful. According to such logic, as time passes and resentments mount, you have the "right" to get angrier and angrier, becoming a broken record of complaints. But is that the sour person you want to be? Instead, for emotional freedom, work on letting resentments go, permitting compassion to purify them. One friend, in the midst of that process, likened uncovering resentments to "dragging dead bodies out of a well." You don't want moldering negativity rotting your psyche. Also, as my hero Rosa Parks so correctly said when I interviewed her in *Positive Energy:* "If you stay angry at other people, you might miss finding friends among those you were angry with." Surrendering old hurts can feel difficult, even impossible at times. You may resist the whole idea. But to be an extraordinary person, one who values compassion over hatred, forgiveness is essential.

Guideline 2: Cultivate Forgiveness

Forgiveness is the spiritual act of compassionately releasing resentments, anger, or the desire to punish someone or yourself for an offense. It's a state of grace, nothing you can force or pretend. No shortcuts there. Mistakenly, some of my patients, earnestly wanting to be "spiritual," have prematurely tried to go straight to forgiveness after someone emotionally knifes them in the gut. No can do. First, you must feel anger before you can begin to forgive. In Energy Psychiatry, I *gradually* guide patients to the large-heartedness of forgiving injuries either caused by others or self-inflicted. A Stanford research study shows that practicing forgiveness decreases stress, anger, and psychosomatic symptoms. Forgiveness comes from your highest self, an expansion of vision. Ultimately it does more for you than for anyone else because it liberates you from negativity and lets you move forward. Forgiving might not make anger totally dissolve, but it will give you the freedom of knowing you are so much more. I repeat: forgiveness refers to the actor, not to the act—not to the offense but to the woundedness of the offender. This doesn't mean you'll run back to your battering spouse because of compassion for the damaged person he or she is. Of course you want to spare yourself mistreatment. However, from a distance, you can try to forgive the conscious or unconscious suffering that motivates people. Our desire to transform anger is a summoning of peace, well worth the necessary soul stretching.

As part of forgiveness, take this reality check: people bring a lifetime of wounds to relationships, which may make their behavior more about them than you. You might justifiably say, as one of my patients did, "I'm hurt and furious my spouse left me and refused to even talk about it. Isn't it reasonable to want that?" Naturally it is. But your need doesn't take into consideration your spouse's terror of intimacy, or that he or she would do anything to escape it in your relationship or any other. Unfortunately, your spouse's fears and inadequacies won out over your needs. To find forgiveness while endeavoring to heal anger, you must evaluate whom you're dealing with, the good and the bad. Often, people are just doing the best they can—which may not amount to a hill of beans where you're concerned, but it does represent the sad truth of the situation. Accepting the truth of someone's limitations will help you to forgive. It will get you past the paralysis of old resentments so you can achieve the happiness, peace, and love that you desire.

Compassion opens a hidden door to a secret world that exists beyond anger. Notwithstanding, the feelings of anger or forgiveness aren't mutually exclusive. You can simultaneously experience varying degrees of both. Perhaps at first you're a little forgiving and a lot angry. But when you progress with the Seventh Transformation, the scales increasingly tip toward forgiveness as your attachment to anger recedes.

Guideline 3: Make Amends

If you've been angry in a nonconstructive manner, there's always the option of apologizing and making other amends, including changing your behavior, in an ongoing way or taking steps to undo or minimize harm. Granted, it can stick in our craw to set aside our ego-driven need to be "right," or to admit we were insensitive or wrong. Still, it's a caring, humble act others appreciate. As I've noted, anger isn't limited to just exploding at someone. There are gradations. It can take the form of, say, being bitchy, imperious, judgmental, or condescending. I tend to displace my anger away from its source by pointing out picayune, unrelated things that irritate me about others: a friend brakes "too much" in heavy traffic, my cleaning person didn't get the dust behind a plant. When I catch myself lapsing into this mode instead of addressing the issue with the appropriate person, I apologize by saying, "I'm sorry for being so critical or if I hurt your feelings. Please forgive me." Inwardly, I try to clarify the real cause of my anger, which is usually linked to larger disappointments, rather than continuing to be that wretch of a nitpicker. However you express anger, try to make amends as quickly as possible. Most apologies can be short and sweet, though some require lengthier discussions. Picking up the phone to sincerely say "I'm sorry" will help clear the atmosphere so that resentments don't build. This isn't simply spouting an excuse; it's sincerely admitting you were wrong. In addition, sometimes concrete reparations are called for. You can ask the person, "What can I do to make this up to you?" For instance, you might agree on a payment schedule to relieve a debt, or set straight a harmful rumor you started with those you spread it to. In the case of many emotional breaches, sometimes the best amends involve apologizing, hearing the person out, and acknowledging the hurt you caused, then consistently treating that person well.

Guideline 4: Resist Revenge

Revenge is the desire to get even when someone does you wrong. It's natural to feel angry, to say "I'm not going to let that **** get away with this," whatever "this" is. However, revenge reduces you to your worst self, putting you on the same level with those spiteful people we claim to abhor. Sure, if someone hits you with a stick, you have the impulse to hit them back—that's the basis for wars. To thrive personally and as a species, we must resist this predictable lust for revenge, and seek to right wrongs more positively. This doesn't make you a pushover; you're just refusing to act in a tediously destructive way antithetical to ever finding peace. What I'm suggesting is a version of "turn the other cheek" while still doing everything to preserve what's important to you. The really hard part, though, is watching someone "get away with something" when there isn't anything you can do about it. Yes, your wife left you for the yoga instructor. Yes, your weaselly colleague sold you out. When I confront this kind of galling situation in my life, I take solace in the notion of karma, that sooner or later what goes around comes around. For me, this isn't a rationalization, but something I firmly believe. Also know that the best revenge is your success, your happiness, and the triumph of not giving vindictive people any dominion over your peace of mind.

To directly experience forgiveness, try this exercise. Do it in conjunction with the process of healing and transforming anger.

Emotional Action Step

BE BIGGER THAN ANGER—
PRACTICE FORGIVENESS NOW

1. *Identify one person you're angry with.* Start with someone low on your list, not your rageaholic father. Then you can get a taste of forgiveness quickly. After that you can proceed to tackle more challenging targets.

2. *Honestly address your feelings.* Talk to friends, your therapist, or other supportive people, but get the anger out. I also recommend writing your feelings down in a journal to purge negativity. Then decide whether you want to raise the issue with that person. If so, use the Rules for Compassionate Communication, presented later in this chapter.

3. *Begin to forgive.* Hold the person you're angry with clearly in your mind's eye. Then ask yourself, "What emotional shortcomings caused him or her to treat me poorly?" This is what you want to have compassion for, the area to forgive. Definitely do everything possible not to subject yourself to shabby treatment, but reach for compassion for the person's emotional blindness or cold heart. Forgiveness from hurt flows from this.

Here are a few suggestions of how forgiveness can work in a range of situations where you'd have every right to be angry. It establishes a kinder mind-set whether or not you decide to confront someone.

- *A good friend acts inconsiderately when she's having a bad day.* Remember, nobody's perfect. You may want to let the incident slide. If you do mention it, don't make this onetime slight into a big deal. Give your friend a break—forgive the lapse.
- *Your teenager keeps screaming at you and treats you disrespectfully.* Set consistent, appropriate limits on the behavior; let him or her know it's unacceptable. But instead of simply getting mad in response and leaving it there, try to have compassion for the pain that motivates the anger. Do what you can to find the cause of your teenager's acting out, which will generally go beyond just you.
- *A coworker takes credit for your ideas.* Do damage control, whether it means mentioning this situation to the coworker, your boss, or Human Resources, and don't trust her with ideas in the future. However, try to forgive the coworker for being such a greedy, inse-cure, mean-spirited person that she has to stoop so low as to steal from you.
- *Your mother-in-law is needy or demanding.* Keep setting kind but firm boundaries so that over time you can reach palatable compro-mises. But also have mercy on the insecurities beneath her needi-ness and demands—perhaps fear of being alone, of aging, of being excluded from the family, of not being heard. This will soften your response to her.
- *You suffered childhood abuse.* The healing process of recovering from abuse requires enormous compassion for yourself and is facilitated by support from other abuse survivors, family, friends, or a therapist. Still, if you feel ready to work toward forgiveness of an abuser, it necessitates seeing the brokenness and suffering that would make the person want to commit such grievous harm. You're not excusing the behavior or returning to it, but grasping how emotionally crippled he or she is—a huge stretch of compas-sion, but the path to freedom.

Compassion is a paradigm-shifting spiritual solution for transforming anger. Nonetheless, how you express it must always be guided by intuition and common sense. Buddhist nun Pema Chödrön warns against what she insightfully terms "idiot compassion"—using kindness to avoid conflict when a resounding "no" is required. I completely agree. To preserve our emotional freedom, we must know where to draw the line.

Additionally, beware of the "do-gooder syndrome," also known as "the helping hand strikes again." This is where overenthusiastic compassion can go wrong and unintentionally harm the recipient. Do-gooders sometimes get so caught up in the gratification they feel when doing something nice for someone that they fail to consider whether their actions are truly in the person's best interest. Do-gooders have a plus side and a minus side. They often do a lot of good for others, acts to be proud of. But in some instances, these good acts can lead to undesired results. Sometimes giving, especially donations of money, inadvertently embarrasses the recipients, makes them feel less-than, and hurts their pride. This can foster resentments. I have a compassionate friend who has a touch of do-gooderism. Feeling lonely after his wife died, he struck up a friendship with a homeless man in Venice Beach—not something that everyone would do. My friend brought this appreciative man lovely furnishings for his tent. But one day he was horrified to discover that the man's tent had been ransacked and that he'd been hospitalized, injured while trying to defend his new possessions from thieves. My friend never foresaw these consequences, nor had he thought through the man's vulnerability. This isn't about blame. Still, the incident made my friend ponder the complexity of some acts of compassion and their possible unintended repercussions, as we all need to consider. To be grounded in giving, we must balance both the good giving may do for us and its effect on the recipient.

Conversely, we may feel that our compassion is in short supply, that we have nothing left to give. Once, while I was changing clothes in my gym's locker room, the woman next to me admired my jade pendant. "What does it symbolize?" she asked. When I responded, "Quan Yin, the goddess of compassion," she looked stricken and declared, "My supplies of compassion have been all used up! My family has sucked every last bit of it out of me." I sympathetically nodded, appreciating how easy it is to feel this emotionally spent. So much occurs in life that can burn compassion out. But we must rebel against this. Together, let's stoke compassion's flame brighter and brighter so that anger and hatred wane.

EXPERIENCE THE ENERGETIC POWER OF ANGER AND COMPASSION

Anger is a tempestuous emotional force to be reckoned with and tamed. As an Energy Psychiatrist, I'm sobered by anger's physically destructive effects when it's channeled into psychokinetic energy, which gives thoughts and emotions the ability to affect matter. In a very real way, this emotion can jar your body and surroundings, particularly when it comes at you full-bore. Take Kate, a take-care-of-business but hot-tempered farmer in Kansas who came to my energy workshop scared of her own anger. After a cell-phone screaming match about money with her husband, the picture window beside her suddenly started violently rattling, then cracked. It wasn't the first time something like this had occurred. Previously, when she'd lost her temper, she noticed that car doors jammed, flashlight batteries went dead, and watches stopped. She'd dismissed these incidents as "just too freaky." But the window episode made her think she was in a remake of *The Exorcist*. She came to me desperate to get to the bottom of what was happening.

I conveyed to Kate that I've seen anger do strange things not explained by mainstream science. The energy of anger can inflict chaos on your body and environment, much like a twister ripping through a town. Electronic devices are especially susceptible: computers, fax machines, and cell phones can all frustratingly go on the fritz. My introduction to anger's psychokinetic energy came while working at a UCLA parapsychology lab. One of my duties was investigating ghosts. You wouldn't believe how many people in Los Angeles suspect their houses are haunted. They'd tell us about flying forks and knives and televisions and radios that mysteriously turned themselves on and off. We researchers mostly concluded, though, that even if these occurrences happened, they were misinterpreted. Generally, they seemed to be extensions of household anger; as tempers raged, episodes increased. Even when the family moved, the strange incidents would accompany them—showing how psychokinetic energy can disrupt the stability of physical objects.

What I advised Kate, and suggest to you, is to try to catch anger before it escalates, so that it doesn't implode in your organs or become a poltergeist in your space. In a way, Kate was fortunate. She received instant physical feedback when her anger went over the top. But for emotional freedom, it's vital to catch this emotion at an earlier stage and de-escalate it by invoking the perspective of compassion. You can train yourself to accomplish this by becoming familiar with how the first energetic flickers of anger and compassion register in your body. The following are common qualities of each emotion.

HOW THE ENERGY OF ANGER CAN FEEL

- Red-hot, fiery, steamed-up
- Like machine-gun fire
- Battering, blistering, hurtful
- Impulsive; you want to attack or do harm
- Like pressure building until it bursts

HOW THE ENERGY OF COMPASSION CAN FEEL

- Warm in your chest; your heart opens
- Calming; your body softens and your mind quiets down
- Nourishing; it generates a palpably positive connection to others and to Spirit
- Unconditionally loving; intuitively on-center
- Physically and emotionally cocooning and healing

Recognizing anger's initial signs gives you the opportunity to transform it expediently and with kindness. Even though anger is loud and imposing, the quiet, calm energy of compassion, when focused, can override it. Studies at Fairfield University on Transcendental Meditation (which uses repetitive phrases called mantras) showed that when a test group in high-crime neighborhoods regularly meditated on compassion and nonviolence, crime rates decreased. What extraordinary implications: people nearby could feel the energy field emitted by the meditators. Picture someone about to fly into a rage feeling a wave of that loving energy. What an amazing defuser. Anger and hatred leave a residue of energetic pollution that compassion can clear out. Consider the ramifications of this personally and for the world. As John Lennon said, *imagine.*

Set Energetic Boundaries: Coping with Intrusions into Your Personal Space

If you want to see people flip their lids fast, try invading their personal space. What is personal space? It has two main aspects. First, it's the invisible subtle energy border that surrounds us and sets our comfort level when we interact. Depending on our preferences, it can range from inches to feet and varies with situations, upbringing, and culture. (Elephants have a no-go line of a few feet around them; cross it and you'll hear a noisy bellow or be charged.) Studies indicate that most Americans need an arm's-length bubble around them. Second, personal space refers to the border that guards our physical and psychic privacy. For instance, you can violate it by barging in on your spouse when he or she needs to be alone. Other types of violations can include sound, odors, sneezing on someone if you have a cold, or cyberintrusions such as spam. You can also overstep a line that demarcates someone's property or turf, a breach that can ignite gang violence or wars between nations. To better understand your own energetic needs about personal space and respect others', be aware of the following predictable factors in daily life that stir anger.

TEN COMMON PERSONAL SPACE INTRUSIONS

1. Hearing the blather of someone's cell-phone conversation while waiting in line
2. Telemarketers
3. Loud music, loud people, loud machinery, loud cars
4. A dog lifting its leg preparing to pee on your roses
5. Internet cons, schemes, and spam
6. Gym hogs who won't let others work out on the equipment
7. Air pollution, toxic fumes (for example, car exhaust), strong perfume
8. Tailgaters or slow drivers
9. A person talking too close in your face or backslapping
10. Graffiti and vandalism

What is it about intrusions into our personal space that can make our blood boil? Aside from being obnoxious, rude, dangerous, or unhealthy, they violate a primitive energetic instinct that our well-being isn't respected or safe. This instinct goes beyond getting security codes to guard against intruders, or those scary motion-activated, talking car alarms that announce, "Move away. You're standing too close to the vehicle." When we experience such violations, our brains actually react as if we were still back in 50,000 B.C. Research shows that personal space disputes such as neighbor feuds about overgrown foliage are evolutionarily prompted responses aimed at guarding resources and ensuring survival. People take these intrusions as personal attacks. In fact, a Florida newspaper reported that after a man had his trees cut down by a machete-wielding neighbor, he said, "I should have shot him while I could." How angry we get about these intrusions depends on our stress level. If we're tense or tired, they can push us over the edge. Psychologist David Buss's *The Murderer Next Door* documents how turf conflicts often motivate assaults and murders. Indeed, national statistics indicate that nearly half of road rage incidents involve drivers using firearms and their own cars as weapons against other drivers. But such reactions aren't viable in the twenty-first century.

Rather than leading to added power, food, or resources, they result in alienating others, jail time, injury, or death. With emotional freedom, cooler minds will prevail. As I'll describe, you must learn liberating ways to deal with intrusions into your personal space so you don't let them bring out the worst in you or walk around seething.

Believe me, I know keeping calm isn't always easy. My neighbors on the floor beneath me have a barking dog. I'm a writer who worships quiet, and I'm often at home immersed in my interior life. Though I'm a die-hard animal lover, this downstairs dog is no occasional yipper. He's a champion German shepherd with a booming bark that echoes from the beach side of our building to the alley behind us. He barks intermittently throughout the day, every day, at dogs that pass by— and there are plenty. This drives me crazy. It's the kind of banal puddle you can drown in. Over the last year, I've nicely spoken with my neighbors about this on numerous occasions. At first, I sympathized with this decent couple when they said, "We couldn't have a family. Our dog is our child." But after hearing their "child" bark and bark and bark, I'm sorry, that excuse didn't cut it. Caring parents set limits for their children. These people wouldn't do the same with their dog. Over time, my anger grew. I spoke to them more forcefully about keeping the noise down, ratcheting up my irritation. Our relationship became increasingly strained.

I wish I could report that my attempts at reasoning with my neighbors worked out perfectly. There were some sublime days of relative quiet when we compromised—they agreed to control their dog and I'd be tolerant of minimal barking. I'd thank them for their efforts and apologize for contributing to any strain between us. They apologized too. We'd part congenially, sometimes even hug—but soon the barking would resume. We went through this cycle innumerable times. Clearing the air seemed to grant this couple permission to give their dog free rein.

It wasn't that I was totally depending on them to solve this. On my own, I tried different tactics to detach from the sound: earplugs, white noise machines, meditating to center myself, sending the dog loving energy to quiet him, praying for him and my neighbors. (This of course was testing my faith.) It was a lot of effort with minimal relief.

Then one afternoon, I completely lost it. I got into a yelling match with the neighbors. I'm not ordinarily a yeller, but at my wit's end, I threatened to call animal control and the police to have their dog removed. I don't win any medals for having lashed out, particularly because I could have clarified these consequences in writing sooner and in a centered way. Meanwhile, my neighbors matched me yell for yell: "Go ahead, see if we care." I'd been reluctant to issue these threats before for fear of making our already tense situation worse. I feared my neighbors might strike back by letting the dog bark at night or early in the morning when they were home. Condo dwellers are a bit like Siamese twins: you do have to live with each other. This angry exchange left me exhausted and demoralized. What happened next is a good-news, bad-news story. These days the dog does bark much less. But there's palpable friction between me and my neighbors, though it gradually seems to be decreasing.

I lament that we weren't able to collaborate on a solution that we were both more comfortable with. Problem is, we still see things so differently. My neighbors have their side and are sticking to it: "Judith is too sensitive and overreacts." And I have my side: "Ongoing barking isn't okay. It intrudes on the serenity of my home." So there we have it—a microcosm in my humble condominium complex of why there are wars. Both of us believe we are right. I understand that at one level there's only so much you can do in certain situations, that you have to accept imperfect solutions. Apologizing again to each other for behaving badly—which we have done—is certainly a step in the right direction, but to find a meeting of minds we need more.

I know the way to bring this interaction to a higher level is by stretching our compassion. We can coexist more amicably when we're able to increasingly appreciate how we both feel impinged upon, and put ourselves in the other's shoes. This will create a more enlightened dialogue between us and, thus, the possibility of lasting change. Otherwise, if we stay rigidly fixed in our positions, anger will usurp any hope of peace. Unless one of us moves away, we must interact, as opposed to other relationships—including with people you love—that you can decide to end for various reasons and without blame. However, I don't see this struggle with my neighbors as being just about us. Rather, I deeply believe that learning to resolve and find compromises on even seemingly intractable differences is also the path to global peace. This is a foundation for emotional freedom that I've emphasized throughout this book.

When someone intrudes on your personal space, try to stick to the high road. Though at times you'll have more success than others, do your best to remedy the problem using the techniques I'll suggest below. It's tempting to simply get nasty, but that provides only fleeting satisfaction with no real gains. Still, I admit I got a good chuckle out of George Hayduke's *Don't Get Mad, Get Even: The Big Book of Revenge*, a tongue-in-cheek list of diabolical schemes to make personal space violators pay—for instance, slowing down when someone tailgates you. But the reason I'm so adamantly against "payback" is that it is completely devoid of compassion for the offender or any desire to improve how we humans relate. The following exercise offers strategies for securing your personal space and dealing more sanely with those who violate it.

Emotional Action Step

HONOR YOUR PERSONAL SPACE NEEDS

When someone intrudes on your personal space, do not act impulsively. Take a breath. Stay calm. Decide how you want to respond. Sometimes you'll opt to address the issue directly. If so, it's most effective to express your needs with an even, non-accusatory or angry tone.

Option 1: Set limits.

- *Talk to your family and friends.* We often get short-tempered when we're overwhelmed. Even a brief escape will relieve pressure and lets you emotionally regroup. Plan regular mini-breaks at home. Tell your kids you need five minutes in the bathroom with the door shut and that they may not intrude. Tell your mate you want to read in a separate room when the television is on. Or set limits with a friend by saying you'd like to refrain from late-night phone calls or make an agreement that you can just be quiet during part of your walks together. Conveying your needs with kindness can lead to more loving relationships.

- *Speak up with others.* When you have an ongoing interaction with someone, it's useful to set kind, firm limits, then show appreciation when the offender adheres to them. For instance, in a sweet voice, I asked a man at my gym who's constantly on his cell phone, though they are banned, to please not use it so others could relax. Initially he snapped, "Well, I wouldn't want to disturb you!" but I just smiled back at him and sincerely said, "That is so kind of you, sir. I really appreciate it." Simple as it sounds, in this case sweetness worked. At least around me, he never used the phone again. In some circumstances, though, resolving the conflict might involve more discussion and mutual compromise.

- *Avoid toxic situations.* Avoid or minimize contact with those who don't respect your needs. For instance, don't drive in a car with a rageaholic. (Anger's poisonous energy is intensified in cramped spaces.) Or don't travel with someone who's an obsessively chronic talker if you want to be quiet and unwind.

Option 2: Practice the Zen approach.

- *Let it be.* Sometimes it's more aggravation than it's worth to confront intruders, particularly if you'll never see them again. The motormouth woman in the airport ticket line. The guy who steals your parking space. One go-with-the-flow friend told me, "No one cuts me off in traffic anymore because I let everyone in!" When faced with a "let it be" scenario, your sense of equanimity is the greatest victory. Focus on something positive and keep moving on.

- *View the personal space intruder's insensitivity with compassion.* Remember:

  - They're usually not doing it to you personally.
  - Maybe they're just having a bad day.

○ They lack the good sense or manners not to intrude.

○ They're so egotistical or inconsiderate they're only concerned for themselves, a crippling deficit of heart.

○ If they're being malicious, it's a great weakness and darkness within them.

Drawing on the Energy of Compassion

This section's exploration of the energy of both anger and compassion outlines various ways for the heart to be victorious over our less mindful selves. In all situations cultivating compassion is possible. Setting this intent with people will allow you to make love, not war. You can have compassion even if you don't like someone; even if you're mad, in a bad mood, sick, or tired; or even if practical considerations prevent your personal space needs from being met. Though you may think compassion is beyond you, it's always there to draw on.

Recently my appreciation for this deepened. Following a weeklong intensive course I gave for health care professionals in Los Angeles, I flew to Las Vegas to be a bridesmaid at the wedding of two close friends. I was grouchy from being wiped out, a state that predictably shortens my fuse. I badly needed to be left alone to rejuvenate. Still, I had to postpone that a day. I wouldn't have missed their wedding for the world. An Elvis impersonator married them; I caught the bouquet, a hoot of a celebration. But right after the ceremony, this magical moment, the groom started experiencing uncomfortable twinges in his chest, an unpleasant first. Medically, of course, I saw a remote possibility it might be a heart attack and stayed alert for further signs. In the meantime, I offered him an energy work session to see if his symptoms would dissipate. So we returned to their hotel room. By that time, however, I was so exhausted, I wondered if I had anything left to give. Still, inwardly I prayed, "Let me help my friend." Then I put my hand over his heart and stayed open to be a vessel for healing. By God, despite my leaden fatigue, I soon felt the sun-like energy of compassion flow through my hand into this dear man. He felt it too and quickly relaxed.

Soon his chest discomfort ceased. You can imagine the great relief of both bride and groom. At that point, they saw no need to go to the emergency room, but when they returned home in a few days he planned to see his doctor for a complete physical exam. As it happened, scans revealed that he had one partially blocked coronary artery, not life-threatening but in need of repair. Soon after, he underwent surgery to open it with a stent and the problem was solved.

Reflecting on this experience, what I learned more profoundly than ever is the potency of energy work and that compassion is accessible to me regardless of my irritability or my need for personal space. In your life, believe in compassion. With patients and many others, I've seen how it can lift suffering and invisibly insinuate itself into even the coldest, stoniest hearts. I've seen how it can keep my own heart open when it angrily wants to shut down. Compassion's energy is light at its brightest. It will illuminate you.

MAP THE PSYCHOLOGY OF ANGER AND COMPASSION

On the night of the first January full moon in 1993, my mother left this world angry. Angry at God that she had cancer and was in such pain. Angry at herself and her doctors for not being able to beat it. Angry that she couldn't practice medicine or be with Dad and me anymore. In one of her dreams, she was even angry at her long-deceased parents when they came to gently fetch her to go with them: "Mama, Daddy, I won't go! Leave me alone!" she kept yelling while asleep. She wanted nothing to do with departing this world. During those final days in the hospital, Mother's anger went ballistic. Though she'd always found off-color language distasteful, she swore like a truck driver at the nurses and lambasted me and my father for not doing more. As a physician, I'm well aware that anger can be how the dying cling to life, the unconscious instinct being that anger's obstinate protest can stave off death. It's common knowledge on inpatient units that angry patients, full of fight, live longer. Still, for Dad and me, Mother's wrath was searing, though we loved her with all that was in us. I talked to Mother about her anger, how it was wearing down the staff and hard on us, but she was way beyond adhering to any limits. Staying alive was her obsession. At times, not surprisingly, I felt angry at her anger, but opted not to pursue the issue with her. The days of resolving psychological issues were over for us—and, because of our joint efforts, we'd done a great deal to more respectfully understand each other. But now the focus wasn't on me. It was on how Mother was emotionally negotiating her passage to death. The way she did this, angry or not, was her right.

Ultimately, at her deathbed, it was just Mother and me. Dad had caught a bad flu; he could no longer visit. Mother had forbidden us to tell her friends that she was in the hospital, much less that she was dying. She didn't want them to see her debilitated. In the end, as I sat with her, she wasn't always angry. Sometimes she'd tenderly reminisce or be sad, holding my hand tightly. Or we'd laugh and talk as we always had. Throughout our forty years together we'd had so many amazing conversations, something I treasured about us. At other moments we'd both be quiet as kittens. During such silences, I often felt my maternal grandmother's presence in the room, three generations of women gathered together. Then, on Christmas Day, I looked into Mother's eyes and knew something had changed. As I prepared to leave, bending over to kiss her, she straightened my bangs one last time—still and forever intent on improving me—and whispered, "Judith, I love you." These were her last words. That afternoon she slipped into a coma, and she died ten days later.

The psychology of anger, how it affects living life and leaving it, is enlightening. When I reflect on Mother's anger, both in her dying and in the course of her life, I can see how hard it was for her to find compassion for her own struggles and perceived shortcomings. Before she became ill, I remember us having tea on her balcony, overlooking Westwood, where I grew up. With heartrending sincerity she asked, "Judith, at seventy why am I still so angry?" God, what a question. All I could think to say was, "I see you often getting furious with yourself for not living up to your superwoman expectations." I recognized this as an unforgiving pattern I too have to watch. Much of her anger was directed inward. But she also had very strong opinions about how Dad and I "should" be. Like many people, she felt free to show her harshest side to family members. If things didn't jibe with her vision, she'd nip at my heels, making her case like a prosecuting attorney. Yet there was more. The psychological origins of anger harken back to childhood and our reactions to role models, especially parents. My maternal grandmother, bless her soul, could be sharp-tongued and hypercritical, though also awfully caring, whimsical, wise, and intuitive too. My mother modeled all these qualities; she hardly walked around furious every minute. She was always generously present and so full of love for me. I'll never forget how, on winter days when I was a child, she used to warm my socks on a heater so my feet weren't cold on my walk to school. A very smart cookie, she did realize the cost of carrying anger around, but lacked the skills to transform it. Further, she resisted doing the requisite psychological work to clear anger, such as probing how her parents' style of conveying anger became her own. So there she was, in a bind like so many people, an unwitting bedfellow with an emotion that kept her from becoming free.

I'd like to present three psychological guidelines for transforming anger. They'll help you find more compassion for yourself and others, and improve communication in relationships.

First Guideline: Learn from Your Past

Understanding the psychology of both anger and compassion involves evaluating the formative messages you received about them. We learn how to be angry from our parents. If you had parents who were kind to themselves and you, ones who knew better than to rage and apologized if they did, then you're unusual, and lucky. More likely, parents are well-meaning but inept at expressing anger positively because they weren't shown how. In other cases, such as with alcoholic parents, they might've just been plain abusive. To psychologically explore your relationship with anger, recall how your parents articulated it. Ask yourself: Were they yellers? Criticizers? Verbally assaultive? Did they turn their anger inward? Did they emotionally lacerate themselves? How did their anger impact you? Were you afraid of it? Did you become angry too? Did you frequently hear them arguing? It's scary for children to be within earshot when their parents fight. Erroneously, they believe they caused it. Also note what role, if any, compassion played in tempering anger or as an overall influence in your home. It's useful to write your responses in a journal. Reviewing your history lets you adopt your parents' best virtues and distance yourself from their liabilities. The enemy of compassion is unconscious anger. It can be valuable to consult a therapist or spiritual guide to assist with this. Also, once you apply the Rules for Compassionate Communication I'll discuss below, you'll have tools to mindfully express anger and choose compassionate action.

Second Guideline: Outsmart Bullies

Bullying is a toxic form of anger that harms adults, teenagers, and children. It's such a timely topic because of its chilling association with school violence. After the tragic Columbine shootings in 1999, the Secret Service reported that the experience of being bullied significantly provoked the attackers' massacre of their classmates. One was described as "the kid everyone teased." In response to this landmark finding, twenty-two states passed antibullying laws to prevent harassment in schools. The Department of Justice defines bullying as "repeated acts that involve an imbalance of power" between dominating individuals and meeker ones. They cite three kinds of bullying in kids, which can apply to adults too: physical (spitting, hitting, pushing), verbal (name-calling and making threats), and psychological (social exclusion, extortion, intimidation, spreading rumors, and gossiping). Problematically, bullying is often socially accepted and even encouraged by some adults, video games, and films, which teach kids to be mean. While many of us consider bullying a normal part of childhood, it's now recognized as a behavioral red flag that requires a swift psychological intervention with kids and their families. Bullying can also carry into adulthood with hazardous results.

What causes someone to become a bully? Besides mimicking a parent's behavior, temperament figures in. One friend said of his brother, a big bruiser nicknamed "Tiny" since kindergarten, "He was so mean and angry as a boy he used to go down to the street corner bar and beat sailors up. Now Tiny's the head of a giant oil company, pushing all the rest of us around with high gas prices and pollution." My intuitive read on bullies is that they're power-obsessed, eerily empty, and devoid of empathy. They don't recognize this and see no reason to change, a dangerous kind of ignorance. Anger darkens their hearts. Studies indicate that bullies want control and view themselves as superior to others. While envy and resentments may motivate them, in fact they don't usually suffer from low self-esteem. I'm also intrigued by what dog psychology can teach us about these brutes. Cesar Millan, a masterful canine behavior specialist known as "The Dog Whisperer," stresses two principles in rehabilitating bullying, vicious dogs. The first is using "calm, assertive energy." Since many owners are tense, dogs pick up on this, which only further agitates them. Second, Cesar trains owners to become "pack leaders," which provides the stability and order dogs experience in packs. Once you assume such command, dogs won't take over the household.

If you've been bullied as a child or adult, you know how demeaning it feels. Bullies need to be definitively dealt with. Though you're not setting out to become anyone's pack leader, what you can learn from Cesar Millan is the importance of taking a calm, authoritative stance rather than rolling over in response to a bullying relative, friend, coworker, or boss. Thus, one way or another you'll take control, either by addressing the situation or by leaving it entirely. Your resolve and refusal to cower undermines the bully's game. (In instances of physical coercion, you must secure police or legal protection immediately.) Depending on your situation, enlist one or more of these techniques.

THE BULLY GUIDE

1. *Avoid becoming a target.* Bullies pick on people who're nice, who feel inferior, or who have difficulty standing up for themselves. They have a knack for discerning if you can be thrown off balance. They want to get a rise from you. In any office, there are some workers who bullies go after, others they leave alone. Do not become a victim. A bully respects people who can't be bullied.

2. *If you decide to approach the bully directly:*

- *Stay calm and assertive.* Take a breath. Try not to be emotionally reactive or flustered. Deal with the bully from a centered place, never from a sense of weakness.

- *Talk to the bully in private.* Bullies respond best if you talk to them one-on-one rather than in front of a posse who might support their position; this also avoids embarrassing them. When you begin the conversation, it's useful to define the behavior in question and suggest a specific change. Setting boundaries may help a bully back off. For instance, if a car salesman tries to bully you into making a purchase when you're not ready, say, "I know you're trained to do this, but you're pushing way too hard. I'll have to think it over." Or if a competitor gossips and spreads rumors about you, call her on it; ask her to stop. You may also use this approach with a bully boss but proceed with special caution and take care to document your actions. If you don't get results, become more than an army of one. Report him or her to management and recruit others with similar complaints to bolster your case.

3. *Use humor to deflect a bully's potshots.* It's worth a try. This is one way of showing a bully you aren't intimidated, nor will you engage with such aggression. Keeping things light indicates that you won't be pushed around or go for a bully's bait. Meanwhile, try not to take the bully's comments personally. Treat them like background noise until you've reached your limit and want to consider other options.

4. *Avoid the person or switch jobs.* If a bully won't change after using the suggested techniques, minimize or sever contact. It is unhealthy to subject yourself to ongoing mistreatment. You deserve more.

Third Guideline: Rules for Compassionate Communication

When you're angry or when someone's angry at you, there's an art to responding using a compassionate framework. My spiritual teacher says, "The goal is to win someone's heart, not to angrily control them."

From the start, setting your intention to bring compassion to the interchange radically alters the course of anger. Be the one to create this tone, especially with nasty people.

Here are two ways to better access compassion in enraging situations. Keeping them in focus allows you to have realistic expectations and a more loving heart. The first is to be willing to acknowledge the hurt beneath your anger instead of lashing out combatively and self-righteously. This is a big step. It means taking responsibility for your reaction, beginning to work through it, then seeking a nonhostile solution. You'll be substituting "I'm angry because he _____" with "I'm angry because my need for _____ wasn't met." Then communicate about how to get your need met rather than only feeling "How could he do this to me?" or engaging in the clash of the Titans, responses that will lead you straight for a fall. I witnessed such a vitriolic exchange between two CEOs who were thinking of partnering on a project involving renewable energy that would have benefited them and the world. Both were used to being in control and had confrontational styles. CEO #1 would anger the other by scheduling meetings and canceling them. CEO #2 would bristle, "I can't do everything on your schedule." CEO #1 then hurled the accusation, "You're unprofessional." To top that insult, CEO #2 finally said, "You're impossible. I can't work with you." Sadly, these people were more invested in the power struggle than in trying to understand each other's position so they could both compromise and get their needs met.

Consider this alternative solution. CEO #2 might have reasoned, "I'm hurt because CEO #1 isn't respecting my time. I'm angry because I feel like I'm losing control of this project and if she takes the lead I may not get the credit I deserve." CEO #2 could've asked herself if CEO #1 had done anything else to justify her feelings (such as trying to usurp her authority in other areas) or if she was simply getting insecure. She might have said to CEO #1, "I want to feel like an equal partner in this venture because it's going to do a lot of good. How can we figure out a schedule we're both comfortable with and move ahead?" Reframing the situation in this way would've helped CEO #2 realize that she was reacting because a need wasn't being met. Then she could more calmly move forward to achieve that goal.

The second way to access compassion is to realize that it's not the burden of your mate or anyone else to heal your emotional issues. Read that sentence again. Facilitating such healing is the function of therapists and spiritual guides. While someone may opt to change a behavior, that's very different from him or her fixing you. For instance, your mate might agree to examine his rageaholism so that his temper doesn't flare with you anymore, but that's very different from expecting your mate to heal your low self-esteem which gets inflamed by his outburst.

Anger is deceptive because the view we take of an emotional struggle determines how angry we'll feel. For instance, I might periodically get mad at not having a significant other to pick up the slack in my life, whereas you might be relieved to have that autonomy. In your relationships, convey what your triggers for anger are so that others can be more sensitive to you.

The key to addressing anger is compassionate communication. I'm defining this as an information exchange for the greater good that involves both expressing yourself and empathically listening to another. Then the people in a relationship have the possibility of transformational bonding—the ability to grow deeper as a result of communicating well—rather than pulling away or silencing angry feelings. Of course, it's wise to pick your battles. You don't want to die on just any hill. But once you've determined an issue is worth addressing, the following exercise will yield optimal results.

Emotional Action Step

SEVEN RULES FOR COMPASSIONATE COMMUNICATION

Use these along with this chapter's spiritual strategies for transforming anger.

Rule 1: Calmly express your feelings.

Rule 2: Be specific about why you're angry; stick to one issue.

Rule 3: Request a small, doable change that could meet your need. Clarify how it will benefit your relationship.

Rule 4: Listen nondefensively to another's position; don't interrupt.

Rule 5: Empathize with the person's feelings. Ask yourself: "What pain or shortcoming is causing this person to act so angrily, to behave in a manner that doesn't meet my needs?" Take some quiet moments to intuitively sense where the person's heart is hurting or closed. Then compassion will come more easily.

Rule 6: Work out a compromise or resolution. Don't stay attached to simply being "right."

Rule 7: If a person is unwilling to change, you can either accept the situation as is and try to emotionally detach from it or limit contact.

While communicating, always speak to the best in people, to their intelligence, integrity, or intuition. This will bring out the best in you too. The worst in us is just raring to emerge, but don't go for it. Refrain from being curt, condescending, or mean; it'll backfire. (Any waitress can vouch for the horrors of what happens to a rude customer's food, including being spat into.) Avoid generalizing, becoming vague, or asking for too much. Stay cool: don't explode or issue ultimatums before attempting to find common ground. All this is your meditation. Compassionate communication is a holy exchange, a meeting of hearts that overrides the fascism of malice.

IN THIS FINAL CHAPTER of the book, we can rightfully celebrate how emotional freedom puts us in full possession of ourselves, not subject to the whims of anger or other negative emotions.

When we view anger as something to process and transform, when we see compassion as the prize, we're not just courting liberation, we're living it. By applying the Seventh Transformation, compassion imbues us with a natural authority flowing from the heart rather than simply mind or ego. It permits us to behave in a radically mindful fashion. Never confuse it with weakness. The Buddha teaches: "Compassion is the way out of hell." It's our compass toward the heaven of loving-kindness.

In my own life, I'm so grateful for compassion's grace. The smallest acts are truly miraculous to me. One afternoon a friend and I were relaxing by the hotel pool during a break at a conference. Having forgotten my sunglasses, I was shielding my eyes from the sun with a piece of paper. When he reached over to hold it for me I resisted, but he just smiled, saying with absolute assurance, "I can handle this." Talk about hearing the dream words you'd always yearned for. This friend, a psychologist with keen insight into human nature, had my number. I was so used—too used—to doing everything myself, wary that well-meaning others will only cause me more work. His competent, consoling gesture conveyed such empathy for my reluctance to accept help and actually trust that someone could make my life easier without having to ask. I was touched that he recognized and honored this vulnerability in me.

Compassion also provides the crucible for healing miracles to occur. One of my workshop participants told the following story. Two years before, she'd longed to get pregnant but she had a rare, serious type of kidney disease. Her doctor warned that pregnancy would overly stress her body, even endanger her life. Still, this woman's desire for a baby was so strong she decided to risk it. Fortunately, she stayed well those nine months and her disease stabilized, which isn't typical during pregnancy—a great relief to her, her husband, and the doctor. However, in that same period, her young golden retriever, her constant companion and "soul mate" with whom she was so attuned, was diagnosed with kidney failure. Soon after the birth of her daughter, this loving animal died, as if having held on just long enough to see her through.

Though cynics would dismiss as "mere coincidence" the fact that both contracted the same rare disease—especially when the dog had been perfectly healthy—I read this quite differently. For me, it seems rather to be a moving reminder of the interconnectedness of our hearts and the power of compassion. There was a special love between this woman and her dog. Could it be possible for one life to so empathize with another that it can sense and even assume illness? Certainly, it's something to contemplate. As a physician, I know that love can create miracles that defy logical explanation. Selfless giving resonates with such mystery. How wondrous and far-reaching compassion can be among all living beings. Each of us is capable of limitless love. The monumental implications of this fact continue to reveal themselves over the years, always giving me chills and reclarifying my emotional priorities.

It's been said that when people stop performing random acts of kindness, the net that holds the world together will fall apart. Woe is that day when our compassion ceases, when anger has no means of being counteracted. Instead, together we can cultivate compassion's bounty and rejoice in each other. Be compassionate with people you know and those you don't. We are all sacred. We are all achingly beautiful. Intuition allows us to recognize one another's light. Let's take our cue from poet Mary Oliver when she writes about "seeing through the heavenly visibles to the heavenly invisibles." Compassion grants us the sightedness to behold both the surface of things and their deeper emotional dimensions. It enables us to be more giving, thereby consecrating our relationships. It lets us make the earth a better place than when we came.

Meditation on Freedom

Bestow the Gift of Loving-kindness

Today, go on a compassion spree. Put no holds on your heart or how you'll love others or yourself. View everything benevolently, where we shine as well as our foibles. Take the deepest breath you've ever taken. Let your heart grow larger than it's ever been. Feel good about the person you've become. Compassion's time has arrived. Embrace and share this goodness. Your compassion fills the world with soul.

Another world is not only possible, she is on her way!
On a quiet day, if you listen carefully,
You can hear her breathing.

—ARUNDHATI ROY

AFTERWORD

LIVING IN SERVICE TO THE HEART: THE BLESSING OF EMOTIONAL FREEDOM

EMOTIONAL FREEDOM IS an inner peace movement that is birthed from within each of us, then emanates into the world. The starting place is always you. The more peace you enjoy, the more that energy ripples out to everyone. Becoming liberated from the bondage of negativity—the purpose of this book's transformations—lets you realize your tremendous value as a person. You'll be more connected to your heart and also feel a communion with the whole human family. With this awareness, you can treat others as kindred, as one of your own. Generosity and goodwill soon begin to seem natural.

Achieving emotional freedom gives you ongoing access to your own power center during jubilant times and in adversity. As master of your emotions, you'll have the wherewithal to hold your own with angels, demons, and everything in between. I admire your courage in getting to know yourself. The journey to self-knowledge is an exhilarating yet humbling one. As it unfolds, keep distilling the core message of emotional freedom: Outer events may be the stimulus for an upset, but how you choose to respond determines your experience. Openness to such growth is more important than mere intellectual knowing. Living in service to the heart blesses you with a comprehensively loving perspective. As a result, your presence becomes more radiant. A special beauty emerges from within that is transmitted to others.

Emotional freedom means not only living in service to the heart on a personal level but also pledging allegiance to the well-being of the earth. We are her guardians, her protectors. To fulfill that sacred duty, we must stay apprised of our emotional motivations lest we unconsciously act out inner strife on a global scale. It's daunting to grasp that one emotionally damaged person in a position of power can inflict cataclysmic planetary harm. As a psychiatrist, I believe that people with unresolved anger are more apt to wage war. We don't want to place the fate of peace in the hands of leaders whose decisions are distorted by rage from childhood or anywhere else. The fact is, happy people don't want to blow up the world. Rather, advocates for peace must know what it is to feel peaceful. Then we'll have a far better chance of attaining our goals. Alternatively, it won't benefit you to be a fearful whirlwind of unrest trying to save civilization. This will impede your mission. Therefore each of us must put our own emotional house in order.

Our world is in the midst of a quickening. It feels like time has accelerated, that the years keep flitting by faster and faster. This quickening, however, involves more than simply our altered perception of time as we age, our frantic culture, or anxiety about fulfilling our goals in life. The Hopis say our world is sick and needs to get well. To prevent what geo-biologists call "the sixth great extinction" of earth's species (akin to the disappearance of the dinosaurs), we urgently need to save the planet as well as our souls. Throughout history, human nature seems impelled toward turmoil, just as children by a tranquil lake will inevitably throw pebbles into the water to disrupt the calm. Even so, I have faith that with mindfulness more enduring peace is possible. Who knows the Lords of Peace better than an awakened heart? We're at a crossroads with choices to be made. We can ride the momentum of this quickening either to the depths of our love or to the edge of oblivion. Gone is the luxury of a middle ground. We need prophets who aren't afraid to speak out. It behooves us to heed Albert Einstein's admonition: "I don't know what weapons World War III will be fought with. But World War IV will be fought with sticks and stones." Emotional freedom tilts the tipping point toward goodness. It allows us to experience inner peace so that outer peace can prosper.

Observing the world is the fascination of my life and profession. I am drawn to penetrate to the center of things. But what I live for most are those perfect intuitions that convey I'm on center with my heart. My fondest wish is that this book ignites an excitement in you about this experience, that I've inspired you to rebel against whatever opposes love. Our heart is our greatest legacy. Over time, your emotional insights will refine themselves. Stay with them until they shimmer. Remain loyal to ways of being that feel authentic. During phases of self-doubt or when you falter, keep in mind: a golden compass always points to the heart. That's the direction to freedom.

The overarching message of this book is to manifest love with abandon. Cherish each moment on the widening path to emotional freedom. A dream once told me, "Now is the beginning of forever." With a sense of wonder, let's see what's next for ourselves and hail the mystery of what hasn't yet become. The present makes the future bright, so make your present as bright as possible. About the Master, the Tao te Ching says:

> *He is ready to use all situations*
> *and doesn't waste anything.*
> *This is called embodying the light.*

Accordingly, let's join together in service to the heart as we continue to live and learn. Approach all circumstances with the confidence of someone who knows the strength of loving. Circulate goodness wherever you go. Every day, you create your own karma— good or bad, it's up to you. Our bond with one another, our bond to the world, illuminates the vision of the whole. Carve out a space within where intuition and love can abide. Trusting what's inside so fervently will allow you to have a fully embodied life.

CENTER FOR MINDFULNESS
(stress reduction and meditation programs)
University of Massachusetts Medical School
55 Lake Avenue North
Worcester, MA 01655
508-856-2656
mindfulness@umassmed.edu
www.umassmed.edu/cfm

BENSON-HENRY INSTITUTE FOR MIND-BODY MEDICINE
(stress reduction and meditation programs)
Massachusetts General Hospital
824 Boylston Street
Chestnut Hill, MA 02467
617-732-9130
mindbody@partners.org
www.mbmi.org/home

MINDFUL AWARENESS RESEARCH CENTER (MARC)
(stress reduction and meditation programs)
UCLA Semel Institute for Neuroscience and Human Behavior
760 Westwood Plaza, Room 47-444, Box 951759
Los Angeles, CA 90095-1759
310-206-7503
marcinfo@ucla.edu
www.marc.ucla.edu

ALCOHOLICS ANONYMOUS
(information on alcoholism and national AA meeting locations)
PO Box 459
New York, NY 10163
212-870-3400
www.alcoholics-anonymous.org

CODEPENDENTS ANONYMOUS
(international support group referrals)
PO Box 33577
Phoenix, AZ 85067
24-hour live meeting information: 602-277-7991
www.coda.org

EMOTIONS ANONYMOUS
(national support group referrals)
www.emotionsanonymous.org
PO Box 4245
Saint Paul, MN 55104-0245
651-647-9712
www.emotionsanonymous.org

NATIONAL SUICIDE PREVENTION LIFELINE
(24-hour number for anyone in a suicidal crisis)
1-800-273-TALK (8255)

DEPRESSION IS REAL COALITION
(information and resources to overcome depression)
1-800-SUICIDE
www.depressionisreal.org

SPIRITUAL EMERGENCE NETWORK
(national spiritual psychotherapist referrals)
c/o Association for Transpersonal Psychology
PO Box 50187
Palo Alto, CA 94303
415-453-1106
www.spiritualemergence.info

AMERICAN HOLISTIC MEDICAL ASSOCIATION
(national medical referrals)
One Eagle Valley Court, Suite 201
Broadview Heights, OH 44147
440-838-1010
www.holisticmedicine.org

AMERICAN HOLISTIC NURSES ASSOCIATION
(national holistic nursing referrals)
323 N. San Francisco Street, Suite 201
Flagstaff, AZ 86001
1-800-278-AHNA
www.ahna.org

NURSE-HEALERS—PROFESSIONAL ASSOCIATES INC.
(energy healing referrals)
PO Box 419
Craryville, NY 12521
518-325-1185 or 877-32N-HPAI
nhpai@therapeutic-touch.org
www.therapcutic-touch.org

NATIONAL INSTITUTE OF MENTAL HEALTH
(information about depression, anxiety, and all aspects of mental health)
6001 Executive Boulevard, Room 8184, MSC 9663
Bethesda, Maryland 20892
1-866-615-6464
nimhinfo@nih.gov
www.nimh.nih.gov

NATIONAL CENTER FOR COMPLEMENTARY AND ALTERNATIVE MEDICINE
(information about complementary/holistic approaches to physical and mental health)
National Institutes of Health
9000 Rockville Pike
Bethesda, MD 20892
1-888-644-6226
info@nccam.nih.gov
http://nccam.nih.gov

NATIONAL ALLIANCE ON MENTAL ILLNESS (NAMI)
(education and national support groups for patients and their families)
Colonial Place Three
2107 Wilson Boulevard, Suite 300
Arlington, VA 22201-3042
703-524-7600
Information helpline: 1-800-950-NAMI (6264)
www.nami.org

INSTITUTE OF NOETIC SCIENCES
(research and programs on intuition, healing, and consciousness)
101 San Antonio Road
Petaluma, CA 94952
707-775-3500
www.noetic.org

THE INTERNATIONAL SOCIETY FOR THE STUDY OF SUBTLE ENERGIES AND ENERGY MEDICINE (ISSSEEM)
(education and programs on subtle energies and health)
11005 Ralston Road, Suite 210
Arvada, CO 80004
303-425-4625
www.issseem.org

THE ASSOCIATION FOR COMPREHENSIVE ENERGY PSYCHOLOGY (ACEP)
(programs and education about energy psychology)
303 Park Avenue South, Box 1051
New York, NY 10010-3657
619-861-2237
www.energypsych.org

INSTITUTE OF TRANSPERSONAL PSYCHOLOGY
(training program for spiritual psychology)
1069 East Meadow Circle
Palo Alto, CA 94303
650-493-4430
www.itp.edu

SELECTED READING

Beattie, Melody. *Codependent No More: How to Stop Controlling Others and Start Caring for Yourself.* Hazelton Information Education, 1997.

Bennett-Goleman, Tara. *Emotional Alchemy: How the Mind Can Heal the Heart.* Three Rivers Press, 2002.

Chödrön, Pema. *When Things Fall Apart: Heart Advice for Difficult Times.* Shambhala Press, 2005.

Dalai Lama. *The Art of Happiness: A Handbook for Living.* Riverhead Books. 1999.

———. *Healing Anger: The Power of Patience from a Buddhist Perspective.* Snow Lion Press, 1997.

Dass, Ram. *Be Here Now.* Crown Publishing Group, 1971.

Dossey, Larry. *Healing Words: The Power of Prayer and the Practice of Medicine.* HarperOne, 1997.

Eden, Donna. *Energy Medicine.* Tarcher, 1999.

Feinstein, David. *The Promise of Energy Psychology.* Tarcher, 2005.

Frankl, Viktor. *Man's Search for Meaning.* Simon & Schuster, 1984.

Garfield, Patricia. *Creative Dreaming: Plan and Control Your Dreams to Develop Creativity, Overcome Fears, Solve Problems, and Create a Better Self.* Fireside Books, 1995.

Goleman, Daniel. *Destructive Emotions: A Scientific Dialogue with the Dalai Lama.* Bantam, 2004.

———. *Emotional Intelligence: Why It Can Matter More than IQ.* Bantam, 2006.

Groopman, Jerome. *The Anatomy of Hope: How People Prevail in the Face of Illness.* Random House, 2005.

Jamison, Kay Redfield. *An Unquiet Mind: A Memoir of Moods and Madness.* Picador Books, 1997.

Jung, Carl. *Man and His Symbols.* Dell, 1968.

———. *Memories, Dreams, Reflections.* Vintage Books, 1989.

Kabat-Zinn, Jon. *Full Catastrophe Living.* Piatkus Books, 2001.

———. *The Mindful Way Through Depression.* Guilford Press, 2007.

Kerouac, Jack. *Book of Dreams.* City Lights Books, 2001.

LaBerge, Stephen, *Exploring the World of Lucid Dreaming.* Ballantine Books, 1991.

Lawrence, Brother. *The Practice of the Presence of God.* Baker House Books, 2004.

Leahy, Robert. *The Worry Cure: Seven Steps to Stop Worry from Stopping You.* Three Rivers Press, 2006.

Lynch, James J. *A Cry Unheard: New Insights into the Medical Consequences of Loneliness.* Bancroft Press, 2000.

Myss, Caroline. *Anatomy of the Spirit: The Seven Stages of Power and Healing.* Random House, 1997.

Naparstek, Belleruth. *Your Sixth Sense: Unlocking the Power of Your Intuition.* HarperOne, 1996.

Newberg, Andrew, et al. *Neurotheology: Brain, Science, Spirituality, and Religious Experience.* University Press, 2003.

Oliver, Mary. *Dreamwork.* Atlantic Monthly Press. 1994.

Ornish, Dean. *Love and Survival: The Scientific Basis for the Healing Power of Intimacy.* HarperCollins, 1997.

Pearsall, Paul. *The Heart's Code: Tapping the Wisdom and Power of Our Heart Energy.* Broadway Books, 1999.

Pert, Candace. *Molecules of Emotion: The Science Behind Mind-Body Medicine.* Simon & Schuster, 1999.

Radin, Dean. *Entangled Minds: Extrasensory Experiences in a Quantum Reality.* Paraview Pocket Books, 2006.

Richmond, Cynthia. *Dream Power: How to Use Your Night Dreams to Change Your Life.* Simon & Schuster, 2001.

Rosenberg, Marshall B. *Nonviolent Communication: A Language of Life; Create Your Life, Your Relationships and Your World in Harmony with Your Values.* Puddle Dancer Press, 2003.

Salzberg, Sharon. *Loving Kindness: The Revolutionary Art of Happiness.* Shambhala Publications, 2002.

Schwartz, Stephan. *Opening to the Infinite.* Nemoseen Media, 2007.

Seligman, Martin. *Learned Optimism: How to Change Your Mind and Your Life.* Vintage, 2006.

Shimoff, Marci. *Happy for No Reason: 7 Steps for Being Happy from the In-side Out.* Free Press, 2008.

Targ, Russell. *The End of Suffering: Fearless Living in Troubled Times.* Hampton Roads Publishing, 2006.

Thurman, Robert. *Anger: The Seven Deadly Sins.* Oxford University Press, 2006.

Tolle, Eckhart. *The Power of Now.* New World Library, 1999.

Wallerstein, Gene. *Mind, Stress and Emotions: The New Science of Mood.* Commonwealth Press, 2002.

SELECTED SCIENCE ARTICLES

Arnst, Amy. "The Biology of Being Frazzled." *Science* 280 (Jun 12, 1998): 1711–13. (Discusses the biology of being emotionally off center)

Aston, John A. "The Efficacy of Distant Healing: A Systemized Review of Randomized Trials." *Annals of Internal Medicine* 132, 11 (2000): 903–10. (A review of distant healing studies)

Coan, A. "Spouse but Not Stranger: Handholding Attenuates Activation in Neural Systems Underlying Response to Threat." *Psychophysiology* 42 (2005): 544. (Discusses how holding your spouse's hand in a threatening situation can biologically reduce his or her stress)

Davidson, R. J., and W. Iron. "The Functional Neuroanatomy of Emotion and Affective Style." *Trends in Cognitive Science* 3 (1999): 11–21. (Discusses the neuroanatomy of emotion)

Dijksterhuis, Ap, et al. "On Making the Right Choice: The Deliberation-Without-Attention Effect." *Science* 311 (Aug 11, 2006): 1005–7. (Discusses the importance of "sleeping on" decisions versus figuring them out)

Gozzola, V. "Empathy and the Somatotopic Auditory Mirror System in Humans." *Current Biology* 16 (2006): 1824–29. (Discusses the connection between empathy and mirror neurons)

Gump, Brooks, et al. "Stress, Affiliation, and Emotional Contagion." *Journal of Personality and Social Psychology* 72, 2 (1997): 305–19. (Discusses the concept of emotional contagion and how it relates to stress)

Keltner, Dahser, and Cameron Anderson. "Emotional Convergence Between People over Time." *Journal of Personality and Social Psychology* 84, 5 (2003): 1954–68. (Discusses the concept of emotional merging in relationships)

Kemper, Kathi, et al. "Impact of a Medical School Elective in Cultivating Compassion Through Touch Therapies." *Complementary Health Practice Review* 11, 1 (2006): 47–56. (Discusses the power of therapeutic touch and compassion)

Lieberman, Matthew. "Intuition: A Social Cognitive Neuroscience Approach." *Psychological Bulletin* 126, 1 (2000): 109–37. (Discusses the neuroanatomy of intuition)

Luskin, Frederic. "The Art and Science of Forgiveness." *Stanford Medicine* 16, 4 (1999). (Discusses the heath benefits of forgiveness)

Miller, Greg. "Reflecting on Another's Mind: Mirror Mechanisms Built into the Brain May Help Us Understand Each Other." *Science* 308 (May 13, 2005): 945–47. (Discusses the connection between empathy and mirror neurons)

Mischel, W., Y. Shoda, and M. Rodriguez. "Delay of Gratification in Children." *Science* 244 (May 26, 1989): 933–38. (The famous marshmallow experiment, which linked the ability to delay gratification as a child with future success as an adult)

Newberg, A. B., et al. "The measurement of regional cerebral blood flow during the complex cognitive task of meditation: A preliminary SPECT study." *Psychiatry Research: Neuroimaging* 106 (2001): 113–22. (Discusses the effects of spirituality and meditation on the brain)

Radin, Dean, et al. "Double-Blind Test of the Effects of Distant Intention on Water Crystal Formation." *Explore Journal* 2, 5 (2006). (Discusses the power of intention to create physical change)

Rizzolatti, Giacomo. "The Mirror Neuron System." *Annual Review of Neuroscience* 27 (2004): 169–92. (A review of the body's mirror neurons system and empathy)

Seeman, Teresa. "Social Ties and Support and Neuroendocrine Function." *Annals of Behavioral Medicine* 16 (1994): 95–106. (Discusses the positive effects of emotional support on health)

INDEX

About the Author

Judith Orloff, M.D., is a board-certified psychiatrist and assistant clinical professor of psychiatry at UCLA. She is also author of the bestsellers *Positive Energy, Dr. Judith Orloff's Guide to Intuitive Healing,* and *Second Sight.* Dr. Orloff is an international lecturer and workshop leader on the relationship between medicine, intuition, and emotional freedom. Her work has been featured on CNN, PBS, and NPR and has appeared in *USA Today, O Magazine,* and *Self.* Dr. Orloff is the creator of YouTube's Intuition and Emotional Freedom Channel at www.youtube.com/judithorloffmd. She lives by the ocean in Los Angeles, California.

For information on Dr. Judith Orloff's books and workshop schedule, visit DrJudithOrloff.com or send inquiries to:

Judith Orloff, M.D.
2080 Century Park East, Suite 1811
Los Angeles, CA 90067